CW01035200

Haswell's Engineers' And Mechanics' Pocket-book ..

Haswell, Chas. H. (Charles Haynes), 1809-1907

Nabu Public Domain Reprints:

You are holding a reproduction of an original work published before 1923 that is in the public domain in the United States of America, and possibly other countries. You may freely copy and distribute this work as no entity (individual or corporate) has a copyright on the body of the work. This book may contain prior copyright references, and library stamps (as most of these works were scanned from library copies). These have been scanned and retained as part of the historical artifact.

This book may have occasional imperfections such as missing or blurred pages, poor pictures, errant marks, etc. that were either part of the original artifact, or were introduced by the scanning process. We believe this work is culturally important, and despite the imperfections, have elected to bring it back into print as part of our continuing commitment to the preservation of printed works worldwide. We appreciate your understanding of the imperfections in the preservation process, and hope you enjoy this valuable book.

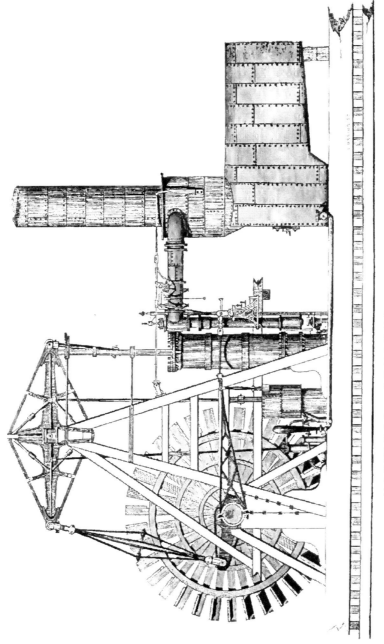

VERTICAL, CONDENSING BEAM ENGINE.

Made by the West Point Foundry Association, New-York.

HASWELL'S

ENGINEERS AND MECHANICS POCKET-BOOK

0 — 13.6

1 — 15.6 — 2/2

2 — 17.5 — 88

3 — 19.87 — 2.37

4 — 8.30

6 — 2.6 — 2.40

7 — 2 8.66

8 — 30.7 — 2.09

9 — 32.6 — 1.9

10 — 3 5

27.6

0 — 11.50

1 — 13.66

2 — 16.25

3 — 18.20

4 — 21.24

5 — 23.30

6 — 25.

7 — 2 8.

8 — 3 0.

9 — 3 2.

10 — 3 5.25

HASWELL'S

ENGINEERS' AND MECHANICS' POCKET-BOOK,

CONTAINING

UNITED STATES AND FOREIGN WEIGHTS AND MEASURES;
TABLES OF AREAS AND CIRCUMFERENCES OF CIRCLES, CIRCULAR SEG-
MENTS, AND ZONES OF A CIRCLE;
SQUARES AND CUBES, SQUARE AND CUBE ROOTS;
LENGTHS OF CIRCULAR AND SEMI-ELLIPTIC ARCS;
AND RULES OF ARITHMETIC.

MENSURATION OF SURFACES AND SOLIDS;

THE MECHANICAL POWERS;
GEOMETRY, TRIGONOMETRY, GRAVITY, STRENGTH
OF MATERIALS, WATER WHEELS, HYDRAULICS, HYDROSTATICS, PNEU-
MATICS, STATICS, DYNAMICS, GUNNERY, HEAT, WINDING EN-
GINES, TONNAGE, SHOT, SHELLS, &c.

STEAM AND THE STEAM-ENGINE;

COMBUSTION, WATER, CABLES AND ANCHORS, FUEL, AIR, GUNS, &c., &c.

TABLES OF THE WEIGHTS OF METALS, PIPES, &c.

MISCELLANEOUS NOTES, AND EXERCISES,
&c., &c.

BY CHARLES H. HASWELL.

CHIEF ENGINEER U. S. NAVY.

An examination of facts is the foundation of science.

NEW-YORK:

HARPER & BROTHERS, 82 CLIFF-STREET.

1844.

Entered, according to Act of Congress, in the year 1844, by
HARPER & BROTHERS,
In the Clerk's Office of the Southern District of New-York.

ERRATA.

Page 140, 27th line, for "common," read *cannon*.

" 142, 12th line, for "$\sqrt{10 \times 64.33}$," read $\sqrt{10 \times 64.33}$.

" 142, 16th and 17th lines, *omit* "and that product, again, by the velocity in feet per second."

Page 142, 20th line, *omit* "$\times 5 = 7500$."

" 158, 15th line, for "594,000," read 59,400.

" 179, 26th line, for "$5\frac{1}{2}$" read $4\frac{1}{2}$.

" 218, last line, after "horses' power," read, *with plain cylindrical boilers*.

Page 226, 17th line, for "Picton," read *Pictou*.

" 240, 19th line, for "brushes," read *bushes*.

" 248, in column 2d, insert $\frac{1}{4}$ opposite to "0.211."

" 251, 3d line from bottom, for "176.7149," read 1767.145; and in bottom line, for "460.6957," read 460.6947.

Page 260, last line, for "92000," read 9200.

Prof. Wm R. Johnson
with the respects of
the Author.

TO

CAPTAIN ROBERT F. STOCKTON,

U. S. NAVY,

S A TRIBUTE TO THE LIBERALITY AND ENTERPRISE HE HAS
EVINCED IN HIS PATRONAGE OF MECHANICAL SCIENCE,
THIS EDITION IS, WITH PERMISSION,

Respectfully Inscribed

BY

THE AUTHOR.

Washington, Aug. 1, 1843.

PREFACE.

THE following work is submitted to the Engineers and Mechanics of the United States by one of their number, who trusts that it will be found a convenient summary for reference to Tables, Results, and Rules connected with the discharge of their various duties.

The Tables have been selected from the latest and best publications, and information has been sought from various sources, to render it useful to the Operative Engineer, Mechanic, or Student.

The want of a work of this description in this country has long been felt, and this is peculiarly fitted to supply that want, in consequence of the adaptation of its rules to the metals, woods, and manufactures of the United States.

Having for many years experienced inconvenience for the want of a compilation of tables and rules by a Practical Mechanic, together with the total absence of *units* for the weights and strengths of American materials, I was induced to attempt the labour of a compilation and the necessary experiments to furnish this work.

The proportions of the parts of the steam-engine and boilers will be found to differ in most instances materially from the English authorities; but as they are based upon the actual results of the most successful experience, I do not hesitate to put them forth, being well assured that an adherence to them will ensure both success and satisfaction.

The sources of information from which I have principally compiled are Adcock, Grier, Gregory, the Library of Useful Knowledge, and the Ordnance Manual; and to the labours of the authors of these valuable works I freely acknowledge my indebtedness.

In my own efforts, I have been materially assisted by the officers of the West Point Foundry Association, who liberally furnished me with the means of making such experiments as were considered necessary, and to the Engineer of that establishment, Mr. B. H. Bartol, I am indebted for much valuable information and assistance.

To the Young Engineer I would say, cultivate a knowledge of physical laws, without which, eminence in his profession can never be securely attained; and if this volume should assist him in the attainment of so desirable a result, the object of the author will be fully accomplished.

We have seen a proof copy of HASWELL's ENGINEERS' AND MECHANICS' POCKET BOOK, and approve of its design and the subjects treated of: a work of this description has long been wanted, and we confidently express a conviction of its usefulness and application, which in extent exceeds that of any work of its class with which we are acquainted.

GOUVERNEUR KEMBLE,
WILLIAM KEMBLE,
ROBERT P. PARROTT,
B. H. BARTOL,
} *West Point Foundry Association, N. Y.*

JAMES P. ALLAIRE,
B. R. M'ILVAINE,
} *Allaire Works, N. Y.*

HORATIO ALLEN,
C. E. DETMOLD,
} *Civil Engineers.*

CHARLES W. HACKLEY, } *Professor of Mathematics, Columbia College, N.Y.*

HOGG & DELAMATER, *Phœnix Foundry, N. Y.*

STILLMAN & Co., *Novelty Works, N. Y.*

T. F. SECOR & Co., } *Steam-Engine Manufacturers, N. Y.*

BROWN & BELL,
SMITH & DIMON,
} *Shipbuilders, N. Y.*

MERRICK & TOWNE, } *Southwark Foundry, Philadelphia.*

CONTENTS.

NOTATION.

1 = I.
2 = II.
3 = III.

} As often as a character is repeated, so many times is its value repeated.

4 = IV.
5 = V.
6 = VI.
7 = VII.

{ A less character before a greater diminishes its value, as IV = I from V, or 1 subtracted from 5 = 4.

8 = VIII.
9 = IX.
10 = X.

{ A less character after a greater increases its value, as XI = X+I, or 10+1 = 11.

20 = XX.
30 = XXX.
40 = XL.
50 = L.
60 = LX.
70 = LXX.
80 = LXXX.
90 = XC.
100 = C.

500 = D, or IƆ.

} For every Ɔ annexed, this becomes 10 times as many.

1,000 = M, or CIƆ.

{ For every C and Ɔ, placed one at each end, it becomes 10 times as many.

2,000 = MM.
5,000 = $\overline{V}$, or IƆƆ.
6,000 = $\overline{VI}$.
10,000 = $\overline{X}$, or CCIƆƆ.
50,000 = $\overline{L}$, or IƆƆƆ.
60,000 = $\overline{LX}$.
100,000 = $\overline{C}$, or CCCIƆƆƆ.
1,000,000 = $\overline{M}$, or CCCCIƆƆƆƆ.
2,000,000 = $\overline{MM}$.

} A bar, thus —, over any number, increases it 1000 times.

EXAMPLES.—1840, MDCCCXL.
18560, $\overline{XVIII}$DLX.

EXPLANATIONS OF THE CHARACTERS USED IN THE FOLLOWING TABLES AND CALCULATIONS.

$=$ *Equal to*, as, 12 inches $=$ 1 foot, or $8 \times 8 = 16 \times 4$.

$+$ *Plus*, or *more*, signifies addition ; as, $4+6+5 = 15$.

$-$ *Minus*, or *less*, signifies subtraction ; as, $15-5 = 10$.

$\times$ *Multiplied by*, or *into*, signifies multiplication ; as, $8 \times 9 = 72$.

$\div$ *Divided by*, signifies division ; as, $72 \div 9 = 8$.

$\left. \begin{array}{l} : \text{ Is to} \\ : : \text{ so is} \\ : \text{ to} \end{array} \right\}$ *Proportion* ; as, $2:4::8:16$; that is, as 2 *is to* 4 *so is* 8 *to* 16.

$\sqrt{}$ Prefixed to any number signifies that the *square root* of that number is required ; as, $\sqrt{16} = 4$; that is, $4 \times 4 = 16$.

$\sqrt[3]{}$ Signifies that the *cube root* of that number is required ; as, $\sqrt[3]{64} = 4$; that is, $4 \times 4 \times 4 = 64$.

^{2} added to a number signifies that that number is to be *squared ;* thus, 4^2 means that 4 is to be multiplied by 4.

^{3} added to a number signifies that that number is to be *cubed ;* thus, 4^3 is $= 4 \times 4 \times 4 = 64$. The *power* or number of times a number is to be multiplied by itself is shown by the number added ; as, ^{2} ^{3} ^{4} ^{5}, &c.

$\overline{\quad}$ The *bar* signifies that the numbers are to be taken together ; as, $\overline{8-2+6} = 12$, or $3 \times \overline{5+3} = 24$.

. *Decimal point*, signifies when prefixed to a number, that that number has a unit (1) for its denominator ; as, .1 is $\frac{1}{10}$, .155 is $\frac{155}{1000}$, &c.

$\backsim$ Signifies *difference*, and is placed between two quantities when it is not evident which of them is the greater.

$^\circ$ *Degrees,* ' *minutes,* " *seconds,* ''' *thirds*.

$<$ Signifies *angle*.

$a-^1, a-^2, a-^3$, &c., denote inverse powers of a, and are equal to $\frac{1}{a^1}, \frac{1}{a^2}, \frac{1}{a^3}$, &c.

γ Is put between two quantities to express that the former is *greater than* the latter ; as, $a \gamma b$, reads a greater than b.

ι Signifies the reverse ; as, $a \iota b$, reads a less than b.

( ) *Parentheses* are used to show that all the figures within them are to be operated upon as if they were only one ; thus, $(3+2) \times 5 = 25$.

p is used to express the ratio of the circumference of a circle to its diameter $= 3.1415926$, &c.

A A' A'' A''' signifies A, A *prime*, A *second*, A *third*, &c.

$a \times d$, $a.d$, or ad, signifies that a is to be multiplied by d.

To ascertain the value of a *decimal of a unit*, see Reduction of Decimals, page 28.

Note. The degrees of temperature used in this work are those of Fahrenheit.

UNITED STATES' WEIGHTS AND MEASURES.

Measures of Length.

	Inches.	Feet.	Yards.	Rods.	Furl.
12 inches = 1 foot.					
3 feet = 1 yard.	36 =	3.			
5½ yards = 1 rod.	198 =	16½ =	5½.		
40 rods = 1 furlong.	7920 =	660 =	220 =	40.	
8 furlongs = 1 mile.	63360 =	5280 =	1760 =	320 =	8.

The inch is sometimes divided into 3 *barley corns*, or 12 *lines*.
A hair's breadth is the 48th of an inch.

Gunter's Chain.

7.92 inches = 1 link.
100 links = 4 rods, or 22 yards.

Ropes and Cables.

6 feet = 1 fathom.
120 fathoms = 1 cable's length.

Geographical and Nautical Measure.

1 degree of a great circle of the earth = 69.77 Statute miles.
1 mile . . . . . . = 2046.5 yards.

Log Lines.

1 knot = 51.1625 feet, or 51 feet 1¾+ inches.
1 fathom = 5.11625 feet, or 5 feet 1⅓+ inches.
Estimating a mile at 6139½ feet, and using a 30″ glass. If a 28″
glass is used, and eight divisions, then
1 knot = 47 feet 9 + inches.
1 fathom = 5 feet 11⅜ inches.
The line should be about 150 fathoms long, having 10 fathoms
between the chip and first knot for stray line.

NOTE.—*Bowditch gives 6120 feet in a sea mile, which, if taken as the length, will make the divisions 51 feet and 5 1-10 feet.*

Cloth.

1 nail = 2¼ inches = $\frac{1}{16}$th of a yard.
1 quarter = 4 nails.
5 quarters = 1 ell English

Pendulums.

6 points = 1 line.
12 lines = 1 inch.

Shoemakers'.

No. 1 is 4⅓ inches in length, and every succeeding number is ⅓ of
an inch.
There are 28 divisions, in two series of numbers, viz., from 1 to
13, and 1 to 15.

B

Circles.

60 seconds = 1 minute.	″
60 minutes = 1 degree.	3600
360 degrees = 1 circle.	1296000 = 21600.

1 day is . . . . . .002739 of a year.
1 minute is . . . . .000694 of a day.

Miscellaneous.

1 palm = 3 inches.	1 span = 9 inches.
1 hand = 4 inches.	1 metre = 3.28174 feet.

The standard of measure is a brass rod, which, at the temperature of 32° Fahrenheit, is the standard yard.

The standard yard of the *State of New-York* bears, to a pendulum vibrating seconds in vacuo, at Columbia College, the relation of 1.000000 to 1.086141 at a temperature of 32° Fahrenheit.

1 yard is . . . . . .000568 of a mile.
1 inch is . . . . . .0000153 of a mile.

Measures of Surface.

144 square inches = 1 square foot.		Inches.
9 square feet = 1 square yard.		1296

Land.

		Yards.	Rods.	Roods.
30¼ square yards	= 1 square rod.			
40 square rods	= 1 square rood.	1210.		
4 square roods				
10 square chains	} = 1 acre.	4840 = 160.		
640 acres	= 1 square mile.	3097600 = 102400 = 2560.		

NOTE.—*208.710321 feet, 69.5701 yards, or 220 by 198 feet square = 1 acre.*

Paper.

24 sheets = 1 quire.		Sheets.
20 quires = 1 ream.		480.

Drawing Paper.

Cap	. . 13 ×16 inches.	Columbier	. 33¾× 23 inches.
Demy	. . 19½×15½ "	Atlas	. . 33 × 26 "
Medium	. 22 ×18 "	Theorem	. 34 × 28 "
Royal	. . 24 ×19 "	Doub. Elephant,	40 × 26 "
Super-royal	. 27 ×19 "	Antiquarian	. 52 × 31 "
Imperial	. 29 ×21¼ "	Emperor	. 40 × 60 "
Elephant	. 27¾×22¼ "	Uncle Sam	. 48 ×120 "

Measures of Capacity.

Liquid.

		Gills.	Pints.
4 gills = 1 pint.		8.	
2 pints = 1 quart.			
4 quarts = 1 gallon.		32 = 8.	

The standard gallon measures 231 cubic inches, and contains

8 3388822 avoirdupois pounds, or 58372.1754 troy grains of distilled water at 39° 83 Fahrenheit ; the barometer at 30 inches.

The gallon of the *State of New-York* contains 221.184 cubic inches, or 8 pounds of pure water at its maximum density.

The *Imperial gallon* (British) contains 277.274 cubic inches.

Dry.

	Pints.	Quarts.	Gallons.
2 pints = 1 quart.	8.		
4 quarts = 1 gallon.			
2 gallons = 1 peck.	16 = 8.		
4 pecks = 1 bushel.	64 = 32 = 8.		

The standard bushel is the *Winchester*, which contains 2150.42 cubic inches, or 77.627413 lbs. avoirdupois of distilled water at its maximum density.

Its dimensions are 18½ inches diameter inside, 19½ inches outside, and 8 inches deep ; and when heaped, the cone must not be less than 6 inches high.

The bushel of the *State of New-York* contains 80 lbs. of pure water at its maximum density, or 2211.84 cubic inches.

Measures of Solidity.

	Inches.
1728 cubic inches = 1 foot.	46656.
27 cubic feet = 1 yard.	

Miscellaneous.

1 chaldron = 36 bushels, or	57.25 cubic feet.
Dry gallon of New-York	276.48 cubic inches.
1 perch of stone	24.75 cubic feet.

Measures of Weight.

Avoirdupois.

	Drachms.	Ounces.	Pounds.
16 drachms = 1 ounce.	256.		
16 ounces = 1 pound.			
112 pounds = 1 cwt.	28672 = 1792.		
20 cwt. = 1 ton.	573440 = 35840 = 2240.		

1 lb. = 14 oz. 11 dwt. 16 gr. troy.

The standard avoirdupois pound is the weight of 27.7015 cubic inches of distilled water weighed in air, at the temperature of the maximum density (39°.83), the barometer being at 30 inches.

Troy.

	Grains.	Dwt.
24 grains = 1 dwt.	480.	
20 dwt. = 1 ounce.		
12 ounces = 1 pound.	5760 = 240.	

Apothecaries.

	Grains.	Scruples.	Drachms.
20 grains = 1 scruple.	60.		
3 scruples = 1 drachm.			
8 drachms = 1 ounce.	480 = 24.		
12 ounces = 1 pound.	5760 = 288 = 96.		

Diamond.

16 parts = 1 grain = 0.8 troy grains.
4 grains = 1 carat = 3.2   "

7000	troy grains =	1 lb. avoirdupois.
175	troy pounds =	144 lbs. "
175	troy ounces =	192 oz. "
437½	troy grains =	1 oz. "
1	troy pound =	.8228+ lb. "

Miscellaneous.

1 cubic foot of anthracite coal from 50 to 55 lbs.
1 cubic foot of bituminous coal from 42 to 55 lbs.
1 cubic foot Cumberland coal = 53 lbs.
1 cubic foot charcoal   .   = 18.5 " (hard wood).
1 cubic foot charcoal   .   = 18.   " (pine wood).
1 bushel bituminous coal   = 80 "
1 stone .   .   .   = 14 "

Coals are usually purchased at the conventional rate of 28 bushels (5 pecks) to a ton.

Measures of Value.

1 eagle = 258 troy grains.
1 dollar = 412.5 "
1 cent = 168   "

The standard of gold and silver is 900 parts of pure metal, and 100 of alloy, in 1000 parts of coin.

Relative Mint Value of Foreign Gold Coins,

By Law of Congress, August, 1834.

	Coin.	Weight. Dwt. Gr.		Value.
BRAZIL.	1 Johannes . . .	18	. .	$17.068
	1 Dobraon	34 12	. .	32.714
	1 Dobra . . .	18 06	. .	17.305
	1 Moidore	6 22	. .	6.560
	1 Crusado	16¼	. .	.638
ENGLAND.	1 Guinea	5 9½	. .	5.116
	1 Sovereign . . .	5 3¼	. .	4.875
FRANCE.	1 Double Louis (1786) .	10 11	. .	9.694
	1 Double Napoleon .	8 7	. .	7.713
COLOMBIA.	1 Doubloon . . .	17 8½	. .	15.538
MEXICO.	1 Doubloon . . .	17 8½	. .	15.538
PORTUGAL.	1 Dobraon . . .	34 12	. .	32.714
	1 Dobra . . .	18 6	. .	17.305
	1 Johannes . . .	18	. .	17.068
	1 Moidore . . .	6 22	. .	6.560
	1 Milrea . . .	19¾	. .	.780
SPAIN.	1 Doubloon (1772) . .	17 8½	. .	16.030
	1 Doubloon (1801) . .	17 9	. . *	15.538
	1 Pistole . . .	4 3¼	. .	3.883

23.2 grains of pure gold = $1.00.

United States Eagle preceding 1834, $10.668.

Mint Value of Foreign Coins.

ENGLAND.	1 Shilling	=	$0.244
FRANCE.	5 Francs	=	0.935
	1 Sous	=	0.0093
AUSTRIA.	1 Crown, or rix dollar	=	0.97
	1 Ducat	=	2.22
PRUSSIA.	1 Ducat	=	2.202
RUSSIA.	1 Ducat = 10 roubles	=	7.724
	1 Rouble	=	0.748
SWEDEN.	1 Ducat	=	2.19
	1 Rix dollar	=	1.08

The relative value of gold and silver is as 1 to $15\frac{11}{27}$.

Measures of Length.

ferred to a manial standard,

BRITISH. Yard is the length of a pendulum vibrating seconds in vacuo in London, at the level of the sea; measured on a brass rod, at the temperature of 62° Fahrenheit, =39.1393 *Imperial inches.*

FRENCH. *Old System.*—
1 Line	= 12 points	= 0.08884 U. S. inches.
1 Inch	= 12 lines	= 1.06604 "
1 Foot	= 12 inches	= 12.7925 "
1 Toise	= 6 feet	= 76.7550 "
1 League	= 2280 toises	(common).
1 League	= 2000 toises	(post).
1 Fathom	= 5 feet.	

New System.—
1 Millimetre	=	.03938 U. S. inches.
1 Centimetre	=	.39380 "
1 Decimetre	=	3.93809 "
1 *Metre*	=	39.38091 "
1 Decametre	=	393.80917 "
1 Hecatometre	=	3938.09171 "

AUSTRIAN	1 Foot	=	12.448 "
PRUSSIAN	1 Foot	=	12.361 "
SWEDISH	1 Foot	=	11.690 "
SPANISH	1 Foot	=	11.034 "
	1 League (common)	=	3.448 U. S. miles.

TABLE showing the relative length of *Foreign Measures* compared with BRITISH.

Places.	Measures.	Inches.	Places.	Measures.	Inches.
Amsterdam	Foot	11.14	Malta	Foot	11.17
Antwerp	"	11.24	Moscow	"	13.17
Bavaria	"	11.42	Naples	Palmo	10.38
Berlin	"	12.19	Prussia	Foot	12.35
Bremen	"	11.38	Persia	Arish	38.27
Brussels	"	11.45	Rhineland	Foot	12.35
China	" Mathematic.	13.12	Riga	"	10.79
"	" Builder's	12.71	Rome	"	11.60
"	" Tradesman's	13.32	Russia	"	13.75
"	" Surveyor's	12.58	Sardinia	Palmo	9.78
Copenhagen	"	12.35	Sicily	"	9.53
Dresden	"	11.14	Spain	Foot	11.12
England	"	12.00	"	Toesas	66.72
Florence	Braccio	21.60	"	Palmo	8.34
France	Pied de Roi	12.79	Strasburgh	Foot	11.39
"	Metre	39.381	Sweden	"	11.69
Geneva	Foot	19.20	Turin	"	12.72
Genoa	Palmo	9.72	Venice	"	13.40
Hamburgh	Foot	11.29	Vienna	"	12.45
Hanover	"	11.45	Zurich	"	11.81
Leipsic	"	11.11	Utrecht	"	10.74
Lisbon	"	12.96	Warsaw	"	14.03
"	Palmo	8.64			

TABLE showing the relative length of *Foreign Road Measures* compared with BRITISH.

Places.	Measures.	Yards.	Places.	Measures.	Yards.
Arabia . . .	Mile	2148	Hungary . .	Mile	9113
Bohemia . .	"	10137	Ireland . . .	"	3038
China . . .	Li	629	Netherlands .	"	1093
Denmark . .	Mile	8244	Persia . . .	Parasang	6086
England. . .	" Statute	1760	Poland . . .	Mile, long	8101
" . . .	" Geograph.	2025	Portugal . .	League	6760
Flanders . .	"	6869	Prussia . . .	Mile	8468
France . . .	League, marine	6075	Rome . . .	"	2025
" . . .	" common	4861	Russia . . .	Verst	1167
" . . .	" post	4264	Scotland . .	Mile	1984
Germany . .	Mile, long	10126	Spain . . .	League, com.	7416
Hamburgh . .	"	8244	Sweden . .	Mile	11700
Hanover . .	"	11559	Switzerland .	"	9153
Holland . . .	"	6395	Turkey . . .	Berri	1826

Measures of Surface.

FRENCH. *Old System.*—1 Square Inch . . = 1.1364 U. S. inches.
                1 Arpent (Paris) . . = 900 square toises.
                1 Arpent (woodland) . = 100 square royal perches.
      New System.—1 Are . . . = 100 square metres.
                1 Decare . . = 10 ares.
                1 Hecatare . . = 100 ares.
                1 Square Metre . . = 1550.85 square inches.
                            or 10.7698 square feet.
                1 Are . . . = 1076.98 "

TABLE showing the relation of *Foreign Measures of Surface* compared with BRITISH.

Places.	Measures.	Sq. yards.	Places.	Measures.	Sq. yards.
Amsterdam .	Morgen . .	9722	Portugal . .	Geira	6970
Berlin . .	" great	6786	Prussia . . .	Morgen	3053
" . .	" small	3054	Rome . . .	Pezza	3158
Canary Isles .	Fanegada	2422	Russia . . .	Dessetina	13066.6
England. . .	Acre	4840	Scotland . .	Acre	6150
Geneva . .	Arpent	6179	Spain . . .	Fanegada	5500
Hamburgh . .	Morgen	11545	Sweden . .	Tunneland	5900
Hanover . .	"	3100	Switzerland .	Faux	7855
Ireland . . .	Acre	7840	Vienna . . .	Joch	6889
Naples . . .	Moggia	3998	Zurich . . .	Common acre	3875.6

Measures of Capacity.

BRITISH. The *Imperial gallon* measures 277.274 cubic inches, containing 10 lbs. avoirdupois of distilled water, weighed in air, at the temperature of 62°, the barometer at 30 inches.
    For Grain. 8 bushels = 1 quarter.
                1 quarter = 10.2694 cubic feet.
    Coal, or heaped measure. 3 bushels = 1 sack.
                12 sacks = 1 chaldron.
    Imperial bushel = 2218.192 *cubic inches.*
    Heaped bushel, 19½ ins. diam., cone 6 ins. high = 2815.4872 cub. ins.
    1 chaldron = 58.658 cubic feet, and weighs 3136 pounds.
    1 chaldron (Newcastle) = 5936 pounds.
FRENCH. *New System.*—1 *Litre* = 1 cub. decimetre, or 61.074 U. S. cub. ins.
    Old System. — 1 Boisseau = 13 litres = 793.964 cub. ins., or 3.43 galls.
                1 Pinte = 0.931 litres, or 56.817 cubic inches.
SPANISH. 1 Wine Arroba = 4.2455 gallons.
    1 Fanega (common measure) = 1.593 bushels.

TABLE showing the relative *Capacity of Foreign Liquid Measures* compared with BRITISH.

Places.	Measures.	Cub. Inch.	Places.	Measures.	Cub.Inch.
Amsterdam .	Anker	2331	Naples . . .	Wine Barille	2544
" . .	Stoop	146	" . . .	Oil Stajo	1133
Antwerp . .	"	194	Oporto . . .	Almude	1555
Bordeaux . .	Barrique	14033	Rome . .' .	Wine Barille	2560
Bremen . . .	Stubgens	194.5	" . . .	Oil "	2240
Canaries . .	Arrobas	949	" . . .	Boccali	80
Constantinople	Almud	319	Russia . . .	Weddras	752
Copenhagen .	Anker	2355	" . . .	Kunkas	94
Florence . .	Oil Barille	1946	Scotland . .	Pint	103.5
" . .	Wine "	2427	Sicily . . .	Oil Caffiri	662
France . . .	Litre	61.07	Spain . . .	Azumbres	22.5
Geneva . . .	Setier	2760	" . . .	Quartillos	30.5
Genoa . . .	Wine Barille	4530	Sweden . . .	Eimer	4794
" . . .	Pinte	90.5	Trieste . . .	Orne	4007
Hamburgh . .	Stubgen	221	Tripoli . . .	Mattari	1376
Hanover . .	"	231	Tunis . . .	Oil "	1157
Hungary . .	Eimer	4474	Venice . . .	Secchio	628
Leghorn. . .	Oil Barille	1942	Vienna . . .	Eimer	3452
Lisbon . . .	Almude	1040	" . . .	Maas	86.33
Malta . . .	Caffiri	1270			

TABLE showing the relative *Capacity of Foreign Dry Measures* compared with BRITISH.

Places.	Measures.	Cub.Inch.	Places.	Measures.	Cub.Inch.
Alexandria .	Rebele	9587	Malta . . .	Salme	16930
" . .	Kislos	10418	Marseilles . .	Charge	9411
Algiers . . .	Tarrie	1219	Milan . . .	Moggi	8444
Amsterdam .	Mudde	6596	Naples . . .	Tomoli	3122
" . .	Sack	4947	Oporto . . .	Alquiere	1051
Antwerp . .	Viertel	4705	Persia . . .	Artaba	4013
Azores . . .	Alquiere	731	Poland . . .	Zorzec	3120
Berlin . . .	Scheffel	3180	Riga	Loop	3978
Bremen . . .	"	4339	Rome . . .	Rubbio	16904
Candia . . .	Charge	9288	" . . .	Quarti	4226
Constantinople	Kislos	2023	Rotterdam .	Sach	6361
Copenhagen .	Toende	8489	Russia . . .	Chetwert	12448
Corsica . . .	Stajo	6014	Sardinia . .	Starelli	2988
Florence . .	Stari	1449	Scotland . .	Firlot	2197
Geneva . . .	Coupes	4739	Sicily . . .	Salme gros	21014
Genoa . . .	Mina	7382	" . . .	" generale	16886
Greece . . .	Medimni	2390	Smyrna . . .	Kislos	2141
Hamburgh . .	Scheffel	6426	Spain . . .	Catrize	41269
Hanover . .	Malter	6868	Sweden . . .	Tunnar	8940
Leghorn . . .	Stajo	1501	Trieste . . .	Stari	4521
" . . .	Sacco	4503	Tripoli . . .	Caffiri	19780
Lisbon . . .	Alquiere	817	Tunis . . .	"	21855
" . . .	Fanega	3268	Venice . . .	Stajo	4945
Madeira . . .	Alquiere	684	Vienna . . .	Metzen	3753
Malaga . . .	Fanega	3783			

Measures of Solidity.

FRENCH.	1 Cubic Foot	=	2093.470 U. S. inches.
	Decistre	=	3.5375 cubic feet.
	Stere (a cubic metre)	=	35.375 "
	Decastere	=	353.75 "
	1 Stere	=	61074.664 cubic inches.

For the *Square* and *Cubic Measures* of other countries, take the length of the measure in table, page 17, and square or cube it as required.

Measures of Weight.

BRITISH.   1 troy Grain   =   .003961 cubic inches of distilled water.
           1 troy Pound = 22.815689 cubic inches of water.
FRENCH.   *Old System.*—1 Grain   .   .   . =   0.8188 grains troy.
                         1 Gros   .   .   . =   58.9548   "
                         1 Once   .   .   . =   1.0780 oz. avoirdupois.
                         1 Livre   .   .   . =   1.0780 lbs.   "
           New System.—Milligramme   .   . =   .01543 troy grains.
                         Centigramme   .   . =   .15433   "
                         Decigramme   .   . =   1.54331   "
                         Gramme   .   . = 15.43315   "
                         Decagramme   .   . = 154.33159   "
                         Hecatogramme .   . = 1543.3159   "
                         1 Millier = 1000 Kilogrammes = 1 ton sea weight.
                         1 Kilogramme   .   = 2.204737 lbs. avoirdupois.
                         1 Pound avoirdupois = 0.4535685 Kilogramme.
                         1 Pound troy   .   = 0.3732223   "
SPANISH .   .   . 1   "   .   . = 1.0152 lbs. avoirdupois.
SWEDISH .   .   . 1   "   .   . = 0.9376   "
AUSTRIAN .   .   . 1   "   .   . = 1.2351   "
PRUSSIAN .   .   . 1   "   .   . = 1.0333   "

NOTE.—*In the new French system, the values of the base of each measure, viz.,
Metre, Litre, Stere, Are, and Gramme, are decreased or increased by the following
words prefixed to them. Thus,*

Milli expresses the 1000th part.	Hecato expresses 100 times the value.
Centi " 100th "	Chilio " 1000 "
Deci " 10th "	Myrio " 10000 "
Deca " 10 times the value.	

TABLE showing the relative value of *Foreign Weights* compared with BRITISH.

Places.	Weights.	Number equal to 100 avoirdupois pounds.	Places.	Weights.	Number equal to 100 avoirdupois pounds.
Aleppo . . .	Rottoli	20.46	Hanover . .	Pound	93.20
" . . .	Oke	35.80	Japan . . .	Catty	76.92
Alexandria .	Rottoli	107.	Leghorn . .	Pound	133.56
Algiers . . .	"	84.	Leipsic . . .	" (common)	97.14
Amsterdam .	Pound	91.8	Lyons . . .	" (silk)	98.81
Antwerp . .	"	96.75	Madeira . .	"	143.20
Barcelona . .	"	112.6	Mocha . . .	Maund	33.33
Batavia . . .	Catty	76.78	Morea . . .	Pound	90.79
Bengal . . .	Seer	53.57	Naples . . .	Rottoli	50.91
Berlin . . .	Pound	96.8	Rome . . .	Pound	133.69
Bologna . . .	"	125.3	Rotterdam .	"	91.80
Bremen . . .	"	90.93	Russia . . .	"	110.86
Brunswick . .	"	97.14	Sicily . . .	"	142.85
Cairo	Rottoli	105.	Smyrna . . .	Oke	36.51
Candia . . .	"	85.9	Sumatra . .	Catty	35.56
China . . .	Catty	75.45	Sweden . .	Pound	106.67
Constantinople	Oke	35.55	" . . .	"	120.68
Copenhagen .	Pound	90.80	Tangiers . .	" (miner's)	94.27
Corsica . . .	"	131.72	Tripoli . . .	Rottoli	89.28
Cyprus . . .	Rottoli	19.07	Tunis . . .	"	90.09
Damascus . .	"	25.23	Venice . . .	Pound (heavy)	94.74
Florence . .	Pound	133.56	" . . .	" (light)	150.
Geneva . . .	" (heavy)	82.35	Vienna . . .	"	81.
Genoa . . .	" "	92.86	Warsaw . .	"	112.25
Hamburgh . .	" "	93.63			

Scripture Long Measures.

	Feet.	Inches.			Feet.	Inches.
A digit	= 0	0.912		A cubit	= 1	9.888
A palm	= 0	3.648		A fathom	= 7	3.552
A span	= 0	10.944				

Grecian Long Measures.

	Feet.	Inches.			Feet.	Inches.
A digit	= 0	0.7554		A stadium	= 604	4.5
A pous (foot)	= 1	0.0875		A mile	= 4835	
A cubit	= 1	1.5984				

A Greek or Olympic foot = 12.108 inches.
A Pythic or natural foot = 9.768 "

Jewish Long Measures.

	Feet			Feet.
A cubit	= 1.824		A mile	= 7296
A Sabbath day's journey	= 3648.		A day's journey (or 33 miles 864 feet).	= 175104

Roman Long Measures.

	Feet.	Inches.			Feet.	Inches.
A digit	= 0	.72575		A cubit	= 1	5.406
An uncia (inch)	= 0	.967		A passus	= 4	10.02
A pes (foot)	= 0	11.604		A mile	= 4835	

Miscellaneous.

	Feet.			Feet.
Arabian foot	= 1.095		Hebrew foot	= 1.212
Babylonian foot	= 1.140		" cubit	= 1.817
Egyptian	= 1.421		" sacred cubit	= 2.002

NOTE.—*The above dimensions are British.*

TABLE *for finding the Distance of Objects at Sea, in Statute Miles.*

Height in feet.	Distance in miles.	Height in feet.	Distance in miles.	Height in feet.	Distance in miles.	Height in feet.	Distance in miles.
*.582	1.	11	4.39	30	7.25	200	18.72
1	1.31	12	4.58	35	7.83	300	22.91
2	1.87	13	4.77	40	8.37	400	26.46
3	2.29	14	4.95	45	8.87	500	29.58
4	2.63	15	5.12	50	9.35	1000	32.41
5	2.96	16	5.29	60	10.25	2000	59.20
6	3.24	17	5.45	70	11.07	3000	72.50
7	3.49	18	5.61	80	11.83	4000	83.7
8	3.73	19	5.77	90	12.55	5000	93.5
9	3.96	20	5.92	100	13.23	1 mile.	96.1
10	4.18	25	6.61	150	16.20		

* 6.99 inches.

The difference in two levels is as the square of the distance. Thus, if the height is required for 2 miles,

$$1^2 : 2^2 :: 6.99 : 27.96 \text{ inches};$$

and if for 100 miles, $1^2 : 100^2 :: 6.99 : 1.103 +$ miles.

For Geographical miles, the distance for one mile is 7.962 inches.

EXAMPLE.—If a man at the foretop-gallant-mast-head of a ship, 100 feet from the water, sees another and a large ship (hull to), how far are the ships apart?

A large ship's bulwarks are, say 20 feet from the water.

$$
\begin{array}{ll}
\text{Then, by table, 100 feet} & = 13.23 \\
\qquad\qquad\quad 20\ \text{``} & = \underline{5.92} \\
\qquad\qquad \text{Distance} & \overline{19.15}\ \text{miles.}
\end{array}
$$

NOTE.—1-13 *should be added for horizontal refraction.*

To Reduce Longitude into Time.

Multiply the number of degrees, minutes, and seconds by 4, and the product is the time.

EXAMPLE.—Required the time corresponding to 50° 31'.

$$
\begin{array}{c}
50^{\circ}\ 31' \\
4 \\
\hline
h.3 \quad 22' \quad 4''\ Ans.
\end{array}
$$

If time is to be reduced, then

$$
\begin{array}{cccc}
 & h. & m. & s. \\
4) & 3 & 22 & 4 \\
\hline
 & 50 & 31 & Ans.
\end{array}
$$

Or, multiplying by 15 : thus,

$$
\begin{array}{ccc}
h. & m. & s. \\
4 & 27 & 13 \times 15 = 66^{\circ}\ 48'\ 15''.
\end{array}
$$

Degrees of longitude are to each other in length, as the cosines of their latitudes.

For every 5° they are as follows :

	Miles.		Miles.
Equator	60.	50°	38.57
5°	59.77	55°	34.41
10°	59.09	60°	30.
15°	57.96	65°	25.36
20°	56.38	70°	20.52
25°	54.38	75°	15.53
30°	51.96	80°	10.42
35°	49.15	85°	5.23
40°	45.96	90°	0.00
45°	42.43		

VULGAR FRACTIONS.

A FRACTION, or broken number, is one or more parts of a UNIT.

EXAMPLE.—12 inches are 1 foot.

Here, 1 *foot* is the unit, and 12 *inches* its parts; 3 *inches*, therefore, are the *one fourth* of a foot, for 3 is the quarter or fourth of 12.

A *Vulgar Fraction* is a fraction expressed by *two numbers* placed one above the other, with a line between them; as, 50 cents is the $\frac{1}{2}$ of a dollar.

The upper number is called the *Numerator*, because it shows the number of parts used.

The lower number is called the *Denominator*, because it denominates, or gives name to the fraction.

The *Terms* of a fraction express both numerator and denominator; as, 6 and 9 are the terms of $\frac{6}{9}$.

A *Proper* fraction has the numerator equal to, or less than the denominator; as, $\frac{1}{2}$, &c.

An *Improper* fraction is the reverse of a proper one; as, $\frac{2}{1}$, &c.

A *Mixed* fraction is a compound of a whole number and a fraction; as, $5\frac{7}{8}$, &c.

A *Compound* fraction is the fraction of a fraction; as, $\frac{1}{2}$ of $\frac{3}{4}$, &c.

A *Complex* fraction is one that has a fraction for its numerator or denominator, or both; as, $\frac{\frac{1}{2}}{6}$, or $\frac{5}{\frac{3}{4}}$, or $\frac{\frac{1}{2}}{\frac{3}{4}}$, or $\frac{3\frac{1}{2}}{6}$, &c.

A Fraction denotes division, and its value is equal to the quotient obtained by dividing the numerator by the denominator; thus, $\frac{12}{4}$ is equal to 3, and $\frac{21}{5}$ is equal to $4\frac{1}{5}$.

REDUCTION OF VULGAR FRACTIONS.

To find the greatest Number that will divide Two or more Numbers without a Remainder.

RULE.—Divide the greater number by the less; then divide the divisor by the remainder; and so on, dividing always the last divisor by the last remainder, until nothing remains.

EXAMPLE.—What is the greatest common measure of 1908 and 936 ?

```
936) 1908 (2
     1872
     ────
      36) 936 (26
          72
         ────
         216
         216
         ────   So 36 is the greatest common measure.
```

To find the least Common Multiple of Two or more Numbers.

RULE.—Divide by any number that will divide two or more of the given numbers without a remainder, and set the quotients with the undivided numbers in a line beneath.

Divide the second line as before, and so on, until there are no two numbers that can be divided; then the continued product of the divisors and quotients will give the multiple required.

EXAMPLE.—What is the least common multiple of 40, 50, and 25 ?

```
5) 40 . 50 . 25
5)  8 . 10 .  5
2)  8 .  2 .  1
    4 .  1 .  1
```

Then 5×5×2×4=200 *Ans.*

To reduce Fractions to their lowest Terms.

RULE.—Divide the terms by any number that will divide them without a remainder, or by their greatest common measure at once.

EXAMPLE.—Reduce $\frac{720}{960}$ of a foot to its lowest terms.

$$\frac{720}{960} \div 10 = \frac{72}{96} \div 8 = \frac{9}{12} \div 3 = \frac{3}{4}, \text{ or } 9 \text{ inches.}$$

To reduce a Mixed Fraction to its equivalent, an Improper Fraction.

NOTE.—*Mixed and improper fractions are the same; thus, $5\frac{1}{2} = \frac{11}{2}$. For illustration, see following examples:*

RULE.—Multiply the whole number by the denominator of the fraction, and to the product add the numerator; then set that sum above the denominator.

EXAMPLE.—Reduce $23\frac{2}{6}$ to a fraction.

$$\frac{23 \times 6 + 2 = 140}{6}$$

EXAMPLE.—Reduce $\frac{123}{6}$ inches to its value in feet.

$$123 \div 6 = 20\frac{3}{6}; \text{ that is, 20 feet and } \frac{3}{6} \text{ or } \frac{1}{2} \text{ of a foot.}$$

To reduce a Whole Number to an equivalent Fraction having a given Denominator.

RULE.—Multiply the whole number by the given denominator, and set the product over the said denominator.

EXAMPLE.—Reduce 8 to a fraction whose denominator shall be 9.

$$8 \times 9 = 72; \text{ then } \frac{72}{9} \text{ the answer.}$$

To reduce a Compound Fraction to an equivalent Simple one.

RULE.—Multiply all the numerators together for a numerator, and all the denominators together for a denominator.

NOTE.—*When there are terms that are common, they may be omitted.*

EXAMPLE.—Reduce $\frac{1}{2}$ of $\frac{3}{4}$ of $\frac{2}{3}$ to a simple fraction.

$$\frac{1}{2} \times \frac{3}{4} \times \frac{2}{3} = \frac{6}{24} = \frac{1}{4}. \text{ Ans.}$$

Or, $\frac{1}{2} \times \frac{3}{4} \times \frac{2}{3} = \frac{1}{4}$, by cancelling the 2's and 3's.

EXAMPLE.—Reduce $\frac{1}{2}$ of $\frac{3}{4}$ of a pound to a simple fraction.

$$\frac{1}{2} \times \frac{3}{4} = \frac{3}{8} \text{ Ans.}$$

To reduce Fractions of different Denominations to equivalent ones having a common Denominator.

RULE.—Multiply each numerator by all the denominators except its own for the new numerators; and multiply all the denominators together for a common denominator.

NOTE.—*In this, as in all other operations, whole numbers, mixed, or compound fractions, must first be reduced to the form of simple fractions.*

EXAMPLE.—Reduce $\frac{1}{2}$, $\frac{2}{3}$, and $\frac{3}{4}$ to a common denominator.

$$\left. \begin{array}{l} 1 \times 3 \times 4 = 12 \\ 2 \times 2 \times 4 = 16 \\ 3 \times 2 \times 3 = 18 \end{array} \right\} = \frac{12}{24} = \frac{16}{24} = \frac{18}{24} \text{ Ans.}$$
$$\overline{2 \times 3 \times 4 = 24}$$

The operation may be performed mentally; thus,

Reduce $\frac{1}{8}$, $\frac{3}{2}$, $\frac{6}{8}$, and $\frac{5}{2}$ to a common denominator.

$$\frac{3}{2} = \frac{12}{8}. \qquad \frac{1}{8} = \frac{1}{8}. \qquad \frac{6}{8} = \frac{6}{8}. \qquad \frac{5}{2} = \frac{20}{8}.$$

To reduce Complex Fractions to Simple ones.

RULE.—Reduce the two parts both to simple fractions; then multiply the numerator of each by the denominator of the other.

EXAMPLE.—Simplify the complex fraction $\frac{2\frac{2}{3}}{4\frac{4}{5}}$.

$$2\frac{2}{3} = \frac{8}{3} \qquad 8 \times 5 = 40 \qquad \frac{5}{9} \; Ans.$$
$$4\frac{4}{5} = \frac{24}{5} \qquad 3 \times 24 = 72$$

ADDITION OF VULGAR FRACTIONS.

RULE.—If the fractions have a common denominator, add all the numerators together, and then place the sum over the denominators.

NOTE.—*If the prepared fractions have not a common denominator, they must be reduced to one. Also, compound and complex must be reduced to simple fractions.*

EXAMPLE.—Add $\frac{1}{4}$ and $\frac{3}{4}$ together.

$$\frac{1}{4} + \frac{3}{4} = \frac{4}{4} = 1 \; Ans.$$

EXAMPLE.—Add $\frac{1}{2}$ of $\frac{3}{4}$ of $\frac{6}{10}$ to $2\frac{1}{8}$ of $\frac{3}{4}$.

$$\frac{1}{2} \times \frac{3}{4} \times \frac{6}{10} = \frac{18}{80}.$$
$$2\frac{1}{8} \text{ of } \frac{3}{4} = \frac{17}{8} \times \frac{3}{4} = \frac{51}{32}. \quad \text{Then, } \frac{18}{80} + \frac{51}{32} = 1\frac{131}{160}. \; Ans.$$

SUBTRACTION OF VULGAR FRACTIONS.

RULE.—Prepare the fractions the same as for other operations, when necessary; then subtract the one numerator from the other, and set the remainder over the common denominator.

EXAMPLE.—What is the difference between $\frac{5}{8}$ and $\frac{1}{8}$?

$$\frac{5}{8} - \frac{1}{8} = \frac{4}{8} \; Ans.$$

EXAMPLE.—Subtract $\frac{6}{8}$ from $\frac{3}{9}$.

$$\left.\begin{array}{l} 6 \times 9 = 54 \\ 3 \times 8 = 24 \\ 8 \times 9 = 72 \end{array}\right\} = \frac{54}{72} - \frac{24}{72} = \frac{30}{72} \; Ans.$$

MULTIPLICATION OF VULGAR FRACTIONS.

RULE.—Prepare the fractions as previously required; multiply all the numerators together for a new numerator, and all the denominators together for a new denominator.

EXAMPLE.—What is the product of $\frac{3}{4}$ and $\frac{3}{9}$?

$$\frac{3}{4} \times \frac{3}{9} = \frac{9}{36} = \frac{1}{4} \; Ans.$$

EXAMPLE.—What is the product of 6 and $\frac{2}{3}$ of 5?

$$\frac{6}{1} \times \frac{2}{3} \text{ of } 5 = \frac{6}{1} \times \frac{10}{3} = \frac{60}{3} = 20 \; Ans.$$

C

DIVISION OF VULGAR FRACTIONS.

RULE.—Prepare the fractions as before; then divide the numerator by the numerator, and the denominator by the denominator, if they will exactly divide; but if not, invert the terms of the divisor, and multiply the dividend by it, as in multiplication.

EXAMPLE.—Divide $\frac{25}{9}$ by $\frac{5}{3}$.

$$\frac{25}{9} \div \frac{5}{3} = \frac{5}{3} = 1\frac{2}{3} \ Ans.$$

To find the Value of a Fraction in Parts of the whole Number.

RULE.—Multiply the whole number by the numerator, and divide by the denominator; then, if anything remains, multiply it by the parts in the next inferior denomination, and divide by the denominator, as before, and so on as far as necessary; so shall the quotients placed in order be the value of the fraction required.

EXAMPLE.—What is the value of $\frac{1}{2}$ of $\frac{2}{3}$ of $9 ?

$$\frac{1}{2} \text{ of } \frac{2}{3} = \frac{2}{6} \times \frac{9}{\cdot} = \frac{18}{6} = \$3 \ Ans.$$

EXAMPLE.—Reduce $\frac{3}{4}$ of a pound to avoirdupois ounces.

$$\begin{array}{c} 3 \\ 1 \\ 4)\overline{3} \ (0 \text{ lbs.} \\ 16 \text{ ounces in a lb.} \\ 4)\overline{48} \\ \overline{12} \text{ ounces, } Ans. \end{array}$$

EXAMPLE.—Reduce $\frac{3}{10}$ of a day to hours.

$$\frac{3}{10} \times \frac{24}{\cdot} = \frac{72}{10} = 7\frac{2}{10} \text{ hours, } Ans.$$

To reduce a Fraction from one Denomination to another.

RULE.—Multiply the number of parts in the next less denominator by the numerator *if the reduction is to be to a less name*, but multiply by the denominator *if to a greater.*

EXAMPLE.—Reduce $\frac{1}{4}$ of a dollar to the fraction of a penny.

$$\frac{1}{4} \times \frac{100}{1} = \frac{100}{4} = \frac{25}{1}, \text{ the answer.}$$

EXAMPLE.—Reduce $\frac{1}{6}$ of an avoirdupois pound to the fraction of an ounce.

$$\frac{1}{6} \times \frac{16}{1} = \frac{16}{6} = \frac{8}{3}, \text{ the answer.}$$

EXAMPLE.—Reduce $\frac{2}{7}$ of a cwt. to the fraction of a lb.

$$\frac{2}{7} \times \frac{4}{1} \times \frac{28}{1} = \frac{224}{7} = \frac{32}{1}, \text{ the answer.}$$

EXAMPLE.—Reduce $\frac{2}{3}$ of $\frac{3}{4}$ of a mile to the fraction of a foot.

$$\frac{2}{3} \text{ of } \frac{3}{4} = \frac{6}{12} \times \frac{5280}{1} = \frac{31680}{1} = \frac{2640}{1}, \text{ the answer.}$$

EXAMPLE.—Reduce $\frac{1}{4}$ of a square foot to the fraction of an inch.

$$\frac{1}{4} \times \frac{144}{1} = \frac{144}{4} = \frac{36}{1} \ Ans.$$

For Rule of Three in Vulgar Fractions, see page 29.

DECIMAL FRACTIONS.

A DECIMAL FRACTION is that which has for its denominator a UNIT (1), with as many ciphers annexed as the numerator has places; it is usually expressed by setting down the numerator only, with a point on the left of it. Thus, $\frac{4}{10}$ is .4, $\frac{85}{100}$ is .85, $\frac{0075}{10000}$ is .0075, and $\frac{125}{100000}$ is .00125. When there is a deficiency of figures in the numerator, prefix ciphers to make up as many places as there are ciphers in the denominator.

Mixed numbers consist of a whole number and a fraction; as, 3.25, which is the same as $3.\frac{25}{100}$, or $\frac{325}{100}$.

Ciphers on the right hand make no alteration in their value; for .4, .40, .400 are decimals of the same value, each being $\frac{4}{10}$, or $\frac{2}{5}$.

ADDITION OF DECIMALS.

RULE.—Set the numbers under each other according to the value of their places, as in whole numbers, in which state the decimal points will stand directly under each other. Then, beginning at the right hand, add up all the columns of numbers as in integers, and place the point directly below all the other points.

EXAMPLE.—Add together 25.125, 56.19, 1.875, and 293.7325.

$$\begin{array}{r} 25.125 \\ 56.19 \\ 1.875 \\ 293.7325 \\ \hline 376.9225 \text{ the sum.} \end{array}$$

SUBTRACTION OF DECIMAL FRACTIONS.

RULE.—Place the numbers under each other as in addition; then subtract as in whole numbers, and point off the decimals as in the last rule.

EXAMPLE.—Subtract 15.150 from 89.1759.

$$\begin{array}{r} 89.1759 \\ 15.150 \\ \hline 74.0259 \text{ Rem.} \end{array}$$

MULTIPLICATION OF DECIMALS.

RULE.—Place the factors, and multiply them together the same as if they were whole numbers; then point off in the product just as many places of decimals as there are decimals in both the factors. But if there be not so many figures in the product, supply the deficiency by prefixing ciphers.

EXAMPLE.—Multiply 1.56 by .75.

$$\begin{array}{r} 1.56 \\ .75 \\ \hline 780 \\ 1092 \\ \hline 1.1700 \text{ Prod.} \end{array}$$

BY CONTRACTION.

To contract the Operation so as to retain only as many Decimal places in the Product as may be thought necessary.

RULE.—Set the unit's place of the multiplier under the figure of the multiplicand whose place is the same as is to be retained for the last in the product, and dispose of the rest of the figures in the contrary order to what they are usually placed in. Then, in multiplying, reject all the figures that are more to the right hand than each multiplying figure, and set down the products, so that their right-hand figures may fall in a column straight below each other; and observe to increase the first figure in every line with what would arise from the figures omitted; thus, add 1 for every result from 5 to 14, 2 from 15 to 24, 3 from 25 to 34, 4 from 35 to 44, &c., &c., and the sum of all the lines will be the product as required.

EXAMPLE.—Multiply 13.57493 by 46.20517, and retain only four places of decimals in the product.

$$\begin{array}{r} 13.574\,93 \\ 71\,502.64 \\ \hline 54\,299\,72 \\ 8\,144\,96 + 2 \text{ for } 18 \\ 271\,50 + 2 \text{ `` } 18 \\ 6\,79 + 4 \text{ `` } 35 \\ 14 + 1 \text{ `` } 5 \\ 9 + 2 \text{ `` } 21 \\ \hline 627.23\,20 \end{array}$$

EXAMPLE.—Multiply 27.14986 by 92.41035, and retain only five places of deci
mals.   *Ans.* 2508.92806.

DIVISION OF DECIMALS.

RULE.—Divide as in whole numbers, and point off in the quotient as many places for decimals as the decimal places in the dividend exceed those in the divisor; but if there are not so many places, supply the deficiency by prefixing ciphers.

EXAMPLE.—Divide 53.00 by 6.75.

$$6.75) \; 53.00 \; (= 7.851+.$$

Here 3 ciphers were annexed to carry out the division.

BY CONTRACTION.

RULE.—Take only as many figures of the divisor as will be equal to the number of figures, both integers and decimals, to be in the quotient, and find how many times they may be contained in the first figures of the dividend, as usual.

Let each remainder be a new dividend; and for every such dividend leave out one figure more on the right-hand side of the divisor, carrying for the figures cut off as in Contraction of Multiplication.

NOTE.—*When there are not so many figures in the divisor as are required to be in the quotient, continue the first operation till the number of figures in the divisor be equal to those remaining to be found in the quotient, after which begin the contraction.*

EXAMPLE.—Divide 2508.92806 by 92.41035, so as to have only four places of decimals in the quotient.

$$
\begin{array}{r}
92.4103|5) \; 2508.928|06 \; (27.1498 \\
1848\,207+1 \\
\hline
660\,721 \\
646\,872+2 \\
\hline
13\,849 \\
9\,241 \\
\hline
4\,608 \\
3\,696 \\
\hline
912 \\
832+4 \\
\hline
80 \\
74+2 \\
\hline
6
\end{array}
$$

EXAMPLE.—Divide 4109.2351 by 230.409, retaining only four decimals in the quotient.   *Ans.* 17.8345.

REDUCTION OF DECIMALS.

To reduce a Vulgar Fraction to its equivalent Decimal.

RULE.—Divide the numerator by the denominator, annexing ciphers to the numerator as far as necessary.

EXAMPLE.—Reduce ⅘ to a decimal.

$$
\begin{array}{r}
5) \; 4.0 \\
\hline
.8 \; \textit{Ans.}
\end{array}
$$

To find the Value of a Decimal in Terms of an Inferior Denomination.

RULE.—Multiply the decimal by the number of parts in the next lower denomination, and cut off as many places for a remainder, to the right hand, as there are places in the given decimal.

Multiply that remainder by the parts in the next lower denomination, again cutting off for a remainder, and so on through all the parts of the integer.

EXAMPLE.—What is the value of .875 dollars ?

$$
\begin{array}{r}
.875 \\
100 \\
\hline
\text{Cents,} \quad 87,500 \\
10 \\
\hline
\text{Mills,} \quad 5.000
\end{array}
$$

Ans. 87 cents 5 mills.

EXAMPLE.—What is the content of .140 cubic feet in inches ?

.140

1728 cubic inches in a cubic foot.

241.920

Ans. 241.$\frac{920}{1000}$ cubic inches.

EXAMPLE.—What is the value of .00129 of a foot ?

Ans. .01548 inches.

EXAMPLE.—What is the value of 1.075 tons in pounds ?

Ans. 2408.

To reduce Decimals to equivalent Decimals of higher Denominations.

RULE.—Divide by the number of parts in the next higher denomination, continuing the operation as far as required.

EXAMPLE.—Reduce 1 inch to the decimal of a foot.

12|1.00000

|.08333, &c., *Ans.*

EXAMPLE.—Reduce 14 minutes to the decimal of a day.

60|14.00000

24| .23333

.00972, &c., *Ans.*

EXAMPLE.—Reduce 14″ 12‴ to the decimal of a minute.

14″ 12‴

60

60|852.‴

60| 14.2″

.23666′, &c., *Ans.*

NOTE.—*When there are several numbers, to be reduced all to the decimal of the highest.*

Reduce them all to the lowest denomination, and proceed as for one denomination.

EXAMPLE.—Reduce 5 feet 10 inches and 3 barleycorns to the decimal of a yard

Feet. Inches. Bc.

  5   10   3

 12

 70

  3

3|213.

12| 71.

3| 5.9166

1.9722, &c., yards, *Ans.*

RULE OF THREE IN DECIMALS.

RULE.—Prepare the terms by reducing the vulgar fractions to decimals, compound numbers to decimals of the highest denomination, the first and third terms to the same name ; then proceed as in whole numbers. See Rule, page 31.

EXAMPLE.—If ½ a ton of iron cost ¾ of a dollar, what will .625 of a ton cost ?

½ = .5 ⎫   .5 : .75 : : .625

¾ = .75 ⎰   .625

.5) .46875

.9375 dollars, *Ans.*

C 2

DUODECIMALS.

In Duodecimals, or Cross Multiplication, the dimensions are taken in feet, inches, and twelfths of an inch.

RULE.—Set down the dimensions to be multiplied together, one under the other, so that feet may stand under feet, inches under inches, &c.

Multiply each term of the multiplicand, beginning at the lowest, by the feet in the multiplier, and set the result of each immediately under its corresponding term, carrying 1 for every 12, from one term to the other. In like manner, multiply all the multiplicand by the inches of the multiplier, and then by the twelfth parts, setting the result of each term one place farther to the right hand for every multiplier. The sum of the products is the answer.

EXAMPLE.—Multiply 1 foot 3 inches by 1 foot one inch.

```
Feet. Inches.
  1     3
  1     1
  -------
  1     3
        1     3
  ---------------
  1     4     3
```

PROOF.—1 foot 3 inches is 15 inches, and 1 foot 1 inch is 13 inches; and 15×13 = 195 square inches. Now the above product reads 1 foot 4 inches and 3 twelfths of an inch, and

```
1 foot    = 144 square inches.
4 inches  =  48      "
3 twelfths =   3      "
           -----
            195
```

EXAMPLE.—How many square inches are there in a board 35 feet 4½ inches long and 12 feet 3¼ inches wide?

```
Feet. Inches. Twelfths.
 35     4      6
 12     3      4
 --------------------
424     6      0         0
  8    10      1         6
       11      9         6      0
 --------------------------------
434     3     11         0      0
```

EXAMPLE.—Multiply 20 feet 6½ inches by 40 feet 6 inches.

By duodecimals, *Ans.* 831 feet 11 inches 3 twelfths equal 831 square feet and 135 square inches.

```
By decimals    .    .   40 feet 6 inches = 40.5
                     20  "   6½  "        = 20.541666, &c.
                 Feet   .   .   .   831.937499
                                           144
                 Square inches   .   134.999856
```

Table showing the value of Duodecimals in Square Feet, and Decimals of an Inch.

		Sq. feet.	Sq. inches.
1 Foot	=	1	or 144.
1 Inch	=	$\frac{1}{12}$	" 12.
1 Twelfth	=	$\frac{1}{144}$	" 1.
$\frac{1}{12}$ of 1 twelfth	=	$\frac{1}{1728}$	" .083333, &c.
$\frac{1}{12}$ of $\frac{1}{12}$ of do.	=	$\frac{1}{20736}$	" .006944. &c.

Application of this Table.

What number of square inches are there in a floor 100½ feet broad and 25 feet 6 inches and 6 twelfths long?

Ans. 2566 feet 11 inches 3 twelfths equal 2566 feet 135 inches.

RULE OF THREE.

The RULE OF THREE teaches how to find a fourth proportional to three given numbers.

It is either DIRECT or INVERSE.

It is Direct when more requires more, or less requires less. Thus, if 3 barrels of flour cost $18, what will 10 barrels cost? Or, if 300 lbs. of lead cost $25.50, what will 10 lbs. cost?

In both of these cases the *Proportion* is *Direct*, and the stating must be,

As   3 : 18   : : 10 :   *Ans.* 60.
300 : 25.50 : : 10 :   *Ans.* .85.

It is Inverse when more requires less, or less requires more. Thus, if 6 men build a certain quantity of wall in 10 days, in how many days will 8 men build the like quantity? Or, if 3 men dig 100 feet of trench in 7 days, in how many days will 2 men perform the same work?

Here the *Proportion* is *Inverse*, and the stating must be,

As 8 : 10 : : 6 :   *Ans.* 7½.
2 : 7 : : 3 :   *Ans.* 10½.

The fourth term is always found by multiplying the 2d and 3d terms together, and dividing the product by the 1st term.

Of the three given numbers necessary for the stating, two of them contain the supposition, and the third a demand.

RULE.—STATE the question by setting down in a straight line the three necessary numbers in the following manner:

Let the 2d term be that number of supposition which is of the same denomination as that the answer, or 4th term, is to be, making the *demanding* number the 3d term, and the other number the 1st term when the question is in *Direct Proportion*, but contrariwise if in *Inverse Proportion*, that is, let the *demanding* number be the 1st term.

Then multiply the 2d and 3d terms together, and divide by the 1st, and the product will be the answer, or 4th term sought, of the same denomination as the 2d term.

NOTE.—*If the first and third terms are of different denominations, reduce them to the same. If, after division, there be any remainder, reduce it to the next lower denomination, and divide by the same divisor as before, and the quotient will be of this last denomination.*

Sometimes two or more statings are necessary, which may always be known by the nature of the question.

EXAMPLE 1.—If 20 tons of iron cost $225, what will 500 tons cost?

Tons. Dolls. Tons.
20 : 225 : : 500
500

2|0) 11250|0

5625 dollars, *Ans.*

EXAMPLE 2.—If 15 men raise 100 tons of iron ore in 12 days, how many men will raise a like quantity in 5 days?

Days. Men. Days.
As 5 : 15 : : 12
12

5) 180

36 men, *Ans.*

EXAMPLE 3.—A wall that is to be built to the height of 36 feet was raised 9 feet high by 16 men in 6 days: how many men could finish it in 4 days at the same rate of working?

Days. Men. Days. Men.
4 : 16 : : 6 : 24 *Ans.*

Then, if 9 feet require 24 men, what will 27 feet require?

9 : 24 : : 27 : 72 *Ans.*

EXAMPLE 4.—If the third of six be three, what will the fourth of twenty be?

Ans. 7½.

COMPOUND PROPORTION.

COMPOUND PROPORTION is the rule by means of which such questions as would require two or more statings in simple proportion (Rule of Three) can be resolved in one.

As the rule, however, is but little used, and not easily acquired, it is deemed preferable to omit it here, and to show the operation by two or more statings.

EXAMPLE.—How many men can dig a trench 135 feet long in 8 days, when 16 men can dig 54 feet in 6 days?

			Feet. Men. Feet. Men.
First	.	.	As 54 : 16 : : 135 : 40

			Days Men. Days. Men.
Second	.	.	As 8 : 40 : : 6 : 30 *Ans.*

EXAMPLE.—If a man travel 130 miles in 3 days of twelve hours each, in how many days of 10 hours each would he require to travel 360 miles?

			Miles. Days. Miles. Days.
First	.	.	As 130 : 3 : : 360 : 8.307

			Hours. Days. Hours. Days.
Second	.	.	As 10 : 8.307 : : 12 : 9.9684 *Ans.*

EXAMPLE.—If 12 men in 15 days of 12 hours build a wall 30 feet long, 6 wide, and 3 deep, in how many days of 8 hours will 60 men build a wall 300 feet long, 8 wide, and 6 deep?   *Ans.* 120 days.

INVOLUTION.

INVOLUTION is the multiplying any number into itself a certain number of times. The products obtained are called POWERS. The number is called the ROOT, or first power.

When a number is multiplied by itself once, the product is the square of that number; twice, the cube; three times, the biquadrate, &c. Thus, of the number 5.

	5 is the Root, or 1st power.	
$5 \times 5 =$ 25	"	Square, or 2d power, and is expressed 5^2.
$5 \times 5 \times 5 =$ 125	"	Cube, or 3d power, and is expressed 5^3.
$5 \times 5 \times 5 \times 5 =$ 625	"	Biquadrate, or 4th power, and is expressed 5^4.

The little figure denoting the power is called the INDEX or EXPONENT.

EXAMPLE.—What is the cube of 9?   *Ans.* 729.

EXAMPLE.—What is the 9th power of 2?   *Ans.* 512.

EXAMPLE.—What is the cube of $\frac{3}{4}$?   *Ans.* $\frac{27}{64}$.

EXAMPLE.—What is the 4th power of 1.5?   *Ans.* 5.0625.

EVOLUTION.

EVOLUTION is finding the ROOT of any number.

The sign $\sqrt{}$ placed before any number, indicates the square root of that number is required or shown.

The same character expresses any other root by placing the index above it.

Thus, $\sqrt{25} = 5$, and $4 + 2 = \sqrt{36}$.

And, $\sqrt[3]{27} = 3$, and $\sqrt[3]{64} =$ 4.

Roots which only approximate are called Surd Roots.

RULE.—Point off the given number from units' place into periods of two figures each.

Find the greatest square in the left-hand period, and place its root in the quotient; subtract the square number from the left-hand period, and to the remainder bring down the next period for a dividend.

Double the root already found for a divisor; find how many times the divisor is contained in the dividend, exclusive of the right-hand figure, place the result in the quotient, and at the right hand of the divisor.

Multiply the divisor by the last quotient figure, and subtract the product from the dividend; bring down the next period, and proceed as before.

NOTE.—*Mixed decimals must be pointed off both ways from units.*

EXAMPLE.—What is the square root of 2 ?

```
 1| 2.000000 (1.414, &c.
 1| 1
24|100
 4| 96
281| 400
  1| 281
2824|11900
   4|11296
2828|  604
```

EXAMPLE.—What is the square root of 144 ?

```
 1| 144 (12 Ans.
 1| 1
22|044
  | 44
   00
```

EXAMPLE.—What is the square root of 12 ?   *Ans.* 3.464101.

SQUARE ROOTS OF VULGAR FRACTIONS.

RULE.—Reduce the fractions to their lowest terms, and that fraction to a decimal, and proceed as in whole numbers and decimals.

NOTE.—*When the terms of the fractions are squares, take the root of each and set one above the other ; as, $\frac{5}{6}$ is the square root of $\frac{25}{36}$.*

EXAMPLE.—What is the square root of $\frac{9}{12}$?   *Ans.* 0.86602540.

To find the 4th root of a number, extract the square root twice, and for the 8th root thrice, &c., &c.

TO EXTRACT THE CUBE ROOT.

RULE.—From the table of Roots (page 99) take the nearest cube to the given number, and call it the assumed cube.

Then say, as the given number added to twice the assumed cube is to the assumed cube added to twice the given number, so is the root of the assumed cube to the required root, *nearly.*

And, by using in like manner the root thus found as an assumed cube, and proceeding as above, another root will be found still nearer, and in the same manner as far as may be deemed necessary.

EXAMPLE.—What is the cube root of 10517.9 ?

Nearest cube, page 99, 10648, root 22.

```
 10648.    10517.9
     2          2
 21296     21035.8
 10517.9   10648.
 31813.9 : 31683.8 : : 22 : 21.9+ Ans.
```

To extract any Root whatever.

Let P represent the number,
    n   "   the index of the power,
    A   "   the assumed power, *r* its root,
    R   "   the required root of P.

Then say, as the sum of $n+1 \times A$ and $n-1 \times P$ is to the sum of $n+1 \times P$ and $n-1 \times A$, so is the assumed root *r* to the required root R.

EXAMPLE.—What is the cube root of 1500 ?

The nearest cube, page 99, is 1331, root 11.

then, $P = 1500$, $n = 3$, $A = 1331$, $r = 11$;

$$n+1 \times A = 5324, \quad n+1 \times P = 6000$$
$$n-1 \times P = 3000, \quad n-1 \times A = 2662$$
$$\overline{8324} \quad : \quad \overline{8662} :: 11 : 11.446+ \; Ans.$$

ARITHMETICAL PROGRESSION.

ARITHMETICAL PROGRESSION is a series of numbers increasing or decreasing by a constant number or difference; as, 1, 3, 5, 7, 9, 15, 12, 9, 6, 3. The numbers which form the series are called *Terms;* the first and last are called the *Extremes*, and the others the *Means*.

When any three of the following parts are given, the remaining two can be found, viz.: The *First* term, the *Last* term, the *Number* of terms, the COMMON DIFFERENCE, and the SUM of all the terms.

When the First Term, the Common Difference, and the Number of Terms are given, to find the Last Term.

RULE.—Multiply the number of terms less one, by the common difference, and to the product add the first term.

EXAMPLE.—A man travelled for 12 days, going 3 miles the first day, 8 the second, and so on; how far did he travel the last day?
$$12-1 \times 5+3 = 58 \; Ans.$$

When the Number of Terms and the Extremes are given, to find the Common Difference.

RULE.—Divide the difference of the extremes, by one less than the number of terms.

EXAMPLE.—The extremes are 3 and 15, and the number of terms 7; what is the common difference?
$$15-3 \div (7-1) = 2 \; Ans.$$

When the Extremes and Number of Terms are given, to find the Sum of all the Terms.

RULE.—Multiply the number of terms by half the sum of the extremes.

EXAMPLE.—How many times does the hammer of a clock strike in 12 hours?
$$12 \times (13 \div 2) = 78 \; Ans.$$

When the Common Difference and the Extremes are given, to find the Number of Terms.

RULE.—Divide the difference of the extremes by the common difference, and add *one* to the quotient.

EXAMPLE.—A man travelled 3 miles the first day, 5 the second, 7 the third, and so on, till he went 57 miles in one day. How many days had he travelled at the close of the last day?
$$57-3 \div 2+1 = 28 \; Ans.$$

To find two Arithmetical Means between two given Extremes.

RULE.—Subtract the less extreme from the greater, and divide the difference by 3, and the quotient will be the common difference, which, being added to the less extreme, or taken from the greater, will give the means.

EXAMPLE.—Find two arithmetical means between 4 and 16.
$$16-4 \div 3 = 4 \text{ com. dif.}$$
$$4+4 = 8 \text{ one mean.}$$
$$16-4 = 12 \text{ second mean.}$$

To find any Number of Arithmetical Means between two Extremes.

RULE.—Subtract the less extreme from the greater, and divide the difference by *one* more than the number of means required to be found, and then proceed as in the foregoing rule.

GEOMETRICAL PROGRESSION.

GEOMETRICAL PROGRESSION is any series of numbers continually increasing by a constant multiplier, or decreasing by a constant divisor.

As, 1, 2, 4, 8, 16, and 15, $7\frac{1}{2}$, $3\frac{3}{4}$.

The constant multiplier or divisor is the RATIO.

When any three of the following parts are given, the remaining two can be found, viz.: The FIRST term, the LAST term, the NUMBER of terms, the RATIO, and the SUM OF ALL THE TERMS.

When the Ratio, Number of Terms, and the First Term are given, to find the Last Term.

RULE.—Write a few of the leading terms of the series, and place their indices over them, beginning with a cipher. Add together the most convenient indices, to make an index less by one than the number of the term sought.

Multiply together the terms of the series or powers belonging to those indices, and the product, multiplied by the first term, will be the answer.

NOTE.—*When the first term is equal to the ratio, the indices must begin with a unit.*

EXAMPLE.—The first term is 1, the ratio 2, and the number of terms 23 ; what is the last term ?

Indices. 0   1   2   3   4   5   6   7
Terms.   1, 2, 4, 8, 16, 32, 64, 128.
$1+2+3+4+5+7 = 22$.
$128 \times 32 \times 16 \times 8 \times 4 \times 2 = 4194304 \times 1 = 4194304$ *Ans.*

EXAMPLE.—If one cent had been put out at interest in 1630, what would it have amounted to in 1834 if it had doubled itself every 12 years ?
$1834 - 1630 = 204 \div 12 = 17$.
0   1   2   3   4   5   6
1, 2, 4, 8, 16, 32, 64, $1+2+3+4+6 = 16$.
$1 \times 2 \times 4 \times 8 \times 16 \times 64 = 65536 \times 2 = \$1.310.72$ *Ans*

When the First Term, the Ratio, and the Number of Terms are given, to find the Sum of the Series.

RULE.—Raise the ratio to a power whose index is equal to the number of terms, from which subtract 1 ; then divide the remainder by the ratio less 1, and multiply the quotient by the first term.

EXAMPLE.—If a man were to buy 12 horses, giving 2 cents for the first horse, 6 cents for the second, and so on, what would they cost him ?
$3^{12} = 531441 - 1 = 531440 \div (3-1) = 2 = 265720 \times 2 = \$5.314.40$ *Ans.*

By another Method, the greater Extreme being known.

$$\frac{(\text{Greater extreme} \times \text{ratio}) - \text{less extreme}}{\text{Ratio} - 1} = \text{Sum of the Series}.$$

Thus . . $\dfrac{354294 \times 3 - 2 = 1062880}{3-1} = \$5.314.40$, *Ans.*, as above.

A TABLE OF GEOMETRICAL PROGRESSION,

Whereby any questions of Geometrical Progression proceeding from 1, *and of double ratio, may be solved by inspection, if the number of terms exceed not* 50.

1	1	8	128	15	16384	22	2097152
2	2	9	256	16	32768	23	4194304
3	4	10	512	17	65536	24	8388608
4	8	11	1024	18	131072	25	16777216
5	16	12	2048	19	262144	26	33554432
6	32	13	4096	20	524288	27	67108864
7	64	14	8192	21	1048576	28	134217728

TABLE—(Continued.)

29	268435456	37	68719476736	44	8796093022208
30	536870912	38	137438953472	45	17592186044416
31	1073741824	39	274877906944	46	35184372088832
32	2147483648	40	549755813888	47	70368744177664
33	4294967296	41	1099511627776	48	140737488355328
34	8589934592	42	2199023255552	49	281474976710656
35	17179869184	43	4398046511104	50	562949953421312
36	34359738368		100		63382530011411470748351602688

PERMUTATION.

PERMUTATION is a rule for finding how many different ways, any given number of things may be varied in their position.

RULE.—Multiply all the terms continually together, and the last product will be the answer.

EXAMPLE.—How many variations will the nine digits admit of?
$$1 \times 2 \times 3 \times 4 \times 5 \times 6 \times 7 \times 8 \times 9 = 362880 \ Ans.$$

COMBINATION.

COMBINATION is a rule for finding how often a less number of things, can be chosen from a greater.

RULE.—Multiply together the natural series, 1, 2, 3, &c., up to the number to be taken at a time. Take a series of as many terms, decreasing by 1, from the number out of which the choice is to be made, and find their continued product. Divide this last product by the former, and the quotient is the answer.

EXAMPLE.—How many combinations may be made of 7 letters out of 12?
$$1 \times 2 \times 3 \times 4 \times 5 \times 6 \times 7 = 5040.$$
$$\overline{12 \times 11 \times 10 \times 9 \times 8 \times 7 \times 6} = 3991680 \div 5040 = 792 \ Ans.$$

EXAMPLE.—How many combinations can be made of 5 letters out of 10?
$$\frac{10 \times 9 \times 8 \times 7 \times 6}{1 \times 2 \times 3 \times 4 \times 5} = 252 \ Ans.$$

POSITION.

POSITION is of two kinds, SINGLE and DOUBLE, and is determined by the number of SUPPOSITIONS.

SINGLE POSITION.

RULE.—Take any number, and proceed with it as though it were the correct one; then say, as the result is to the given sum, so is the supposed number to the number required.

EXAMPLE.—A commander of a vessel, after sending away in boats $\frac{1}{3}$, $\frac{1}{6}$, and $\frac{1}{4}$ of his crew, had left 300; what number had he in command?

Suppose he had   .   600.
$\frac{1}{3}$ of 600 is 200
$\frac{1}{6}$ of 600 is 100
$\frac{1}{4}$ of 600 is 150   450
$$\overline{150} : 300 :: 600 : 1200 \ Ans.$$

EXAMPLE.—A person being asked his age, replied, if $\frac{3}{4}$ of my age be multiplied by 2, and that product added to half the years I have lived, the sum will be 75. How old was he?   Ans. $37\frac{1}{2}$ years.

DOUBLE POSITION.

RULE.—Take any two numbers, and proceed with each according to the conditions of the question; multiply the results or *errors* by the contrary supposition; that is, the first position by the last error, and the last position by the first error.

If the errors be too great, mark them +; and if too little, —.

Then, if the errors are *alike*, divide the *difference* of the products by the *difference* of the errors; but if they are *unlike*, divide the *sum* of the products by the *sum* of the errors.

EXAMPLE.—F asked G how much his boat cost; he replied that if it cost him 6 times as much as it did, and $30 more, it would stand him in $300. What was the price of the boat?

Suppose it cost . . 60 . . . or 30
                        6 times.   6 times.
                        ———   ———
                        360   180
                 and 30 more,   and 30 more.
                        ———   ———
                        390   210
                        300   300
                        ———   ———
                        90+   90—
                        30 2d position.   60 1st position.
              90   2700   5400
              90   5400
              ——— ————
              180) 8100 (45 *Ans.*
                   720
                   ———
                   900
                   900

EXAMPLE.—What is the length of a fish when the head is 9 inches long, the tail as long as its head and half its body, and the body as long as both the head and tail?   *Ans.* 6 feet.

FELLOWSHIP.

FELLOWSHIP is a method of ascertaining gains or losses of individuals engaged in joint operations.

RULE.—As the whole stock is to the whole gain or loss, so is each share to the gain or loss on that share.

EXAMPLE.—Two men drew a prize in a lottery, of $9.500. A paid $3, and B paid $2 for the ticket; how much is each one's share?

                5 : 9.500 : : 3 : 5.700, A's share.
                5 : 9.500 : : 2 : 3.800, B's share.

DOUBLE FELLOWSHIP,

Or Fellowship with Time.

RULE.—Multiply each share by the time of its interest in the Fellowship; then, as the sum of the products is to the product of each interest, so is the whole gain or loss to each share of the gain or loss.

EXAMPLE.—A ship's company take a prize of $10,000, which they divide according to their rate of pay and time of service on board. The officers have been on board 6 months, and the men 3 months; the pay of the lieutenants is $100; midshipmen $50, and men $10 per month; and there are 2 lieutenants, 4 midshipmen, and 50 men. What is each one's share?

        2 lieutenants . . . . . . $100 = 200×6 = 1200
        4 midshipmen   . . . . . .   50 = 200×6 = 1200
       50 men   . . . . . .   10 = 500×3 = 1500
                                                        ————
                                                        3900

   Lieutenants . . 3900 : 1200 : : 10.000 : 3.076.92÷ 2 = $1.538.46
   Midshipmen   . . 3900 : 1200 : : 10.000 : 3.076.92÷ 4 = $769.23
   Men . . . . . 3900 : 1500 : : 10.000 : 3.846.16÷50 = $76.92

D

ALLIGATION.

ALLIGATION is a method of finding the mean rate or quality of different materials when mixed together.

When it is required to find the mean price of the mixture, observe the following

RULE.—Multiply each quantity by its rate, then divide the sum of these products by the sum of the quantities, and the quotient will be the rate of the composition.

EXAMPLE.—If 10 lbs. of copper at 20 cents per lb., 1 lb. of tin at 5 cents, and 1 lb of lead at 4 cents, be mixed together, what is the value of the composition?

$$10 \times 20 = 200$$
$$1 \times 5 = 5$$
$$1 \times 4 = 4$$
$$12 \qquad) \ 209 \ (17.\tfrac{5}{12} \ Ans.$$

When the Prices and Mean Price are given, to find what Quantity of each Article must be taken.

RULE 1.—Connect with a line each price that is *less* than the mean rate with one or more that is *greater.*

Write the difference between the mixture rate and that of each of the simples opposite the price with which it is *connected;* then the sum of the differences against any price will express the quantity to be taken of that price.

EXAMPLE.—How much gunpowder, at 72, 54, and 48 cents per pound, will compose a mixture worth 60 cents a pound?

$$60 \begin{cases} 48 \\ 54 \\ 72 \end{cases} \begin{array}{l} 12, \text{ at } 48 \text{ cents} \\ 12, \text{ at } 54 \text{ cents} \\ 12+6 = 18, \text{ at } 72 \text{ cents} \end{array} \Big\} \ Ans.$$

PROOF.—$12 \times 48 + 12 \times 54 + 18 \times 72 = 2520 \div \overline{12+12+12+6} = 60.$

Should it be required to mix a definite quantity of any one article, the quantities of each, determined by the above rule, must be increased or decreased in the proportion they bear to the defined quantity.

Thus, had it been required to mix 18 pounds at 48 cents, the result would be 18 at 48, 18 at 54, and 27 at 72 cents per pound.

Again, when the whole composition is limited, say,

As the sum of the relative quantities, as found by the above rule, is to the whole quantity required, so is each quantity so found to the required quantity of each.

EXAMPLE.—Were 100 pounds of the above mixture wanting, the result would be obtained thus:

$$\text{As } 42 : 100 : : 12 : 28\tfrac{4}{7}.$$
$$42 : 100 : : 12 : 28\tfrac{4}{7}.$$
$$42 : 100 : : 18 : 42\tfrac{6}{7}.$$

COMPOUND INTEREST.

If any principal be multiplied by the amount (in the following table) opposite the years, and under the rate per cent., the sum will be the amount of that principal at compound interest for the time and rate taken.

EXAMPLE.—What is the amount of $500 for 10 years, at 6 per cent.?

Tabular number   . $1.79084 \times 500 = \$895.42$ *Ans.*

TABLE *showing the amount of £1 or $1, &c., for any number of years not exceeding 24, at the rates of 5 and 6 per cent. compound interest.*

Years.	5 per cent.	6 per cent.	Years.	5 per cent.	6 per cent.
1	1.05	1.06	13	1.88564	2.13292
2	1.1025	1.1236	14	1.97993	2.26090
3	1.15762	1.19101	15	2.07892	2.39655
4	1.21550	1.26247	16	2.18287	2.54035
5	1.27628	1.33822	17	2.29201	2.69277
6	1.34009	1.41851	18	2.40661	2.85433
7	1.40710	1.50363	19	2.52695	3.02559
8	1.47745	1.59384	20	2.65329	3.20713
9	1.55132	1.68947	21	2.78596	3.39956
10	1.62889	1.79084	22	2.92526	3.60353
11	1.71033	1.89829	23	3.07152	3.81974
12	1.79585	2.01219	24	3.22509	4.04893

DISCOUNT.

The Time, Rate per Cent., and Interest being given, to find the Principal.

RULE.—Divide the given interest by the interest of $1, for the given rate and time.

EXAMPLE.—What sum of money at 6 per cent. will in 14 months gain $14 ?

As .07÷$14 = $200 *Ans.*

The Principal, Interest, and Time being given, to find the Rate per Cent.

RULE.—Divide the given interest by the interest of the given sum, for the time, at 1 per cent.

EXAMPLE.—A broker received $32.66 interest for the use of $400, 14 months; what was that per cent. ?

The interest on $32.66 for 14 months, is 4.66.

Then, as 4.66÷32.66 = 7 per cent., *Ans.*

The Principal, Rate per Cent., and Interest being given, to find the Time.

RULE.—Divide the given interest by the interest of the sum at the rate per cent. for one year.

EXAMPLE.—In what time will $108 gain 11.34, at 7 per cent. ?

The interest on $108 for one year is 7.56.

Then, as 7.56÷11.34 = 1.5 years, *Ans.*

EQUATION OF PAYMENTS.

Multiply each sum by its time of payment in days, and divide the sum of the products by the sum of the payments.

EXAMPLE.—A owes B $300 in 15 days, $60 in 12 days, and $350 in 20 days; when is the whole due ?

$$300 \times 15 = 4500$$
$$60 \times 12 = 720$$
$$350 \times 20 = 7000$$
$$\overline{710} \qquad) \overline{12220} \ (17 + \text{days, } Ans.$$

ANNUITIES.

The Annuity, Time, and Rate of Interest given, to find the Amount.

RULE.—Raise the ratio to a power denoted by the time, from which subtract 1; divide the remainder by the ratio less 1, and the quotient, multiplied by the annuity, will give the amount.

NOTE.—$1 or £1 *added to the given rate per cent. is the ratio, and the preceding table in Compound Interest is a table of ratios.*

EXAMPLE.—What is the amount of an annual pension of $100, interest 5 per cent., which has remained unpaid for four years?
1.05 ratio; then $1.05^4 = 1.21550625 - 1 = .21550625 \div (1.05-1).05 = 4.310125 \times 100 = $ 431.0125 dollars.

The Annuity, Time, and Rate given, to find the Present Worth.

RULE.—Divide the annuity by the ratio involved to the time, ~~subtract the quotient from the annuity,~~ and the remainder will be the present worth.

EXAMPLE.—What is the present worth of a pension or salary of $500, to continue 10 years at 6 per cent. compound interest?
$500, by the last rule, is worth $6590.3975, which, divided by 1.06^{10} (by table, page 39, is 1.79084) = $3680.05 *Ans.*

Or, by the following table, multiply the tabular number by the given annuity, and the product will be the present worth:

TABLE *showing the present worth of $1 or £1 annuity, at 5 and 6 per cent. compound interest, for any number of years under 34.*

Years.	5 per cent.	6 per cent.	Years.	5 per cent.	6 per cent.
1	0.95238	0.94339	18	11.68958	10.8276
2	1.85941	1.83339	19	12.08532	11.15811
3	2.72325	2.67301	20	12.46221	11.46992
4	3.54595	3.4651	21	12.82115	11.76407
5	4.32948	4.21236	22	13.163	12.04158
6	5.07569	4.91732	23	13.48397	12.30338
7	5.78637	5.58238	24	13.79864	12.55035
8	6.46321	6.20979	25	14.09394	12.78335
9	7.10782	6.80169	26	14.37518	13.00316
10	7.72173	7.36008	27	14.64303	13.21053
11	8.30641	7.88687	28	14.89813	13.40616
12	8.86325	8.38384	29	15.14107	13.59072
13	9.39357	8.85268	30	15.37245	13.76483
14	9.89864	9.29498	31	15.59281	13.92908
15	10.37966	9.71225	32	15.80268	14.08398
16	10.83777	10.10589	33	16.00255	14.22917
17	10.27407	10.47726	34	16.1929	14.36613

EXAMPLE.—Same as above; 10 years at 6 per cent. gives
$7.36008 \times 500 = $3680.04 *Ans.*

When annuities do not commence till a certain period of time, they are said to be in REVERSION.

To find the Present Worth of an Annuity in Reversion.

RULE.—Take two numbers under the rate in the above table, viz., that opposite the sum of the two given times and that of the time of reversion, and multiply their difference by the annuity, and the product is the present worth.

EXAMPLE.—What is the present worth of a reversion of a lease of $40 per annum, to continue for six years, but not to commence until the end of 2 years, allowing 6 per cent. to the purchaser?

By table, 8 years 6.20979
  "   2   " 1.83339
                                 ————————
                                 4.37640 × 40 = $175.05 *Ans.*

For half yearly and quarterly payments, the amount for the given time, multiplied by the number in the following table, will be the true amount:

Rate per ct.	Half yearly.	Quarterly.	Rate per ct.	Half yearly.	Quarterly.
3	1.007445	1.011181	5½	1.013567	1.020395
3½	1.008675	1.013031	6	1.014781	1.022257
4	1.009902	1.014877	6½	1.015993	1.024055
4½	1.011126	1.016720	7	1.017204	1.025880
5	1.012348	1.018559	.		

EXAMPLE.—What will an annuity of $50, payable yearly, amount to in 4 years at 5 per cent., and what if payable half yearly ?

By table, page 39,
$$1.21550 - 1 \div (1.05 - 1) = 4.310 \times 50 = \$215.50 \; Ans., \text{ for yearly payment,}$$
and . . $215.50 \times 1.012348 = \$218.16$ " half yearly do.

PERPETUITIES.

PERPETUITIES are such annuities as continue forever.

RULE.—Divide the annuity by the rate per cent., multiply by the tabular number above, and the quotient will be the answer.

EXAMPLE.—What is the present worth of a $100 annuity, payable semi-annually, at 5 per cent. ?
$$100 \div .05 = 2000 \times 1.012348 \text{ (from preceding table)} = \$2.024.70 \; Ans.$$

For *Perpetuities in Reversion*, subtract the present worth of the annuity for the time of reversion from the worth of the annuity, to commence immediately.

EXAMPLE.—What is the present worth of an estate of $50 per annum, at 5 per cent., to commence in 4 years ?
$$50 \div .05 \quad . \qquad . \qquad . \qquad . \qquad . \qquad . = 1000.$$
$$\$50, \text{ for 4 years, at 5 per cent.} = 3.54595 \text{ (from table)} \times 50 = \underline{\quad 177.29}$$
$$\$822.71 \; Ans.,$$
which in 4 years, at 5 per cent. compound interest, would produce $1000.

CHRONOLOGICAL PROBLEMS.

The Golden Number is a period of 19 years, in which the changes of the moon fall on the same days of the month as before.

To find the Golden Number, or Lunar Cycle.

RULE.—Add one to the given year; divide the sum by 19, and the remainder is the golden number.

NOTE.—*If 0 remain, it will be 19.*

EXAMPLE.—What is the golden number for 1830 ?
$$1830 + 1 \div 19 = 96 \text{ rem. : } 7 \; Ans.$$

To find the Epact.

RULE.—Divide the centuries of the given year by 4; multiply the remainder by 17, and to this product add the quotient, multiplied by 43; divide this sum plus 86 by 25, multiplying the golden number by 11, from which subtract the last quotient, and, rejecting the 30's, the remainder will be the answer.

EXAMPLE.—Required the epact for 1830.

Centuries. $18 \div 4 = 4\frac{2}{4}$. $2 \times 17 = 34$. $4 \times 43 = 172 + 34 = 206 + 86 = 292 \div 25 = 11$, last quotient.

Golden number, as ascertained above, $7 \times 11 = 77 - 11$ (last quotient) $= 66$, rejecting 30's $= 6 \; Ans.$

EXAMPLE.—What is the epact for 1839 ?   *Ans.* 15.

TO FIND THE MOON'S AGE ON ANY GIVEN DAY.

RULE.—To the day of the month add the epact and number of the month, then reject the 30's, and the answer will be the moon's age.

Numbers of the Month.

January 0,	April 2,	July 5,	October 8,
February 2,	May 3,	August 6,	November 10,
March 1,	June 4,	September 8,	December 10.

EXAMPLE.—For 5th February, 1841.

```
Given day      .    .    5 ⎫
Epact          .    .    7 ⎬ 14, age of the moon.
Number of month .        2 ⎭
```

The CYCLE OF THE SUN is the 28 years before the days of the week return to the same days of the month.

TABLE of Epacts, Dominical Letters, and an Almanac, from 1776 to 1875.

February, March, November.	February,* August.	May.	January. October.	January,* April, July.	September, December.	June.
1	2	3	4	5	6	7
8	9	10	11	12	13	14
15	16	17	18	19	20	21
22	23	24	25	26	27	28
29	30	31				

N. B.—In leap-year, January and February must be taken in the columns marked *.

Years	Days.	Dom. Letters.	Epact.	Years	Days.	Dom. Letters.	Epact.	Years	Days.	Dom. Letters.	Epact.	Years	Days	Dom. Letters.	Epact.
1776	Friday*	GF	9	1801	Sunday.	D	15	1826	Wedn'y.	A	22	1851	Sat'y.	E	28
1777	Saturd'y	E	20	1802	Monday.	C	26	1827	Thursd.	G	3	1852	Mon.*	DC	9
1778	Sunday.	D	1	1803	Tuesd'y.	B	7	1828	Saturd.*	FE	14	1853	Tues.	B	20
1779	Monday.	C	12	1804	Thurs.*	AG	18	1829	Sunday.	D	25	1854	Wedn.	A	1
1780	Wedn.*	BA	23	1805	Friday.	F	29	1830	Monday.	C	6	1855	Thur.	G	12
1781	Thursd.	G	4	1806	Saturd'y	E	11	1831	Tuesd'y.	B	17	1856	Sat'y*	FE	23
1782	Friday.	F	15	1807	Sunday.	D	22	1832	Thurs.*	AG	28	1857	Sund.	D	4
1783	Saturd'y	E	26	1808	Tuesd.*	CB	3	1833	Friday	F	9	1858	Mond.	C	15
1784	Mond.*	DC	7	1809	Wedn'y.	A	14	1834	Saturd'y	E	20	1859	Tues.	B	26
1785	Tuesd'y	B	18	1810	Thursd.	G	25	1835	Sunday.	D	1	1860	Thu.*	AG	7
1786	Wedn'y.	A	29	1811	Friday.	F	6	1836	Tuesd *	CB	12	1861	Friday	F	18
1787	Thursd.	G	11	1812	Sunday*	ED	17	1837	Wedn'y.	A	23	1862	Satur.	E	29
1788	Saturd.*	FE	22	1813	Monday.	C	28	1838	Thursd.	G	4	1863	Sund.	D	11
1789	Sunday.	D	3	1814	Tuesd'y.	B	9	1839	Friday.	F	15	1864	Tue.*	CB	22
1790	Monday.	C	14	1815	Wedn'y.	A	20	1840	Sund'y.*	ED	26	1865	Wedn.	A	3
1791	Tuesd'y.	B	25	1816	Friday.*	GF	1	1841	Monday.	C	7	1866	Thur.	G	14
1792	Thurs.*	AG	6	1817	Saturd'y	E	12	1842	Tuesd'y.	B	18	1867	Friday	F	25
1793	Friday.	F	17	1818	Sunday.	D	23	1843	Wedn'y.	A	29	1868	Sun.*	ED	6
1794	Saturd'y	E	28	1819	Monday.	C	4	1844	Friday.*	GF	11	1869	Mond.	C	17
1795	Sunday.	D	9	1820	Wedn.*	BA	15	1845	Saturd'y	E	22	1870	Tues	B	28
1796	Tuesd.*	CB	20	1821	Thursd.	G	26	1846	Sunday.	D	3	1871	Wedn.	A	9
1797	Wedn'y.	A	1	1822	Friday.	F	7	1847	Monday.	C	14	1872	Frid.*	GF	20
1798	Thursd.	G	12	1823	Saturd'y	E	18	1848	Wed'y.*	BA	25	1873	Satur.	E	1
1799	Friday.	F	23	1824	Mond'y*	DC	29	1849	Thursd.	G	6	1874	Sund.	D	12
1800	Saturd'y	E	4	1825	Tuesd'y.	B	11	1850	Friday.	F	17	1875	Mond.	C	23

* Distinguishes the *leap-years*.

Use of the above Table—To find the day of the week on which any given day of the month falls in any year from 1776 to 1875.

EXAMPLE.—The great fire occurred in New-York on the 16th December, 1835; what was the day of the week ?

Against 1835 we find Sunday, and at top, under December, we find that the 13th was Sunday; consequently, the 16th was Wednesday.

PROMISCUOUS QUESTIONS.

1. If $100 principal gain $5 interest in one year, what amount will gain $20 in 8 months?

As 12 months : 5 : : 8 months : 3.33, the interest for 8 months. And, as 3.33 : : 100 : : 20 : 600 the answer.

2. A reservoir has two cocks, through which it is supplied ; by one of them it will fill in 40 minutes, and by the other in 50 minutes ; it has also a discharging cock, by which, when full, it may be emptied in 25 minutes. If the three cocks are left open, in what time would the cistern be filled, assuming the velocity of the water to be uniform?

The least common multiple of 40, 50, and 25 is 200.

Then . . the 1st cock will fill it 5 times in 200 minutes,
the 2d " 4 " 200 "

or both 9 times in 200 minutes ; and, as the discharge-cock will empty it 8 times in 200 minutes, then 9—8 = 1, or once in 3.20 hours, *Ans.*

3. Out of a pipe of wine, containing 84 gallons, 10 gallons were drawn off, and the vessel replenished with water ; after which 10 gallons of the mixture was likewise drawn off, and then 10 gallons more of water were poured in, and so on for a third and fourth time. It is required to find how much pure wine remained in the vessel, supposing the two fluids to have been thoroughly mixed?

$$84—10 = 74$$
As 84 : 10 : : 74   : 8.80952
84 : 10 : : 65.19048 : 7.76077
84 : 10 : : 57.42971 : 6.83687
6.83687
————————
50.59284 *Ans.*

4. A traveller leaves New-York at 8 o'clock in the morning, and walks towards New-London at the rate of 3 miles an hour, without intermission ; another traveller sets out from New-London at 4 o'clock the same evening, and walks for New-York at the rate of 4 miles an hour, constantly ; now, supposing the distance between the two cities to be 130 miles, whereabout on the road will they meet?

From 8 o'clock till 4 o'clock is 8 hours; therefore, 8×3 = 24 miles, performed by A before B set out from New-London ; and, consequently, 130—24 = 106 are the miles to travel between them after that. Hence, as $7 = 3+4 : 3 : : 106 : \frac{318}{7} = 45\frac{3}{7}$ more miles travelled by A at the meeting; consequently, $24+45\frac{3}{7} = 69\frac{3}{7}$ miles from New-York is the place of their meeting.

5. What part of $3 is a third part of $2?

$$\tfrac{1}{3} \text{ of } \tfrac{2}{1} \text{ of } \tfrac{1}{3} = \tfrac{1}{3} \times \tfrac{2}{1} \times \tfrac{1}{3} = \tfrac{2}{9} \ Ans.$$

6. The hour and minute hand of a clock are exactly together at 12; when are they next together?

As the minute hand runs 11 times as fast as the hour hand; then, $11 : 60 : : 1 : 5$ min. $5\frac{5}{11}$ sec. The time, then, is 5 min. $5\frac{5}{11}$ sec. past 1 o'clock.

7. The time of the day is between 4 and 5, and the hour and minute hands are exactly together; what is the time?

The speed of the hands is as 1 to 11.

4 hours $\times 60 = 240$, which $\div 11 = 21\frac{9}{11}$ min. added to 4 hours, *Ans.*

8. A can do a piece of work in 3 weeks, B can do thrice as much in 8 weeks, and C five times as much in 12 weeks; in what time can they finish it jointly?

Week. Week. Week.

As $3 : 1 : : 1 : \frac{1}{3}$ work done by A in one week.

$8 : 3 : : 1 : \frac{3}{8}$ " B "

$12 : 5 : : 1 : \frac{5}{12}$ " C "

Then, by addition, $\frac{1}{3} + \frac{3}{8} + \frac{5}{12}$ will be the work done by them all in one week; these, reduced to a common denominator, become $\frac{24}{72} + \frac{27}{72} + \frac{30}{72} = \frac{81}{72} = \frac{9}{8}$; whence, $9 : 6 : : 8 : 5\frac{1}{3}$ *Ans.*

9. A cistern, containing 60 gallons of water, has 3 unequal cocks for discharging it; one cock will empty it in 1 hour, a second in 2 hours, and a third in 3 hours; in what time will it be emptied if they all run together?

First, $\frac{1}{2}$ would run out in 1 hour by the second cock, and $\frac{1}{3}$ by the third; consequently, by the 3 was the reservoir supplied one hour. $\frac{1}{2} + \frac{1}{3} + 1 = \frac{3}{6} + \frac{2}{6} + \frac{6}{6}$ being reduced to a common denominator, the sum of these $3 = \frac{11}{6}$; whence the proportion, $11 : 60 : : 6 : 32\frac{8}{12}$ minutes, the time required.

10. What will a body, weighing 10 lbs. troy, lose by being carried to the height of 7 miles above the surface of the earth?

As the gravitation or weight of a body above the earth is inversely as the square of its distance, and the earth's diameter being, say 3993 miles, then $3993 + 7 = 4000$.

And, as $4000^2 : 3993^2 : : 10 : 9.965$ lbs., *Ans.*

11. Suppose a cubic inch of common glass weighs 1.49 ounces troy, the same of sea water .59, and of brandy .53. A gallon of this liquor in a glass bottle, which weighs 3.84 lbs., is thrown into the water. It is proposed to determine if it will sink; and if so, how much force will just buoy it up?

$3.84 \times 12 \div 1.49 = 30.92$ cubic inches of glass in the bottle.

231 cubic inches in a gallon $\times .53 = 122.43$ ounces of brandy.

Then, bottle and brandy weigh $3.84 \times 12 + 122.43 = 168.51$ ounces, and contain 261.92 cubic inches, which, $\times .59 = 154.53$ ounces, the weight of an equal bulk of salt water.

And, $168.51 - 154.53 = 13.98$ ounces, the weight necessary to support it in the water.

12. How many fifteens can be counted with four fives? *Ans.* 4.

13. What is the radius of a circular acre?

(Side of a square $\times 1.128 =$ diameter of an equal circle.)

208.710321, the side of a square acre, $\times 1.128 = 235.50 \div 2$ (for radius) $= 117.75$ feet, *Ans.*

14. From Caldwell's to Newburg is 18 miles; the current of the river is such as to accelerate a boat descending, or retard one ascending $1\frac{1}{2}$ miles per hour. Suppose two boats, driven uniformly at the rate of 15 miles per hour through the water, were to start one from each place at the same time, where will they meet?

Call x the distance from N to the place of meeting; its distance from C, then, will be $18 - x$.

Speed of descending boat, $15 + 1.5 = 16.5$ miles per hour.
Speed of ascending boat, $15 - 1.5 = 13.5$ miles per hour.

$\frac{x}{16.5} =$ time of boat descending to point of meeting.

$\frac{18-x}{13.5} =$ time of boat ascending to point of meeting.

These times are, of course, equal; therefore, $\dfrac{x}{16.5} = \dfrac{18-x}{13.5}$.

Then, $13.5x = 297 - 16.5x$, and $13.5x + 16.5x = 297$, or $30x = 297$.

Hence, $x = \dfrac{297}{30} = 9.9$ miles, the distance from Newburgh, *Ans.*

15. A steamboat, going at the rate of 10 miles per hour through the water, descends a river, the velocity of which is 4 miles per hour, and returns in 10 hours; how far did she proceed?

Let $x =$ distance required, $\dfrac{x}{10+4} =$ time of going, $\dfrac{x}{10-4} =$ time of returning.

$\dfrac{x}{14} + \dfrac{x}{6} = 10$; $6x + 14x = 840$; $20x = 840$; $840 \div 20 = 42$, *Ans.*

16. The flood tide wave of a river runs 20 miles per hour, the current of it is 3 miles per hour. Assume the air to be quiescent, and a floating body set in motion at the commencement of the flow of the tide; how long will the body drift in one direction, the tide flowing six hours from each point of the river?

Let x be the time required; $20x =$ distance the tide has run up, together with the distance which the floating body has moved; $3x =$ whole distance which the body has floated.

Then $20x - 3x = 6 \times 20$, or the length in miles of a tide.

$x = \dfrac{20}{20-3} \times 6 = 7$ hours, 3 minutes, $31\frac{752}{1000}$ seconds, *Ans.*

17. If a steamboat, going uniformly at the rate of 15 miles in an hour through the water, were to run for 1 hour with a current of 5 miles per hour; then, to return against that current; what length of time would she require to reach the place from whence she started?

$15 + 5 = 20$ miles, the distance gone during the hour.

Then $15 - 5 = 10$ miles, is her effective velocity per hour when returning, and $20 \div 10 = 2$ hours, the time of returning, and $2 + 1 = 3$ hours, or the whole time occupied, *Ans.*

GEOMETRY.

Definitions.

A *Point* has position, but not magnitude.

A *Line* is length without breadth, and is either *Right*, *Curved*, or *Mixed*.

A *Right Line* is the shortest distance between two points.

A *Mixed Line* is composed of a right and a curved line.

A *Superficies* has length and breadth only, and is plane or curved.

A *Solid* has length, breadth, and thickness.

An *Angle* is the opening of two lines having different directions, and is either *Right*, *Acute*, or *Obtuse*.

A *Right Angle* is made by a line perpendicular to another, falling upon it.

An *Acute Angle* is less than a right angle.

An *Obtuse Angle* is greater than a right angle.

A *Triangle* is a figure of three sides.

An *Equilateral Triangle* has all its sides equal.

An *Isosceles Triangle* has two of its sides equal

A *Scalene Triangle* has all its sides unequal.

A *Right-angled Triangle* has one right angle.

An *Obtuse-angled Triangle* has one obtuse angle.

An *Acute-angled Triangle* has all its angles acute.

A *Quadrangle* or *Quadrilateral* is a figure of four sides, and has the following particular names, viz. :

A *Parallelogram*, having its opposite sides parallel.

A *Square*, having length and breadth equal.

A *Rectangle*, a parallelogram having a right angle.

A *Rhombus* (or *Lozenge*), having equal sides, but its angles not right angles.

A *Rhomboid*, a parallelogram, its angles not being right angles.

A *Trapezium*, having unequal sides.

A *Trapezoid*, having only one pair of opposite sides parallel.

NOTE.—*A Triangle is sometimes called a Trigon, and a Square a Tetragon.*

POLYGONS are plane figures having more than four sides, and are either Regular or Irregular, according as their sides and angles are equal or unequal, and they are named from the number of their sides or angles. Thus :

A Pentagon	has	five	sides.
A Hexagon	"	six	"
A Heptagon	"	seven	"
An Octagon	"	eight	"
A Nonagon	"	nine	"
A Decagon	"	ten	"
An Undecagon	"	eleven	"
A Dodecagon	"	twelve	"

A CIRCLE is a plane figure bounded by a curve line, called the *Circumference* (or *Periphery*).

An *Arc* is any part of the circumference of a circle.

A *Chord* is a right line joining the extremities of an arc.

A *Segment* of a circle is any part bounded by an arc and its chord.

The *Radius* of a circle is a line drawn from the centre to the circumference.

A *Sector* is any part of a circle bounded by an arc and its two radii.

A *Semicircle* is half a circle.

A *Quadrant* is a quarter of a circle.

A *Zone* is a part of a circle included between two parallel chords and their arcs.

A *Lune* is the space between the intersecting arcs of two eccentric circles.

A *Gnomon* is the space included between the lines forming two similar parallelograms, of which the smaller is inscribed within the larger, so as to have one angle in each common to both.

A *Secant* is a line that cuts a circle, lying partly within and partly without it.

A *Cosecant* is the secant of the complement of an arc.

A *Sine* of an arc is a line running from one extremity of an arc perpendicular to a diameter passing through the other extremity, and the sine of an angle is the sine of the arc that measures that angle.

The *Versed Sine* of an arc or angle is the part of the diameter intercepted between the sine and the arc.

The *Cosine* of an arc or angle is the part of the diameter intercepted between the sine and the centre.

A *Tangent* is a right line that touches a circle without cutting it.

A *Cotangent* is the tangent of the complement of the arc.

The *Circumference* of every circle is supposed to be divided into 360 equal parts called *Degrees* ; each degree into 60 *Minutes*, and each minute into 60 *Seconds*, and so on.

The *Complement* of an angle is what remains after subtracting the angle from 90 degrees.

The *Supplement* of an angle is what remains after subtracting the angle from 180 degrees.

To exemplify these definitions, let A c b, in the following diagram, be an assumed arc of a circle described with the radius A B.

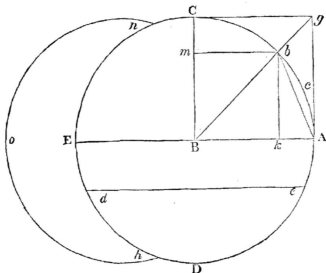

A c b, an Arc of the circle A C E D.

A b, the Chord of that arc.

e D d, a Segment of the circle.

A B, the Radius.

A B b c, a Sector.

A D E B, a Semicircle.

C B E, a Quadrant.

A e d E, a Zone.

n o h, a Lune.

B g, the Secant of the arc A c b.

b k, the Sine of   do.

A k, the Versed Sine of   do.

B k, the Cosine of the arc A c b.

A g, the Tangent of   do.

C B b, the Complement, and b B E, the Supplement of the arc A c b.

C g, the *Cotangent* of the arc, written cot.

B g, the *Cosecant* of the arc, written cosec.

m b, the *Coversed sine* of the arc, or, by convention, of the angle A B b; written coversin.

A *Prism* is a solid of which the sides are parallelograms, and are of three, four, five, or more sides, and are *upright* or *oblique*.

A *Parallelopipedon* is a solid terminated by six parallelograms: thus, a four-sided prism is a parallelopipedon.

A *Pyramid* is a solid bounded by a number of planes, its base being a rectilinear figure, and its faces triangles, terminating in one point, called the *summit* or *vertex*.

It is regular or irregular, upright or oblique, and triangular, quadrangular, and so on, from its equality of sides, inclination, or number of sides.

A *Cylinder* is a solid formed by the rotation of a rectangle about one of its sides, at rest; this side is called the *axis* of the cylinder. It is right or oblique as the axis is perpendicular or inclined.

An *Ellipse* is a section of a cylinder oblique to the axis. (*See* CONIC SECTIONS, page 54.)

A *Sphere* is a solid bounded by one continued surface, every point of which is equally distant from a point within the sphere, called the centre.

The *Altitude*, or height of a figure, is a perpendicular let fall from its vertex to the opposite side, called the base.

The *Measure* of an angle is an arc of a circle contained between the two lines that form the angle, and is estimated by the number of degrees in the arc.

A *Prismoid* has its two ends as any unlike parallel plane figures of the same number of sides, the upright sides being trapezoids.

A *Spheroid* is a solid resembling the figure of a sphere, but not exactly round, one of its diameters being longer than the other.

A *Spindle* is a solid formed by the revolution of some curve round its base.

A *Segment* is a part cut off by a plane, parallel to the base.

A *Frustum* is the part remaining after the segment is cut off.

A *Cycloid* is a curve formed by a point in the circumference of a circle, revolving on a right line the length of that circumference.

An *Epicycloid* is a curve generated by a point in one circle which revolves about another circle, either on the concavity or convexity of its circumference.

An *Ungula* is the bottom part cut off by a plane passing obliquely through the base of a cone or cylinder.

The *Perimeter* of a figure is the sum of all its sides.

A *Problem* is something proposed to be done.

A *Postulate* is something required.

A *Theorem* is something proposed to be demonstrated.

A *Lemma* is something premised, to render what follows more easy.

A *Corollary* is a truth consequent upon a preceding demonstration.

A *Scholium* is a remark upon something going before it.

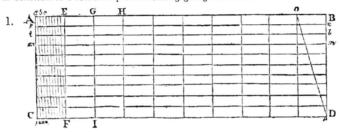

To construct a Diagonal Scale upon any Line, as A B—*fig.* 1.

Divide the line into as many divisions as there are hundreds of feet, spaces of ten feet, feet, or inches required.

Draw perpendiculars from every division to a parallel line C D.

Divide these perpendiculars and one of the divisions A E, C F, into spaces of ten if for feet and hundredths, and into twelve if for inches; draw the lines A 1, a 2, b 3, &c., and they will complete the scale required.

Thus: The line A B representing ten feet; A to E, E to G, &c., will measure one foot; A to a, C to 1, 1 to 2, &c., will measure 1-10th of a foot; and the several lines A 1, a 2, &c., will measure upon the lines k k, l l, &c., 1-100th of a foot; and o p will measure upon k k, l l, &c., 1-10th of a foot.

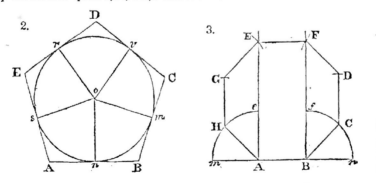

To circumscribe a Pentagon about a given Circle—*fig.* 2.

RULE.—Inscribe a pentagon in the circle, defining the points *s r v m n.*

From the centre o, draw o r, o v, &c.

Through n, m, &c., draw A B, B C, &c., perpendicular to o n, o m, and complete the figure.

NOTE.—*Any other polygon may be made in a similar manner, by drawing tangents to the points, first defining them in the circle.*

Upon a given Line A B, to form an Octagon—fig. 3.

RULE.—On the extremities of A B, erect indefinite perpendiculars A F, B E, produce A B to m and n, and bisect the angles m A e and n B f with A H and B C.

Make A H and B C equal to A B, and draw H G, C D, parallel to A F, and equal to A B.

From G and D, as centres with a radius equal to A B, describe arcs cutting A F, B E, in F and E. Join G F, F E, and E D, and the figure is made.

Circles and Squares.

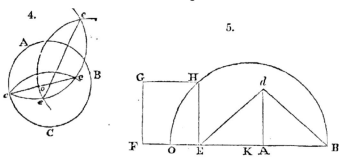

4.   5.

To describe a Circle that shall pass through any three given Points, as A B C—fig. 4.

RULE.—Upon the points A and B, with any opening of the dividers, describe two arcs to intersect each other, as at e e; on the points A C describe two more to intersect each other in the points c c; draw the lines e e and c c, and where these two lines intersect o, place one foot of the dividers, and extend the other to A, B, or C, and it will pass through the three given points as required.

To make a Square equal to a given Triangle—fig. 5.

Let B d E be the triangle given.

RULE.—Extend the side of the triangle B E to O, making E O equal to half the length of the perpendicular of the triangle A d. Divide B O into two equal parts in K, and with the distance K B describe the semicircle B H O. Upon E erect the perpendicular E H, which will be the side of a square, equal to the triangle B d E.

Triangles and Squares.

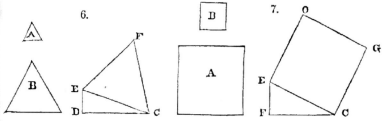

6.   7.

To make an Equilateral Triangle equal to two given Equilateral Triangles—fig. 6.

Let the given equilateral triangles be A and B.

RULE.—Draw a right line C D equal in length to one side of the triangle B. Erect the perpendicular D E, equal in length to one side of the triangle A.

Draw C E, and complete the equilateral triangle C E F, which shall be equal in quantity to the two given equilateral triangles A and B.

To make a Square equal to two given Squares—fig. 7.

Let the two squares given be A and B.

E

RULE.—Draw the line C F, equal in length to one side of the largest square **A**
Raise the perpendicular E F, equal in length to one side of the smallest square **B**.
Draw C E, and C E is the side of the square C E G O, which is equal in quantity
to the two given squares A and B.

Circles and Ellipse.

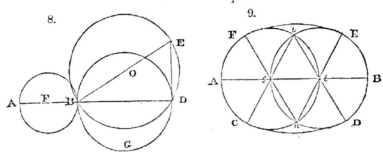

Two Circles, F and G, being given, to make another of equal quantity—fig. 8.

RULE.—Upon the diameter of the largest of the two circles at the point D, erect
the perpendicular D E, equal in length to the diameter A B of the least circle.
   Draw B E, and divide it into two equal parts in O ; take the distance B O or O E,
and describe a circle. This circle will be equal in quantity to the two given circles F
and G.

To describe an Ellipse of any given length, without regard to breadth—fig. 9.

Let A B be the given length.
   RULE.—Divide it into three equal parts, as A *s i* B. Then, with the radius A *s*,
describe A F *o i n* C ; and from *i*, the circle B D *n s o* E ; then with *n* F and *o* C describe F E and C D, and you have the ellipse required.

10.   Ellipses.   11.

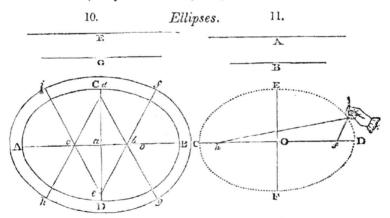

To describe an Ellipse to any length and breadth given—fig. 10.

Let the longest diameter given be the line F, and the shortest G.
   RULE.—Make A B equal to F, and C D to G, dividing A B equally at right angles
in *a*.
   Make A *o* equal to D C, and dividing *o* B into three equal parts, set off two of
those parts from *a* to *b* and from *a* to *c*, then with the distance *c b* make the two
equilateral triangles *c d b* and *c e b*, whose angles are the centres, and the sides being
continued are the lines of direction for the several arcs of the oval A C B D.

NOTE.—*Carpenters, Bricklayers, and Masons are oftentimes obliged to work an
architrave, &c., about windows, of this form : they may, by the help of the four centres
c, d, b, e, and the lines of direction h d, e f, d g, e i, describe another line around the
former, and at any distance required, as h i f g.*

To describe an Ellipse to any length and breadth required, another way—fig. 11.

Let the longest diameter be A, and the shortest B.

RULE.—Draw the line C D equal in length to A ; also E F equal in length to B, and at right angles with C D.

Take the distance C O or O D, and with it, from the point E and F, describe the arcs *h* and *f* upon the diameter C D.

Strike in a nail or pin at *h* and at *f*, and put a string around them, of such a length that the two ends may just reach to E or F.

Introduce a pencil, and bearing upon the string, carry it around the centre O, and it will describe the ellipse required.

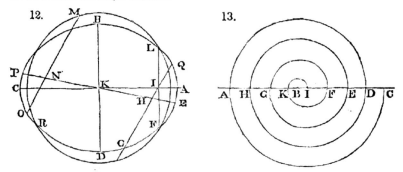

To find the Centre and two diameters of an Ellipse—fig. 12.

Let A B C D be the ellipse.

RULE.—Draw at pleasure two lines, Q G, M O, parallel to each other; bisect them in the points H N, and draw the line P E; bisect it in K, and upon K, as a centre, describe a circle at pleasure, as F L R, cutting the figure in the points F L; draw the right line F L, bisect it in I, and through the points I K draw the greatest diameter A C, and through the centre K draw the least diameter B D, parallel to the line F L.

To draw a Spiral Line about a given Point—fig. 13.

Let B be the centre.

RULE.—Draw A C, and divide it into twice the number of parts that there are to be revolutions of the line. Upon B describe K I, G F, H E, &c., and upon I describe K F, G E, &c.

Polygons.

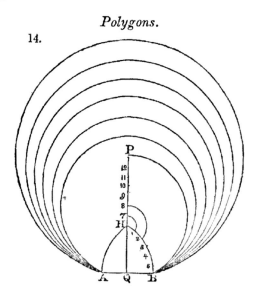

Upon a given line, to describe any Polygon beyond a Pentagon—fig. 14.

Let A B be the given line.

RULE.—Bisect the line A B in Q, and erect the perpendicular Q P. From the point A describe the arc B H, and from B the arc A H, and divide B H into equal parts, as H 1, 2, 3, 4, 5, B.

Let a pentagon be required. From the point H, with the interval H 1, describe the arc I 7, and the point I will be the centre of a circle containing the given line A B five times, the interval I B being the radius thereof. Take the point H for the centre of another circle, and H B for the radius; this circle will contain the line A B six times. From the point 7, with the radius 7 B, a circle drawn will contain A B seven times. From the point H, with the interval H 2, describe the arc 2 8; and from the point 8, with the radius 8 B, draw a circle, and A B shall be the side of an octagon. From 9, with the radius 9 B, you form a nine-sided figure; from 10 a ten-sided figure; and so on to 12.

Arches.

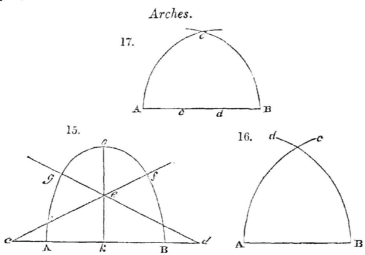

To describe an Elliptic Arch on the Conjugate Diameter—fig. 15.

RULE.—Draw the diameter A B, and in the middle at *k*, erect the perpendicular *k o*, equal to the height of the arch; divide the perpendicular *k o* into two equal parts at *e*; continue the line A B on both sides at pleasure, and from the point *k*, with the distance *k o*, define *c* and *d*; through *c e, d e*, draw *c e f* and *d e g* at pleasure; *d* and *c* are centres for the arcs A *g* and B *f*, and *e* the centre for the arc *g o f*, which will form the arch required.

To draw a Gothic Arch—fig. 16.

RULE 1.—Take the length of the line A B, and on the points A and B describe the arcs A *c* and B *d*, and it will complete the arch required.

RULE 2, *fig.* 17.—Divide the line A B into three equal parts, at *c* and *d*; take A *d* or B *c*, and describe B *e* or A *e*, and it will give an arch of another form.

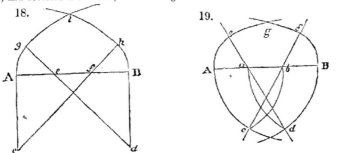

RULE 3, *fig.* 18.—Divide the line A B also into three equal parts, *e f*; from the points A and B let fall the perpendiculars A c and B d, equal in length to two of the divisions of the line A B; draw the lines c h and d g: from the points e f, with the length of f B, describe the arcs A g and B h, and from the points c d describe the arcs g i and i h, and it will complete another Gothic arch.

RULE 4, *fig.* 19.—As before, divide the line A B into three equal parts at a and b, and on the points A u, b B, with the distance of two divisions, make four arcs intersecting at c d. Through the points c d and the divisions a b, draw the lines c f and d e, and on the points a and b describe the arcs A e and B f, and on the points c d the arcs e g and f g, and it will complete another Gothic arch.

E 2

CONIC SECTIONS.

Definitions.

A *Cone* is a solid figure having a circle for its base, and terminated in a vertex.

Conic Sections are the figures made by a plane cutting a cone.

An *Ellipse* is the section of a cone when cut by a plane obliquel through both sides.

A *Parabola* is the section of a cone when cut by a plane paralle to its side.

A *Hyperbola* is the section of a cone when cut by a plane, making a greater angle with the base than the side of the cone makes.

The *Transverse Axis* is the longest straight line that can be drawn in an ellipse.

The *Conjugate Axis* is a line drawn through the centre, at right angles to the transverse axis.

An *Ordinate* is a right line drawn from any point of the curve perpendicular to either of the diameters.

An *Abscissa* is a part of any diameter contained between its vertex and an ordinate.

The *Parameter* of any diameter is a third proportional to that diameter and its conjugate.

The *Focus* is the point in the axis where the ordinate is equal to half the parameter.

A *Conoid* is a solid generated by the revolving of a parabola or hyperbola around its axis.

A *Spheroid* is a solid generated in like manner to a conoid by an ellipse.

To construct a Parabola—fig. 1.

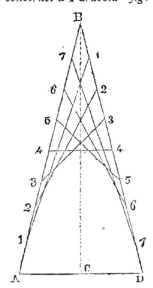

Draw an isosceles triangle, A B D, whose base shall be equal to that of the proposed parabola, and its altitude, C B, twice that of it.

Divide each side, A B, D B, into 8, or any number of equal parts; then draw lines 1 1, 2 2, 3 3, &c., and their intersection will define the curve of a parabola.

NOTE.—*The following figures are drawn to a scale of 100 parts to an inch.*

To construct an Hyperbola,* the Transverse and Conjugate Diameters being given—fig. 2.

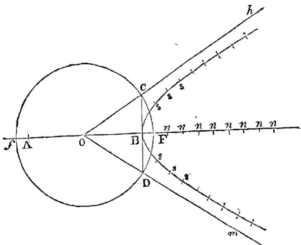

Make A B the transverse diameter, and C D, perpendicular to it, the conjugate.

Bisect A B in O, and from O, with the radius O C or O D, describe the circle D *f c* F, cutting A B produced in F and *f*, which points will be the foci.

In A B produced take any number of points, *n n*, &c., and from F and *f*, as centres, with B *n*, A *n*, as radii, describe arcs, cutting each other in *s s*, &c.

Through *s s*, &c., draw the curve *s* B *s*, and it will be the hyperbola required.

3. ELLIPSE.

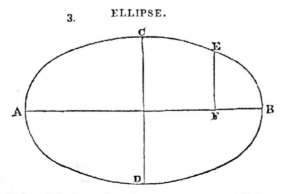

* To describe hyperbolas by another method, see Gregory's Mathematics, p. 160.

To find the length of the Ordinate, E F, *of an Ellipse, the Transverse,* A B, *Conjugate,* C D, *and Abscissæ,* A F *and* F B, *being known—fig.* 3.

RULE.—As the transverse diameter is to the conjugate, so is the square root of the product of the abscissæ to the ordinate which divides them.

EXAMPLE.—The transverse axis, A B, is 100; the conjugate, C D, is 60; one abscissa, B F, is 20; the other, A F, is (100—20) = 80.

$$100 : 60 : : \sqrt{20 \times 80} : 24 \; Ans.$$

The Transverse and Conjugate diameters, and an Ordinate being known, to find the Abscissæ—fig. 3.

RULE.—As the conjugate diameter is to the transverse, so is the square root of the difference of the squares of the ordinate and semi-conjugate to the distance between the ordinate and centre; and this distance, being added to and subtracted from the semi-transverse, will give the abscissas required.

EXAMPLE.—The transverse diameter, A B, is 100; the conjugate, C D, is 60; and the ordinate, F E, is 24.

$$60 : 100 : : \sqrt{24^2 - 30^2} : 30, \text{ distance between the}$$
ordinate and centre;
then $100 \div 2 - 30 = 20$, one abscissa;
$100 \div 2 + 30 = 80$, the other abscissa.

When the Conjugate, Ordinate, and Abscissæ are known, to find the Transverse—fig. 3.

RULE.—To or from the semi-conjugate, according as the greater or less abscissa is used, add, or subtract the square root of the difference of the squares of the ordinate and semi-conjugate. Then, as this sum or difference is to the abscissa, so is the conjugate to the transverse.

EXAMPLE.—The ordinate, F E, is 24; the less abscissa, F B, is 20; and the conjugate, C D, is 60.

$$30 - \sqrt{24^2 - 30^2} = 12;$$
then $12 : 20 : : 60 : 100 \; Ans.$

The Transverse, Ordinate, and Abscissæ being given, to find the Conjugate—fig. 3.

RULE.—As the square root of the product of the abscissæ is to the ordinate, so is the transverse diameter to the conjugate.

EXAMPLE.—The transverse is 100, the ordinate 24, one abscissa 20, the other 80.

$$\sqrt{80 \times 20} : 24 : : 100 : 60 \; Ans.$$

PARABOLAS.

Any three of the four following terms being given, viz., any two Ordinates and their Abscissæ, to find the fourth—fig. 4.

RULE.—As any abscissa is to the square of its ordinate, so is another abscissa to the square of its ordinate.

4.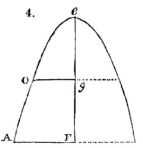

EXAMPLE.—The abscissa, *e g*, is 50, its ordinate, *c g*, 35.35 ; required the ordinate A F, whose abscissa, *e* F, is 100.

$$50 : 35.35^2 : : 100 : \sqrt{2500} = 50 \ Ans.$$

HYPERBOLAS.

5.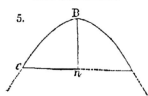

When the Transverse, the Conjugate, and the less Abscissa, B n, are given, to find an Ordinate, e n—fig. 5.

NOTE.—*In hyperbolas, the less abscissa, added to the axis, gives the greater.*

RULE.—As the transverse diameter is to the conjugate, so is the square root of the product of the abscissæ to the ordinate required.

When the Transverse, the Conjugate, and an Ordinate are given, to find the Abscissæ—fig. 5.

RULE.—To the square of half the conjugate add the square of the ordinate, and extract the square root of that sum.

Then, as the conjugate diameter is to the transverse, so is the square root to half the sum of the abscissæ.

To this half sum add half the transverse diameter for the greater abscissa, and subtract it for the less.

When the Transverse, the Abscissæ, and Ordinate are given, to find the Conjugate—fig. 5.

RULE.—As the square root of the product of the abscissæ is to the ordinate, so is the transverse diameter to the conjugate.

When the Conjugate, the Ordinate, and the Abscissæ are given, to find the Transverse—fig. 5.

RULE.—Add the square of the ordinate to the square of half the conjugate, and extract the square root of that sum.

To this root add half the conjugate when the less abcissa is used, and subtract it when the greater is used, reserving the difference or sum.

Then, as the square of the ordinate is to the product of the abscissa and conjugate, so is the sum, or difference above found, to the transverse diameter.

Examples.—In the hyperbola, *figs.* 2 and 5, the transverse dian eter is 100, the conjugate 60, and the abscissa, B *n*, is 40 ; required the ordinate *e n*.

$$100 : 60 : : \sqrt{(40+100 \times 40)} = 74.8 : 44.8 \quad Ans.$$

The transverse is 100, the conjugate 60, and ordinate *e n*, 44.8 ; what are the abscissæ ?   *Ans.* 40 and 140.

The transverse is 100, the ordinate 44.8, the abscissæ 140 and 40 ; what is the conjugate ?   *Ans.* 60.

The conjugate is 60, the ordinate 44.8, and the less abscissa 40 ; what is the transverse ?   *Ans.* 100.

MENSURATION OF SURFACES.

OF FOUR-SIDED FIGURES.

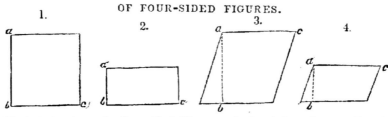

To find the Area of a four-sided Figure, whether it be a Square, Parallelogram, Rhombus, or a Rhomboid.

RULE.—Multiply the length by the breadth or perpendicular height, and the product will be the area.

OF TRIANGLES.

To find the Area of a Triangle—figs. 5 and 6.

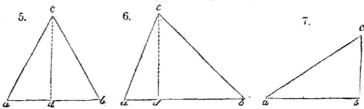

RULE.—Multiply the base *a b* by the perpendicular height *c d*, and half the product will be the area.

To find the Area of a Triangle by the length of its sides.

RULE.—From half the sum of the three sides subtract each side separately; then multiply the half sum and the three remainders continually together, and the square root of the product will be the area.

To find the Length of one side of a Right-angled Triangle, when the Length of the other two sides are given—fig. 7.

RULE.—*To find the hypothenuse a c.* Add together the square of the two legs *a b* and *a c*, and extract the square root of that sum.

To find one of the legs. Subtract the square of the leg, of which the length is known, from the square of the hypothenuse, and the square root of the difference will be the answer.

NOTE.—*For Spherical Triangles, see page 68.*

OF TRAPEZIUMS AND TRAPEZOIDS.

To find the Area of a Trapezium—fig. 8.

RULE.—Multiply the diagonal *a c* by the sum of the two perpendiculars falling upon it from the opposite angles, and half the product will be the area.

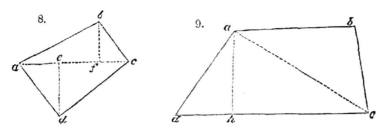

To find the Area of a Trapezoid—fig. 9.

RULE.—Multiply the sum of the parallel sides *a b, d c*, by *a h*, the perpendicular distance between them, and half the product will be the area.

OF REGULAR POLYGONS.

RULE.—Multiply half the perimeter of the figure by the perpendicular, falling from its centre upon one of the sides, and the product will be the area.

To find the Area of a Regular Polygon, when the side only is given.

RULE.—Multiply the square of the side by the multiplier opposite to the name of the polygon in the following table, and the product will be the area.

No. of Sides.	Name of Polygon.	Angle.	Angle of Polygon.	Area.	A	B	C
3	Trigon	120°	60°	0.433012	2.	1.732	.5773
4	Tetragon	90	90	1.000000	1.41	1.414	.7071
5	Pentagon	72	108	1.720477	1.238	1.175	.8506
6	Hexagon }	60	120	2.598076	1.156	=Radius	{ =l'gth of side
7	Heptagon	51$\frac{3}{7}$	128$\frac{4}{7}$	3.633912	1.11	.8677	1.152
8	Octagon	45	135	4.828427	1.08	.7653	1.3065
9	Nonagon	40	140	6.181824	1.06	.6840	1.4619
10	Decagon	36	144	7.694208	1.05	.6180	1.6180
11	Undecagon	32$\frac{3}{11}$	147$\frac{3}{11}$	9.365640	1.04	.5634	1.7747
12	Dodecagon	30	150	11.196152	1.037	.5176	1.9318

Additional uses of the foregoing Table.

The third and fourth columns of the table will greatly facilitate the construction of these figures, with the aid of the sector. Thus, if it is required to describe an *octagon*, opposite to it, in column third, is 45; then, with the chord of 60 on the sector as radius, describe a circle, taking the length 45 on the same line of the sector; mark this distance off on the circumference, which, being repeated around the circle, will give the points of the sides.

The fourth column gives the angle which any two adjoining sides of the respective figures make with each other.

Take the length of a perpendicular drawn from the centre to one of the sides of a polygon, and multiply this by the numbers in column A, the product will be the radius of the circle that contains the figure.

The radius of a circle multiplied by the number in column B, will give the length of the side of the corresponding figure which that circle will contain.

The length of the side of a polygon multiplied by the corresponding number in the column C, will give the radius of the circumscribing circle.

OF REGULAR BODIES.

To find the Superficies of any Regular Body.

RULE.—Multiply the tabular *surface* in the following table by the square of the linear edge, and the product will be the superficies.

Number of Sides.	Names.	Surfaces.
4	Tetrahedron	1.73205
6	Hexahedron.	6.00000
8	Octahedron.	3.46410
12	Dodecahedron.	20.64573
20	Icosahedron.	8.66025

OF IRREGULAR FIGURES.

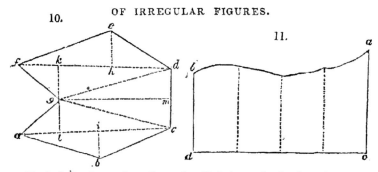

To find the Area of an Irregular Polygon, a b c d e f g—fig. 10.

RULE.—Draw diagonals to divide the figure into trapeziums and triangles ; find the area of each separately, and the sum of the whole will give the area required.

To find the Area of a Long Irregular Figure, b d c a—fig. 11.

RULE.—Take the breadth in several places, and at equal distances apart ; add them together, and divide the sum by the number of breadths for the mean breadth ; then multiply that by the length of the figure, and the product will be the area.

OF CIRCLES.

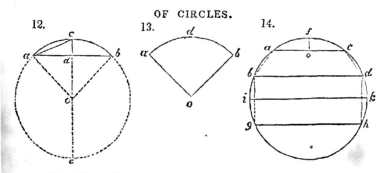

To find the Diameter and Circumference of any Circle.

RULE 1.—Multiply the diameter by 3.1416, and the product will be the circumference.

F

Rule 2.—Divide the circumference by 3.1416, and the quotient will be the diameter.

Rule 3.—Or, as 7 is to 22, so is the diameter to the circumference.

Or, as 22 is to 7, so is the circumference to the diameter.

Or, as 113 is to 355, so is the diameter to the circumference, &c

To find the Area of a Circle.

Rule 1.—Multiply the square of the diameter by .7854, or the square of the circumference by .07958, and the product will be the area.

Rule 2.—Multiply half the circumference by half the diameter.

Rule 3.—As 14 is to 11, so is the square of the diameter to the area , or, as 88 is to 7, so is the square of the circumference to the area.

To find the Length of any Arc of a Circle—fig. 12.

Rule 1.—From 8 times the chord of half the arc $a\,c$, subtract the chord $a\,b$ of the whole arc ; one third of the remainder will be the length nearly.

Rule 2.—Multiply the radius $a\,o$ of the circle by .0174533, and that product by the degrees in the arc.

Rule 3.—As 180 is to the number of degrees in the arc, so is 3.1416 times the radius to its length.

1. When the Chord of the Arc and the Versed Sine of half the Arc are given.

Rule 4.—To 15 times the square of the chord $a\,b$, add 33 times the square of the versed sine $c\,d$, and reserve the number.

To the square of the chord add 4 times the square of the versed sine, and the square root of the sum will be *twice the chord of half the arc.*

Multiply twice the chord of half the arc by 10 times the square of the versed sine, divide the product by the reserved number, and add the quotient to twice the chord of half the arc : the sum will be the length of the arc very nearly.

Note.—1. diameter   × .8862 = side of an equal square.
2. circumference × .2821 = "   "   "
3. diameter   × .7071 = " of the inscribed square.
4. circumference × .2251 = "   "   "
5. area   × .9003 = "   "   "
6. side of a square × 1.4142 = diam. of its circums. circle.
7. "   "   × 4.443 = circum.   "   "
8. "   "   × 1.128 = diam. of an equal circle.
9. "   "   × 3.545 = circum.   "   "
10. square inches × 1.273 = round inches.

When the Chord of the Arc, and the Chord of half the Arc are given.

Rule 5.—From the square of the chord of half the arc subtract

Note.—If the length for any number of degrees, minutes, &c., is required (see page 67 for the units, radius being 1), multiply them by the number of degrees, &c. in the arc, and the answer is the length.

the square of half the chord of the arc, and the remainder will be the square of the versed sine : then proceed as above.

NOTE.—The chord of half the arc is equal to the square root of the sum of the squares of the versed sine or height, and half the chord of the entire arc.

When the Diameter and the Versed Sine of half the Arc are given.

RULE 6.—From 60 times the diameter *c o*, subtract 27 times *c d* the versed sine, and reserve the number.

Multiply the diameter by the versed sine, and the square root of the product will be the *chord of half the arc.*

Multiply twice the chord of half the arc by 10 times the versed sine, divide the product by the reserved number, and add the quotient to twice the chord of half the arc : the sum will be the length of the arc very nearly.

NOTE. — When the diameter and chord of the arc are given, the versed sine may be found thus : From the square of the diameter subtract the square of the chord, and extract the square root of the remainder. Subtract this root from the diameter, and half the remainder will give the versed sine of half the arc.

The square of the chord of half the arc being divided by the diameter, will give the versed sine ; or, being divided by the versed sine, will give the diameter.

To find the Area of a Sector of a Circle—fig. 13.

RULE 1.—Multiply the length of the arc *a d b* by half the length of the radius *a o*.

RULE 2.—As 360 is to the degrees in the arc of the sector, so is the area of the circle to the area of the sector.

NOTE.—If the diameter or radius is not given, add the square of half the chord of the arc to the square of the versed sine of half the arc ; this sum being divided by the versed sine, will give the diameter.

To find the Area of a Segment of a Circle—fig. 12.

(See table of Areas, page 72.)

RULE 1.—Find the area of the sector having the same arc with the segment, then find the area of the triangle formed by the chord of the segment and the radii of the sector, and the difference of these areas, according as the segment is greater or less than a semicircle, will be the area required.

RULE 2.—To the chord *a b* of the whole arc, add the chord *a c* of half the arc, and ⅓ of it more ; then multiply the sum by the versed sine *c d*, and $\frac{4}{10}$ of the product will be the area.

RULE 3.—Multiply the chord of the segment by the versed sine, divide the product by 3, and multiply the remainder by 2.

Cube the height, find how often twice the length of the chord is contained in it, and add the quotient to the former product, and it will give the area nearly.

To find the Area of a Circular Zone—fig. 14.

(See table of Areas, page 80.)

RULE 1.—*When the zone is less than a semicircle.* To the area of the trapezoid *a b c d* add the area of the segments *a b, c d;* their sum is the area.

RULE 2.—*When the zone is greater than a semicircle.* To the area of the parallelogram *b g d h*, add the area of the segments *b i g, d k h;* their sum is the area.

To find the Convex Surface of any Zone or Segment—figs. 38 and 39.

RULE.—Multiply the height *c b*, or *b d*, of the zone or segment by the circumference of the sphere, and the product is the surface.

OF UNGULAS.

To find the Convex Surface of the Ungulas—figs. 27, 28, 29, and 30.

RULES.—For fig. 27, multiply the length of the arc line *a b c* of the base by the height *a d*.

For fig. 28, multiply the circumference of the base of the cylinder *e f g* by half the sum of the greater and less lengths *a c, c f.*

For fig. 29, multiply the sine *a d*, of half the arc *a g*, of the base *a c g*, by the diameter *e g* of the cylinder, and from this product subtract the product[*] of the arc *a g c* and cosine *d f.* Multiply the difference thus found by the quotient of the height *g b*, divided by the versed sine *c d.*

For fig. 30 (conceive the section to be continued till it meets the side of the cylinder produced), then find the surface of each of the ungulas thus formed, and their difference is the surface required.

NOTE.—For rules to ascertain the surface of conical ungulas, see *Ryan's Bonnycastle's Mensuration,* page 136 (1839).

To find the Area of a Circular Ring or Space included between two Concentric Circles—fig. 54.

RULE.—Find the areas of the two circles *a d, b c* separately, and their difference will be the area of the ring.

OF ELLIPSES.

15.   16.

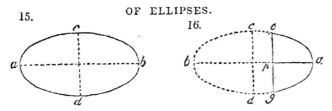

To find the Circumference of an Ellipse—fig. 15.

RULE.—Square the two axes *a b* and *c d*, and multiply the square root of half their sum by 3.1416 ; the product will be the circumference.

To find the Area of an Ellipse—fig. 15.

RULE.—Multiply the two diameters together, and the product by .7854.

---

[*] When this product exceeds the other, add them together, and when the cosine is 0, the product is 0.

To find the Area of an Elliptic Segment, a e g—fig. 16.

RULE.—Divide the height of the segment *a p* by the axis *a b*, of which it is a part, and find in the table of circular segments, page 72, a segment having the same versed sine as this quotient; then multiply the segment thus found and the two axes of the ellipse together, and the product will give the area.

OF PARABOLAS.

17. 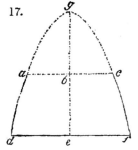   18.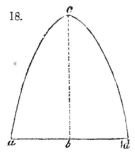

To find the Area of a Parabola—fig. 17.

RULE.—Multiply the base *d f* by the height *g e*, and $\frac{2}{3}$ of the product will be the area.

To find the Area of a Frustrum of a Parabola—fig. 17.

RULE.—Multiply the difference of the cubes of the two ends of the frustrum *a c d f* by twice its altitude *b e*, and divide the product by three times the difference of the squares of the ends.

To find the Length of a Parabolic Curve cut off by a Double Ordinate— fig. 18.

RULE.—To the square of the ordinate *a b* add $\frac{4}{3}$ of the square of the abscissa *c b;* the square root of that sum, multiplied by 2, will give the length of the curve nearly.

OF HYPERBOLAS.

19. 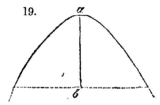   20.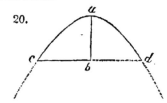

To find the Area of a Hyperbola—fig. 19.

RULE.—To the product of the transverse and abscissa add $\frac{5}{7}$ of the square of the abscissa *a b,* and multiply the square root of the sum by 21. Add 4 times the square root of the product of the transverse and abscissa to the product last found, and divide the sum by 75.

Divide 4 times the product of the conjugate and abscissa by the transverse, and this last quotient, multiplied by the former, will give the area nearly.

F 2

To find the Length of a Hyperbolic Curve—fig. 20.

RULE.—As the transverse is to the conjugate, so is the conjugate to the parameter. To 21 times the parameter of the axis add 19 times the transverse, and to 21 times the parameter add 9 times the transverse, and multiply each of these sums by the quotient of the abscissa *b a*, divided by the transverse. To each of these two products add 15 times the parameter, and divide the former by the latter; multiply this quotient by the ordinate, and the product is the length of half the curve nearly.

OF CYLINDRICAL RINGS.

To find the Convex Surface of a Cylindrical Ring—fig. 54.

RULE.—To the thickness of the ring *a b* add the inner diameter *c*; multiply this sum by the thickness, and the product by 9.8696, nd it will give the surface required.

To find the Area of a Circular Ring—fig. 54.

RULE.—The difference of the areas of the two circles will be the area of the ring.

OF LUNES.

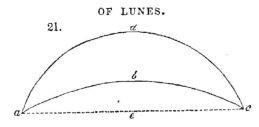

21.

To find the Area of a Lune—fig. 21.

RULE.—Find the areas of the two segments *a d c b, a b c e* from which the lune is formed, and their difference will be the area required.*

OF CYCLOIDS.

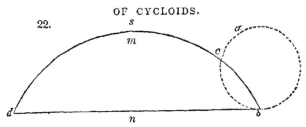

22.

To find the Area of a Cycloid—fig. 22.

RULE.—Multiply area of generating circle *a b c* by 3, and the product is the area.

* If semicircles be described on the three sides of a right-angled triangle as diameters, two lunes will be formed, their united areas being equal to the area of the triangle.

$dsb = 4mn.$

OF CYLINDERS.

To find the Convex Surface of a Cylinder—fig. 25.

RULE.—Multiply the circumference by the length, and the product will be the surface.

OF CONES OR PYRAMIDS.

To find the Convex Surface of a Right Cone or Pyramid—figs. 31 and 33.

RULE.—Multiply the perimeter or circumference of the base by the slant height, and half the product will be the surface.

To find the Convex Surface of a Frustrum of a Right Cone or Pyramid—figs. 32 and 34.

RULE.—Multiply the sum of the perimeters of the two ends by the slant height or side, and half the product will be the surface.

OF SPHERES.

To find the Convex Surface of a Sphere or Globe—fig. 37.

RULE —Multiply the diameter of the sphere by its circumference, and the product is the surface.

OF CIRCULAR SPINDLES.

To find the Convex Surface of a Circular Spindle—fig. 45.

RULE.—Multiply the length fc of the spindle by the radius oc of the revolving arc; multiply the said arc fac by the central distance oe, or distance between the centre of the spindle and centre of the revolving arc. Subtract this last product from the former, double the remainder, multiply it by 3.1416, and the product is the surface.

NOTE.—The same rule will serve for any zone or segment, cut off perpendicularly to the chord of the revolving arc ; in this case, then, the particular length of the part, and the part of the arc which describes it, must be taken, in lieu of the whole length and whole arc.

BY MATHEMATICAL FORMULÆ.

LINES.   CIRCLE.

Ratio of circumference to diameter, $p = 3.1416$.

Length of an arc $= \dfrac{8c'-c}{3}$ nearly ; c the chord of the arc, and c' the chord of half the arc.

Length of 1 degree, radius being 1, $= .0174533$
  "   1 *minute,* $= .0002909$
  "   1 *second,* $= .0000048$

ELLIPSE.

Circumference $= \frac{199}{200}p\sqrt{\frac{1}{2}(a^2+b^2)}$ nearly, a and b being the axes.

PARABOLA.

Length of an arc, commencing at the vertex, $= \sqrt{\left(\dfrac{4a^2}{3}+b^2\right)}$ nearly, a being the abscissa, and b the ordinate.

QUADRILATERALS.

Half the product of the diagonals × the sine of their angle.

CIRCLE.

pr^2; or diam.^{2} ×.78539816; or circum.^{2} ×.0795774.

CYLINDER.

Curved surface = height × perimeter of base.

SPHERICAL ZONE OR SEGMENT.

$2prh$; or, the height of the zone or segment × the circumference of the sphere.

CIRCULAR SPINDLE.

$2p(rc - a\sqrt{r^2 - \frac{1}{4}c^2})$; a being the length of the arc, and c its chord, or the length of the spindle.

SPHERICAL TRIANGLE.

$pr^2 \dfrac{s - 180°}{180°}$; s being the sum of the three angles.

ANY SURFACE OF REVOLUTION.

$2pr \times l$; or, the length of the generating element × the circumference described by its centre of gravity.

ILLUSTRATIONS.—Let $a\,b\,c$ be the side of a *cylinder*, $b\,r$ the radius; then $a\,b\,c$ is the generating element, b the centre of gravity (of the line), and $b\,r$ the radius of the circle described by $a\,b\,c$.

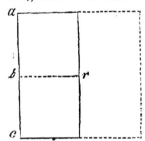

Then, if $a\,b\,c = 10$, $b\,r = 5$: $10 \times (5 + 5 \times 3.1416) = 314.16$.

Parabola.

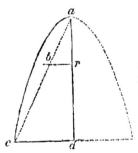

$ac \times (2br \times p)$, p being in this and all other instances = 3.1416, b the centre of gravity, and $b\,r$ the radius of its circumference.

Or, take a uniform piece of board or thick pasteboard, and cut out the figure of which the area is required; weigh both pieces together, and then the figure separately, and say, as the gross weight is to the entire surface, so is the weight of the figure to its surface.

CAPILLARY TUBE.

Let the tube be weighed when empty, and again when filled with mercury; let w be the difference of those weights in troy grains, and l the length of the tube in inches.

$$\text{Diameter} = .019252\sqrt{\frac{w}{l}}.$$

USEFUL FACTORS,

In which p represents the Circumference of a Circle whose Diameter is 1.

Then $p = 3.1415926535897932384626+$

$2p = 6.283185307179+$

$4p = 12.566370614359+$

$\frac{1}{2}p = 1.570796326794+$

$\frac{1}{4}p = 0.785398163397+$

$\frac{4}{3}p = 4.188790$

$\frac{1}{6}p = .523598$

$\frac{1}{8}p = .392699$

$\frac{1}{12}p = .261799$

$\frac{1}{360}p = .008726$

$\frac{1}{p} = .318309$

$\frac{2}{p} = .636619$

$\frac{4}{p} = 1.273239$

$\frac{1}{4p} = .079577$

$\sqrt{p} = 1.772453$

$\frac{1}{2}\sqrt{p} = .886226$

$2\sqrt{p} = 3.544907$

$\sqrt{\frac{2}{p}} = .797884$

$\sqrt{\frac{1}{p}} = .564189$

$\frac{360}{p} = 114.591559$

$\frac{2}{3}p = 2.094395$

$\frac{6}{p} = 1.909859$

$36p = 113.097335$

Examples in Illustration of the foregoing Rules.

Required the area, 1. Of the rhombus, fig. 3, ac 12 feet 6 inches, and its he.
ab, 9 feet 3 inches.   *Ans.* 115.625 feet.

2. Of the triangle abc, fig. 5, ab being 10 feet, and cd 5 feet.   *Ans.* 25 feet.

3. Of the triangle abc, fig. 7, its three sides measuring respectively 24, 36, and 48 feet.   *Ans.* 418.282.

4. In the right-angled triangle abc, fig. 7, the base is 56, and the height 33; what is the hypothenuse?   *Ans.* 65.

5. If the hypothenuse of a triangle be 53, and the base 45, what is the perpendicular?   *Ans.* 28.

6. Required the area of the trapezium, fig. 8, the diagonal ac 84, the perpendiculars 21 and 28.   *Ans.* 2058.

7. Of the trapezoid, fig. 9, ab 10, dc 12, and ah 6 feet.   *Ans.* 66.

8. Of an octagon, the side being 5. $5^2 = 25 \times 4.828427 = 120.710675$ *Ans.*

9. The length of a perpendicular from the centre to one of the sides of an octagon is 12; what is the radius of the circumscribing circle?
12×1.08 (table, page 60) $= 12.96$ *Ans.*

10. The radius of a circle being 12.96, what will be the length of one side of an inscribed octagon? $12.96 \times .765$ (page 60) $= 9.914$ *Ans.*

11. The length of the side of a decagon is 10; what is the radius of the circumscribing circle? 10×1.618 (page 60) $= 16.18$ *Ans.*

12. The chord ab, fig. 12, is 48, and the versed sine cd 18; what is the length of the arc?
By Rule 4, twice the chord of half the arc is 60, then $60 \div 2 = 30$, chord of half the arc, and $30 \times 8 = 240 - 48 = 192 \div 3 = 64$ *Ans.*

13. The diameter co, fig. 12, is 50, and the versed sine cd 18; what is the length of the arc?
By rule 6   .   .   . $50 \times 60 + \overline{18 \times 27} = 2514 \sqrt{50 \times 18} = 900 = 30.$
Then $30 \times 2 = 60 \times \overline{10 \times 18} = 10800 \div 2514 = 4.2959 + 30 \times 2 = 64.2959$ *Ans.*

14. The diameter of a circle is 50, and the chord of half the arc 30; what is the length of the arc?   *Ans.* 64.2959.

15. What is the area of a sector, the chord of the arc being 40, and the versed sine 15?   *Ans.* 558.125.

16. The radius of a sector ob, fig. 13, is 20, and the degrees in its arc 22; what is the area?   *Ans.* 76.7947.

17. The radius oc is 10, and the chord ac 10; what is the area of the segment $acbd$, fig. 12?   *Ans.* 52.36.

18. The greater chord, bd, fig. 14, is 96, the lesser, ac, 60, and the breadth 26; what is the area of the zone?   *Ans.* 2136.75.

19. The sine of half the arc, fig. 29, is 7, the diameter of the cylinder 15, the cosine on eg, at the intersection of ac, 2.7, the versed sine 4.8, and the height, bg, 12; what is the convex surface?   *Ans.* 196.

20. The height, ap, of an elliptic segment, fig. 16, is 10, and the axes 25 and 35 respectively; what is the area?
$10 \div 35 = .2857$ tabular versed sine, and segment $= .185153 \times 35 \times 25 = 162.0088$ *Ans.*

21. In the parabolic frustrum, $acdf$, fig. 17, the ends ac and df are 6 and 10, and the height be is 5; what is the area?
$$\frac{10^3 - 6^3}{10^2 - 6^2} = \frac{784}{64} = 12.25 \times \tfrac{2}{3} \text{ of } 5 = 40.8 \text{ } Ans.$$

22. The abscissa cb, fig. 18, is 12, and its ordinate ab 6; what is the length of acd?   *Ans.* 30.198.

23. The transverse and conjugate diameters of a hyperbola, fig. 19, are 100 and 60, and the abscissa ab 60; what is the area?   *Ans.* 4320.

24. What is the curve acd of the hyperbola, fig. 20, the abscissa ab 40?
                                            Ans. 59.85.

25. The chord *a c*, fig. 21, is 19, the heights *e d* 6.9, and *e b* 2.4 ; what is the area of the lune ?   *Ans.* 65.3.

26. The generating circle *a b c*, fig. 22, is 4 inches diameter ; what is the area of the cycloid *b c d ?*   *Ans.* 37.6992.

27. The base of a cone, fig. 31, is 3 feet, and the slant height 15 feet ; what is the convex surface ?   *Ans.* 70.686.

28. The thickness of a cylindric ring, fig. 54, is 3 inches, and the inner diameter 12 inches ; what is the convex surface ?   *Ans.* 444.132.

29. What is the convex surface of a globe, fig. 37, 17 inches in diameter ?
                    Ans. 6.305 square feet.

30. What is the surface of the circular spindle, fig. 45, the length *f c* 14.142, the radius *o c* 10, and the central distance *o e* 7.071 inches ?   *Ans.* 190.82 inches.

31. What is the surface of an octahedron, the linear side being 2 inches ?
                    $2^2 \times 3.46410$ (tabular surface) $= 13.85640$ *Ans.*

32. What is the convex surface of a cylinder, fig. 25, the diameter of the base *a b* 10, and the height *b c* 10 inches ?   *Ans.* 314.16.

TABLE *of the Areas of the Segments of a Circle, the diameter of which is Unity, and supposed to be divided into* 1000 *equal Parts.*

Versed Sine.	Seg. Area.	Versed Sine.	Seg. Area.	Versed Sine.	Seg. Area.	Versed Sine.	Seg. Area.
.001	.00004	.055	.01691	.109	.04638	.163	.08332
.002	.00011	.056	.01736	.110	.04700	.164	.08405
.003	.00021	.057	.01783	.111	.04763	.165	.08480
.004	.00033	.058	.01829	.112	.04826	.166	.08554
.005	.00047	.059	.01876	.113	.04889	.167	.08628
.006	.00061	.060	.01923	.114	.04952	.168	.08703
.007	.00077	.061	.01971	.115	.05016	.169	.08778
.008	.00095	.062	.02019	.116	.05080	.170	.08853
.009	.00113	.063	.02068	.117	.05144	.171	.08928
.010	.00132	.064	.02116	.118	.05209	.172	.09004
.011	.00153	.065	.02165	.119	.05273	.173	.09079
.012	.00174	.066	.02215	.120	.05338	.174	.09155
.013	.00196	.067	.02265	.121	.05403	.175	.09231
.014	.00219	.068	.02315	.122	.05468	.176	.09307
.015	.00243	.069	.02365	.123	.05534	.177	.09383
.016	.00268	.070	.02416	.124	.05600	.178	.09460
.017	.00294	.071	.02468	.125	.05666	.179	.09536
.018	.00320	.072	.02519	.126	.05732	.180	.09613
.019	.00347	.073	.02571	.127	.05799	.181	.09690
.020	.00374	.074	.02623	.128	.05865	.182	.09767
.021	.00403	.075	.02676	.129	.05932	.183	.09844
.022	.00432	.076	.02728	.130	.05999	.184	.09922
.023	.00461	.077	.02782	.131	.06067	.185	.09999
.024	.00492	.078	.02835	.132	.06134	.186	.10077
.025	.00523	.079	.02889	.133	.06202	.187	.10155
.026	.00554	.080	.02943	.134	.06270	.188	.10233
.027	.00586	.081	.02997	.135	.06338	.189	.10311
.028	.00619	.082	.03052	.136	.06407	.190	.10390
.029	.00652	.083	.03107	.137	.06476	.191	.10468
.030	.00686	.084	.03162	.138	.06544	.192	.10547
.031	.00720	.085	.03218	.139	.06614	.193	.10626
.032	.00755	.086	.03274	.140	.06683	.194	.10705
.033	.00791	.087	.03330	.141	.06752	.195	.10784
.034	.00827	.088	.03387	.142	.06822	.196	.10863
.035	.00863	.089	.03444	.143	.06892	.197	.10943
.036	.00900	.090	.03501	.144	.06962	.198	.11022
.037	.00938	.091	.03558	.145	.07032	.199	.11102
.038	.00976	.092	.03616	.146	.07103	.200	.11182
.039	.01014	.093	.03674	.147	.07174	.201	.11262
.040	.01053	.094	.03732	.148	.07245	.202	.11342
.041	.01093	.095	.03790	.149	.07316	.203	.11423
.042	.01133	.096	.03849	.150	.07387	.204	.11503
.043	.01173	.097	.03908	.151	.07458	.205	.11584
.044	.01214	.098	.03968	.152	.07530	.206	.11665
.045	.01255	.099	.04027	.153	.07602	.207	.11746
.046	.01297	.100	.04087	.154	.07674	.208	.11827
.047	.01339	.101	.04147	.155	.07746	.209	.11908
.048	.01381	.102	.04208	.156	.07819	.210	.11989
.049	.01424	.103	.04268	.157	.07892	.211	.12071
.050	.01468	.104	.04329	.158	.07964	.212	.12152
.051	.01511	.105	.04390	.159	.08038	.213	.12234
.052	.01556	.106	.04452	.160	.08111	.214	.12316
.053	.01600	.107	.04513	.161	.08184	.215	.12398
.054	.01645	.108	.04575	.162	.08258	.216	.12481

TABLE—(Continued).

Versed Sine.	Seg. Area.	Versed Sine.	Seg. Area.	Versed Sine.	Seg. Area.	Versed Sine.	Seg. Area.
.217	.12563	.272	.17286	.327	.22321	.382	.27580
.218	.12645	.273	.17375	.328	.22415	.383	.27677
.219	.12728	.274	.17464	.329	.22509	.384	.27774
.220	12811	.275	.17554	.330	.22603	.385	.27872
.221	.12894	.276	.17643	.331	.22697	.386	.27969
.222	.12977	.277	.17733	.332	.22791	.387	.28066
.223	.13060	.278	.17822	.333	.22885	.388	.28164
.224	.13143	.279	.17912	.334	.22980	.389	.28261
.225	.13227	.280	.18001	.335	.23074	.390	.28359
.226	.13310	.281	.18091	.336	.23168	.391	.28456
.227	.13394	.282	.18181	.337	.23263	.392	.28554
.228	.13478	.283	.18271	.338	.23358	.393	.28652
.229	.13562	.284	.18361	.339	.23452	.394	.28749
.230	.13646	.285	.18452	.340	.23547	.395	.28847
.231	.13730	.286	.18542	.341	.23642	.396	.28945
.232	.13815	.287	.18632	.342	.23736	.397	.29043
.233	.13899	.288	.18723	.343	.23831	.398	.29141
.234	.13984	.289	.18814	.344	.23926	.399	.29239
.235	.14068	.290	.18904	.345	.24021	.400	.29336
.236	.14153	.291	.18995	.346	.24116	.401	.29434
.237	.14238	.292	.19086	.347	.24212	.402	.29533
.238	.14323	.293	.19177	.348	.24307	.403	.29631
.239	.14409	.294	.19268	.349	.24402	.404	.29729
.240	.14494	.295	.19359	.350	.24498	.405	.29827
.241	.14579	.296	.19450	.351	.24593	.406	.29925
.242	.14665	.297	.19542	.352	.24688	.407	.30023
.243	.14751	.298	.19633	.353	.24784	.408	.30122
.244	.14837	.299	.19725	.354	.24880	.409	.30220
.245	.14923	.300	.19816	.355	.24975	.410	.30318
.246	.15009	.301	.19908	.356	.25071	.411	.30417
.247	.15095	.302	.20000	.357	.25167	.412	.30515
.248	.15181	.303	.20092	.358	.25263	.413	.30614
.249	.15268	.304	.20184	.359	.25359	.414	.30712
.250	.15354	.305	.20276	.360	.25455	.415	.30811
.251	.15441	.306	.20368	.361	.25551	.416	.30909
.252	.15528	.307	.20460	.362	.25647	.417	.31008
.253	.15614	.308	.20552	.363	.25743	.418	.31106
.254	.15701	.309	.20645	.364	.25839	.419	.31205
.255	.15789	.310	.20737	.365	.25935	.420	.31304
.256	.15876	.311	.20830	.366	.26032	.421	.31402
.257	.15963	.312	.20922	.367	.26128	.422	.31501
.258	.16051	.313	.21015	.368	.26224	.423	.31600
.259	.16138	.314	.21108	.369	.26321	.424	.31699
.260	.16226	.315	.21201	.370	.26417	.425	.31798
.261	.16314	.316	.21294	.371	.26514	.426	.31897
.262	.16401	.317	.21387	.372	.26611	.427	.31995
.263	.16489	.318	.21480	.373	.26707	.428	.32094
.264	.16578	.319	.21573	.374	.26804	.429	.32193
.265	.16666	.320	.21666	.375	.26901	.430	.32292
.266	.16754	.321	.21759	.376	.26998	.431	.32391
.267	.16843	.322	.21853	.377	.27095	.432	.32490
.268	.16931	.323	.21946	.378	.27192	.433	.32590
.269	.17020	.324	.22040	.379	.27289	.434	.32689
.270	.17108	.325	.22134	.380	.27386	.435	.32788
.271	.17197	.326	.22227	.381	.27483	.436	.32887

G

TABLE—(Continued).

Versed Sine.	Seg. Area.	Versed Sine.	Seg. Area.	Versed Sine.	Seg. Area.	Versed Sine.	Seg. Area.
.437	.32986	.453	.34576	.469	.36171	.485	.37770
.438	.33085	.454	.34676	.470	.36271	.486	.37870
.439	.33185	.455	.34775	.471	.36371	.487	.37970
.440	.33284	.456	.34875	.472	.36471	.488	.38070
.441	.33383	.457	.34975	.473	.36571	.489	.38169
.442	.33482	.458	.35074	.474	·36671	.490	.38269
.443	.33582	.459	.35174	.475	.36770	.491	.38369
.444	.33681	.460	.35274	.476	.36870	.492	.38469
.445	.33781	.461	.35373	.477	.36970	.493	.38569
.446	.33880	.462	.35473	.478	.37070	.494	.38669
.447	.33979	.463	.35573	.479	.37170	.495	.38769
.448	.34079	.464	.35673	.480	.37276	.496	.38869
.449	.34178	.465	.35772	.481	.37370	.497	.38969
.450	.34278	.466	.35872	.482	.37470	.498	.39069
.451	.34377	.467	.35972	.483	.37570	.499	.39169
.452	.34477	.468	.36072	.484	.37670	.500	.39269

USE OF THE ABOVE TABLE.

To find the Area of a Segment of a Circle.

RULE.—Divide the height or versed sine by the diameter of the circle, and find the quotient in the column of versed sines. Take the area noted in the next column, and multiply it by the square of the diameter, and it will give the area required.

EXAMPLE.—Required the area of a segment; its height being 10, and the diameter of the circle 50 feet.

$10 \div 50 = .2$, and $.2$, per table, $= .11182$; then $.11182 \times 50^2 = 279.55$ *Ans.*

TABLE *of the Lengths of Circular Arcs.*

Height.	Length.	Height.	Length.	Height.	Length.	Height.	Length.
.100	1.0265	.156	1.0637	.212	1.1158	.268	1.1816
.101	1.0270	.157	1.0645	.213	1.1169	.269	1.1829
.102	1.0275	.158	1.0653	.214	1.1180	.270	1.1843
.103	1.0281	.159	1.0661	.215	1.1190	.271	1.1856
.104	1.0286	.160	1.0669	.216	1.1201	.272	1.1869
.105	1.0291	.161	1.0678	.217	1.1212	.273	1.1882
.106	1.0297	.162	1.0686	.218	1.1223	.274	1.1897
.107	1.0303	.163	1.0694	.219	1.1233	.275	1.1908
.108	1.0308	.164	1.0703	.220	1.1245	.276	1.1921
.109	1.0314	.165	1.0711	.221	1.1256	.277	1.1934
.110	1.0320	.166	1.0719	.222	1.1266	.278	1.1948
.111	1.0325	.167	1.0728	.223	1.1277	.279	1.1961
.112	1.0331	.168	1.0737	.224	1.1289	.280	1.1974
.113	1.0337	.169	1.0745	.225	1.1300	.281	1.1989
.114	1.0343	.170	1.0754	.226	1.1311	.282	1.2001
.115	1.0349	.171	1.0762	.227	1.1322	.283	1.2015
.116	1.0355	.172	1.0771	.228	1.1333	.284	1.2028
.117	1.0361	.173	1.0780	.229	1.1344	.285	1.2042
.118	1.0367	.174	1.0789	.230	1.1356	.286	1.2056
.119	1.0373	.175	1.0798	.231	1.1367	.287	1.2070
.120	1.0380	.176	1.0807	.232	1.1379	.288	1.2083
.121	1.0386	.177	1.0816	.233	1.1390	.289	1.2097
.122	1.0392	.178	1.0825	.234	1.1402	.290	1.2120
.123	1.0399	.179	1.0834	.235	1.1414	.291	1.2124
.124	1.0405	.180	1.0843	.236	1.1425	.292	1.2138
.125	1.0412	.181	1.0852	.237	1.1436	.293	1.2152
.126	1.0418	.182	1.0861	.238	1.1448	.294	1.2166
.127	1.0425	.183	1.0870	.239	1.1460	.295	1.2179
.128	1.0431	.184	1.0880	.240	1.1471	.296	1.2193
.129	1.0438	.185	1.0889	.241	1.1483	.297	1.2206
.130	1.0445	.186	1.0898	.242	1.1495	.298	1.2220
.131	1.0452	.187	1.0908	.243	1.1507	.299	1.2235
.132	1.0458	.188	1.0917	.244	1.1519	.300	1.2250
.133	1.0465	.189	1.0927	.245	1.1531	.301	1.2264
.134	1.0472	.190	1.0936	.246	1.1543	.302	1.2278
.135	1.0479	.191	1.0946	.247	1.1555	.303	1.2292
.136	1.0486	.192	1.0956	.248	1.1567	.304	1.2306
.137	1.0493	.193	1.0965	.249	1.1579	.305	1.2321
.138	1.0500	.194	1.0975	.250	1.1591	.306	1.2335
.139	1.0508	.195	1.0985	.251	1.1603	.307	1.2349
.140	1.0515	.196	1.0995	.252	1.1616	.308	1.2364
.141	1.0522	.197	1.1005	.253	1.1628	.309	1.2378
.142	1.0529	.198	1.1015	.254	1.1640	.310	1.2393
.143	1.0537	.199	1.1025	.255	1.1653	.311	1.2407
.144	1.0544	.200	1.1035	.256	1.1665	.312	1.2422
.145	1.0552	.201	1.1045	.257	1.1677	.313	1.2436
.146	1.0559	.202	1.1055	.258	1.1690	.314	1.2451
.147	1.0567	.203	1.1065	.259	1.1702	.315	1.2465
.148	1.0574	.204	1.1075	.260	1.1715	.316	1.2480
.149	1.0582	.205	1.1085	.261	1.1728	.317	1.2495
.150	1.0590	.206	1.1096	.262	1.1740	.318	1.2510
.151	1.0597	.207	1.1006	.263	1.1753	.319	1.2524
.152	1.0605	.208	1.1117	.264	1.1766	.320	1.2539
.153	1.0613	.209	1.1127	.265	1.1778	.321	1.2554
.154	1.0621	.210	1.1137	.266	1.1791	.322	1.2569
.155	1.0629	.211	1.1148	.267	1.1804	.323	1.2584

TABLE—(Continued).

Height.	Length.	Height.	Length.	Height.	Length.	Height.	Length.	Height.	Length.
.324	1.2599	.369	1.3307	.413	1.4061	.457	1.4870		
.325	1.2614	.370	1.3323	.414	1.4079	.458	1.4889		
.326	1.2629	.371	1.3340	.415	1.4097	.459	1.4908		
.327	1.2644	.372	1.3356	.416	1.4115	.460	1.4927		
.328	1.2659	.373	1.3373	.417	1.4132	.461	1.4946		
.329	1.2674	.374	1.3390	.418	1.4150	.462	1.4965		
.330	1.2689	.375	1.3406	.419	1.4168	.463	1.4984		
.331	1.2704	.376	1.3423	.420	1.4186	.464	1.5003		
.332	1.2720	.377	1.3440	.421	1.4204	.465	1.5022		
.333	1.2735	.378	1.3456	.422	1.4222	.466	1.5042		
.334	1.2750	.379	1.3473	.423	1.4240	.467	1.5061		
.335	1.2766	.380	1.3490	.424	1.4258	.468	1.5080		
.336	1.2781	.381	1.3507	.425	1.4276	.469	1.5099		
.337	1.2786	.382	1.3524	.426	1.4295	.470	1.5119		
.338	1.2812	.383	1.3541	.427	1.4313	.471	1.5138		
.339	1.2827	.384	1.3558	.428	1.4331	.472	1.5157		
.340	1.2843	.385	1.3574	.429	1.4349	.473	1.5176		
.341	1.2858	.386	1.3591	.430	1.4367	.474	1.5196		
.342	1.2874	.387	1.3608	.431	1.4386	.475	1.5215		
.343	1.2890	.388	1.3625	.432	1.4404	.476	1.5235		
.344	1.2905	.389	1.3643	.433	1.4422	.477	1.5254		
.345	1.2921	.390	1.3660	.434	1.4441	.478	1.5274		
.346	1.2937	.391	1.3677	.435	1.4459	.479	1.5293		
.347	1.2952	.392	1.3694	.436	1.4477	.480	1.5313		
.348	1.2968	.393	1.3711	.437	1.4496	.481	1.5332		
.349	1.2984	.394	1.3728	438	1.4514	.482	1.5352		
.350	1.3000	.395	1.3746	.439	1.4533	.483	1.5371		
.351	1.3016	.396	1.3763	.440	1.4551	.484	1.5391		
.352	1.3032	.397	1.3780	.441	1.4570	.485	1.5411		
.353	1.3047	.398	1.3797	.442	1.4588	.486	1.5430		
.354	1.3063	.399	1.3815	.443	1.4607	.487	1.5450		
.355	1.3079	.400	1.3832	.444	1.4626	.488	1.5470		
.356	1.3095	.401	1.3850	.445	1.4644	.489	1.5489		
.357	1.3112	.402	1.3867	.446	1.4663	.490	1.5509		
.358	1.3128	.403	1.3885	.447	1.4682	.491	1.5529		
.359	1.3144	.404	1.3902	.448	1.4700	.492	1.5549		
.360	1.3160	.405	1.3920	.449	1.4719	.493	1.5569		
.361	1.3176	.406	1.3937	.450	1.4738	.494	1.5585		
.362	1.3192	.407	1.3955	.451	1.4757	.495	1.5608		
.363	1.3209	.408	1.3972	.452	1.4775	.496	1.5628		
.364	1.3225	.409	1.3990	.453	1.4794	.497	1.5648		
.365	1.3241	.410	1.4008	.454	1.4813	.498	1.5668		
.366	1.3258	.411	1.4025	.455	1.4832	.499	1.5688		
.367	1.3274	.412	1.4043	.456	1.4851	.500	1.5708		
.368	1.3291								

To find the Length of an Arc of a Circle by the foregoing Table.

RULE.—Divide the height by the base, find the quotient in the column of heights, and take the length of that height from the next right-hand column. Multiply the length thus obtained by the base of the arc, and the product will be the length of the arc required.

EXAMPLE.—What is the length of an arc of a circle, the span or base being 100 feet, and the height 25 feet?

25÷100 = .25, and .25, per table, gives 1.1591; which, being multiplied by 100, = 115.9100, the length.

NOTE.—*When great accuracy is required, if, in the division of a height by the base, there should be a remainder.*

Find the lengths of the curves from the two nearest tabular heights, and subtract the one length from the other. Then, as the base of the arc of which the length is required is to the remainder *in the operation of division*, so is the difference of the lengths of the curves to the complement required, to be added to the length.

EXAMPLE.—What is the length of an arc of a circle, the base of which is 35 feet, and the height or versed sine 8 feet?

$8 \div 35 = .228 \frac{20}{35}$, $.228 = 1.1333$, $.229 = 1.1344$, $1.1333 \times 35 = 39.6655$, $1.1344 \times 35 = 39.7040$, $39.7040 - 39.6655 = .0385$, difference of lengths.

Hence, as $35 : 20 : : .0385 : .0220$, the length for the remainder, and $.0220 + 39.6655 = 39.6875$, and $.6875 \times 12$, for inches $= 8\frac{1}{4}$, making the length of the arc 39 feet $8\frac{1}{4}$ inches.

To find the length of an Elliptic Curve which is less than half of the entire Figure.

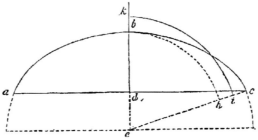

GEOMETRICALLY.—*Let the curve of which the length is required be a b c.*

Extend the versed sine *b d* to meet the centre of the curve in *e*.

Draw the line *c e*, and from *e*, with the distance *e b*, describe *b h*; bisect *c h* in *i*, and from *e*, with the radius *e i*, describe *k i*, and it is equal half the arc *a b c*.

To find the length when the Curve is greater than half the entire Figure.

RULE.—Find by the above problem the curve of the less portion of the figure, and subtract it from the circumference of the ellipse, and the remainder will be the length of the curve required.

G 2

TABLE *of the Lengths of Semi-elliptic Arcs.*

Height.	Length.	Height.	Length.	Height.	Length.	Height.	Length.	Height.	Length.
.100	1.0416	.315	1.2960	.545	1.6409	.775	2.0187		
.101	1.0426	.320	1.3038	.550	1.6488	.780	2.0273		
.102	1.0436	.325	1.3106	.555	1.6567	.785	2.0360		
.103	1.0446	.330	1.3175	.560	1.6646	.790	2.0446		
.104	1.0456	.335	1.3244	.565	1.6725	.795	2.0533		
.105	1.0466	.340	1.3313	.570	1.6804	.800	2.0620		
.110	1.0516	.345	1.3383	.575	1.6883	.805	2.0708		
.115	1.0567	.350	1.3454	.580	1.6963	.810	2.0795		
.120	1.0618	.355	1.3525	.585	1.7042	.815	2.0883		
.125	1.0669	.360	1.3597	.590	1.7123	.820	2.0971		
.130	1.0720	.365	1.3669	.595	1.7203	.825	2.1060		
.135	1.0773	.370	1.3741	.600	1.7283	.830	2.1148		
.140	1.0825	.375	1.3815	.605	1.7364	.835	2.1237		
.145	1.0879	.380	1.3888	.610	1.7444	.840	2.1326		
.150	1.0933	.385	1.3961	.615	1.7525	.845	2.1416		
.155	1.0989	.390	1.4034	.620	1.7606	.850	2.1505		
.160	1.1045	.395	1.4107	.625	1.7687	.855	2.1595		
.165	1.1106	.400	1.4180	.630	1.7768	.860	2.1685		
.170	1.1157	.405	1.4253	.635	1.7850	.865	2.1775		
.175	1.1213	.410	1.4327	.640	1.7931	.870	2.1866		
.180	1.1270	.415	1.4402	.645	1.8013	.875	2.1956		
.185	1.1327	.420	1.4476	.650	1.8094	.880	2.2047		
.190	1.1384	.425	1.4552	.655	1.8176	.885	2.2139		
.195	1.1442	.430	1.4627	.660	1.8258	.890	2.2230		
.200	1.1501	.435	1.4702	.665	1.8340	.895	2.2322		
.205	1.1560	.440	1.4778	.670	1.8423	.900	2.2414		
.210	1.1620	.445	1.4854	.675	1.8505	.905	2.2506		
.215	1.1680	.450	1.4931	.680	1.8587	.910	2.2597		
.220	1.1741	.455	1.5008	.685	1.8670	.915	2.2689		
.225	1.1802	.460	1.5084	.690	1.8753	.920	2.2780		
.230	1.1864	.465	1.5161	.695	1.8836	.925	2.2872		
.235	1.1926	.470	1.5238	.700	1.8919	.930	2.2964		
.240	1.1989	.475	1.5316	.705	1.9002	.935	2.3056		
.245	1.2051	.480	1.5394	.710	1.9085	.940	2.3148		
.250	1.2114	.485	1.5472	.715	1.9169	.945	2.3241		
.255	1.2177	.490	1.5550	.720	1.9253	.950	2.3335		
.260	1.2241	.495	1.5629	.725	1.9337	.955	2.3429		
.265	1.2306	.500	1.5709	.730	1.9422	.960	2.3524		
.270	1.2371	.505	1.5785	.735	1.9506	.965	2.3619		
.275	1.2436	.510	1.5863	.740	1.9599	.970	2.3714		
.280	1.2501	.515	1.5941	.745	1.9675	.975	2.3810		
.285	1.2567	.520	1.6019	.750	1.9760	.980	2.3906		
.290	1.2634	.525	1.6097	.755	1.9845	.985	2.4002		
.295	1.2700	.530	1.6175	.760	1.9931	.990	2.4098		
.300	1.2767	.535	1.6253	.765	2.0016	.995	2.4194		
.305	1.2834	.540	1.6331	.770	2.0102	.1000	2.4291		
.310	1.2901								

To find the Length of the Curve of a Right Semi-Ellipse.

Proceed with the foregoing table by the rules for ascertaining the lengths of circular arcs, page 76.

EXAMPLE.—What is the length of the curve of the arch of a bridge, the span being 70 feet, and the height 30.10 feet?

30.10÷70 = .430 = per table, 1.4627, and 1.4627×70 = 102.3890, the length required.

When the Curve is not that of a Right Semi-Ellipse, the height being half of the Transverse Diameter.

RULE.—Divide half the base by twice the height; then proceed as in the forego-ing example, and multiply the tabular length by twice the height, and the product will be the length required.

EXAMPLE.—What is the length of the profile of arch (it being that of a semi-el-lipse), the height measuring 35 feet and the base 60 feet?

$60 \div 2 = 30 \div \overline{35 \times 2} = .428$, the tabular length of which is 1.4597.

Then, $1.4597 \times \overline{35 \times 2} = 102.1790$, the length required.

NOTE.—*When the quotient is not given in the column of heights, divide the dif-ference between the two nearest heights by .5; multiply the quotient by the excess of the height given and the height in the table first above it, and add this sum to the tabular area of the least height. Thus, if the height is 118,*

.115, per table, $= 1.0567$
.120,   " $= 1.0618$

$\overline{.0051} \div .5 = .00102 \times (118 - 115) = .00306$,

which, added to $1.0567 = 1.05976$, the length for 118.

TABLE *of the Areas of the Zones of a Circle.*

Height.	Area.	Height.	Area.	Height.	Area.	Height.	Area.
.001	.00100	.115	.11397	.245	.23480	.375	.33604
.002	.00300	.120	.11883	.250	.23915	.380	.33931
.003	.00300	.125	.12368	.255	.24346	.385	.34253
.004	.00400	.130	.12852	.260	.24775	.390	.34569
.005	.00500	.135	.13334	.265	.25201	.395	.34879
.010	.01000	.140	.13814	.270	.25624	.400	.35182
.015	.01499	.145	.14294	.275	.26043	.405	.35479
.020	.01999	.150	.14772	.280	.26459	.410	.35769
.025	.02499	.155	.15248	.285	.26871	.415	.36051
.030	.02998	.160	.15722	.290	.27280	.420	.36326
.035	.03497	.165	.16195	.295	.27686	.425	.36594
.040	.03995	.170	.16667	.300	.28088	.430	.36853
.045	.04494	.175	.17136	.305	.28486	.435	.37104
.050	.04992	.180	.17603	.310	.28880	.440	.37346
.055	.05489	.185	.18069	.315	.29270	.445	.37579
.060	.05985	.190	.18532	.320	.29657	.450	.37805
.065	.06482	.195	.18994	.325	.30039	.455	.38015
.070	.06977	.200	.19453	.330	.30416	.460	.38216
.075	.07472	.205	.19910	.335	.30790	.465	.38466
.080	.07965	.210	.20365	.340	.31159	.470	.38853
.085	.08458	.215	.20818	.345	.31523	.475	.38747
.090	.08951	.220	.21268	.350	.31883	.480	.38895
.095	.09442	.225	.21715	.355	.32237	.485	.39026
.100	.09933	.230	.22161	.360	.32587	.490	.39137
.105	.10422	.235	.22603	.365	.32931	.495	.39223
.110	.10910	.240	.23043	.370	.33270	.500	.39270

To find the Area of a Zone by the above Table.

RULE 1.—*When the zone is greater than a part of a semicircle*, take the height on each side of the diameter of the circle, of which it is a part; divide the heights by the diameter; find the respective quotients in the column of heights, and take out the areas opposite to them, multiplying the areas thus found by the square of the diameter or chord, and the products, added together, will be the area required.

NOTE.—*When the quotient is not given in the column of heights, divide the difference between the two nearest heights by 5, and multiply the quotient by the excess between the height given and the height in the table first above it, and add this sum to the tabular area of the least height.* Thus, if the height is .333,

.30416—.30790 = .00374÷5 = .000748×3 (excess of 333 over 330) = .002244+.30416 = .306404, the area for 333.

EXAMPLE.—What is the area of zone, the diameter of the circle being 100, and the heights respectively 20 and 10, upon each side of it?

$$20÷100 = .200, \text{ and } 200, \text{ per table,} = .19453×100^2 = 1945.3.$$
$$10÷100 = .100, \text{ and } 100, \text{ per table,} = .09933×100^2 = 993.3.$$
$$\text{Hence, } 1945.3+993.3 = 2938.6 \text{ } Ans.$$

RULE.—*When the zone is less than a semicircle*, proceed as in rule 1 for one height.

EXAMPLE.—What is the area of a zone, the longest chord being 10, and the height 4?

$$4÷10 = .400 = .35182×10^2 = 35.182 \text{ } Ans.$$

MENSURATION OF SOLIDS.

23. OF CUBES AND PARALLELOPIPEDONS.

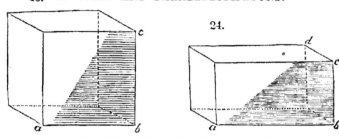

24.

To find the Solidity of a Cube—fig. 23.

RULE.—Multiply the side of the cube by itself, and that product again by the side, and this last product will be the solidity.

To find the Solidity of a Parallelopipedon—fig. 24.

RULE.—Multiply the length by the breadth, and that product by the depth, and this product is the solidity.

OF REGULAR BODIES.

To find the Solidity of any Regular Body.

RULE.—Multiply the tabular *solidity* in the following table by the cube of the linear edge, and the product is the solidity.

TABLE *of the Solidities of the Regular Bodies when the Linear Edge is*

Number of Sides.	Names.	Solidities.
4	Tetrahedron.	0.11785
6	Hexahedron.	1.00000
8	Octahedron.	0.47140
12	Dodecahedron.	7.66312
20	Icosahedron.	2.18169

OF CYLINDERS, PRISMS, AND UNGULAS.

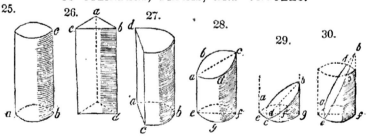

25. 26. 27. 28. 29. 30.

To find the Solidity of Cylinders, Prisms, and Ungulas—figs. 25, 26, and 27.

RULE.—Multiply the area of the base by the height, and the product is the solidity.

To find the Solidity of an Ungula, fig. 28, *when the section passes obliquely through the cylinder, a b c d.*

Rule.—Multiply the area of the base of the cylinder by half the sum of the greater and less heights *a e, c f* of the ungula, and the product is the solidity.

When the Section passes through the base of the Cylinder and one of its sides—fig. 29, *a b c.*

Rule.—From $\frac{2}{3}$ of the cube of the right sine *a d*, of half the arc *a g* of the base, subtract the product of the area of the base, and the cosine *d f* of said half arc. Multiply the difference thus found by the quotient of the height, divided by the versed sine, and the product is the solidity.

When the Section passes obliquely through both ends of the Cylinder, a d c e—fig. 30.

Rule.—Find the solidities of the ungulas *a d c e* and *d b c*, and the difference is the solidity required (*conceiving* the section to be continued till it meets the side of the cylinder).

Note.—For rules to ascertain the solidity of conical ungulas, see *Ryan's Bonnycastle's Mensuration*, page 136 (1839).

OF CONES AND PYRAMIDS.

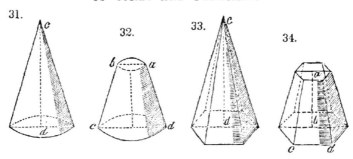

To find the Solidity of a Cone or Pyramid—figs. 31 *and* 33.

Rule.—Multiply the area of the base by the height *c d*, and $\frac{1}{3}$ the product will be the content.

To find the Solidity of the Frustrum of a Cone—fig. 32.

Rule.—Divide the difference of the cubes of the diameters *a b, c d* of the two ends by the difference of the diameters ; this quotient, multiplied by .7854, and again by $\frac{1}{3}$ of the height, will give the solidity.

To find the Solidity of the Frustrum of a Pyramid—fig. 34.

Rule.—Add to the areas of the two ends of the frustrum the square root of their product, and this sum, multiplied by $\frac{1}{3}$ of the height *a b*, will give the solidity.

OF WEDGES AND PRISMOIDS.

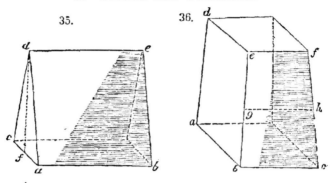

To find the Solidity of a Wedge—fig. 35.

RULE.—To the length of the edge of the wedge *d e* add twice the length of the back *a b;* multiply this sum by the height of the wedge *d f*, and then by the breadth of the back *c a*, and $\frac{1}{6}$ of the product will be the solid content.

To find the Solidity of a Prismoid—fig. 36.

RULE.—Add the areas of the two ends *a b c, d e f*, and four times the middle section *g h*, parallel to them, together ; multiply this sum by $\frac{1}{6}$ of the height, and it will give the solidity.

OF SPHERES.

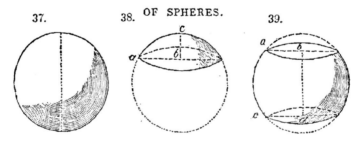

To find the Solidity of a Sphere—fig. 37.

RULE.—Multiply the cube of the diameter by .5236, and the product is the solidity.

To find the Solidity of a Spherical Segment—fig. 38.

RULE.—To three times the square of the radius of its base *a b*, add the square of its height *c b;* then multiply this sum by the height, and the product by .5236.

To find the Solidity of a Spherical Zone or Frustrum—fig. 39.

RULE.—To the sum of the squares of the radius of each end *a b, c d*, add $\frac{1}{3}$ of the square of the height *b d* of the zone ; and this sum, multiplied by the height, and the product by 1.5708, will give the solidity.

OF SPHEROIDS.*

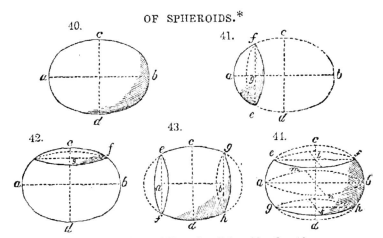

To find the Solidity of a Spheroid—fig. 40.

RULE.—Multiply the square of the revolving axis *c d* by the fixed axis *a b*; the product, multiplied by .5236, will give the solidity.

To find the Solidity of the Segment of a Spheroid—figs. 41 *and* 42.

RULE.—*When the base e f is circular, or parallel to the revolving axis c d,* fig. 41. Multiply the fixed axis *a b* by 3, the height of the segment *a g* by 2, and subtract the one product from the other; then multiply the remainder by the square of the height of the segment, and the product by .5236. Then, as the square of the fixed axis is to the square of the revolving axis, so is the last product to the content of the segment.

RULE.—*When the base e f is perpendicular to the revolving axis c d,* fig. 42. Multiply the revolving axis by 3, and the height of the segment *c g* by 2, and subtract the one from the other; then multiply the remainder by the square of the height of the segment, and the product by .5236. Then, as the revolving axis is to the fixed axis, so is the last product to the content.

To find the Solidity of the Middle Frustrum of a Spheroid—figs. 43 *and* 44.

RULE.—*When the ends e f and g h are circular, or parallel to the revolving axis c d,* fig. 43. To twice the square of the revolving axis *c d*, add the square of the diameter of either end, *e f* or *g h*; then multiply this sum by the length *a b* of the frustrum, and the product again by .2618, and this will give the solidity.

RULE.—*When the ends e f and g h are elliptical, or perpendicular to the revolving axis c d,* fig. 44. To twice the product of the transverse and conjugate diameters of the middle section *a b*, add the product of the transverse and conjugate of either end; multiply this sum by the length *l k* of the frustrum, and the product by .2618, and this will give the solidity.

---

* Spheroids are either *Prolate* or *Oblate.* They are prolate when produced by the revolution of a semi-ellipse about its transverse diameter, and oblate when produced by an ellipse revolving about its conjugate diameter.

OF CIRCULAR SPINDLES.

45.

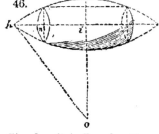

46.

To find the Solidity of a Circular Spindle—fig. 45.

RULE.—Multiply the central distance *o c* by half the area of the revolving segment *a c e f*. Subtract the product from ⅓ of the cube *f e* of half the length ; then multiply the remainder by 12.5664 (or four times 3.1416), and the product is the solidity.

To find the Solidity of the Frustrum, or Zone of a Circular Spindle— fig. 46.

RULE.—From the square of half the length *h i* of the whole spindle, take ⅓ of the square of half the length *n i* of the frustrum, and multiply the remainder by the said half-length of the frustrum ; multiply the central distance *o i* by the revolving area* which generates the frustrum ; subtract the last product from the former, and the remainder, multiplied by 6.2832 (or twice 3.1416), will give the solidity.

47.   OF ELLIPTIC SPINDLES.

48.

To find the Solidity of an Elliptic Spindle—fig. 47.

RULE.—To the square of the greatest diameter *a b*, add the square of twice the diameter *e f* at ¼ of its length ; multiply the sum by the length, and the product by .1309, and it will give the solidity nearly.

To find the Solidity of a Frustrum or Segment of an Elliptic Spindle— fig. 48.

RULE.—Proceed as in the last rule for this or any other solid formed by the revolution of a conic section about an axis, viz. : Add together the squares of the greatest and least diameters, *a b, c d*, and the square of double the diameter in the middle, between the two ; multiply the sum by the length *e f*, and the product by .1309, and it will give the solidity.

NOTE.—For all such solids, this rule is exact when the body is formed by the conic section, or a part of it, revolving about the axis of the section, and will always be very near when the figure revolves about another line.

---

* The area of the frustrum can be obtained by dividing its central plane into segments of a circle, and triangles or parallelograms.

OF PARABOLIC CONOIDS AND SPINDLES.

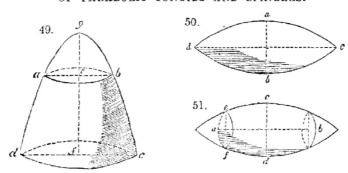

To find the Solidity of a Parabolic Conoid*—fig. 49.

RULE.—Multiply the area of the base $d\,c$ by half the altitude $f\,g$, and the product will be the solidity.

NOTE.—This rule will hold for any segment of the paraboloid, whether the base be perpendicular or oblique to the axis of the solid.

To find the Solidity of a Frustrum of a Paraboloid—fig. 49.

RULE.—Multiply the sum of the squares of the diameters $a\,b$ and $d\,c$ by the height $e\,f$, and the product by .3927.

To find the Solidity of a Parabolic Spindle—fig. 50.

RULE.—Multiply the square of the diameter $a\,b$ by the length $d\,c$, and the product by .4188, and it will give the solidity.

To find the Solidity of the Middle Frustrum of a Parabolic Spindle—fig. 51.

RULE.—Add together 8 times the square of the greatest diameter $c\,d$, 3 times the square of the least diameter $e\,f$, and 4 times the product of these two diameters; multiply the sum by the length $a\,b$, and the product by .05236, and it will give the solidity.

OF HYPERBOLOIDS AND HYPERBOLIC CONOIDS.

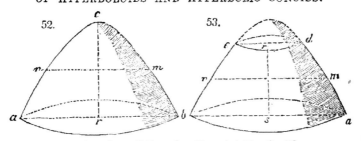

To find the Solidity of a Hyperboloid—fig. 52.

RULE.—To the square of the radius of the base $a\,b$, add the square of the middle diameter $n\,m$; multiply this sum by the height $c\,r$, and the product again by .5236, and it will give the solidity.

* The parabolic conoid is $=\frac{1}{2}$ its circumscribing cylinder.

To find the Solidity of the Frustrum of a Hyperbolic Conoid—fig. 53.

RULE.—Add together the squares of the greatest and least semi-diameters $a\,s$ and $d\,r$, and the square of the whole diameter $n\,m$ in the middle of the two; multiply this sum by the height $r\,s$, and the product by .5236, and it will give the solidity.

OF CYLINDRICAL RINGS.

54.

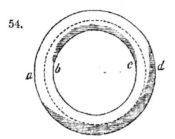

To find the Solidity of a Cylindrical Ring—fig. 54.

RULE.—To the thickness of the ring $a\,b$, add the inner diameter $b\,c$; then multiply the sum by the square of the thickness, and the product by 2.4674, and it will give the solidity.

BY MATHEMATICAL FORMULÆ.

FRUSTRUM OF A RIGHT TRIANGULAR PRISM.
The base $\times \frac{1}{3}(h+h'+h'')$, h being the heights.

FRUSTRUM OF ANY RIGHT PRISM.
The base $\times$ its distance from the centre of gravity of the section.

CYLINDRICAL SEGMENT.
Contained between the base and an oblique plane passing through a diameter of the base, twice the height $\times$ the quotient of the square of the radius $\div 3$; or $\frac{2}{3}h r^2$, r being the radius and h the height.

SPHERICAL SEGMENT.
$\frac{ph}{6}(3r^2+h^2)$, r being the radius of the base, and h the height of the segment.

SPHERICAL ZONE.
$\frac{ph}{6}(3R^2+3r^2+h^2)$, Rr being the radii of the bases.

SPHERICAL SECTOR.
$\frac{1}{3}r \times$ the surface of the segment or zone.

ELLIPSOID.
$\frac{pa^2b}{6}$, a being the revolving diameter, and b the axis of revolution.

PARABOLOID.

$\frac{1}{2}$ area of the base $\times$ the height.

CIRCULAR SPINDLE.

$p(\frac{1}{6}c^3 - 2s\sqrt{r^2 - \frac{1}{4}c^2})$, s being the area of the revolving segment, and c its chord.

ANY SOLID OF REVOLUTION.

$2prs$; or, the area of the generating surface $\times$ the circumference described by its centre of gravity.

NOTE.—If bounded by a curved surface, find the area by the rule for irregular plane figures.

To find a Cylinder of a Given Solidity (b) with the Least Surface.

Let a = altitude, and d = diameter of base.

Then $\dfrac{pd^2 a}{4} = b$, and $\dfrac{pd^2}{2}$ = sum of bases.

Convex surface   . = pda, or $\dfrac{4b}{d}$.

Therefore   . $\dfrac{pd^2}{2} + \dfrac{4b}{d}$ = a minimum.

CASK GAUGING.

Casks are usually comprised under the following figures, viz.:
1. The middle frustrum of a spheroid.
2. The middle frustrum of a parabolic spindle.
3. The two equal frustrums of a paraboloid.
4. The two equal frustrums of a cone,

and their contents can be computed by the preceding rules for these figures.

To find the Content of a Cask by four Dimensions.

RULE.—Add together the squares of the bung and head diameters, and the square of double the diameter taken in the middle between the bung and head; multiply the sum by the length of the cask, and the product by .1309.

Or, l .1309 $(d^2 + D^2 + 2M^2)$, l being the length, d D the head and bung diameters, and M a diameter midway between them.

Or, $l\left(\dfrac{d + D + M}{3}\right)$, d D M being the areas of the diameters.

Or, $l \times$ area of $\dfrac{2D + d}{3}$.

ULLAGE CASKS.

When the Cask is standing.

$l \times \left(\dfrac{d + D + M}{3}\right)$, l being the height of the fluid.

When the Cask is on its bilge.

RULE.—Divide the wet inches by the bung diameter, and opposite to the quotient in the column of versed sines, page 72, take the area of the segment; multiply this area by the content of the cask in inches or gallons, and the product by 1.25 for the ullage required.

EXAMPLE.—What is the ullage of a cask that contains 25689 cubic inches, and has 8 inches of liquor on its bilge, the bung diameter 32 inches?   *Ans.* 4930.

Examples in Illustration of the foregoing Rules.

1. The side of a cube *a b c*, fig. 23, is 5 inches; what is the solidity?   *Ans.* 125.

2. The length of a parallelopipedon *a b*, fig. 24, is 8 inches, its depth *b c* and breadth *c d* 4 inches; what is the solidity?   *Ans.* 128.

3. The base of a cylinder *a b*, fig. 25, is 30 inches, and the height *b c* 50 inches; what is the solidity?   *Ans.* 20.4531 cubic feet.

4. The sides of a prism *a b*, *b c*, fig. 26, are each 5 inches, and the height *b d* 10 inches; what is the solidity?

$$\frac{5+5+5}{2} = 7.5; \text{ then } 7.5-5 \cdot 7.5-5 \cdot 7.5-5 = 2.5 \cdot \sqrt{7.5\times2.5\times2.5\times2.5}\times10 =$$

108.6 *Ans.*

5. The base of an ungula, fig. 27, is a semicircle, the radius 5 inches, and the height of the figure 25 inches; what is the solidity?   *Ans.* 981.75.

6. The base of an ungula, fig. 28, is a circle, the radius 8 inches, and the heights of the sides 2 and 4 inches; what is the solidity?   *Ans.* 603.180.

7. The base of a cone, fig. 31, is 20 inches, and the height *c d* 24; what is the solidity?   *Ans.* 2513.28.

8. The diameter of the greater end *c d* of the frustrum of a cone, fig. 32, is 5 feet, the less end *a b* 3 feet, and the perpendicular height 9 feet; what is the solidity?   *Ans.* 115.4538.

9. What is the solidity of the frustrum of a hexagonal pyramid, fig. 34, a side *c d* of the greater end being 4 feet, and one of the lesser end 3 feet, and the height *a b* 9 feet?   *Ans.* 288.3864.

10. How many solid feet are there in a wedge, fig. 35, the base *a b* is 64 inches long, *c a* 9 inches, *d e* 42 inches, and the height *d f* 28 inches?   *Ans.* 4.1319.

11. What is the solidity of a rectangular prismoid, fig. 36, the base being 12 by 14 inches, the top 4 by 6 inches, and the perpendicular height 18 feet?   *Ans.* 10.666.

12. What is the solidity of the sphere, fig. 37, the diameter being 17 inches?   *Ans.* 2572.4468.

13. The segment of a sphere, fig. 38, has a radius *a b* of 7 inches for its base, and its height *b c* is 4 inches; what is the solidity?   *Ans.* 341.3872.

14. The greater and less diameters of a spherical zone, fig. 39, are each 3 feet, and the height *d b* 4 feet; what is the solidity in cubic feet?   *Ans.* 61.7843.

15. In the prolate spheroid, fig. 40, the fixed axis *a b* is 100, and the revolving axis *c d* is 60; what is the solidity?   *Ans.* 188496.

16. The segment of a spheroid, fig. 41, is cut from a spheroid, the fixed axis of which, *a b*, is 100 inches, the height of the segment *a g* is 10, and the revolving axis 60; what is the solidity of it?   *Ans.* 14660.8.

17. The fixed axis *c d*, fig. 42, is 60, the revolving axis 100, and the height of the segment *c g* 8 inches; what is its solidity?   *Ans.* 9159.509.

18. What is the solidity of the middle frustrum of a spheroid, fig. 43, the middle diameter *c d* being 60, *e f* and *g h* each 36, and the length *a b* 80?   *Ans.* 177940.224.

19. In the middle frustrum *e f g h*, fig. 44, *an oblate* spheroid, the diameters of the ends are 40 by 24 inches, the middle diameters are 50 and 30, and the height *l k* is 18 inches; what is the solidity ? *Ans.* 18661.104.

20. What is the solidity of a circular spindle, fig. 45, the distance *o e* 7.07 inches, the length *f e* 7.07 inches, and the radius *o c* 10 inches? *Ans.* 210.96.

21. The length of an elliptic spindle *a b*, fig. 47, is 85, its greatest diameter *c d* 25, and the diameter *e f*, at ¼ of its length, 20 inches ; what is its solidity ? *Ans.* 24756.4625.

22. What is the solidity of the parabolic conoid, fig. 49 ; its height *g f* is 60, and the diameter *d c* of its base 100 inches ? *Ans.* 235620.

23. What is the solidity of the parabolic frustrum *a b c d*, fig. 49, its diameters *d c* 58, *a b* 30, and height *e f* 18 inches? *Ans.* 30140.5104.

24. What is the solidity of the parabolic spindle, fig. 50, *a b* being 40, and *c d* 100 inches ? *Ans.* 67008.8.

25. The middle frustrum of a parabolic spindle, fig. 51, has *a b* 60, *c d* 40, and *e f* 30 inches ; what is its solidity ? *Ans.* 63774.48.

26. In the hyperboloid, fig. 52, the height *c r* is 10, the radius *a r* 12, and the middle diameter *n m* 15.8745; what is the solidity ? *Ans.* 2073.454691.

27. The frustrum of the hyperbolic conoid, fig. 53, has *r s* 12, *a b* 10, *d e* 6, and *n m* 8.5 inches ; what is the solidity ? *Ans.* 667.59.

28. The thickness *a b*, fig. 54, of a cylindric ring is 3 inches, and the inner diameter *c b* 8 inches ; what is the solidity ? *Ans.* 244.2726.

29. Required the solidity of an icosahedron, its linear edge being 2 ? *Ans.* 17.45352.

30. Required the content of a cask, the length being 40, the bung and head diameters 24 and 32, and the middle diameter 28.75 inches. *Ans.* 25689.125.

Areas of Circles, *from* 1 *to* 100.

Diameter	Area.	Diameter.	Area.	Diameter.	Area.	Diameter.	Area.
1/64	.00019	5.	19.635	12.	113.09	19.	283.52
1/32	.00076	.1/8	20.629	.1/8	115.46	.1/8	287.27
1/16	.00306	.1/4	21.647	.1/4	117.85	.1/4	291.03
1/8	.01227	.3/8	22.690	.3/8	120.27	.3/8	294.83
3/16	.02761	.1/2	23.758	.1/2	122.71	.1/2	298.64
1/4	.04908	.5/8	24.850	.5/8	125.18	.5/8	302.48
5/16	.07669	.3/4	25.967	.3/4	127.67	.3/4	306.35
3/8	.1104	.7/8	27.108	.7/8	130.19	.7/8	310.24
7/16	.1503	6.	28.274	13.	132.73	20.	314.16
1/2	.1963	.1/8	29.464	.1/8	135.29	.1/8	318.09
9/16	.2485	.1/4	30.679	.1/4	137.88	.1/4	322.06
5/8	.3067	.3/8	31.919	.3/8	140.50	.3/8	326.05
11/16	.3712	.1/2	33.183	.1/2	143.13	.1/2	330.06
3/4	.4417	.5/8	34.471	.5/8	145.80	.5/8	334.10
13/16	.5184	.3/4	35.784	.3/4	148.48	.3/4	338.16
7/8	.6013	.7/8	37.122	.7/8	151.20	.7/8	342.25
15/16	.6902	7.	38.484	14.	153.93	21.	346.36
1.	.7853	.1/8	39.871	.1/8	156.69	.1/8	350.49
.1/8	.9940	.1/4	41.282	.1/4	159.48	.1/4	354.65
.1/4	1.227	.3/8	42.718	.3/8	162.29	.3/8	358.84
.3/8	1.484	.1/2	44.178	.1/2	165.13	.1/2	363.05
.1/2	1.767	.5/8	45.663	.5/8	167.98	.5/8	367.28
.5/8	2.073	.3/4	47.173	.3/4	170.87	.3/4	371.54
.3/4	2.405	.7/8	48.707	.7/8	173.78	.7/8	375.82
.7/8	2.761	8.	50.265	15.	176.71	22.	380.13
2.	3.141	.1/8	51.848	.1/8	179.67	.1/8	384.46
.1/8	3.546	.1/4	53.456	.1/4	182.65	.1/4	388.82
.1/4	3.976	.3/8	55.088	.3/8	185.66	.3/8	393.20
.3/8	4.430	.1/2	56.745	.1/2	188.69	.1/2	397.60
.1/2	4.908	.5/8	58.426	.5/8	191.74	.5/8	402.03
.5/8	5.411	.3/4	60.132	.3/4	194.82	.3/4	406.49
.3/4	5.939	.7/8	61.862	.7/8	197.93	.7/8	410.97
.7/8	6.491	9.	63.617	16.	201.06	23.	415.47
3.	7.068	.1/8	65.396	.1/8	204.21	.1/8	420.00
.1/8	7.669	.1/4	67.200	.1/4	207.39	.1/4	424.55
.1/4	8.295	.3/8	69.029	.3/8	210.59	.3/8	429.13
.3/8	8.946	.1/2	70.882	.1/2	213.82	.1/2	433.73
.1/2	9.621	.5/8	72.759	.5/8	217.07	.5/8	433.30
.5/8	10.320	.3/4	74.662	.3/4	220.35	.3/4	443.01
.3/4	11.044	.7/8	76.588	.7/8	223.65	.7/8	447.69
.7/8	11.793	10.	78.539	17.	226.98	24.	452.39
4.	12.566	.1/8	80.515	.1/8	230.33	.1/8	457.11
.1/8	13.364	.1/4	82.516	.1/4	233.70	.1/4	461.86
.1/4	14.186	.3/8	84.540	.3/8	237.10	.3/8	466.63
.3/8	15.033	.1/2	86.590	.1/2	240.52	.1/2	471.43
.1/2	15.904	.5/8	88.664	.5/8	243.97	.5/8	476.25
.5/8	16.800	.3/4	90.762	.3/4	247.45	.3/4	481.10
.3/4	17.720	.7/8	92.885	.7/8	250.94	.7/8	485.97
.7/8	18.665	11.	95.033	18.	254.46	25.	490.87
		.1/8	97.205	.1/8	258.01	.1/8	495.79
		.1/4	99.402	.1/4	261.58	.1/4	500.74
		.3/8	101.62	.3/8	265.18	.3/8	505.71
		.1/2	103.86	.1/2	268.80	.1/2	510.70
		.5/8	106.13	.5/8	272.44	.5/8	515.72
		.3/4	108.43	.3/4	276.11	.3/4	520.70
		.7/8	110.75	.7/8	279.81	.7/8	525.83

Table—(Continued).

Diameter	Area	Diameter	Area	Diameter	Area	Diameter	Area
26.	530.93	33.	855.30	40.	1256.6	47.	1734.9
1/8	536.04	1/8	861.79	1/8	1264.5	1/8	1744.1
1/4	541.18	1/4	868.30	1/4	1272.3	1/4	1753.4
3/8	546.35	3/8	874.84	3/8	1280.3	3/8	1762.7
1/2	551.54	1/2	881.41	1/2	1288.2	1/2	1772.0
5/8	556.76	5/8	888.00	5/8	1296.2	5/8	1781.3
3/4	562.00	3/4	894.61	3/4	1304.2	3/4	1790.7
7/8	567.26	7/8	901.25	7/8	1312.2	7/8	1800.1
27.	572.55	34.	907.92	41.	1320.2	48.	1809.5
1/8	577.87	1/8	914.61	1/8	1328.3	1/8	1818.9
1/4	583.20	1/4	921.32	1/4	1336.4	1/4	1828.4
3/8	588.57	3/8	928.06	3/8	1344.5	3/8	1837.9
1/2	593.95	1/2	934.82	1/2	1352.6	1/2	1847.4
5/8	599.37	5/8	941.60	5/8	1360.8	5/8	1856.9
3/4	604.80	3/4	948.41	3/4	1369.0	3/4	1866.5
7/8	610.26	7/8	955.25	7/8	1377.2	7/8	1876.1
28.	615.75	35.	962.11	42.	1385.4	49.	1885.7
1/8	621.26	1/8	968.99	1/8	1393.7	1/8	1895.3
1/4	626.79	1/4	975.90	1/4	1401.9	1/4	1905.0
3/8	632.35	3/8	982.84	3/8	1410.2	3/8	1914.7
1/2	637.94	1/2	989.80	1/2	1418.6	1/2	1924.4
5/8	643.54	5/8	996.78	5/8	1426.9	5/8	1934.1
3/4	649.18	3/4	1003.7	3/4	1435.3	3/4	1943.9
7/8	654.83	7/8	1010.8	7/8	1443.7	7/8	1953.6
29.	660.52	36.	1017.8	43.	1452.2	50.	1963.5
1/8	666.22	1/8	1024.9	1/8	1460.6	1/8	1973.3
1/4	671.95	1/4	1032.0	1/4	1469.1	1/4	1983.1
3/8	677.71	3/8	1039.1	3/8	1477.6	3/8	1993.0
1/2	683.49	1/2	1046.3	1/2	1486.1	1/2	2002.9
5/8	689.29	5/8	1053.5	5/8	1494.7	5/8	2012.8
3/4	695.12	3/4	1060.7	3/4	1503.3	3/4	2022.8
7/8	700.98	7/8	1067.9	7/8	1511.9	7/8	2032.8
30.	706.86	37.	1075.2	44.	1520.5	51.	2042.8
1/8	712.76	1/8	1082.4	1/8	1529.1	1/8	2052.8
1/4	718.69	1/4	1089.7	1/4	1537.8	1/4	2062.9
3/8	724.64	3/8	1097.1	3/8	1546.5	3/8	2072.9
1/2	730.61	1/2	1104.4	1/2	1555.2	1/2	2083.0
5/8	736.61	5/8	1111.8	5/8	1564.0	5/8	2093.2
3/4	742.64	3/4	1119.2	3/4	1572.8	3/4	2103.3
7/8	748.69	7/8	1126.6	7/8	1581.6	7/8	2113.5
31.	754.76	38.	1134.1	45.	1590.4	52.	2123.7
1/8	760.86	1/8	1141.5	1/8	1599.2	1/8	2133.9
1/4	766.99	1/4	1149.0	1/4	1608.1	1/4	2144.1
3/8	773.14	3/8	1156.6	3/8	1617.0	3/8	2154.4
1/2	779.31	1/2	1164.1	1/2	1625.9	1/2	2164.7
5/8	785.51	5/8	1171.7	5/8	1634.9	5/8	2175.0
3/4	791.73	3/4	1179.3	3/4	1643.8	3/4	2185.4
7/8	797.97	7/8	1186.9	7/8	1652.8	7/8	2195.7
32.	804.24	39.	1194.5	46.	1661.9	53.	2206.1
1/8	810.54	1/8	1202.2	1/8	1670.9	1/8	2216.6
1/4	816.86	1/4	1209.9	1/4	1680.0	1/4	2227.0
3/8	823.21	3/8	1217.6	3/8	1689.1	3/8	2237.5
1/2	829.57	1/2	1225.4	1/2	1698.2	1/2	2248.0
5/8	835.97	5/8	1233.1	5/8	1707.3	5/8	2258.5
3/4	842.39	3/4	1240.9	3/4	1716.5	3/4	2269.0
7/8	848.83	7/8	1248.7	7/8	1725.7	7/8	2279.6

TABLE—(Continued).

Diameter	Area.	Diameter.	Area.	Diameter.	Area.	Diameter.	Area.
54.	2290.2	61.	2922.4	68.	3631.6	75.	4417.8
1/8	2300.8	1/8	2934.4	1/8	3645.0	1/8	4432.6
1/4	2311.4	1/4	2946.4	1/4	3658.4	1/4	4447.3
3/8	2322.1	3/8	2958.5	3/8	3671.8	3/8	4462.1
1/2	2332.8	1/2	2970.5	1/2	3685.2	1/2	4476.9
5/8	2343.5	5/8	2982.6	5/8	3698.7	5/8	4491.8
3/4	2354.2	3/4	2994.7	3/4	3712.2	3/4	4506.6
7/8	2365.0	7/8	3006.9	7/8	3725.7	7/8	4521.5
55.	2375.8	62.	3019.0	69.	3739.2	76.	4536.4
1/8	2386.6	1/8	3031.2	1/8	3752.8	1/8	4551.4
1/4	2397.4	1/4	3043.4	1/4	3766.4	1/4	4566.3
3/8	2408.3	3/8	3055.7	3/8	3780.0	3/8	4581.3
1/2	2419.2	1/2	3067.9	1/2	3793.6	1/2	4596.3
5/8	2430.1	5/8	3080.2	5/8	3807.3	5/8	4611.3
3/4	2441.0	3/4	3092.5	3/4	3821.0	3/4	4626.4
7/8	2452.0	7/8	3104.8	7/8	3834.7	7/8	4641.5
56.	2463.0	63.	3117.2	70.	3848.4	77.	4656.6
1/8	2474.0	1/8	3129.6	1/8	3862.2	1/8	4671.7
1/4	2485.0	1/4	3142.0	1/4	3875.9	1/4	4686.9
3/8	2496.1	3/8	3154.4	3/8	3889.8	3/8	4702.1
1/2	2507.1	1/2	3166.9	1/2	3903.6	1/2	4717.3
5/8	2518.2	5/8	3179.4	5/8	3917.4	5/8	4732.5
3/4	2529.4	3/4	3191.9	3/4	3931.3	3/4	4747.7
7/8	2540.5	7/8	3204.4	7/8	3945.2	7/8	4763.0
57.	2551.7	64.	3216.9	71.	3959.2	78.	4778.3
1/8	2562.9	1/8	3229.5	1/8	3973.1	1/8	4793.7
1/4	2574.1	1/4	3242.1	1/4	3987.1	1/4	4809.0
3/8	2585.4	3/8	3254.8	3/8	4001.1	3/8	4824.4
1/2	2596.7	1/2	3267.4	1/2	4015.1	1/2	4839.8
5/8	2608.0	5/8	3280.1	5/8	4029.2	5/8	4855.2
3/4	2619.3	3/4	3292.8	3/4	4043.2	3/4	4870.7
7/8	2630.7	7/8	3305.5	7/8	4067.3	7/8	4886.1
58.	2642.0	65.	3318.3	72.	4071.5	79.	4901.6
1/8	2653.4	1/8	3331.0	1/8	4085.6	1/8	4917.2
1/4	2664.9	1/4	3343.8	1/4	4099.8	1/4	4932.7
3/8	2676.3	3/8	3356.7	3/8	4114.0	3/8	4948.3
1/2	2687.8	1/2	3369.5	1/2	4128.2	1/2	4963.9
5/8	2699.3	5/8	3382.4	5/8	4142.5	5/8	4979.5
3/4	2710.8	3/4	3395.3	3/4	4156.7	3/4	4995.1
7/8	2722.4	7/8	3408.2	7/8	4171.0	7/8	5010.8
59.	2733.9	66.	3421.2	73.	4185.3	80.	5026.5
1/8	2745.5	1/8	3434.1	1/8	4199.7	1/8	5042.2
1/4	2757.1	1/4	3447.1	1/4	4214.1	1/4	5058.0
3/8	2768.8	3/8	3460.1	3/8	4228.5	3/8	5073.7
1/2	2780.5	1/2	3473.2	1/2	4242.9	1/2	5089.5
5/8	2792.2	5/8	3486.3	5/8	4257.3	5/8	5105.4
3/4	2803.9	3/4	3499.3	3/4	4271.8	3/4	5121.2
7/8	2815.6	7/8	3512.5	7/8	4286.3	7/8	5137.1
60.	2827.4	67.	3525.6	74.	4300.8	81.	5153.0
1/8	2839.2	1/8	3538.8	1/8	4315.3	1/8	5168.9
1/4	2851.0	1/4	3552.0	1/4	4329.9	1/4	5184.8
3/8	2862.8	3/8	3565.2	3/8	4344.5	3/8	5200.8
1/2	2874.7	1/2	3578.4	1/2	4359.1	1/2	5216.8
5/8	2886.6	5/8	3591.7	5/8	4373.8	5/8	5232.8
3/4	2898.5	3/4	3605.0	3/4	4388.4	3/4	5248.8
7/8	2910.5	7/8	3618.3	7/8	4403.1	7/8	5264.9

TABLE—(Continued).

Diameter	Area.	Diameter.	Area.	Diameter.	Area.	Diameter.	Area.
82.	5281.0	87.	5944.6	92.	6647.6	97.	7389.8
.1/8	5297.1	.1/8	5961.7	.1/8	6665.7	.1/8	7408.8
.1/4	5313.2	.1/4	5978.9	.1/4	6683.8	.1/4	7427.9
.3/8	5329.4	.3/8	5996.0	.3/8	6701.9	.3/8	7447.0
.1/2	5345.6	.1/2	6013.2	.1/2	6720.0	.1/2	7466.2
.5/8	5361.8	.5/8	6030.4	.5/8	6738.2	.5/8	7485.3
.3/4	5378.0	.3/4	6047.6	.3/4	6756.4	.3/4	7504.5
.7/8	5394.3	.7/8	6064.8	.7/8	6776.4	.7/8	7523.7
83.	5410.6	88.	6082.1	93.	6792.9	98.	7542.9
.1/8	5426.9	.1/8	6099.4	.1/8	6811.1	.1/8	7562.2
.1/4	5443.2	.1/4	6116.7	.1/4	6829.4	.1/4	7581.5
.3/8	5459.6	.3/8	6134.0	.3/8	6847.8	.3/8	7600.8
.1/2	5476.0	.1/2	6151.4	.1/2	6866.1	.1/2	7620.1
.5/8	5492.4	.5/8	6168.8	.5/8	6884.5	.5/8	7639.4
.3/4	5508.8	.3/4	6186.2	.3/4	6902.9	.3/4	7658.8
.7/8	5525.3	.7/8	6203.6	.7/8	6921.3	.7/8	7678.2
84.	5541.7	89.	6221.1	94.	6939.7	99.	7697.7
.1/8	5558.2	.1/8	6238.6	.1/8	6958.2	.1/8	7717.1
.1/4	5574.8	.1/4	6256.1	.1/4	6976.7	.1/4	7736.6
.3/8	5591.3	.3/8	6273.6	.3/8	6995.2	.3/8	7756.1
.1/2	5607.9	.1/2	6291.2	.1/2	7013.8	.1/2	7775.6
.5/8	5624.5	.5/8	6308.8	.5/8	7032.3	.5/8	7795.2
.3/4	5641.1	.3/4	6326.4	.3/4	7050.9	.3/4	7814.7
.7/8	5657.8	.7/8	6344.0	.7/8	7069.5	.7/8	7834.3
85.	5674.5	90.	6361.7	95.	7088.2	100.	7853.9
.1/8	5691.2	.1/8	6379.4	.1/8	7106.9		
.1/4	5707.9	.1/4	6397.1	.1/4	7125.5		
.3/8	5724.6	.3/8	6414.8	.3/8	7144.3		
.1/2	5741.4	.1/2	6432.6	.1/2	7163.0		
.5/8	5758.2	.5/8	6450.4	.5/8	7181.8		
.3/4	5775.0	.3/4	6468.2	.3/4	7200.5		
.7/8	5791.9	.7/8	6486.0	.7/8	7219.4		
86.	5808.8	91.	6503.8	96.	7238.2		
.1/8	5825.7	.1/8	6521.7	.1/8	7257.1		
.1/4	5842.6	.1/4	6539.6	.1/4	7275.9		
.3/8	5859.5	.3/8	6557.6	.3/8	7294.9		
.1/2	5876.5	.1/2	6575.5	.1/2	7313.8		
.5/8	5893.5	.5/8	6593.5	.5/8	7332.8		
.3/4	5910.5	.3/4	6611.5	.3/4	7351.7		
.7/8	5927.6	.7/8	6629.5	.7/8	7370.7		

CIRCUMFERENCES OF CIRCLES, *from* 1 *to* 100.

Diameter	Circumference.	Diameter.	Circumference.	Diameter.	Circumference.	Diameter.	Circumfer'ce
1/64	.0490	5.	15.70	12.	37.69	19.	59.69
1/32	.0981	1/8	16.10	1/8	38.09	1/8	60.08
1/16	.1963	1/4	16.49	1/4	38.48	1/4	60.47
1/8	.3926	3/8	16.88	3/8	38.87	3/8	60.86
3/16	.5890	1/2	17.27	1/2	39.27	1/2	61.26
1/4	.7854	5/8	17.67	5/8	39.66	5/8	61.65
5/16	.9817	3/4	18.06	3/4	40.05	3/4	62.04
3/8	1.178	7/8	18.45	7/8	40.44	7/8	62.43
7/16	1.374	6.	18.84	13.	40.84	20.	62.83
1/2	1.570	1/8	19.24	1/8	41.23	1/8	63.22
9/16	1.767	1/4	19.63	1/4	41.62	1/4	63.61
5/8	1.963	3/8	20.02	3/8	42.01	3/8	64.01
11/16	2.159	1/2	20.42	1/2	42.41	1/2	64.40
3/4	2.356	5/8	20.81	5/8	42.80	5/8	64.79
13/16	2.552	3/4	21.20	3/4	43.19	3/4	65.18
7/8	2.748	7/8	21.57	7/8	43.58	7/8	65.58
15/16	2.945	7.	21.99	14.	43.98	21.	65.97
1.	3.141	1/8	22.38	1/8	44.37	1/8	66.36
1/8	3.534	1/4	22.77	1/4	44.76	1/4	66.75
1/4	3.927	3/8	23.16	3/8	45.16	3/8	67.15
3/8	4.319	1/2	23.56	1/2	45.55	1/2	67.54
1/2	4.712	5/8	23.95	5/8	45.94	5/8	67.93
5/8	5.105	3/4	24.34	3/4	46.33	3/4	68.32
3/4	5.497	7/8	24.74	7/8	46.73	7/8	68.72
7/8	5.890	8.	25.13	15.	47.12	22.	69.11
2.	6.283	1/8	25.52	1/8	47.51	1/8	69.50
1/8	6.675	1/4	25.91	1/4	47.90	1/4	69.90
1/4	7.068	3/8	26.31	3/8	48.30	3/8	70.29
3/8	7.461	1/2	26.70	1/2	48.69	1/2	70.68
1/2	7.854	5/8	27.09	5/8	49.08	5/8	71.07
5/8	8.246	3/4	27.48	3/4	49.48	3/4	71.47
3/4	8.639	7/8	27.88	7/8	49.87	7/8	71.86
7/8	9.032	9.	28.27	16.	50.26	23.	72.25
3.	9.424	1/8	28.66	1/8	50.65	1/8	72.64
1/8	9.817	1/4	29.05	1/4	51.05	1/4	73.04
1/4	10.21	3/8	29.45	3/8	51.44	3/8	73.43
3/8	10.60	1/2	29.84	1/2	51.83	1/2	73.82
1/2	10.99	5/8	30.23	5/8	52.22	5/8	74.21
5/8	11.38	3/4	30.63	3/4	52.62	3/4	74.61
3/4	11.78	7/8	31.02	7/8	53.01	7/8	75.
7/8	12.17	10.	31.41	17.	53.40	24.	75.39
4.	12.56	1/8	31.80	1/8	53.79	1/8	75.79
1/8	12.95	1/4	32.20	1/4	54.19	1/4	76.18
1/4	13.35	3/8	32.59	3/8	54.58	3/8	76.57
3/8	13.74	1/2	32.98	1/2	54.97	1/2	76.96
1/2	14.13	5/8	33.37	5/8	55.37	5/8	77.36
5/8	14.52	3/4	33.77	3/4	55.76	3/4	77.75
3/4	14.92	7/8	34.16	7/8	56.16	7/8	78.14
7/8	15.31	11.	34.55	18.	56.54	25.	78.54
		1/8	34.95	1/8	56.94	1/8	78.93
		1/4	35.34	1/4	57.33	1/4	79.32
		3/8	35.73	3/8	57.72	3/8	79.71
		1/2	36.12	1/2	58.11	1/2	80.10
		5/8	36.52	5/8	58.51	5/8	80.50
		3/4	36.91	3/4	58.90	3/4	80.89
		7/8	37.30	7/8	59.29	7/8	81.28

Table—(Continued).

Diameter	Circumference	Diameter	Circumference	Diameter	Circumference	Diameter	Circumfer'ce
26.	81.68	33.	103.6	40.	125.6	47.	147.6
1/8	82.07	1/8	104.	1/8	126.	1/8	148.
1/4	82.46	1/4	104.4	1/4	126.4	1/4	148.4
3/8	82.85	3/8	104.8	3/8	126.8	3/8	148.8
1/2	83.25	1/2	105.2	1/2	127.2	1/2	149.2
5/8	83.64	5/8	105.6	5/8	127.6	5/8	149.6
3/4	84.03	3/4	106.	3/4	128.	3/4	150.
7/8	84.43	7/8	106.4	7/8	128.4	7/8	150.4
27.	84.82	34.	106.8	41.	128.8	48.	150.7
1/8	85.21	1/8	107.2	1/8	129.1	1/8	151.1
1/4	85.60	1/4	107.5	1/4	129.5	1/4	151.5
3/8	86.	3/8	107.9	3/8	129.9	3/8	151.9
1/2	86.39	1/2	108.3	1/2	130.3	1/2	152.3
5/8	86.78	5/8	108.7	5/8	130.7	5/8	152.7
3/4	87.17	3/4	109.1	3/4	131.1	3/4	153.1
7/8	87.57	7/8	109.5	7/8	131.5	7/8	153.5
28.	87.96	35.	109.9	42.	131.9	49.	153.9
1/8	88.35	1/8	110.3	1/8	132.3	1/8	154.3
1/4	88.75	1/4	110.7	1/4	132.7	1/4	154.7
3/8	89.14	3/8	111.1	3/8	133.1	3/8	155.
1/2	89.53	1/2	111.5	1/2	133.5	1/2	155.5
5/8	89.92	5/8	111.9	5/8	133.9	5/8	155.9
3/4	90.32	3/4	112.3	3/4	134.3	3/4	156.2
7/8	90.71	7/8	112.7	7/8	134.6	7/8	156.6
29.	91.10	36.	113.	43.	135.	50.	157.
1/8	91.49	1/8	113.4	1/8	135.4	1/8	157.4
1/4	91.89	1/4	113.8	1/4	135.8	1/4	157.8
3/8	92.28	3/8	114.2	3/8	136.2	3/8	158.2
1/2	92.67	1/2	114.6	1/2	136.6	1/2	158.6
5/8	93.06	5/8	115.	5/8	137.	5/8	159.
3/4	93.46	3/4	115.4	3/4	137.4	3/4	159.4
7/8	93.85	7/8	115.8	7/8	137.8	7/8	159.8
30.	94.24	37.	116.2	44.	138.2	51.	160.2
1/8	94.64	1/8	116.6	1/8	138.6	1/8	160.6
1/4	95.03	1/4	117.	1/4	139.	1/4	161.
3/8	95.42	3/8	117.4	3/8	139.4	3/8	161.3
1/2	95.81	1/2	117.8	1/2	139.8	1/2	161.7
5/8	96.21	5/8	118.2	5/8	140.1	5/8	162.1
3/4	96.60	3/4	118.6	3/4	140.5	3/4	162.5
7/8	96.99	7/8	118.9	7/8	140.9	7/8	162.9
31.	97.38	38.	119.3	45.	141.3	52.	163.3
1/8	97.78	1/8	119.7	1/8	141.7	1/8	163.7
1/4	98.17	1/4	120.1	1/4	142.1	1/4	164.1
3/8	98.56	3/8	120.5	3/8	142.5	3/8	164.5
1/2	98.96	1/2	120.9	1/2	142.9	1/2	164.9
5/8	99.35	5/8	121.3	5/8	143.3	5/8	165.3
3/4	99.74	3/4	121.7	3/4	143.7	3/4	165.7
7/8	100.1	7/8	122.1	7/8	144.1	7/8	166.1
32.	100.5	39.	122.5	46.	144.5	53.	166.5
1/8	100.9	1/8	122.9	1/8	144.9	1/8	166.8
1/4	101.3	1/4	123.3	1/4	145.2	1/4	167.2
3/8	101.7	3/8	123.7	3/8	145.6	3/8	167.6
1/2	102.1	1/2	124.	1/2	146.	1/2	168.
5/8	102.4	5/8	124.4	5/8	146.4	5/8	168.4
3/4	102.8	3/4	124.8	3/4	146.8	3/4	168.8
7/8	103.2	7/8	125.2	7/8	147.2	7/8	169.2

Table—(Continued).

Diameter	Circumference	Diameter.	Circumference	Diameter.	Circumference	Diameter.	Circumfer'ce
54.	169.6	61.	191.6	68.	213.6	75.	235.6
⅛	170.	⅛	192.	⅛	214.	⅛	236.
¼	170.4	¼	192.4	¼	214.4	¼	236.4
⅜	170.8	⅜	192.8	⅜	214.8	⅜	236.7
½	171.2	½	193.2	½	215.1	½	237.1
⅝	171.6	⅝	193.6	⅝	215.5	⅝	237.5
¾	172.	¾	193.9	¾	215.9	¾	237.9
⅞	172.3	⅞	194.3	⅞	216.3	⅞	238.3
55.	172.7	62.	194.7	69.	216.7	76.	238.7
⅛	173.1	⅛	195.1	⅛	217.1	⅛	239.1
¼	173.5	¼	195.5	¼	217.5	¼	239.5
⅜	173.9	⅜	195.9	⅜	217.9	⅜	239.9
½	174.3	½	196.3	½	218.3	½	240.3
⅝	174.7	⅝	196.7	⅝	218.7	⅝	240.7
¾	175.1	¾	197.1	¾	219.1	¾	241.1
⅞	175.5	⅞	197.5	⅞	219.5	⅞	241.5
56.	175.9	63.	197.9	70.	219.9	77.	241.9
⅛	176.3	⅛	198.3	⅛	220.3	⅛	242.2
¼	176.7	¼	198.7	¼	220.6	¼	242.6
⅜	177.1	⅜	199.	⅜	221.	⅜	243.
½	177.5	½	199.4	½	221.4	½	243.4
⅝	177.8	⅝	199.8	⅝	221.8	⅝	243.8
¾	178.2	¾	200.2	¾	222.2	¾	244.2
⅞	178.6	⅞	200.6	⅞	222.6	⅞	244.6
57.	179.	64.	201.	71.	223.	78.	245.
⅛	179.4	⅛	201.4	⅛	223.4	⅛	245.4
¼	179.8	¼	201.8	¼	223.8	¼	245.8
⅜	180.2	⅜	202.2	⅜	224.2	⅜	246.2
½	180.6	½	202.6	½	224.6	½	246.6
⅝	181.	⅝	203.	⅝	225.	⅝	247.
¾	181.4	¾	203.4	¾	225.4	¾	247.4
⅞	181.8	⅞	203.8	⅞	225.8	⅞	247.7
58.	182.2	65.	204.2	72.	226.1	79.	248.1
⅛	182.6	⅛	204.5	⅛	226.5	⅛	248.5
¼	182.9	¼	204.9	¼	226.9	¼	248.9
⅜	183.3	⅜	205.3	⅜	227.3	⅜	249.3
½	183.7	½	205.7	½	227.7	½	249.7
⅝	184.1	⅝	206.1	⅝	228.1	⅝	250.1
¾	184.5	¾	206.5	¾	228.5	¾	250.5
⅞	184.9	⅞	206.9	⅞	228.9	⅞	250.9
59.	185.3	66.	207.3	73.	229.3	80.	251.3
⅛	185.7	⅛	207.7	⅛	229.7	⅛	251.7
¼	186.1	¼	208.1	¼	230.1	¼	252.1
⅜	186.5	⅜	208.5	⅜	230.5	⅜	252.5
½	186.9	½	208.9	½	230.9	½	252.8
⅝	187.3	⅝	209.3	⅝	231.3	⅝	253.2
¾	187.7	¾	209.7	¾	231.6	¾	253.6
⅞	188.1	⅞	210.	⅞	232.	⅞	254.
60.	188.4	67.	210.4	74.	232.4	81.	254.4
⅛	188.8	⅛	210.8	⅛	232.8	⅛	254.8
¼	189.2	¼	211.2	¼	233.2	¼	255.2
⅜	189.6	⅜	211.6	⅜	233.6	⅜	255.6
½	190.	½	212.	½	234.	½	256.
⅝	190.4	⅝	212.4	⅝	234.4	⅝	256.4
¾	190.8	¾	212.8	¾	234.8	¾	256.8
⅞	191.2	⅞	213.2	⅞	235.2	⅞	257.2

I

Table—(Continued).

Diameter	Circumference	Diameter	Circumference	Diameter	Circumference	Diameter	Circumfer'ce
82.	257.6	87.	273.3	92.	289.	97.	304.7
.1/8	258.	.1/8	273.7	.1/8	289.4	.1/8	305.1
.1/4	258.3	.1/4	274.1	.1/4	289.8	.1/4	305.5
.3/8	258.7	.3/8	274.4	.3/8	290.2	.3/8	305.9
.1/2	259.1	.1/2	274.8	.1/2	290.5	.1/2	306.3
.5/8	259.5	.5/8	275.2	.5/8	290.9	.5/8	306.6
.3/4	259.9	.3/4	275.6	.3/4	291.3	.3/4	307.
.7/8	260.3	.7/8	276.	.7/8	291.7	.7/8	307.4
83.	260.7	88.	276.4	93.	292.1	98.	307.8
.1/8	261.1	.1/8	276.8	.1/8	292.5	.1/8	308.2
.1/4	261.5	.1/4	277.2	.1/4	292.9	.1/4	308.6
.3/8	261.9	.3/8	277.6	.3/8	293.3	.3/8	309.0
.1/2	262.3	.1/2	278.	.1/2	293.7	.1/2	309.4
.5/8	262.7	.5/8	278.4	.5/8	294.1	.5/8	309.8
.3/4	263.1	.3/4	278.8	.3/4	294.5	.3/4	310.2
.7/8	263.5	.7/8	279.2	.7/8	294.9	.7/8	310.6
84.	263.8	89.	279.6	94.	295.3	99.	311.0
.1/8	264.2	.1/8	279.9	.1/8	295.7	.1/8	311.4
.1/4	264.6	.1/4	280.3	.1/4	296.	.1/4	311.8
.3/8	265.	.3/8	280.7	.3/8	296.4	.3/8	312.1
.1/2	265.4	.1/2	281.1	.1/2	296.8	.1/2	312.5
.5/8	265.8	.5/8	281.5	.5/8	297.2	.5/8	312.9
.3/4	266.2	.3/4	281.9	.3/4	297.6	.3/4	313.3
.7/8	266.6	.7/8	282.3	.7/8	298.	.7/8	313.7
85.	267.	90.	282.7	95.	298.4	100.	314.1
.1/8	267.4	.1/8	283.1	.1/8	298.8		
.1/4	267.8	.1/4	283.5	.1/4	299.2		
.3/8	268.2	.3/8	283.9	.3/8	299.6		
.1/2	269.6	.1/2	284.3	.1/2	300.		
.5/8	268.9	.5/8	284.7	.5/8	300.4		
.3/4	269.3	.3/4	285.1	.3/4	300.8		
.7/8	269.7	.7/8	285.4	.7/8	301.2		
86.	270.1	91.	285.8	96.	301.5		
.1/8	270.5	.1/8	286.2	.1/8	301.9		
.1/4	270.9	.1/4	286.6	.1/4	302.3		
.3/8	271.3	.3/8	287.	.3/8	302.7		
.1/2	271.7	.1/2	287.4	.1/2	303.1		
.5/8	272.1	.5/8	287.8	.5/8	303.5		
.3/4	272.5	.3/4	288.2	.3/4	303.9		
.7/8	272.9	.7/8	288.6	.7/8	304.3		

TABLE *of Squares, Cubes, and Square and Cube Roots, of all Numbers from* 1 *to* 1000.

Number.	Square.	Cube.	Square Root.	Cube Root.
1	1	1	1.	1.
2	4	8	1.414213	1.259921
3	9	27	1.732050	1.442250
4	16	64	2.	1.587401
5	25	125	2.236068	1.709976
6	36	216	2.449489	1.817121
7	49	343	2.645751	1.912933
8	64	512	2.828427	2.
9	81	729	3.	2.080084
10	100	1000	3.162277	2.154435
11	121	1331	3.316624	2.223980
12	144	1728	3.464101	2.289428
13	169	2197	3.605551	2.351335
14	196	2744	3.741657	2.410142
15	225	3375	3.872983	2.466212
16	256	4096	4.	2.519842
17	289	4913	4.123105	2.571282
18	324	5832	4.242640	2.620741
19	361	6859	4.358898	2.668402
20	400	8000	4.472136	2.714418
21	441	9261	4.582575	2.758923
22	484	10648	4.690415	2.802039
23	529	12167	4.795831	2.843867
24	576	13824	4.898979	2.884499
25	625	15625	5.	2.924018
26	676	17576	5.099019	2.962496
27	729	19683	5.196152	3.
28	784	21952	5.291502	3.036589
29	841	24389	5.385164	3.072317
30	900	27000	5.477225	3.107232
31	961	29791	5.567764	3.141381
32	1024	32768	5.656854	3.174802
33	1089	35937	5.744562	3.207534
34	1156	39304	5.830951	3.239612
35	1225	42875	5.916079	3.271066
36	1296	46656	6.	3.301927
37	1369	50653	6.082762	3.332222
38	1444	54872	6.164414	3.361975
39	1521	59319	6.244998	3.391211
40	1600	64000	6.324555	3.419952
41	1681	68921	6.403124	3.448217
42	1764	74088	6.480740	3.476027
43	1849	79507	6.557438	3.503398
44	1936	85184	6.633249	3.530348
45	2025	91125	6.708203	3.556893
46	2116	97336	6.782330	3.583048
47	2209	103823	6.855654	3.608826
48	2304	110592	6.928203	3.634241
49	2401	117649	7.	3.659306
50	2500	125000	7.071067	3.684031
51	2601	132651	7.141428	3.708430
52	2704	140608	7.211102	3.732511
53	2809	148877	7.280109	3.756286
54	2916	157464	7.348469	3.779763
55	3025	166375	7.416198	3.802953

TABLE—(Continued).

Number.	Square.	Cube.	Square Root.	Cube Root.
56	3136	175616	7.483314	3.825862
57	3249	185193	7.549834	3.848501
58	3364	195112	7.615773	3.870877
59	3481	205379	7.681145	3.892996
60	3600	216000	7.745966	3.914867
61	3721	226981	7.810249	3.936497
62	3844	238328	7.874007	3.957892
63	3969	250047	7.937253	3.979057
64	4096	262144	8.	4.
65	4225	274626	8.062257	4.020726
66	4356	287496	8.124038	4.041240
67	4489	300763	8.185352	4.061548
68	4624	314432	8.246211	4.081656
69	4761	328509	8.306623	4.101566
70	4900	343000	8.366600	4.121285
71	5041	357911	8.426149	4.140818
72	5184	373248	8.485281	4.160168
73	5329	389017	8.544003	4.179339
74	5476	405224	8.602325	4.198336
75	5625	421875	8.660254	4.217163
76	5776	438976	8.717797	4.235824
77	5929	456533	8.774964	4.254321
78	6084	474552	8.831760	4.272659
79	6241	493039	8.888194	4.290841
80	6400	512000	8.944271	4.308870
81	6561	531441	9.	4.326749
82	6724	551368	9.055385	4.344481
83	6889	571787	9.110433	4.362071
84	7056	592704	9.165151	4.379519
85	7225	614125	9.219544	4.396830
86	7396	636056	9.273618	4.414005
87	7569	658503	9.327379	4.431047
88	7744	681472	9.380831	4.447960
89	7921	704969	9.433981	4.464745
90	8100	729000	9.486833	4.481405
91	8281	753571	9.539392	4.497942
92	8464	778688	9.591663	4.514357
93	8649	804357	9.643650	4.530655
94	8836	830584	9.695359	4.546836
95	9025	857375	9.746794	4.562903
96	9216	884736	9.797959	4.577857
97	9409	912673	9.848857	4.594701
98	9604	941192	9.899494	4.610436
99	9801	970299	9.949874	4.626065
100	10000	1000000	10.	4.641589
101	10201	1030301	10.049875	4.657010
102	10404	1061208	10.099504	4.672330
103	10609	1092727	10.148891	4.687548
104	10816	1124864	10.198039	4.702669
105	11025	1157625	10.246950	4.717694
106	11236	1191016	10.295630	4.732624
107	11449	1225043	10.344080	4.747459
108	11664	1259712	10.392304	4.762203
109	11881	1295029	10.440306	4.776856
110	12100	1331000	10.488088	4.791420
111	12321	1367631	10.535653	4.805896

TABLE—(Continued).

Number.	Square.	Cube.	Square Root.	Cube Root.
112	12544	1404928	10.583005	4.820284
113	12769	1442897	10.630145	4.834588
114	12996	1481544	10.677078	4.848808
115	13225	1520375	10.723805	4.862944
116	13456	1560896	10.770329	4.876999
117	13689	1601613	10.816653	4.890973
118	13924	1643032	10.862780	4.904868
119	14161	1685159	10.908712	4.918685
120	14400	1728000	10.954451	4.932424
121	14641	1771561	11.	4.946088
122	14884	1815848	11.045361	4.959675
123	15129	1860867	11.090536	4.973190
124	15376	1906624	11.135528	4.986631
125	15625	1953125	11.180339	5.
126	15876	2000376	11.224972	5.013298
127	16129	2048383	11.269427	5.026526
128	16384	2097152	11.313708	5.039684
129	16641	2146689	11.357816	5.052774
130	16900	2197000	11.401754	5.065797
131	17161	2248091	11.445523	5.078753
132	17424	2299968	11.489125	5.091643
133	17689	2352637	11.532562	5.104469
134	17956	2406104	11.575836	5.117230
135	18225	2460373	11.618950	5.129928
136	18496	2515456	11.661903	5.142563
137	18769	2571353	11.704699	5.155137
138	19044	2628072	11.747344	5.167649
139	19321	2685619	11.789826	5.180101
140	19600	2744000	11.832159	5.192494
141	19881	2803221	11.874342	5.204828
142	20164	2863288	11.916375	5.217103
143	20449	2924207	11.958260	5.229321
144	20736	2985984	12.	5.241482
145	21025	3048625	12.041594	5.253588
146	21316	3112136	12.083046	5.265637
147	21609	3176523	12.124355	5.277632
148	21904	3241792	12.165525	5.289572
149	22201	3307949	12.206555	5.301459
150	22500	3375000	12.247448	5.313293
151	22801	3442951	12.288205	5.325074
152	23104	3511808	12.328828	5.336803
153	23409	3581577	12.369316	5.348481
154	23716	3652264	12.409673	5.360108
155	24025	3723875	12.449899	5.371685
156	24336	3796416	12.489996	5.383231
157	24649	3869893	12.529964	5.394690
158	24964	3944312	12.569805	5.406120
159	25281	4019679	12.609520	5.417501
160	25600	4096000	12.649110	5.428835
161	25921	4173281	12.688577	5.440122
162	26244	4251528	12.727922	5.451362
163	26569	4330747	12.767145	5.462556
164	26896	4410944	12.806248	5.473703
165	27225	4492125	12.845232	5.484806
166	27556	4574296	12.884098	5.495865
167	27889	4657463	12.922848	5.506879

TABLE—(Continued).

Number.	Square.	Cube.	Square Root.	Cube Root.
168	28224	4741632	12.961481	5.517848
169	28561	4826809	13.	5.528775
170	28900	4913000	13.038404	5.539658
171	29241	5000211	13.076696	5.550499
172	29584	5088448	13.114877	5.561298
173	29929	5177717	13.152946	5.572054
174	30276	5268024	13.190906	5.582770
175	30625	5359375	13.228756	5.593445
176	30976	5451776	13.266499	5.604079
177	31329	5545233	13.304134	5.614673
178	31684	5639752	13.341664	5.625226
179	32041	5735339	13.379088	5.635741
180	32400	5832000	13.416407	5.646216
181	32761	5929741	13.453624	5.656652
182	33124	6028568	13.490737	5.667051
183	33489	6128487	13.527749	5.677411
184	33856	6229504	13.564660	5.687734
185	34225	6331625	13.601470	5.698019
186	34596	6434856	13.638181	5.708267
187	34969	6539203	13.674794	5.718479
188	35344	6644672	13.711309	5.728654
189	35721	6751269	13.747727	5.738794
190	36100	6859000	13.784048	5.748897
191	36481	6967871	13.820275	5.758965
192	36864	7077888	13.856406	5.768998
193	37249	7189057	13.892444	5.778996
194	37636	7301384	13.928388	5.788960
195	38025	7414875	13.964240	5.798890
196	38416	7529536	14.	5.808786
197	38809	7645373	14.035668	5.818648
198	39204	7762392	14.071247	5.828476
199	39601	7880599	14.106736	5.838272
200	40000	8000000	14.142135	5.848035
201	40401	8120601	14.177446	5.857765
202	40804	8242408	14.212670	5.867464
203	41209	8365427	14.247806	5.877130
204	41616	8489664	14.282856	5.886765
205	42025	8615125	14.317821	5.896368
206	42436	8741816	14.352700	5.905941
207	42849	8869743	14.387494	5.915481
208	43264	8998912	14.422205	5.924991
209	43681	9123329	14.456832	5.934473
210	44100	9261000	14.491376	5.943911
211	44521	9393931	14.525839	5.953341
212	44944	9528128	14.560219	5.962731
213	45369	9663597	14.594519	5.972091
214	45796	9800344	14.628738	5.981426
215	46225	9938375	14.662878	5.990727
216	46656	10077696	14.696938	6.
217	47089	10218313	14.730919	6.009244
218	47524	10360232	14.764823	6.018463
219	47961	10503459	14.798648	6.027650
220	48400	10648000	14.832397	6.036811
221	48841	10793861	14.866068	6.045943
222	49284	10941048	14.899664	6.055048
223	49729	11089567	14.933184	6.064126

TABLE—(Continued).

Number.	Square.	Cube.	Square Root.	Cube Root.
224	50176	11239424	14.966629	6.073177
225	50625	11390625	15.	6.082201
226	51076	11543176	15.033296	6.091199
227	51529	11697083	15.066519	6.100170
228	51984	11852352	15.099668	6.109115
229	52441	12008989	15.132746	6.118032
230	52900	12167000	15.165750	6.126925
231	53361	12326391	15.198684	6.135792
232	53824	12487168	15.231546	6.114634
233	54289	12649337	15.264337	6.153449
234	54756	12812904	15.297058	6.162239
235	55225	12977875	15.329709	6.171005
236	55696	13144256	15.362291	6.179747
237	56169	13312053	15.394804	6.188463
238	56644	13481272	15.427248	6.197154
239	57121	13651919	15.459624	6.205821
240	57600	13824000	15.491933	6.214464
241	58081	13997521	15.524174	6.223083
242	58564	14172488	15.556349	6.231678
243	59049	14348907	15.588457	6.240251
244	59536	14526784	15.620499	6.248800
245	60025	14706125	15.652475	6.257324
246	60516	14886936	15.684387	6.265826
247	61009	15069223	15.716233	6.274304
248	61504	15252992	15.748015	6.282760
249	62001	15438249	15.779733	6.291194
250	62500	15625000	15.811388	6.299604
251	63001	15813251	15.842979	6.307992
252	63504	16003008	15.874507	6.316359
253	64009	16194277	15.905973	6.324704
254	64516	16387064	15.937377	6.333025
255	65025	16581375	15.968719	6.341325
256	65536	16777216	16.	6.349602
257	66049	16974593	16.031219	6.357859
258	66564	17173512	16.062378	6.366095
259	67081	17373979	16.093476	6.374310
260	67600	17576000	16.124515	6.382504
261	68121	17779581	16.155494	6.390676
262	68644	17984728	16.186414	6.398827
263	69169	18191447	16.217274	6.406958
264	69696	18399744	16.248076	6.415068
265	70225	18609625	16.278820	6.423157
266	70756	18821096	16.309506	6.431226
267	71289	19034163	16.340134	6.439275
268	71824	19248832	16.370705	6.447305
269	72361	19465109	16.401219	6.455314
270	72900	19683000	16.431676	6.463304
271	73441	19902511	16.462077	6.471274
272	73984	20123648	16.492422	6.479224
273	74529	20346417	16.522711	6.487153
274	75076	20570824	16.552945	6.495064
275	75625	20796875	16.583124	6.502956
276	76176	21024576	16.613247	6.510829
277	76729	21253933	16.643317	6.518684
278	77284	21484952	16.673332	6.526519
279	77841	21717639	16.703293	6.534335

TABLE—(Continued).

Number.	Square.	Cube.	Square Root.	Cube Root.
280	78400	21952000	16.733200	6.542132
281	78961	22188041	16.763054	6.549911
282	79524	22425768	16.792855	6.557672
283	80089	22665187	16.822603	6.565415
284	80656	22906304	16.852299	6.573139
285	81225	23149125	16.881943	6.580844
286	81796	23393656	16.911534	6.588531
287	82369	23639903	16.941074	6.596202
288	82944	23887872	16.970562	6.603854
289	83521	24137569	17.	6.611488
290	84100	24389000	17.029386	6.619106
291	84681	24642171	17.058722	6.626705
292	85264	24897088	17.088007	6.634287
293	85849	25153757	17.117242	6.641851
294	86436	25412184	17.146428	6.649399
295	87025	25672375	17.175564	6.656930
296	87616	25934336	17.204650	6.664443
297	88209	26198073	17.233687	6.671940
298	88804	26463592	17.262676	6.679419
299	89401	26730899	17.291616	6.686882
300	90000	27000000	17.320508	6.694328
301	90601	27270901	17.349351	6.701758
302	91204	27543608	17.378147	6.709172
303	91809	27818127	17.406895	6.716569
304	92416	28094464	17.435595	6.723950
305	93025	28372625	17.464249	6.731316
306	93636	28652616	17.492855	6.738665
307	94249	28934443	17.521415	6.745997
308	94864	29218112	17.549928	6.753313
309	95481	29503629	17.578395	6.760614
310	96100	29791000	17.606816	6.767899
311	96721	30080231	17.635192	6.775168
312	97344	30371328	17.663521	6.782422
313	97969	30664297	17.691806	6.789661
314	98596	30959144	17.720045	6.796884
315	99225	31255875	17.748239	6.804091
316	99856	31554496	17.776388	6.811284
317	100489	31855013	17.804493	6.818461
318	101124	32157432	17.832554	6.825624
319	101761	32461759	17.860571	6.832771
320	102400	32768000	17.888543	6.839903
321	103041	33076161	17.916472	6.847021
322	103684	33386248	17.944358	6.854124
323	104329	33698267	17.972200	6.861211
324	104976	34012224	18.	6.868284
325	105625	34328125	18.027756	6.875343
326	106276	34645976	18.055470	6.882388
327	106929	34965783	18.083141	6.889419
328	107584	35287552	18.110770	6.896435
329	108241	35611289	18.138357	6.903436
330	108900	35937000	18.165902	6.910423
331	109561	36264691	18.193405	6.917396
332	110224	36594368	18.220867	6.924355
333	110889	36926037	18.248287	6.931300
334	111556	37259704	18.275666	6.938232
335	112225	37595375	18.303005	6.945149

TABLE—(Continued).

Number.	Square.	Cube.	Square Root.	Cube Root.
336	112896	37933056	18.330302	6.952053
337	113569	38272753	18.357559	6.958943
338	114244	38614472	18.384776	6.965819
339	114921	38958219	18.411952	6.972682
340	115600	39304000	18.439088	6.979532
341	116281	39651821	18.466185	6.986369
342	116964	40001688	18.493242	6.993491
343	117649	40353607	18.520259	7.
344	118336	40707584	18.547237	7.006796
345	119025	41063625	18.574175	7.013579
346	119716	41421736	18.601075	7.020349
347	120409	41781923	18.627936	7.027106
348	121104	42144192	18.654758	7.033850
349	121801	42508549	18.681541	7.040581
350	122500	42875000	18.708286	7.047208
351	123201	43243551	18.734994	7.054003
352	123904	43614208	18.761663	7.060696
353	124609	43986977	18.788294	7.067376
354	125316	44361864	18.814887	7.074043
355	126025	44738875	18.841443	7.080698
356	126736	45118016	18.867962	7.087341
357	127449	45499293	18.894443	7.093970
358	128164	45882712	18.920887	7.100588
359	128881	46268279	18.947295	7.107193
360	129600	46656000	18.973666	7.113786
361	130321	47045881	19.	7.120367
362	131044	47437928	19.026297	7.126935
363	131769	47832147	19.052558	7.133492
364	132496	48228544	19.078784	7.140037
365	133225	48627125	19.104973	7.146569
366	133956	49027896	19.131126	7.153090
367	134689	49430863	19.157244	7.159599
368	135424	49836032	19.183326	7.166095
369	136161	50243409	19.209372	7.172580
370	136900	50653000	19.235384	7.179054
371	137641	51064811	19.261360	7.185516
372	138384	51478848	19.287301	7.191966
373	139129	51895117	19.313207	7.198405
374	139876	52313624	19.339079	7.204832
375	140625	52734375	19.364916	7.211247
376	141376	53157376	19.390719	7.217652
377	142129	53582633	19.416487	7.224045
378	142884	54010152	19.442222	7.230427
379	143641	54439939	19.467922	7.236797
380	144400	54872000	19.493588	7.243156
381	145161	55306341	19.519221	7.249504
382	145924	55742968	19.544820	7.255841
383	146689	56181887	19.570385	7.262167
384	147456	56623104	19.595917	7.268482
385	148225	57066625	19.621416	7.274786
386	148996	57512456	19.646882	7.281079
387	149769	57960603	19.672315	7.287362
388	150544	58411072	19.697715	7.293633
389	151321	58863869	19.723082	7.299893
390	152100	59319000	19.748417	7.306143
391	152881	59776471	19.773719	7.312383

Table—(Continued).

Number.	Square.	Cube.	Square Root.	Cube Root.
392	153664	60236288	19.798989	7.318611
393	154449	60698457	19.824227	7.324829
394	155236	61162984	19.849432	7.331037
395	156025	61629875	19.874606	7.337234
396	156816	62099136	19.899748	7.343420
397	157609	62570773	19.924858	7.349596
398	158404	63044792	19.949937	7.355762
399	159201	63521199	19.974984	7.361917
400	160000	64000000	20.	7.368063
401	160801	64481201	20.024984	7.374198
402	161604	64964808	20.049937	7.380322
403	162409	65450827	20.074859	7.386437
404	163216	65939264	20.099751	7.392542
405	164025	66430125	20.124611	7.398636
406	164836	66923416	20.149441	7.404720
407	165649	67419143	20.174241	7.410794
408	166464	67911312	20.199009	7.416859
409	167281	68417929	20.223748	7.422914
410	168100	68921000	20.248456	7.428958
411	168921	69426531	20.273134	7.434993
412	169744	69934528	20.297783	7.441018
413	170569	70444997	20.322401	7.447033
414	171396	70957944	20.346989	7.453039
415	172225	71473375	20.371548	7.459036
416	173056	71991296	20.396078	7.465022
417	173889	72511713	20.420577	7.470999
418	174724	73034632	20.445048	7.476966
419	175561	73560059	20.469489	7.482924
420	176400	74088000	20.493901	7.488872
421	177241	74618461	20.518284	7.494810
422	178084	75151448	20.542638	7.500740
423	178929	75686967	20.566963	7.506660
424	179776	76225024	20.591260	7.512571
425	180625	76765625	20.615528	7.518473
426	181476	77308776	20.639767	7.524365
427	182329	77854483	20.663978	7.530248
428	183184	78402752	20.688160	7.536121
429	184041	78953589	20.712315	7.541986
430	184900	79507000	20.736441	7.547841
431	185761	80062991	20.760539	7.553688
432	186624	80621568	20.784609	7.559525
433	187489	81182737	20.808652	7.565353
434	188356	81746504	20.832666	7.571173
435	189225	82312875	20.856653	7.576984
436	190096	82881856	20.880613	7.582786
437	190969	83453453	20.904545	7.588579
438	191844	84027672	20.928449	7.594363
439	192721	84604519	20.952326	7.600138
440	193600	85184000	20.976177	7.605905
441	194481	85766121	21.	7.611662
442	195364	86350388	21.023796	7.617411
443	196249	86938307	21.047565	7.623151
444	197136	87528384	21.071307	7.628883
445	198025	88121125	21.095023	7.634606
446	198916	88716536	21.118712	7.640321
447	199809	89314623	21.142374	7.646027

TABLE—(Continued).

Number.	Square.	Cube.	Square Root.	Cube Root.
448	200704	89915392	21.166010	7.651725
449	201601	90518849	21.189620	7.657414
450	202500	91125000	21.213203	7.663094
451	203401	91733851	21.236760	7.668766
452	204304	92345408	21.260291	7.674430
453	205209	92959677	21.283796	7.680085
454	206116	93576664	21.307275	7.685732
455	207025	94196375	21.330729	7.691371
456	207936	94818816	21.354156	7.697002
457	208849	95443993	21.377558	7.702624
458	209764	96071912	21.400934	7.708238
459	210681	96702579	21.424285	7.713844
460	211600	97336000	21.447610	7.719442
461	212521	97972181	21.470910	7.725032
462	213144	98611128	21.494185	7.730614
463	214369	99252847	21.517434	7.736187
464	215296	99897344	21.540659	7.741753
465	216225	100544625	21.563858	7.747310
466	217156	101194696	21.587033	7.752860
467	218089	101847563	21.610182	7.758402
468	219024	102503232	21.633307	7.763936
469	219961	103161709	21.656407	7.769462
470	220900	103823000	21.679483	7.774980
471	221841	104487111	21.702534	7.780490
472	222784	105154048	21.725561	7.785992
473	223729	105823817	21.748563	7.791487
474	224676	106496424	21.771541	7.796974
475	225625	107171875	21.794494	7.802453
476	226576	107850176	21.817424	7.807925
477	227529	108531333	21.840329	7.813389
478	228484	109215352	21.863211	7.818845
479	229441	109902239	21.886068	7.824294
480	230400	110592000	21.908902	7.829735
481	231361	111284641	21.931712	7.835168
482	232324	111980168	21.954498	7.840594
483	233289	112678587	21.977261	7.846013
484	234256	113379904	22.	7.851424
485	235225	114084125	22.022715	7.856828
486	236196	114791256	22.045407	7.862224
487	237169	115501303	22.068076	7.867613
488	238144	116214272	22.090722	7.872994
489	239121	116930169	22.113344	7.878368
490	240100	117649000	22.135943	7.883734
491	241081	118370771	22.158519	7.889094
492	242064	119095488	22.181073	7.894446
493	243049	119823157	22.203603	7.899791
494	244036	120553784	22.226110	7.905129
495	245025	121287375	22.248595	7.910460
496	246016	122023936	22.271057	7.915784
497	247009	122763473	22.293496	7.921100
498	248004	123505992	22.315913	7.926408
499	249001	124251499	22.338307	7.931710
500	250000	125000000	22.360679	7.937005
501	251001	125751501	22.383029	7.942293
502	252004	126506008	22.405356	7.947573
503	253009	127263527	22.427661	7.952847

TABLE—(Continued).

Number.	Square.	Cube.	Square Root.	Cube Root.
504	254016	128024064	22.449944	7.958114
505	255025	128787625	22.472205	7.963374
506	256036	129554216	22.494443	7.968627
507	257049	130323843	22.516660	7.973873
508	258064	131096512	22.538855	7.979112
509	259081	131872229	22.561028	7.984344
510	260100	132651000	22.583179	7.989569
511	261121	133432831	22.605309	7.994788
512	262144	134217728	22.627417	8.
513	263169	135005697	22.649503	8.005205
514	264196	135796744	22.671568	8.010403
515	265225	136590875	22.693611	8.015595
516	266256 *	137388096	22.715633	8.020779
517	267289	138188413	22.737634	8.025957
518	268324	138991832	22.759613	8.031129
519	269361	139798359	22.781571	8.036293
520	270400	140608000	22.803508	8.041451
521	271441	141420761	22.825424	8.046603
522	272484	142236648	22.847319	8.051748
523	273529	143055667	22.869193	8.056886
524	274576	143877824	22.891046	8.062018
525	275625	144703125	22.912878	8.067143
526	276676	145531576	22.934689	8.072262
527	277729	146363183	22.956480	8.077374
528	278784	147197952	22.978250	8.082480
529	279841	148025889	23.	8.087579
530	280900	148877000	23.021728	8.092672
531	281961	149721291	23.043437	8.097758
532	283024	150568768	23.065125	8.102838
533	284089	151419437	23.086792	8.107912
534	285156	152273304	23.108440	8.112980
535	286225	153130375	23.130067	8.118041
536	287296	153990656	23.151673	8.123096
537	288369	154854153	23.173260	8.128144
538	289444	155720872	23.194827	8.133186
539	290521	156590819	23.216373	8.138223
540	291600	157464000	23.237900	8.143253
541	292681	158340421	23.259406	8.148276
542	293764	159220088	23.280893	8.153293
543	294849	160103007	23.302360	8.158304
544	295936	160989184	23.323807	8.163309
545	297025	161878625	23.345235	8.168308
546	298116	162771336	23.366642	8.173302
547	299209	163667323	23.388031	8.178289
548	300304	164566592	23.409399	8.183269
549	301401	165469149	23.430749	8.188244
550	302500	166375000	23.452078	8.193212
551	303601	167284151	22.473389	8.198175
552	304704	168196608	23.494680	8.203131
553	305809	169112377	23.515952	8.208082
554	306916	170031464	23.537204	8.213027
555	308025	170953875	23.558438	8.217965
556	309136	171879616	23.579652	8.222898
557	310249	172808693	23.600847	8.227825
558	311364	173741112	23.622023	8.232746
559	312481	174676879	23.643180	8.237661

TABLE—(Continued).

Number.	Square.	Cube.	Square Root.	Cube Root.
560	313600	175616000	23.664319	8.242570
561	314721	176558481	23.685438	8.247474
562	315844	177504328	23.706539	8.252371
563	316969	178453547	23.727621	8.257263
564	318096	179406144	23.748684	8.262149
565	319225	180362125	23.769728	8.267029
566	320356	181321496	23.790754	8.271903
567	321489	182284263	23.811761	8.276772
568	322624	183250432	23.832750	8.281635
569	323761	184220009	23.853720	8.286493
570	324900	185193000	23.874672	8.291344
571	326041	186169411	23.895606	8.296190
572	327184	187149248	23.916521	8.301030
573	328329	188132517	23.937418	8.305865
574	329476	189119224	23.958297	8.310694
575	330625	190109375	23.979157	8.315517
576	331776	191102976	24.	8.320335
577	332929	192100033	24.020824	8.325147
578	334084	193100552	24.041630	8.329954
579	335241	194104539	24.062418	8.334755
580	336400	195112000	24.083189	8.339551
581	337561	196122941	24.103941	8.344341
582	338724	197137368	24.124676	8.349125
583	339889	198155287	24.145392	8.353904
584	341056	199176704	24.166091	8.358678
585	342225	200201625	24.186773	8.363446
586	343396	201230056	24.207436	8.368209
587	344569	202262003	24.228082	8.372966
588	345744	203297472	24.248711	8.377718
589	346921	204336469	24.269322	8.382465
590	348100	205379000	24.289915	8.387206
591	349281	206425071	24.310491	8.391942
592	350464	207474688	24.331050	8.396673
593	351649	208527857	24.351591	8.401398
594	352836	209584584	24.372115	8.406118
595	354025	210644875	24.392621	8.410832
596	355216	211708736	24.413111	8.415541
597	356409	212776173	24.433583	8.420245
598	357604	213847192	24.454038	8.424944
599	358801	214921799	24.474476	8.429638
600	360000	216000000	24.494897	8.434327
601	361201	217081801	24.515301	8.439009
602	362404	218167208	24.535688	8.443687
603	363609	219256227	24.556058	8.448360
604	364816	220348864	24.576411	8.453027
605	366025	221445125	24.596747	8.457689
606	367236	222545016	24.617067	8.462347
607	368449	223648543	24.637370	8.466999
608	369664	224755712	24.657656	8.471647
609	370881	225866529	24.677925	8.476289
610	372100	226981000	24.698178	8.480926
611	373321	228099131	24.718414	8.485557
612	374544	229220928	24.738633	8.490184
613	375769	230346397	24.758836	8.494806
614	376996	231475544	24.779023	8.499423
615	378225	232608375	24.799193	8.504034

K

TABLE.—(Continued).

Number.	Square.	Cube.	Square Root.	Cube Root.
616	379456	233744896	24.819347	8.508641
617	380689	234885113	24.839484	8.513243
618	381924	236029032	24.859605	8.517840
619	383161	237176659	24.879710	8.522432
620	384700	238328000	24.899799	8.527018
621	385641	239483061	24.919871	8.531600
622	386884	240641848	24.939927	8.536177
623	388129	241804367	24.959967	8.540749
624	389376	242970624	24.979992	8.545317
625	390625	244140625	25.	8.549879
626	391876	245314376	25.019992	8.554437
627	393129	246491883	25.039968	8.558990
628	394384	247673152	25.059928	8.563537
629	395641	248858189	25.079872	8.568080
630	396900	250047000	25.099800	8.572618
631	398161	251239591	25.119713	8.577152
632	399424	252435968	25.139610	8.581680
633	400689	253636137	25.159491	8.586204
634	401956	254840104	25.179356	8.590723
635	403225	256047875	25.199206	8.595238
636	404496	257259456	25.219040	8.599747
637	405769	258474853	25.238858	8.604252
638	407044	259694072	25.258661	8.608752
639	408321	260917119	25.278449	8.613248
640	409600	262144000	25.298221	8.617738
641	410881	263374721	25.317977	8.622224
642	412164	264609288	25.337718	8.626706
643	413449	265847707	25.357444	8.631183
644	414736	267089984	25.377155	8.635655
645	416025	268336125	25.396850	8.640122
646	417316	269586136	25.416530	8.644585
647	418609	270840023	25.436194	8.649043
648	419904	272097792	25.455844	8.653497
649	421201	273359449	25.475478	8.657946
650	422500	274625000	25.495007	8.662301
651	423801	275894451	25.514701	8.666831
652	425104	277167808	25.534290	8.671266
653	426409	278445077	25.553864	8.675697
654	427716	279726264	25.573423	8.680123
655	429025	281011375	25.592967	8.684545
656	430336	282300416	25.612496	8.688963
657	431649	283593393	25.632011	8.693376
658	432964	284890312	25.651510	8.697784
659	434281	286191179	25.670995	8.702188
660	435600	287496000	25.690465	8.706587
661	436921	288804781	25.709920	8.710982
662	438244	290117528	25.720360	8.715373
663	439569	291434247	25.748786	8.719759
664	440896	292754944	25.768197	8.724141
665	442225	294079625	25.787593	8.728518
666	443556	295408296	25.806975	8.732891
667	444889	296740963	25.826343	8.737260
668	446224	298077632	25.845696	8.741624
669	447561	299418309	25.865034	8.745984
670	448900	300763000	25.884358	8.750340
671	450241	302111711	25.903667	8.754691

TABLE—(Continued).

Number.	Square.	Cube.	Square Root.	Cube Root.
672	451584	303464448	25.922962	8.759038
673	452929	304821217	25.942243	8.763380
674	454276	306182024	25.961510	8.767719
675	455625	307546875	25.980762	8.772053
676	456976	308915776	26.	8.776382
677	458329	310288733	26.019223	8.780708
678	459684	311665752	26.038433	8.785029
679	461041	313046839	26.057628	8.789346
680	462400	314432000	26.076809	8.793659
681	463761	315821241	26.095976	8.797967
682	465124	317214568	26.115129	8.802272
683	466489	318611987	26.134268	8.806572
684	467856	320013504	26.153393	8.810868
685	469225	321419125	26.172504	8.815159
686	470596	322828856	26.191601	8.819447
687	471969	324242703	26.210684	8.823730
688	473344	325660672	26.229754	8.828009
689	474721	327082769	26.248809	8.832285
690	476100	328509000	26.267851	8.836556
691	477481	329939371	26.286878	8.840822
692	478864	331373888	26.305892	8.845085
693	480249	332812557	26.324893	8.849344
694	481636	334255384	26.343879	8.853598
695	483025	335702375	26.362852	8.857849
696	484416	337153536	26.381811	8.862095
697	485809	338608873	26.400757	8.866337
698	487204	340068392	26.419689	8.870575
699	488601	341532099	26.438608	8.874809
700	490000	343000000	26.457513	8.879040
701	491401	344472101	26.476404	8.883266
702	492804	345948088	26.495282	8.887488
703	494209	317428927	26.514147	8.891706
704	495616	348913664	26.532998	8.895920
705	497025	350402625	26.551836	8.900130
706	498436	351895816	26.570660	8.904336
707	499849	353393243	26.589471	8.908538
708	501264	354894912	26.608269	8.912736
709	502681	356400829	26.627053	8.916931
710	504100	357911000	26.645825	8.921121
711	505521	359425431	26.664583	8.925307
712	506944	360944128	26.683328	8.929490
713	508369	362467097	26.702059	8.933668
714	509796	363994344	26.720778	8.937843
715	511225	365525875	26.739483	8.942014
716	512656	367061696	26.758176	8.946180
717	514089	368601813	26.776855	8.950343
718	515524	370146232	26.795522	8.954502
719	516961	371694959	26.814175	8.958658
720	518400	373248000	26.832815	8.962809
721	519841	374805361	26.851443	8.966957
722	521284	376367048	26.870057	8.971100
723	522729	377933067	26.888659	8.975240
724	524176	379503424	26.907248	8.979376
725	525625	381078125	26.925824	8.983508
726	527076	382657176	26.944387	8.987637
727	528529	384240583	26.962937	8.991762

Table—(Continued).

Number.	Square.	Cube.	Square Root.	Cube Root.
728	529984	385828352	26.981475	8.995883
729	531441	387420489	27.	9.
730	532900	389017000	27.018512	9.004113
731	534361	390617891	27.037011	9.008222
732	535824	392223168	27.055498	9.012328
733	537289	393832837	27.073972	9.016430
734	538756	395446904	27.092434	9.020529
735	540225	397065375	27.110883	9.024623
736	541696	398688256	27.129319	9.028714
737	543169	400315553	27.147743	9.032802
738	544644	401947272	27.166155	9.036885
739	546121	403583419	27.184554	9.040965
740	547600	405224000	27.202941	9.045041
741	549081	406869021	27.221315	9.049114
742	550564	408518488	27.239676	9.053183
743	552049	410172407	27.258026	9.057248
744	553536	411830784	27.276363	9.061309
745	555025	413493625	27.294688	9.065367
746	556516	415160936	27.313000	9.069422
747	558009	416832723	27.331300	9.073472
748	559504	418508992	27.349588	9.077519
749	561001	420189749	27.367864	9.081563
750	562500	421875000	27.386127	9.085603
751	564001	423564751	27.404379	9.089639
752	565504	425259008	27.422618	9.093672
753	567009	426957777	27.440845	9.097701
754	568516	428661064	27.459060	9.101726
755	570025	430368875	27.477263	9.105748
756	571536	432081216	27.495454	9.109766
757	573049	433798093	27.513633	9.113781
758	574564	435519512	27.531799	9.117793
759	576081	437245479	27.549954	9.121801
760	577600	438976000	27.568097	9.125805
761	579121	440711081	27.586228	9.129806
762	580644	442450728	27.604347	9.133803
763	582169	444194947	27.622454	9.137797
764	583696	445943744	27.640549	9.141788
765	585225	447697125	27.658633	9.145774
766	586756	449455096	27.676705	9.149757
767	588289	451217663	27.694764	9.153737
768	589824	452984832	27.712812	9.157713
769	591361	454756609	27.730849	9.161686
770	592900	456533000	27.748873	9.165656
771	594441	458314011	27.766886	9.169622
772	595984	460099648	27.784898	9.173585
773	597529	461889917	27.802877	9.177544
774	599076	463684824	27.820855	9.181500
775	600625	465484375	27.838821	9.185452
776	602176	467288576	27.856776	9.189401
777	603729	469097433	27.874719	9.193347
778	605284	470910952	27.892651	9.197289
779	606841	472729139	27.910571	9.201228
780	608400	474552000	27.928480	9.205164
781	609961	476379541	27.946377	9.209096
782	611524	478211768	27.964262	9.213025
783	613089	480048687	27.982137	9.216950

TABLE—(Continued).

Number.	Square.	Cube.	Square Root.	Cube Root.
784	614656	481890304	28.	9.220872
785	616225	483736025	28.017851	9.224791
786	617796	485587656	28.035691	9.228706
787	619369	487443403	28.053520	9.232618
788	620944	489303872	28.071337	9.237527
789	622521	491169069	28.089143	9.240433
790	624100	493039000	28.106938	9.244335
791	625681	494913671	28.124722	9.248234
792	627264	496793088	28.142494	9.252130
793	628849	498677257	28.160255	9.256022
794	630436	500566184	28.178005	9.259911
795	632025	502459875	28.195744	9.263797
796	633616	504358336	28.213472	9.267679
797	635209	506261573	28.231188	9.271559
798	636804	508169592	28.248893	9.275435
799	638401	510082399	28.266588	9.279308
800	640000	512000000	28.284271	9.283177
801	641601	513922401	28.301943	9.287044
802	643204	515849608	28.319604	9.290907
803	644809	517781627	28.337254	9.294767
804	646416	519718464	28.354893	9.298623
805	648025	521660125	28.372521	9.302477
806	649636	523606616	28.390139	9.306327
807	651249	525557943	28.407745	9.310175
808	652864	527514112	28.425340	9.314019
809	654481	529475129	28.442925	9.317859
810	656100	531441000	28.460498	9.321697
811	657721	533411731	28.478061	9.325532
812	659344	535387328	28.495613	9.329363
813	660969	537366797	28.513154	9.333191
814	662596	539353144	28.530685	9.337016
815	664225	541343375	28.548204	9.340838
816	665856	543338496	28.565713	9.344657
817	667489	545338513	28.583211	9.348473
818	669124	547343432	28.600699	9.352285
819	670761	549353259	28.618176	9.356095
820	672400	551368000	28.635642	9.359901
821	674041	553387661	28.653097	9.363704
822	675684	555412248	28.670542	9.367505
823	677329	557441767	28.687976	9.371302
824	678976	559476224	28.705400	9.375096
825	680625	561515625	28.722813	9.378887
826	682276	563559976	28.740215	9.372675
827	683929	565609283	28.757607	9.386460
828	685584	567663552	28.774989	9.390241
829	687241	569722789	28.792360	9.394020
830	688900	571787000	28.809720	9.397796
831	690561	573856191	28.827070	9.401569
832	692224	575930368	28.844410	9.405338
833	693889	578009537	28.861739	9.409105
834	695556	580093704	28.879058	9.412869
835	697225	582182875	28.896366	9.416630
836	698896	584277056	28.913664	9.420387
837	700569	586376253	28.930952	9.424141
838	702244	588480472	28.948229	9.427893
839	703921	590589719	28.965496	9.431642

K 2

TABLE—(Continued).

Number.	Square.	Cube.	Square Root.	Cube Root.
840	705600	592704000	28.982753	9.435388
841	707281	594823321	29.	9.439130
842	708964	596947688	29.017236	9.442870
843	710649	599077107	29.034462	9.446607
844	712336	601211584	29.051678	9.450341
845	714025	603351125	29.068883	9.454071
846	715716	605495736	29.086079	9.457799
847	717409	607645423	29.103264	9.461524
848	719104	609800192	29.120439	9.465247
849	720801	611960049	29.137604	9.468966
850	722500	614125000	29.154759	9.472682
851	724201	616295051	29.171904	9.476395
852	725904	618470208	29.189039	9.480106
853	727609	620650477	29.206163	9.483813
854	729316	622835864	29.223278	9.487518
855	731025	625026375	29.240383	9.491219
856	732736	627222016	29.257477	9.494918
857	734449	629422793	29.274562	9.498614
858	736164	631628712	29.291637	9.502307
859	737881	633839779	29.308701	9.505998
860	739600	636056000	29.325756	9.509685
861	741321	638277381	29.342801	9.513369
862	743044	640503928	29.359836	9.517051
863	744769	642735647	29.376861	9.520730
864	746496	644972544	29.393876	9.524406
865	748225	647214625	29.410882	9.528079
866	749956	649461896	29.427877	9.531749
867	751689	651714363	29.444863	9.535417
868	753424	653972032	29.461839	9.539081
869	755161	656234909	29.478805	9.542743
870	756900	658503000	29.495762	9.546402
871	758641	660776311	29.512709	9.550058
872	760384	663054848	29.529646	9.553712
873	762129	665338617	29.546573	9.557363
874	763876	667627624	29.563491	9.561010
875	765625	669921875	29.580398	9.564655
876	767376	672221376	29.597297	9.568297
877	769129	674526133	29.614185	9.571937
878	770884	676836152	29.631064	9.575574
879	772641	679151439	29.647932	9.579208
880	774400	681472000	29.664793	9.582839
881	776161	683797841	29.681644	9.586468
882	777924	686128968	29.698484	9.590093
883	779689	688465387	29.715315	9.593716
884	781456	690807104	29.732137	9.597337
885	783225	693154125	29.748949	9.600954
886	784996	695506456	29.765752	9.604569
887	786769	697864103	29.782545	9.608181
888	788544	700227072	29.799328	9.611791
889	790321	702595369	29.816103	9.615397
890	792100	704969000	29.832867	9.619001
891	793881	707347971	29.849623	9.622603
892	795664	709732288	29.866369	9.626201
893	797449	712121957	29.883105	9.629797
894	799236	714516984	29.899832	9.633390
895	801025	716917375	29.916550	9.636981

TABLE—(Continued).

Number.	Square.	Cube.	Square Root.	Cube Root.
896	802816	719323136	29.933259	9.640569
897	804609	721734273	29.949958	9.644154
898	806404	724150792	29.966648	9.647736
899	808201	726572699	29.983328	9.651316
900	810000	729000000	30.	9.654893
901	811804	731432701	30.016662	9.658468
902	813604	733870808	30.033314	9.662040
903	815409	736314327	30.049958	9.665609
904	817216	738763264	30.066592	9.669176
905	819025	741217625	30.083217	9.672740
906	820836	743677416	30.099833	9.676301
907	822649	746142643	30.116440	9.679860
908	824464	748613312	30.133038	9.683416
909	826281	751089429	30.149626	9.686970
910	828100	753571000	30.166206	9.690521
911	829921	756058031	30.182776	9.694069
912	831744	758550528	30.199337	9.697615
913	833569	761048497	30.215889	9.701158
914	835396	763551944	30.232432	9.704698
915	837225	766060875	30.248966	9.708236
916	839056	768575296	30.265491	9.711772
917	840889	771095213	30.282007	9.715305
918	842724	773620632	30.298514	9.718835
919	844561	776151559	30.315012	9.722363
920	846400	778688000	30.331501	9.725888
921	848241	781229961	30.347981	9.729410
922	850084	783777448	30.364452	9.732930
923	851929	786330467	30.380915	9.736448
924	853776	788889024	30.397368	9.739963
925	855625	791453125	30.413812	9.743475
926	857476	794022776	30.430248	9.746985
927	859329	796597983	30.446674	9.750493
928	861184	799178752	30.463092	9.753998
929	863041	801765089	30.479501	9.757500
930	864900	804357000	30.495901	9.761000
931	866761	806954491	30.512292	9.764497
932	868624	809557568	30.528675	9.767992
933	870489	812166237	30.545048	9.771484
934	872356	814780504	30.561413	9.774974
935	874225	817400375	30.577769	9.778461
936	876096	820025856	30.594117	9.782946
937	877969	822656953	30.610455	9.785428
938	879844	825293672	30.626785	9.788908
939	881721	827936019	30.643106	9.792386
940	883600	830584000	30.659419	9.795861
941	885481	833237621	30.675723	9.799333
942	887364	835896888	30.692018	9.802803
943	889249	838561807	30.708305	9.806271
944	891136	841232384	30.724583	9.809736
945	893025	843908625	30.740852	9.813198
946	894916	846590536	30.757113	9.816659
947	896809	849278123	30.773365	9.820117
948	898704	851971392	30.789608	9.823572
949	900601	854670349	30.805843	9.827025
950	902500	857375000	30.822070	9.830475
951	904401	860085351	30.838287	9.833923

Table—(Continued).

Number.	Square.	Cube.	Square Root.	Cube Root.
952	906304	862801408	30.854497	9.837369
953	908209	865523177	30.870698	9.840812
954	910116	868250664	30.886890	9.844253
955	912025	870983875	30.903074	9.847692
956	913936	873722816	30.919249	9.851128
957	915849	876467493	30.935416	9.854561
958	917764	879217912	30.951575	9.857992
959	919681	881974079	30.967725	9.861421
960	921600	884736000	30.983866	9.864848
961	923521	887503681	31.	9.868272
962	925444	890277128	31.016124	9.871694
963	927369	893056347	31.032241	9.875113
964	929296	895841344	31.048349	9.878530
965	931225	898632125	31.064449	9.881945
966	933156	901428696	31.080540	9.885357
967	935089	904231063	31.096623	9.888767
968	937024	907039232	31.112698	9.892174
969	938961	909853209	31.128764	9.895580
970	940900	912673000	31.144823	9.898983
971	942841	915498611	31.160872	9.902383
972	944784	918330048	31.176914	9.905781
973	946729	921167317	31.192947	9.909177
974	948676	924010424	31.208973	9.912571
975	950625	926859375	31.224990	9.915962
976	952576	929714176	31.240998	9.919351
977	954529	932574833	31.256999	9.922738
978	956484	935441352	31.272991	9.926122
979	958441	938313739	31.288975	9.929504
980	960400	941192000	31.304951	9.932883
981	962361	944076141	31.320919	9.936261
982	964324	946966168	31.336879	9.939636
983	966289	949862087	31.352830	9.943009
984	968256	952763904	31.368774	9.946379
985	970225	955671625	31.384709	9.949747
986	972196	958585256	31.400636	9.953113
987	974169	961504803	31.416556	9.956477
988	976144	964430272	31.432467	9.959839
989	978121	967361669	31.448370	9.963198
990	980100	970299000	61.464265	9.966554
991	982081	973242271	31.480152	9.969909
992	984064	976191488	31.496031	9.973262
993	986049	979146657	31.511902	9.976612
994	988036	982107784	31.527765	9.979959
995	990025	985074875	31.543620	9.983304
996	992016	988047936	31.559467	9.986648
997	994009	991026973	31.575306	9.989990
998	996004	994011992	31.591138	9.993328
999	998001	997002999	31.606961	9.996665
1000	1000000	1000000000	31.622776	10.

Additional use of this table can be made by the aid of the following Rules :

To find the Square of a Number above 1000 = when the Number is divisible by any Number without leaving a Remainder.

Rule.—If the number exceed by 2, 3, or any other number of times, any number contained in the table, let the square affixed to that number in the table be multiplied by the square of 2, 3, 4, 5, or 6, &c., and the product will be the answer.

EXAMPLE.—Required the square of 1550.

1550 is 10 times 155, and the square of 155 in the table is 24025.
Then $24025 \times 10^2 = 2402500$ *Ans.*

When the Number is an Odd Number.

RULE.—Find the two numbers nearest to each other, which, added together, make that sum; then the sum of the squares of these two numbers, as per table, multiplied by 2, will give the answer, exceeded by 1, which is to be subtracted, and the remainder is the answer required.

EXAMPLE.—What is the square of 1345 ?

The nearest two numbers are $\left\{ \begin{array}{c} 673 \\ 672 \end{array} \right\} = 1345.$

Then, per table, $\left\{ \begin{array}{l} 673^2 = 452929 \\ 672^2 = 451584 \end{array} \right.$
$$\overline{904513} \times 2 = 1809026 - 1 = 1809025 \ \textit{Ans.}$$

To find the Cube of a Number greater than is contained in the Table.

RULE.—Proceed as in squares to find how many times the number exceeds one of the tabular numbers. Multiply the cube of that number by the cube of the number of times the number sought exceeds the number in the table, and the product will be the answer.

EXAMPLE.—What is the cube of 1200 ?

1200 is 3 times 400, and the cube of 400 is 64000000.
Then $64000000 \times 3^3 = 1728000000 \ \textit{Ans.}$

To find the Squares of Numbers following each other in Arithmetical Progression.

RULE.—Find the squares of the two first numbers in the usual way, and subtract the less from the greater. Add the difference to the greatest square, with the addition of 2 as a constant quantity; the sum will be the square of the next number.

EXAMPLE.—What are the squares of 1001, 1002, 1003, 1004, and 1005 ?

$$1000^2 = 1000000$$
$$999^2 = 998001$$

$$\overline{1999}$$

Add . 2
Add $1000^2 = 1000000$

$$\overline{1002001} \ \text{Square of 1001.}$$
Difference, $2001 + 2 = 2003$

$$\overline{1004004} \ \text{Square of 1002.}$$
Difference, $2003 + 2 = 2005$

$$\overline{1006009} \ \text{Square of 1003.}$$
Difference, $2005 + 2 = 2007$

$$\overline{1008016} \ \text{Square of 1004.}$$
Difference, $2007 + 2 = 2009$

$$\overline{1010025} \ \text{Square of 1005.}$$

To find the Cubes of Numbers following each other in Arithmetical Progression.

RULE.—Find the cubes of the two first numbers, and subtract the less from the greater; then multiply the least of the two numbers cubed, by 6; add the product, with the addition of 6, to the difference, and continue this the first series of differences.

For the second series of differences, add the cube of the highest of the above numbers to the difference, and the sum will be the cube of the next number.

EXAMPLE.—What are the cubes of 1001, 1002, and 1003?

First Series.

Cube of 1000 = 1000000000
Cube of 999 = 997002999
  —————————
  2997001 Difference.
999×6+6 =   6000
  —————————
  3003001 Difference of 1000.
6000   +6 =   6006
  —————————
  3009007 Difference of 1001.
6006   +6 =   6012
  —————————
  3015019 Difference of 1002.

Second Series.

Cube of 1000   = 1000000000
Difference for 1000,   3003001
  —————————
  1003003001 = Cube of 1001.
Difference for 1001,   3009007
  —————————
  1006012008 = Cube of 1002.
Difference for 1002,   3015019
  —————————
  1009027027 = Cube of 1003.

To find the Cube or Square Root of a higher Number than is contained in the Table.

RULE.—Find in the column of Squares or Cubes the number nearest to that number whose root is required, and the number from which that square or cube is derived will be the answer when decimals are not of importance.

EXAMPLE.—What is the square root of 562500 ?
In the table of Squares, this number is the square of 750; therefore 750 is the square root required.

EXAMPLE.—What is the cube root of 2248090 ?
In the table of Cubes, 2248091 is the cube of 131; therefore 131— is the cube root required, nearly.

To find the Cube Root of any Number over 1000.

RULE.—Find by the table the nearest cube to the number given, and call it the assumed cube. Multiply the assumed cube and the given number respectively by 2; to the product of the assumed cube add the given number, and to the product of the given number add the assumed cube.

Then, as the sum of the assumed cube is to the sum of the given number, so is the root of the assumed cube to the root of the given number.

EXAMPLE.—What is the cube root of 224809 ?

By table, the nearest cube is 216000, and its root is 60.
$$216000\times2+224809 = 656809,$$
And $224809\times2+216000 = 665618.$
Then, as 656809 : 665618 : : 60 : 60.804+

To find the Sixth Root of a Number.

RULE.—Take the cube root of its square root.
EXAMPLE.—What is the $\sqrt[6]{}$ of 441 ?
$$\sqrt{441} = 21, \text{ and } \sqrt[3]{21} = 2.7589 \text{ } Ans.$$

TO FIND THE CUBE OR SQUARE ROOT OF A NUMBER CONSISTING OF INTEGERS AND DECIMALS.

RULE.—Multiply the difference between the root of the integer part and the root of the next higher integer by the decimal, and add the product to the root of the integer given ; the sum will be the root of the number required.

This is correct for the square root to three places of decimals, and in the cube root to seven.

EXAMPLE.—What is the square root of 53.75, and the cube root of 843.75 ?

√	54 =	7.3484		∛844	=	9.4503
√	.53 =	7.2801		∛843	=	9.4466
		.0683				.0037
		.75				.75
		.051225				.002775
√	53 = 7.2801			∛843	= 9.4466	
√53.75 =	7.331325			∛843.75 =	9.449375	

TABLE *of the Sides of Squares—equal in Area to a Circle of any Diameter, from* 1 *to* 100.

Diameter.	Side of equal Square.	Diameter.	Side of equal Square.	Diameter.	Side of equal Square.	Diameter.	Side of equal Square.
1.00	0.886	15.	13.293	29.	25.700	43.	38.107
.25	1.107	.25	13.514	.25	25.922	.25	38.329
.5	1.329	.5	13.736	.5	26.143	.5	38.550
.75	1.550	.75	13.958	.75	26.365	.75	38.772
2.	1.772	16.	14.179	30.	26.586	44.	38.993
.25	1.994	.25	14.401	.25	26.808	.25	39.215
.5	2.215	.5	14.622	.5	27.029	.5	39.437
.75	2.437	.75	14.844	.75	27.251	.75	39.658
3.	2.658	17.	15.065	31.	27.473	45.	39.880
.25	2.880	.25	15.287	.25	27.694	.25	40.101
.5	3.101	.5	15.508	.5	27.916	.5	40.323
.75	3.323	.75	15.730	.75	28.137	.75	40.544
4.	3.544	18.	15.952	32.	28.359	46.	40.766
.25	3.766	.25	16.173	.25	28.580	.25	40.987
.5	3.988	.5	16.395	.5	28.802	.5	41.209
.75	4.209	.75	16.616	.75	29.023	.75	41.431
5.	4.431	19.	16.838	33.	29.245	47.	41.652
.25	4.652	.25	17.059	.25	29.467	.25	41.874
.5	4.874	.5	17.281	.5	29.688	.5	42.095
.75	5.095	.75	17.502	.75	29.910	.75	42.317
6.	5.317	20.	17.724	34.	30.131	48.	42.538
.25	5.538	.25	17.946	.25	30.353	.25	42.760
.5	5.760	.5	18.167	.5	30.574	.5	42.982
.75	5.982	.75	18.389	.75	30.796	.75	43.203
7.	6.203	21.	18.610	35.	31.017	49.	43.425
.25	6.425	.25	18.832	.25	31.239	.25	43.646
.5	6.646	.5	19.053	.5	31.461	.5	43.868
.75	6.868	.75	19.275	.75	31.682	.75	44.089
8.	7.089	22.	19.496	36.	31.904	50.	44.311
.25	7.311	.25	19.718	.25	32.125	.25	44.532
.5	7.532	.5	19.940	.5	32.347	.5	44.754
.75	7.754	.75	20.161	.75	32.568	.75	44.976
9.	7.976	23.	20.383	37.	32.790	51.	45.197
.25	8.197	.25	20.604	.25	33.011	.25	45.419
.5	8.419	.5	20.826	.5	33.233	.5	45.640
.75	8.640	.75	21.047	.75	33.455	.75	45.862
10.	8.862	24.	21.269	38.	33.676	52.	46.083
.25	9.083	.25	21.491	.25	33.898	.25	46.305
.5	9.305	.5	21.712	.5	34.119	.5	46.526
.75	9.526	.75	21.934	.75	34.341	.75	46.748
11.	9.748	25.	22.155	39.	34.562	53.	46.970
.25	9.970	.25	22.377	.25	34.784	.25	47.191
.5	10.191	.5	22.598	.5	35.005	.5	47.413
.75	10.413	.75	22.820	.75	35.227	.75	47.634
12.	10.634	26.	23.041	40.	35.449	54.	47.856
.25	10.856	.25	23.263	.25	35.670	.25	48.077
.5	11.077	.5	23.485	.5	35.892	.5	48.299
.75	11.299	.75	23.706	.75	36.113	.75	48.520
13.	11.520	27.	23.928	41.	36.335	55.	48.742
.25	11.742	.25	24.149	.25	36.556	.25	48.964
.5	11.964	.5	24.371	.5	36.778	.5	49.185
.75	12.185	.75	24.592	.75	36.999	.75	49.407
14.	12.407	28.	24.814	42.	37.221	56.	49.628
.25	12.628	.25	25.035	.25	37.443	.25	49.850
.5	12.850	.5	25.257	.5	37.664	.5	50.071
.75	13.071	.75	25.479	.75	37.886	.75	50.293

TABLE—(Continued).

Diameter.	Side of equal Square.	Diameter.	Side of equal Square.	Diameter.	Side of equal Square.	Diameter.	Side of equal Square
57.	50.514	68.	60.263	79.	70.011	90.	79.760
.25	50.736	.25	60.484	.25	70.233	.25	79.981
.5	50.958	.5	60.706	.5	70.455	.5	80.203
.75	51.179	.75	60.928	.75	70.676	.75	80.425
58.	51.401	69.	61.149	80.	70.898	91.	80.646
.25	51.622	.25	61.371	.25	71.119	.25	80.868
.5	51.844	.5	61.592	.5	71.341	.5	81.089
.75	52.065	.75	61.814	.75	71.562	.75	81.311
59.	52.287	70.	62.035	81.	71.784	92.	81.532
.25	52.508	.25	62.257	.25	72.005	.25	81.754
.5	52.730	.5	62.478	.5	72.227	.5	81.975
.75	52.952	.75	62.700	.75	72.449	.75	82.197
60.	53.173	71.	62.922	82.	72.670	93.	82.419
.25	53.395	.25	63.143	.25	72.892	.25	82.640
.5	53.616	.5	63.365	.5	73.113	.5	82.862
.75	53.838	.75	63.586	.75	73.335	.75	83.083
61	54.059	72.	63.808	83.	73.556	94.	83.305
.25	54.281	.25	64.029	.25	73.778	.25	83.526
.5	54.502	.5	64.251	.5	73.999	.5	83.748
.75	54.724	.75	64.473	.75	74.221	.75	83.970
62.	54.946	73.	64.694	84.	74.443	95.	84.191
.25	55.167	.25	64.916	.25	74.664	.25	84.413
.5	55.389	.5	65.137	.5	74.886	.5	84.634
.75	55.610	.75	65.359	.75	75.107	.75	84.856
63.	55.832	74.	65.580	85.	75.329	96.	85.077
.25	56.053	.25	65.802	.25	75.550	.25	85.299
.5	56.275	.5	66.023	.5	75.772	.5	85.520
.75	56.496	.75	66.245	.75	75.993	.75	85.742
64.	56.718	75.	66.467	86.	76.215	97.	85.964
.25	56.940	.25	66.688	.25	76.437	.25	86.185
.5	57.161	.5	66.910	.5	76.658	.5	86.407
.75	57.383	.75	67.191	.75	76.880	.75	86.628
65.	57.604	76.	67.353	87.	77.101	98.	86.850
.25	57.826	.25	67.574	.25	77.323	.25	87.071
.5	58.047	.5	67.796	.5	77.544	.5	87.293
.75	58.269	.75	68.017	.75	77.766	.75	87.514
66.	58.490	77.	68.239	88.	77.987	99.	87.736
.25	58.712	.25	68.461	.25	78.209	.25	87.958
.5	58.934	.5	68.682	.5	78.431	.5	88.179
.75	59.155	.75	68.904	.75	78.652	.75	88.401
67.	59.377	78.	69.125	89.	78.874	100.	88.622
.25	59.598	.25	69.347	.25	79.095	.25	88.844
.5	59.820	.5	69.568	.5	79.317	.5	89.065
.75	60.041	.75	69.790	.75	79.538	.75	89.287

USE OF THIS TABLE.

To find a Square that shall have the same Area as a Given Circle.

EXAMPLE.—What is the side of a square that has the same area as a circle of 1¼ inches ?

By table of Areas, page 93, opposite to 73.25 is its area, 4214.1; and in the above table, page 121, is 64.916, the side of a square that has the same area as a circle of 1¼ inches in diameter.

EXAMPLE.—What should be the side of a square that would give the same area as a board that is 18 inches wide and 10 feet long ?

L

18 inches is   .   1.5   feet.
                               10
                             ――――――
                             15.0 feet.
                             14 4 square inches in a foot.
                             ――――――
                             60 0
                             600
                             150
                             ――――――
                             2160.0 inches area.

By table, page 120, 2164.75 inches area have a diameter of 52.5 inches, which in the above table gives an equal side of 46.526, which is the answer very nearly.

PLANE TRIGONOMETRY.

A B C the three angles (A the right angle) ; *a b c* the three sides respectively opposite to them ; R the tabular radius (1 or 1000000) ; S the area of the triangle, and half its perimeter $= \left(\frac{a+b+c}{2}\right)$.

RIGHT-ANGLED TRIANGLES.

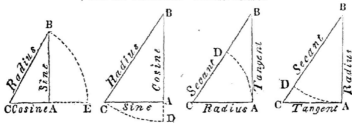

$a = \sqrt{b^2+c^2}$, $b = \sqrt{(a^2-c^2)}$, $c = \sqrt{(a^2-b^2)}$, $b = c \dfrac{\text{tang. B}}{\text{R}}$, also $= a \dfrac{\text{sin. B}}{\text{R}}$.

GIVEN. *To find* A C *and* B A.

Hyp. B C, { R : B C : : sin. B : A C,
and Angles. { R : B C : : sin. C : B A.

GIVEN. *To find* B A *and* B C.

A C, { R : A C : : tan. C : B A,
and Angles. { { R : A C : : sec. C : B C,
        { or sin. B . A C : : R : B C.

GIVEN. *To find Angles and* A C.

Hyp. B C, { B C : R : : B A : sin. C, whose comp. is B.
and leg B A. { R : B C : : sin. B : A C.

GIVEN. *To find Angles and* B C.

Both legs. { A C : R : : B A : tan. C, whose comp. is B.
      } { Sin. C : B A : : R : B C,
        { or R : A C : : sec. C : B C.

NOTE.—*By sin. or tan. B or C is meant the sine or tangent of the angle B or C.*

Let A B C be a right-angled triangle, in which A B is assumed to be radius ; B C is the tangent of A, and A C its ᵗcant to that radius ; or, dividing each of these by the base, ₂ shall have the tangent and secant of A respectively to ᴅius 1. Tracing the consequences of assuming B C and ᵗC each for radius, we obtain the following expressions :

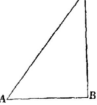

$\dfrac{\text{perp.}}{\text{base}} = \text{tan. angle A.}$ $\dfrac{\text{base}}{\text{perp.}} = \text{tan. angle C.}$

$\dfrac{\text{hyp.}}{\text{base}} = \text{sec. angle A.}$ $\dfrac{\text{hyp.}}{\text{perp.}} = \text{sec. angle C}$

$\dfrac{\text{perp.}}{\text{hyp.}} = \text{sin. angle A.}$ $\dfrac{\text{base}}{\text{hyp.}} = \text{sin. angle C.}$

OBLIQUE-ANGLED TRIANGLES.

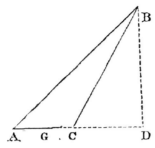 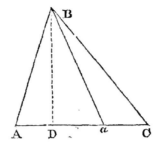

GIVEN, *the Angles and Side* A B, *to find* B C *and* A C.

Sin. C : A B : : sin. A : B C.
Sin. C : A B : : sin. B : A C.

GIVEN, *two Sides* A B, B C, *and the Angle* C, *to find Angle* A *and* B, *and Side* A C.

A B : sin. C : : B C : sin. A, which, added to C, and the sum subtracted from 180°, will give B.

Sin. C : A B : : sin. B : A C.

GIVEN, A C, A B, *and the included Angle* A, *to find Angles* C *and* B, *and Side* B C.

Subtract half the given angle A from 90°; the remainder is half the sum of the other angles. Then, as the sum of the sides A C, A B is to their difference, so is the tangent of the half sum of the other angles to the tangent of half their difference, which, added to and subtracted from the half sum, will give the two angles B and C, the greatest angle being opposite to the greatest side.

Sin. B : A C : : sin. A : B C.

GIVEN, *all three Sides, to find all the Angles.*

Let fall a perpendicular B D opposite to the required angle; then, as A C : sum of A B, B C : : their difference : twice D G, the distance of the perpendicular from the middle of the base; hence A D, C D are known, and the triangle A B C is divided into two right-angled triangles B C D, B A D; then, by the rules in right-angled triangles, find the angle A or C.

TABLE of *Natural Sines, Cosines, and Tangents.*

D. M.	Sine.	Cosine.	Tangent.	D. M.	Sine.	Cosine.	Tangent.
.15	00436	99999	00436	14.	24192	97030	24933
.30	00872	99996	00873	.15	24615	96923	25397
.45	01309	99991	01309	.30	25038	96815	25862
1.	01745	99985	01745	.45	25460	96705	26328
.15	02181	99976	02182	15.	25882	96593	26794
.30	02618	99966	02619	.15	26303	96479	27263
.45	03054	99953	03055	.30	26724	96363	27732
2.	03490	99939	03492	.45	27144	96246	28203
.15	03926	99923	03929	16.	27564	96126	28675
.30	04362	99905	04366	.15	27983	96005	29147
.45	04798	99885	04803	.30	28402	95882	29621
3.	05234	99863	05241	.45	28820	95757	30097
.15	05669	99839	05678	17.	29237	95630	30573
.30	06105	99813	06116	.15	29654	95502	31051
.45	06540	99786	06554	.30	30071	95372	31530
4.	06976	99756	06993	.45	30486	95240	32010
.15	07411	99725	07431	18.	30902	95106	32492
.30	07846	99692	07870	.15	31316	94970	32975
.45	08281	99657	08309	.30	31730	94832	33460
5.	08716	99619	08749	.45	32144	94693	33945
.15	09150	99580	09189	19.	32557	94552	34433
.30	09585	99540	09629	.15	32970	94409	34922
.45	10019	99497	10069	.30	33381	94264	35412
6.	10453	99452	10510	.45	33792	94118	35904
.15	10887	99406	10952	20.	34202	93969	36397
.80	11320	99357	11394	.15	34612	93819	36892
.45	11754	99307	11836	.30	35021	93667	37388
7.	12187	99255	12278	.45	35429	93514	37887
.15	12620	99200	12722	21.	35837	93358	38386
.30	13053	99144	13165	.15	36244	93201	38888
.45	13485	99087	13609	.30	36650	93042	39391
8.	13917	99027	14054	.45	37056	92881	39896
.15	14349	98965	14499	22.	37461	92718	40403
.30	14781	98902	14945	.15	37865	92554	40911
.45	15212	98836	15391	.30	38268	92388	41421
9.	15643	98769	15838	.45	38671	92230	41933
.15	16074	98700	16286	23.	39073	92050	42447
.30	16505	98629	16734	.15	39474	91879	42983
.45	16935	98556	17183	.30	39875	91706	43481
0.	17365	98481	17633	.45	40275	91531	44001
.15	17794	98404	18083	24.	40674	91355	44522
.30	18224	98325	18534	.15	41072	91176	45046
.45	18652	98245	18986	.30	41469	90996	45572
1.	19081	98163	19438	.45	41866	90814	46100
.15	19509	98079	19891	25.	42262	90631	46630
.30	19937	97992	20345	.15	42657	90446	47163
.45	20364	97905	20800	.30	43051	90259	47697
2.	20791	97815	21256	.45	43445	90070	48234
.15	21218	97723	21712	26.	43837	89879	48773
.30	21644	97630	22169	.15	44229	89687	49314
.45	22070	97534	22628	.30	44620	89493	49858
3.	22495	97437	23087	.45	45010	89298	50404
.15	22920	97338	23547	27.	45399	89101	50952
.30	23345	97237	24008	.15	45787	88902	51503
.45	23769	97134	24470	.30	46175	88701	52056
				.45	46561	88499	52612

TABLE—(Continued).

D. M.	Sine.	Cosine.	Tangent.	D M.	Sine.	Cosine.	Tangent.
28.	46947	88295	53170	37.	60182	79864	75355
.15	47332	88089	53731	.15	60529	79600	76041
.30	47716	87882	54295	.30	60876	79335	76732
.45	48099	87673	54861	.45	61222	79069	77428
29.	48481	87462	55430	38.	61566	78801	78128
.15	48862	87250	56002	.15	61909	78532	78833
.30	49242	87036	56577	.30	62251	78261	79543
.45	49622	86820	57154	.45	62592	77988	80258
30.	50000	86603	57735	39.	62932	77715	80978
.15	50377	86384	58318	.15	63271	77439	81703
.30	50754	86163	58904	.30	63608	77162	82433
.45	51129	85941	59493	.45	63944	76884	83169
31.	51504	85717	60086	40.	64279	76604	83910
.15	51877	85491	60681	.15	64612	76323	84656
.30	52250	85264	61280	.30	64945	76041	85408
.45	52621	85035	61881	.45	65276	75756	86165
32.	52992	84805	62486	41.	65606	75471	86928
.15	53361	84573	63095	.15	65935	75184	87697
.30	53730	84339	63707	.30	66262	74896	88472
.45	54097	84104	64392	.45	66588	74606	89253
33.	54464	83867	64940	42.	66913	74314	90040
.15	54829	83629	65562	.15	67237	74022	90833
.30	55194	83389	66188	.30	67559	73728	91633
.45	55557	83147	66817	.45	67880	73432	92439
34.	55919	82904	67450	43.	68200	73135	93251
.15	56280	82659	68087	.15	68518	72837	94070
.30	56641	82413	68728	.30	68835	72537	94896
.45	57000	82165	69372	.45	69151	72236	95729
35.	57358	81915	70020	44.	69466	71934	96568
.15	57715	81664	70673	.15	69779	71630	97415
.30	58070	81412	71329	.30	70091	71325	98269
.45	58425	81157	71989	.45	70401	71019	99131
36.	58779	80902	72654	45.	70710	70710	1.00000
.15	59131	80644	73323	.15	71019	70401	1.00876
.30	59482	80386	73996	.30	71325	70091	1.01760
.45	59832	80125	74673				

TANGENTS FROM 45° TO 90°.

D.	Tangent.	D.	Tangent.	D.	Tangent.	D.	Tangent.	D.	Tangent.
46	1.0355	55	1.4281	64	2.0503	73	3.2708	82	7.1153
47	1.0724	56	1.4826	65	2.1445	74	3.4874	83	8.1443
48	1.1106	57	1.5399	66	2.2460	75	3.7321	84	9.5144
49	1.1504	58	1.6003	67	2.3558	76	4.0107	85	11.4301
50	1.1918	59	1.6643	68	2.4751	77	4.3314	86	14.3007
51	1.2349	60	1.7321	69	2.6051	78	4.7046	87	19.0811
52	1.2799	61	1.8040	70	2.7475	79	5.1445	88	28.6363
53	1.3270	62	1.8807	71	2.9042	80	5.6712	89	57.2900
54	1.3764	63	1.9626	72	3.0776	81	6.3137	90	Infinite.

To find the Sine or Cosine of any Angle exceeding 45°, by the foregoing Table.

Subtract the angle given from 90, look in the table for the remainder, and opposite to it take out the sine for the cosine, and the cosine for the sine of the angle given.

EXAMPLE.—What is the sine and the cosine of 85°?

85°—90° = 5°, and opposite to 5° in the table is 08716 and 99619, which are respectively the cosine and sine of 85°.

The sine of 90° is 100000, cosine 0.

The sine of an arc, divided by the cosine, gives the natural tangent of that arc.

To compute Tangents and Secants.

Cos. : sin. : : rad. : tangent.
Cos. : rad. : : rad. : secant.
Sin. : cos. : : rad. : cotangent.
Sin. : rad. : : rad. : cosecant.

To find the Secant of an Angle.

Divide 1 by the cosine of that angle.

EXAMPLE.—The cosine of 21° 30′ is .93041;

$$\frac{1}{.93041} = 1.07479.$$

To find the Cosecant of an Angle.

Divide 1 by the sine of the angle.

EXAMPLE.—The sine of 21° 30′ is .36650;

$$\frac{1}{.36650} = 2.72951.$$

To find the Versed Sine.

Subtract the cosine from 1.

EXAMPLE.—The cosine of 21° 30′ is .93042;

$$1 - .93042 = .06958.$$

To find the Coversed Sine.

Subtract the sine of the angle from 1.

EXAMPLE.—The sine of 21° 30′ is .36650;

$$1 - .36650 = .6335.$$

To find the Chord of any Angle.

Take the sine of half the angle and double it.

EXAMPLE.—The chord of 21° 30′ is required.

$$\text{Sine of } \frac{21° \ 30′}{2} = .18652 \times 2 = .37304.$$

MECHANICAL POWERS.

Power is a compound of *weight*, or the expansion of a body, multiplied by its *velocity*: it cannot be increased by mechanical means.

The Science of Mechanics is based upon *Weight* and *Power*, or *Force* and *Resistance*.

The weight is the resistance to be overcome, the power is the requisite force to overcome that resistance. When they are equal no motion can take place.

The Powers are three *in number, viz.,* Lever, Inclined Plane, *and* Pulley.

Note.—The Wheel and Axle is a *continual* or *revolving* lever, the Wedge is a *double* inclined plane, and the Screw is a *revolving* inclined plane.

LEVER.

When the Fulcrum (or Support) of the Lever is between the Weight and the Power.

Rule.—Divide the weight to be raised by the power, and the quotient is the difference of leverage, or the distance from the fulcrum at which the power supports the weight.

Or, multiply the weight by its distance from the fulcrum, and the power by its distance from the same point, and the weight and power will be to each other as their products.

Example.—A weight of 1600 lbs. is to be raised by a force of 80 lbs. ; required the length of the longest arm of the lever, the shortest being 1 foot.

$$\frac{1600 \times 1}{80} = 20 \text{ feet}, \textit{Ans.}$$

Proof, by second rule.

$$1600 \times 1 = 1600.$$
$$80 \times 20 = 1600.$$

Example.—A weight of 2460 lbs. is to be raised with a lever 7 feet long and 300 lbs. ; at what part of the lever must the fulcrum be placed?

$\frac{2460}{300} = 8.2$; that is, the weight is to the power as 8.2 to 1 ; therefore the whole length $\frac{7 \times 12}{8.2 + 1} = \frac{84}{9.2} = 9.13$ inches, the distance of the fulcrum from the weight.

Example.—A weight of 400 lbs. is placed 15 inches from the fulcrum of a lever ; what force will raise it, the length of the other arm being 10 feet?

$$\frac{400 \times 15}{120} = 50 \text{ lbs.}, \textit{Ans.}$$

Note.—Pressure upon fulcrum equal the sum of weight and power.

When the Fulcrum is at one Extremity of the Lever, and the Power, or the Weight, at the other.

RULE.—As the distance between the power or weight and fulcrum is to the distance between the weight or power and fulcrum, so is the effect to the power.

EXAMPLE.—What power will raise 1500 lbs., the weight being 5 feet from it, and 2 feet from the fulcrum?

$$5+2 = 7 : 2 :: 1500 : 428.5714 + Ans.$$

EXAMPLE.—What is the weight on each support of a beam that is 30 feet long, supported at both ends, and bearing a weight of 6000 lbs. 10 feet from one end?

30 : 20 : : 6000 : 4000 lbs. at the end nearest the weight; and
30 : 10 : : 6000 : 2000 lbs. at the end farthest from the weight.

NOTE.—Pressure upon fulcrum is the difference of the weight and the power.

The GENERAL RULE, therefore, for ascertaining the relation of POWER to WEIGHT in a lever, whether it be straight or curved, is, the power multiplied by its distance from the fulcrum, is equal to the weight multiplied by its distance from the fulcrum.

Let P be called the power, W the weight, p the distance of P from the fulcrum, and w the distance of W from the fulcrum; then

$$P : W :: w : p, \text{ or } P \times p = W \times w;$$

and

$$\frac{W \times w}{p} = P. \qquad \frac{P \times p}{w} = W.$$

$$\frac{W \times w}{P} = p. \qquad \frac{P \times p}{W} = w.$$

If several weights or powers act upon one or both ends of the lever, the condition of equilibrium is

$$P \times p + P' \times p' + P'' \times p'', \&c., = W \times w + W' \times w', \&c.$$

In a system of levers, either of similar, compound, or mixed kinds, the condition is

$$\frac{P \times p \times p' \times p''}{w \times w' \times w''} = W.$$

Let P = 1 lb., p and p' each 10 feet, p'' 1 foot; and if w and w' be each 1 foot, and w'' 1 inch, then

$$\frac{1 \times 120 \times 120 \times 12}{12 \times 12 \times 1} = \frac{172800}{144} = 1200;$$ that is, 1 lb. will balance

1200 lbs. with levers of the lengths above given.

NOTE.—The weights of the levers in the above formulæ are not considered, the centre of gravity being assumed to be over the fulcrums.

If the arms of the lever be equally bent or curved, the distances from the fulcrum must be measured upon perpendiculars, drawn from the lines of direction of the weight and power, to a line running horizontally through the fulcrum; and if unequally curved, measure the distances from the fulcrum upon a line running horizontally through it till it meets perpendiculars falling from the ends of the lever.

WHEEL AND AXLE.

THE power multiplied by the radius of the wheel is equal to the weight multiplied by the radius of the axle.

As the radius of the wheel is to the radius of the axle, so is the effect to the power.

When a series of wheels and axles act upon each other, either by belts or teeth, the weight or velocity will be to the power or unity as the product of the radii, or circumferences of the wheels, to the product of the radii, or circumferences of the axles.

EXAMPLE.—If the radii of a series of wheels are 9, 6, 9, 10, and 12, and their pinions have each a radius of 6 inches, and the weight applied be 10 lbs., what weight will it raise?

$$\frac{10 \times 9 \times 6 \times 9 \times 10 \times 12}{6 \times 6 \times 6 \times 6 \times 6} = 75 \text{ lbs. weight.}$$

Or, if the 1st wheel make 10 revolutions, the last will make 75 in the same time.

NOTE.—For a fuller treatise on wheels, see *Grier's Mechanic's Calculator*, pages 130 to 136.

To find the Power of Cranes, &c.

RULE.—Divide the product of the driven teeth by the product of the drivers, and the quotient is the relative velocity, which, multiplied by the length of the winch and the force in lbs., and divided by the radius of the barrel, will give the weight that can be raised.

EXAMPLE.—A force of 18 lbs. is applied to the winch of a crane, the length being 8 inches; the pinion having 6, the wheel 72 teeth, and the barrel 6 inches diameter.

$$\frac{6}{72} = 12 \times 8 \times 18 = 1728 \div 3 = 576 \text{ lbs. weight.}$$

Let w represent length of winch,
r "   radius of barrel,
P   "   force applied,
v "   velocity,
W   "   weight raised.

$$\frac{rvP}{r} = W.$$

$$Wr = vwP.$$

$$\frac{Wr}{vw} = P.$$

EXAMPLE.—A weight of 94 tons is to be raised 360 feet in 15 minutes, by a force the velocity of which is 220 feet per minute; what is the power required?

$$\frac{360}{15} = 24 \text{ feet per minute.}$$

$$\frac{24 \times 94}{220} = 10.2542 \text{ tons.}$$

In a wheel and axle, where the axle has two diameters, the condition of equilibrium is

$$W : P :: R : \tfrac{1}{2}\left(r - r'\right);$$
$$\text{or, } P \times R = W \times \tfrac{1}{2}\left(r - r'\right);$$

that is, the weight is to the power as the lever by which the **power** works, is to half the difference of the radii of the axle;

R representing radius of wheel,
r "   radius of large axle,
r' "   radius of less axle.

INCLINED PLANE.

RULE.—As the length of the plane is to its height, so is the weight to the power.

EXAMPLE.—Required the power necessary to raise 1000 lbs. up an inclined plane 6 feet long and 4 feet high.

As 6 : 4 : : 1000 : 666.66 *Ans.*

Let W represent weight,
h "   height of plane,
l "   length of plane,
P   "   power,
b "   base of plane,
p' "   pressure on plane.

$$\frac{W \times h}{l} = P.$$

$$\frac{P \times l}{h} = W.$$

$$\frac{W \times b}{l} = p'.$$

To find the Length of the Base, Height, or Length of the Plane, when any two of them are given.

RULE. — *For the length of the base,* subtract the square of the height from the square of the length of the plane, and the square root of the remainder will be the length of the base.

For the length of the plane, add the squares of the two other dimensions together, and the square root of their sum will be the length required.

For the height, subtract the square of the base from the square of the length of the plane, and the square root of the remainder is the height required.

EXAMPLE.—The height of an inclined plane is 20 feet, and its length 100 ; what is its base, and the pressure of 1000 lbs. upon the plane?

$$\sqrt{20^2 - 100^2} = 9600 = 97.98 \text{ the base.}$$

As 100 : 20 : : 1000 : 200 lbs. necessary power to raise the 1000 lbs., and $\dfrac{1000 \times 97.98}{100} = 979.8$ the pressure upon the plane.

If two bodies on two inclined planes sustain each other by the aid of a cord over a pulley, their weights are directly as the lengths of the planes.

EXAMPLE.—If a body of 50 lbs. weight, upon an inclined plane, of 10 feet rise in 100, be sustained by another weight on an opposite plane, of 10 feet rise to 90 of an inclination, what is the weight of the latter ?

As 100 : 90 : : 50 : 45, the answer.

When a body is supported by two planes, and if the weight be represented by the sine of the angle between the two planes. The pressures upon them are reciprocally as the sines of the inclinations of those planes to the horizon, viz. :

The weight,
The pressure upon one plane,   } are as
The pressure upon the other plane,

{ Sine of the angle between the planes.
Sine of the angle of one plane.
Sine of the angle of the other plane.

Thus, if the angle between the planes was 90°, of one plane 60°, and the other 30°—since the natural sines of 90°, 60°, and 30° are 1, .866, and .500—if the body weighed 100 lbs., the pressure upon the plane of 30° would be 86.6 lbs., and upon the plane of 60°, 50 lbs. = the centre of gravity being in the centre of the body.

When the power does not act parallel to the plane, draw a line perpendicular to the direction of the power's action from the end of the base line (at the back of the plane), and the intersection of this line on the length will determine the length and height of the plane.

Note.—When the line of direction of the power is parallel to the plane, the power is least.

The space which a body describes upon an inclined plane, when descending on the plane by the force of gravity, is to the space it would freely fall in the same time, as the height is to the length of the plane; and the spaces being the same, the times will be inversely in this proportion.

Example.—If a body be placed upon an inclined plane 300 feet long and 25 feet high, what space will it roll down in one second by the force of gravity alone?

As 300 : 25 : : *16.08 : 1.33 feet, *Ans.*

If a body be *projected down an inclined plane* with a given velocity, then the distance which the body will be from the point of projection in a given time will be $t \times v + \frac{h}{l} \times 16.08 t^2$; but if the body be

---

* The distance a body will freely fall in one second by the force of gravity.

The force of an inclined plane bears the same proportion to the force of gravity as the height of the plane bears to its length; that is, the force which accelerates a body down an inclined plane is that fractional part of the force of gravity which is represented by the height of the plane divided by its length.

Let h represent the height of the plane, l its length, t the time in seconds, s the space which a body will move through in a given time, v the velocity, and i the angle of inclination $\left(\sin. i = \frac{h}{l} \right).$

$$s = \frac{16.08\, h t^2}{l}, \text{ or } \frac{tv}{2}, \text{ or } \frac{l v^2}{64.3 h}, \text{ or } \frac{v^2}{64.3 \sin. i}, \text{ or } \sin. i \times 16.08 t^2.$$

$$v = \frac{2s}{t}, \text{ or } \frac{32.16\, h t}{l}, \text{ or } \sqrt{\frac{64.3\, hs}{l}}, \text{ or } \sin. i \times 32.16 t, \text{ or } \sqrt{\sin. i \times 64.3 s}.$$

$$t = \frac{2s}{v}, \text{ or } \frac{l v}{32.16\, h}, \text{ or } \sqrt{\frac{l s}{16.08\, h}}, \text{ or } \frac{v}{32.16 \sin. i}, \text{ or } \sqrt{\frac{s}{16.08 \sin. i}}.$$

$$\frac{h}{l}, \text{ or } \sin. i = \frac{v}{32.16\, t}, \text{ or } \frac{s}{16.08\, t^2}, \text{ or } \frac{v^2}{64.3\, s}.$$

The accelerating force on the plane is to the accelerating force of gravity as v^2 is to 64.3 × s.

If $\sin. i = \frac{1}{2}$, it shows that the length of the plane is twice its height, or $\frac{1}{2} = 30°$.

If the proportion which the length of the plane bears to the height be given, substitute these proportions for the length and height in the above rules, and the conclusions will be equally true.

projected upward, then the distance of the body from the point of projection will be $t \times v - \dfrac{h}{l} \times 16.08 t^2$.

WEDGE.

When two Bodies are forced from one another, in a direction Parallel to the back of the Wedge.

RULE.—As the length of the wedge is to half its back, so is the resistance to the force.

EXAMPLE.—The length of the back of a double wedge is 6 inches, and the length of it through the middle 10 inches ; what is the power necessary to separate a substance having a resistance of 150 lbs. ?

As 10 : 3 : : 150 : 45 lbs., *Ans.*

When only one of the Bodies is Movable.

RULE.—As the length of the wedge is to its back, so is the resistance to the power.

EXAMPLE.—What power, applied to the back of a wedge, will raise a weight of 15,000 lbs., the wedge being 6 inches deep, and 100 long on its base.

As 100 : 6 : : 15000 : 900 lbs., *Ans.*

NOTE.—As the power of the wedge in practice depends upon the split or rift in the wood to be cleft, or in the body to be raised, the above rules are only theoretical where a rift exists.

SCREW.

As the screw is an inclined plane wound round a cylinder, the length of the plane is found by adding the square of the circumference of the screw to the square of the distance between the threads, and taking the square root of the sum, and the height is the distance between the consecutive threads.

RULE.—As the length of the inclined plane is to the pitch or height of it, so is the weight to the power.

When a wheel or capstan is applied to turn the screw, the length of the lever is the radius of the circle described by the handle of the wheel or capstan bar.

Let P represent power,
      R   "   length of lever,
      W   "   weight,
      l   "   length of the inclined plane,
      p   "   pitch of screw or height of plane,
      x   "   effect of power at circumference of screw,
      r   "   radius of screw.

M

Then, by the above rules,

$$
\begin{aligned}
\text{As } l &: p :: W : P, \\
l &: W :: p : P, \\
W &: l :: P : p, \\
p &: l :: P : W, \\
P &: W :: p : l, \\
r &: R :: P : x, \\
P &: x :: r : R, \\
R &: r :: x : P.
\end{aligned}
$$

EXAMPLE.—What is the power requisite to raise a weight of 8000 lbs. by a screw of 12 inches circumference and 1 inch pitch?

$$12^2 + 1^2 = 145, \text{ and } \sqrt{145} = 12.04159.$$

Then, $12.0416 :: 1 :: 8000 : 664.36$ lbs., *Ans.*

And if a lever of 30 inches length was added to the screw,

$$12 \div 3.1416 = 3.819 \div 2 + 30 = 31.9095, \text{ length of lever.}$$

Then, as $31.9095 : 1.9095 :: 664.363 : 39.756$ lbs., *Ans.*

Or, when the circumference described by the power is used (C), we have

$$
\begin{aligned}
P &: W :: p : C, \\
C &: p :: W : P, \\
P \times C &= W \times p;
\end{aligned}
$$

thus, $39.756 : 8000 :: 1 : 201.227 =$ circumference described by lever, which is the hypothenuse of the triangle formed by the base and height of the inclined plane.

When a hollow screw revolves upon one of less diameter and pitch (as designed by Mr. Hunter), the effect is the same as that of a single screw, in which the distance between the threads is equal to the difference of the distances between the threads of the two screws.

If one screw has 20 threads in an inch pitch, and the other 21, the power is to the weight as the difference between $\frac{1}{20}$ and $\frac{1}{21}$, or $\frac{1}{420}$ $= 1$ to 420.

In a complex machine, composed of the screw, and wheel, and axle, the relation between the weight and power is thus:

Let x represent the effect of the power on the wheel,
R   "   the radius of the wheel,
p "   the pitch of the screw,
r "   the radius of the axle,
C   "   the circumference described by the power.

Then, by the properties of the screw,

$$P \times C = x \times p;$$

and of the wheel and axle,

$$x \times R = W \times r.$$

Hence we have

$$P \times C \times x \times R = x \times p \times W \times r.$$

Omitting the common multiplier, x,

$$
\begin{aligned}
P \times C \times R &= W \times p \times r; \\
\text{or}\quad P : W &:: p \times r : C \times R, \\
\text{and } p \times r &: C \times R :: P : W.
\end{aligned}
$$

EXAMPLE.—What weight can be raised with a power of 10 lbs. applied to a crank 32 inches long, turning an endless screw of $3\frac{1}{2}$ inches diameter and one inch pitch, applied to a wheel and axle of 20 and 5 inches in diameter respectively?

Circumference of 64 = 201.

$$1 : 201 : : 10 : 2010.$$

Radii of wheel and axle, 10 and 2.5.

$$2.5 \quad : \quad 10 : : 2010 \quad : 8040 \text{ lbs., } Ans.,$$

or $2.5 \times 1 : 201 \times 10 : : 10 : 8040.$

And when a series of wheels and axles act upon each other, the weight will be to the power as the continued product of the radii of the wheels to the continued product of the radii of the axles;

thus, $W : P : : R^3 : r^3$;

or, $r^3 : R^3 : : P : W$,

there being three wheels and axles of the same proportion to each other.

EXAMPLE.—If an endless screw, with a pitch of half an inch, and a handle of 20 inches radius, be turned with a power of 150 lbs., and geared to a toothed wheel, the pinion of which turns another wheel, and the pinion of the second wheel turns a third wheel, to the pinion or barrel of which is hung a weight, it is required to know what weight can be sustained in that position, the diameter of the wheels being 18, and the pinions 2 inches?

$$p \times r^3 : \quad C \times R^3 : : P : W;$$

or $.5 \times 1^3 : 125.6 \times 9^3 : : : 150;$

which, when extended, gives

$$.5 : 91562.4 : : 150 : 27468720 \text{ lbs., } Ans.$$

PULLEY.

When only one Cord or Rope is used.

RULE.—Divide the weight to be raised by the number of parts of the rope engaged in supporting the lever or movable block.

EXAMPLE.—What power is required to raise 600 lbs. when the lower block contains six sheaves and the end of the rope is fastened to the upper block, and what power when fastened to the lower block?

$$\frac{600}{6 \times 2} = 50 \text{ lbs., 1st } Ans.$$

$$\frac{600}{6 \times 2 + 1} = 46.15 \text{ lbs., 2d } Ans.;$$

or $W = n \times P,$

n signifying the number of parts of the rope which sustain the lower block.

When more than one Rope is used.

In a *Spanish burton*, where there are two ropes, two moveable pulleys, and one fixed and one stationary pulley, with the ends of one rope fastened to the support and upper moveable pulley, and the ends of the other fastened to the lower block and the power, the weight is to the power as 5 to 1.

And in one where the ends of one rope are fastened to the support and the power, and the ends of the other to the lower and upper blocks, the weight is to the power as 4 to 1.

In a system of pulleys, with any number of ropes, the ends being fastened to the support,

$$W = 2^n \times P,$$

n expressing the number of ropes.

EXAMPLE.—What weight will a power of 1 lb. sustain in a system of 4 movable pulleys and 4 ropes?

$$1 \times 2 \times 2 \times 2 \times 2 = 16 \text{ lbs}, \; Ans.$$

When fixed pulleys are used in the place of hooks, to attach the ends of the rope to the support,

$$W = 3^n \times P.$$

EXAMPLE.—What weight will a power of 5 lbs. sustain with 4 moveable and 4 fixed pulleys, and 4 ropes?

$$5 \times 3 \times 3 \times 3 \times 3 = 405 \text{ lbs.}, \; Ans.$$

When the ends of the rope, or the fixed pulleys, are fastened to the weight,

$$W = (2^n - 1) \times P,$$
$$\text{and } W = (3^n - 1) \times P,$$

which would give, in the above examples,

$$1 \times 2 \times 2 \times 2 \times 2 = 16 - 1 = 15 \text{ lbs.},$$
$$5 \times 3 \times 3 \times 3 \times 3 = 405 - 1 = 404 \text{ lbs.}$$

CENTRES OF GRAVITY.

THE CENTRE OF GRAVITY of a body, or any system of bodies connected together, is the point about which, if suspended, all the parts are in equilibrio.

If the centres of gravities of two bodies B C be connected by a line, the distances of B and C from the common centre of gravity A will be as the weights of the bodies ;

thus, $B : C :: C A : A B$.

SURFACES.

1. *To find the Centre of Gravity of a Circular Arc.*

$$\frac{\text{Radius of circle} \times \text{chord of arc}}{\text{length of the arc}} = \text{distance from the centre of the}$$

circle.

2. *Of a Parallelogram, Rhombus, Rhomboid, Circle, Ellipse, Regular Polygon, or Lune.*

The geometrical centre of these figures is their centre of gravity.

3. *Of a Triangle.*

On a line drawn from any angle to the middle of the opposite side, at $\frac{2}{3}$ of the distance from the angle.

4. *Of a Trapezium.*

Draw the two diagonals, and find the centres of gravity of each of the four triangles thus formed ; join each opposite pair of these centres, and the intersection of the two lines will be the centre of gravity of the figure.

5. *Of a Trapezoid.*

On a line *a*, joining the middle points of the two parallel sides B *b*, the distance from $B = \frac{a}{3} \times \left(\frac{B+2b}{B+b}\right)$.

6. *Of a Sector of a Circle.*

$$\frac{2 \times \text{chord of arc} \times \text{radius of circle}}{3 \times \text{length of arc}} = \text{distance from the centre of}$$

the circle.

7. *Of a Semicircle.*

$$\frac{4 \times \text{radius of circle}}{3 \times 3.1416} = \text{distance from centre.}$$

8. *Of a Segment of a Circle.*

$$\frac{\text{Chord of the segment}^3}{12 \times \text{area of segment}} = \text{distance from the centre.}$$

9. *Of a Parabola.*

Distance from the vertex, $\frac{3}{5}$ of the abscissa.

M 2

10. *Of any Plane Figure.*

Divide it into triangles, and find the centre of gravity of each; connect two centres together, and find their common centre; then connect this and the centre of a third, and find the common centre of these, and so on, always connecting the last found common centre to another centre till the whole are included, and the last common centre will be that which is required.

11. *Of a Cylinder, Cone, Frustum of a Cone, Pyramid, Frustum of a Pyramid, or Ungula.*

The centre of gravity is at the same distance from the base as that of the parallelogram, triangle, or trapezoid, which is a right section of either of the above figures.

12. *Of a Sphere, Spherical Segment, or Zone.*

At the middle of their height.

SOLIDS.

1. *Of a Sphere, Cylinder, Cube, Regular Polygon, Spheroid, Ellipsoid, Cylindrical Ring, or any Spindle.*

The geometrical centre of these figures is their centre of gravity.

2. *Of a Right Ungula, Prism, or Wedge.*

At the middle of the line joining the centres of the two ends.

3. *Of a Prismoid, or Ungula.*

At the same distance from the base as that of the trapezoid or triangle, which is a right section of them.

4. *Of a Pyramid, or Cone.*

Distance from the base, $\frac{1}{4}$ of the line joining the vertex and centre of gravity of the base.

5. *Of a Frustum of a Cone, or Pyramid.*

Distance from the centre of the smaller end,

$$= \frac{1}{4} \text{ height} \times \frac{(R+r)^2 + 2R^2}{(R+r)^2 - Rr} \; ;$$

R and r radii of the greater and less ends in a cone, and the sides of a pyramid.

6. *Of a Paraboloid.*

Distance from the vertex, $\frac{2}{3}$ of the abscissa.

7. *Of a Frustum of a Paraboloid.*

Distance on the abscissa from the centre of the less end,

$$\tfrac{1}{3} h \frac{2R^2 + r^2}{R^2 + r^2}, \; h \text{ being the height.}$$

8. *Of a Spherical Segment.*

Distance from the centre,

$$\frac{3.1416 \, v^2 \left(\frac{r-v}{2}\right)^2}{s}, \; v \text{ being the versed sine, } s \text{ the solid contents of the}$$

segment, and r the radius of the sphere.

9. *Of a Spherical Sector.*

Distance from the centre, $\frac{3}{4}\left(r-\frac{v}{2}\right)$.

10. *Of any System of Bodies.*

Distance from a given plane,

$$=\frac{BD+B'D'+B''D''+,\ \&c.}{B+B'+B'',\ \&c.},$$ B being the solid contents or weights,

and D the distances of their respective centres of gravity from the given plane.

GRAVITATION.

In bodies descending freely by their own weight, the velocities are as the times, and the spaces as the square of the times.

The times, then, will be 1, 2, 3, 4, &c. ;

The velocities, then, will be 1, 2, 3, 4, &c. ;

The spaces passed through as 1, 4, 9, 16, &c. ;

And the spaces for each time as 1, 3, 5, 7, 9, &c.

A body falling freely will descend through 16.0833 feet in the first second of time, and will then have acquired a velocity which will carry it through 32.166 feet in the next second.

TABLE *exhibiting the Relation of Time, Space, and Velocities.*

Seconds from the beginning of the descent.	Velocity acquired at the end of that time.	Squares.	Space fallen through in that time.	Spaces.	Space fallen through in the last second of the fall.
1	32.166	1	16.08	1	16.08
2	64.333	4	64.33	·3	48.25
3	96.5	9	144.75	5	80.41
4	128.665	16	257.33	7	112.58
5	160.832	25	402.08	9	144.75
6	193.	36	579.	11	176.91
7	225.166	49	788.08	13	209.08
8	257.333	64	1029.33	15	241.25
9	289.5	81	1302.75	17	273.42
10	321.666	100	1608.33	19	305.58
11	353.832	121	1946.08	21	337.75
12	386.	144	2316. ·	23	369.92

and in the same manner the table might be continued to any extent.

To find the Velocity a Falling Body will acquire in any Given Time.

RULE.—Multiply the time in seconds by 32.166, and it will give the velocity acquired in feet per second.

EXAMPLE.—Required the velocity in 12 seconds.

$$12\times32.166=386\text{ feet, }Ans.$$

To find the Time which a Body will be in falling through a Given Space.

RULE.—Divide the space in feet by 16.083, and the square root of the quotient will give the required time in seconds.

EXAMPLE.—How long will a body be in falling through 402.08 feet of space?

$$\sqrt{402.08 \div 16.083} = 5, \ Ans.$$

To find the Space through which a Body will fall in any Given Time.

RULE.—Multiply the square of the time in seconds by 16.083, and it will give the space in feet.

EXAMPLE.—Required the space fallen through in 5 seconds.
$$5^2 = 25 \times 16.083 = 402.08 \text{ feet}, \ Ans.$$

To find the Velocity a Body will acquire by falling from any Given Height.

RULE.—Multiply the space in feet by 64.333, and the square root of the product will be the velocity acquired in feet per second.

EXAMPLE.—Required the velocity a ball has acquired in descending through 579 feet.
$$\sqrt{579 \times 64.333} = 193 \text{ feet}, \ Ans.$$

OR, *when the time is given,* multiply the time in seconds by 32.166. Thus, the time for 579 feet is 6 seconds; then, $6 \times 32.166 = 192.996$, *Ans.*

To find the Space fallen through, the Velocity being given.

RULE.—Divide the velocity by 8, and the square of the quotient will be the distance fallen through to acquire that velocity.

EXAMPLE.—If the velocity of a common ball is 579 feet per second, from what height must a body fall to acquire the same velocity?
$$579 \div 8 = 72.375^2 = 5237 \text{ feet}, \ Ans.$$

To find the Time, the Velocity per Second being given.

RULE.—Divide the given velocity by 8, and $\frac{1}{4}$ of the quotient is the answer.

EXAMPLE.—How long must a bullet be falling to acquire a velocity of 800 feet per second?
$$800 \div 8 = 100 \div 4 = 25 \text{ seconds}, \ Ans.$$

Let *s* represent the space described by any falling body, *t* the time, and *v* the velocity acquired in feet.

$$\text{Then } s = 16.08 \, t^2, \text{ or } \frac{tv}{2}, \text{ or } \frac{v^2}{64.3}.$$

$$t = \sqrt{\frac{s}{16.08}}, \text{ or } \frac{v}{32.16}, \text{ or } \frac{2s}{v}.$$

$$v = 2\sqrt{16.08 \, s}, \text{ or } 32.16 \, t, \text{ or } \frac{2s}{t}.$$

The distance fallen through in feet is very nearly equal to the square of the time in fourths of a second.

EXAMPLE.—A bullet being dropped from the spire of a church, was 4 seconds in reaching the ground; what was the height?

$$4 \times 4 \times 16 = 256 \text{ feet, } Ans.$$

EXAMPLE.—What is the depth of a well, a bullet being 2 seconds in reaching the bottom?

$$2 \times 4 \times 8 = 64 \text{ feet, } Ans.$$

Or, more correctly, as in case 2,

$$4 \times 4 \times 16.0833 = 257.33 \text{ feet,}$$
$$\text{and } 2 \times 2 \times 16.0833 = 64.33 \text{ feet.}$$

By Inversion.

In what time will a bullet fall through 256 feet?

$$\sqrt{256} = 16, \text{ and } 16 \div 4 = 4 \text{ seconds, } Ans.$$

Ascending bodies are retarded in the same ratio that descending bodies are accelerated.

To find the Space moved through by a Body projected upward or downward with a Given Velocity.

If projected downward.

RULE.—Multiply the square of the time in seconds by 16.083, the velocity of the projection in feet by the number of seconds the body is in motion, and the sum of these products is the answer.

If projected upward.

Then the difference of the above products will give the distance of the body from the point of projection.

Or, $t \times v \pm 16.083 \times t^2$.

EXAMPLE.—If a shot discharged from a gun return to the earth in 12 seconds, how high did it ascend?

The shot is half the time in ascending.

$$12 \div 2 = 6, \text{ and } 6^2 \times 16.08^3 = 579 \text{ feet, } Ans.$$

Or, $6^2 \times 16.083 - \overline{192.96 \times 6}$.

EXAMPLE.—If a body be projected upward with a velocity of 30 feet per second, through what space will it ascend before it begins to return?

$$30^2 \div 64.3 = 13.9 \text{ feet, } Ans.$$

EXAMPLE.—If a body be projected upward with a velocity of 100 feet per second, it is required to find the place of the body at the end of 10 seconds.

$100 \times 10 = 1000$, the space if gravity did not act, and $16.083 \times 10^2 = 1608.3$, the loss arising from gravity.

Hence $1000 - 1608.3 = 608.3$ feet below the point of projection.

To find the Velocity of a Falling Stream of Water per Second (the perpendicular distance being given) at the End of any Given Time.

NOTE.—If two bodies begin to descend from rest, and from the same point, the one on an inclined plane, and the other falling freely, their velocities at all equal heights below the surface will be equal.

The space through which a body will descend on an inclined plane is to the space through which it would fall freely in the same time as the height of the plane to its length.

If a body descend in a curve, it suffers no loss of velocity.

EXAMPLE.—One end of a sluice is 30 inches lower than the other, what is the velocity of the stream per second?

By case 4, 30 inches $= 2.5$ feet, $\times 64.33 = 160.82$, and $\sqrt{160.82} = 12.65$ feet, *Ans.*

What is the distance a stream of water will descend on an inclined plane 10 feet high, and 100 feet long at the base, in 5 seconds?

$5^2 \times 16.083 = 402.08$, and $100 : 10 :: 402.08 : 40.20$ feet, *Ans.*

The momentum with which a falling body strikes is equal to its weight multiplied by its velocity.

If a weight of 4500 lbs. fall through 10 feet, with what force does it strike?

$$\sqrt{10 \times 64.33} = 25.35 \times 4500 = 114075 \text{ lbs., } Ans.$$

If a stream of salt water, running at the rate of 5 feet per second, strike a dam 15 by 4 feet, what is the pressure of the stream?

RULE.—Multiply the height of the fall by the weight of the fluid, and the product by the area of the resisting body, and that product, again, by the velocity in feet per second.

By case 5, $5 \div 8 = .625^2 = .390625$, the height of the fall of the water, $\times 64$ lbs., the weight per cubic foot, $= 25$ lbs. $\times (15 \times 4)60 = 1500 \times 5 = 7500$ pounds, *Ans.*

NOTE.—Water being a yielding substance, an allowance for loss of power should be made.

PROMISCUOUS EXAMPLES.

1. Suppose a bullet to be 1 minute in falling, how far will it fall in the last second?

Space fallen through equal the square of the time; then 1 minute $= 60$ seconds.

$60^2 \times 16.083 = 57898$ distance for 60 seconds,
$59^2 \times 16.083 = \underline{55984}$ "   " 59   "
$ 1914$ "   "   1   " *Ans.*

2. Find the time of generating a velocity of 193 feet per second, and the whole space descended.

$193 \div 32.166 = 6$ seconds, $\Big\}$ *Ans.*
$6^2 \times 16.083 = 579$ feet,

The velocity acquired at any period is equal to twice the mean velocity during that period.

3. Then, if a ball fall through 2316 feet in 12 seconds, with what velocity will it strike?

$2316 \div 12 = 193 \times 2 = 386$ feet, *Ans.*

GRAVITIES OF BODIES.

The gravity of a body, or its weight above the earth's surface, decreases as the square of its distance from the earth's centre in semi-diameters of the earth.

Example.—If a body weigh 900 lbs. at the surface of the earth, what will it weigh 2000 miles above the surface?
The earth's semi-diameter is 3993 miles (say 4000).
Then $2000+4000=6000$ or $1\frac{1}{2}$ semi-diameters,
and $900\div1.5^2=400$ lbs., *Ans.*

Inversely, if a body weigh 400 lbs. at 2000 miles from the earth's surface, what will it weigh at the surface?
$$400\times1.5^2=900 \text{ lbs.}, Ans.$$

Example.—A body at the earth's surface weighs 360 lbs.; how high must it be elevated to weigh 40 lbs.?
$\sqrt{360\div40}=3$, or 3 semi-diameters from the earth's surface, *Ans.*

Example.—At what height must a body be raised to lose half its weight?
$$\sqrt{4000^2\times2}=5656-4000=1656 \text{ miles}, Ans.$$

If the diameters of two globes be equal and their densities different, the weight of a body on their surfaces will be as their densities.

If their densities be equal and their diameters different, the weight of them will be as their diameters.

If the diameters and densities are both different, the weight will be as their products.

Example.—If a body weigh 10 lbs. at the surface of the earth, what will it weigh at the surface of the sun? their densities being 392 and 100, and their diameters 8000 and 883000 miles.
$$883000\times100\times10\div8000\times392=281.5 \text{ lbs.}, Ans.$$

SPECIFIC GRAVITIES.

The specific gravity of a body is the proportion it bears to the weight of another body of known density, and water is well adapted for the standard; and as a cubic foot of it weighs 1000 ounces avoirdupois, its weight is taken as the unit, viz., 1000.

To find the Specific Gravity of a Body heavier than Water.

Rule.—Weigh it both in and out of water, and take the difference; then, as the weight lost in water is to the whole weight, so is 1000 to the specific gravity of the body.

Example.—What is the specific gravity of a stone which weighs 15 lbs., but in water only 10 lbs.?
$$15-10=5. \quad 5:15::1000:3000, Ans.$$

When the Body is lighter than Water.

Rule.—Annex to it a piece of metal or stone, weigh the piece added and the compound mass separately, both in and out of water, find how much each loses in water by subtracting its weight in water from its weight in air, and subtract the less of these differences from the greater ; then,

As the last remainder is to the weight of the light body in air, so is 1000 to the specific gravity of the body.

Example.—What is the specific gravity of a piece of wood that weighs 20 lbs. in air ; annexed to it is a piece of metal that weighs 24 lbs. in air and 21 lbs. in water, and the two pieces in water weigh 8 lbs. ?

$$20+24-8=36$$
$$24-21\quad = 3$$
$$\overline{33} : 20 : : 1000 : 606, \textit{Ans}.$$

Of a Fluid.

Rule.—Take a body of known specific gravity, weigh it in and out of the fluid ; then, as the weight of the body is to the loss of weight, so is the specific gravity of the body to that of the fluid.

Example.—What is the specific gravity of a fluid in which a piece of copper (s. g.=9000) weighs 70 lbs. in, and 80 lbs. out of it ?

$$80 : 80-70 : : 9000 : 1125, \textit{Ans}.$$

To find the Quantities of two Ingredients in a Compound, or to discover Adulteration in Metals.

Rule.—Take the differences of each specific gravity of the ingredients and the specific gravity of the compound, then multiply the gravity of the one by the difference of the other ; and, as the sum of the products is to the respective products, so is the specific gravity of the body to the weights of the ingredients.

Example.—A body compounded of gold (s. g.=18.888) and silver (s. g.=10.535) has a specific gravity of 14 ; what is the weight of each quantity of metal ?

$$18.888-14=4.888\times10.535=51.595 \text{ silver,}$$
$$14.-10.535=3.465\times18.888=65.447 \text{ gold,}$$
$$65.447+51.495 : 65.447 : : 14 : 7.835 \text{ gold,} \quad \Big\}$$
$$65.447+51.495 : 51.495 : : 14 : 6.165 \text{ silver,} \Big\} \textit{Ans}.$$

Proof of Spirituous Liquors.

A cubic inch of *proof spirits* weighs 234 grains ; then, if an inch cube of any heavy body weigh 234 grains less in spirits than air, it shows that the spirit in which it was weighed is *proof*.

If it lose less of its weight, the spirit is above proof ; and if it lose more, it is below proof.

The magnitude of a body in cubic feet multiplied by its specific gravity, in the following table, gives its weight in avoirdupois ounces.

SOLIDS.

Divide the Specific Gravity by 16, and the quotient is the weight of a Cubic Foot in pounds.	Specific Gravity	Weight of a Cubic In.	Divide the Specific Gravity by 16, and the quotient is the weight of a Cubic Foot in pounds.	Specific Gravity	Weight of a Cubic In.
METALS.		*Lbs.*	Walnut	.671	*Lbs.* .024
Antimony	6.712	.244	Willow	.585	.021
Arsenic	5.763	.208	Yew, Dutch	.788	.028
Bismuth	9.823	.355	Spanish	.807	.029
Brass, common	7.820	.282			
Bronze, gun metal	8.700	.315	*Well-seasoned Am., 1839.*		
Copper, cast	8.788	.317	Ash	.722	.026
wire-drawn	8.878	.320	Beech	.624	.023
Gold, pure, cast	19.258	.697	Cherry	.606	.022
hammered	19.361	.700	Cypress	.441	.016
22 carats fine	17.486	.633	Hickory, red	.838	.030
20 carats fine	15.709	.568	Mahogany, St. Domingo	.720	.026
Iron, cast	7.207	.260	White Oak, upland	.687	.025
bars	7.788	.281	James River	.759	.027
Lead, cast	11.352	.410	Pine, yellow	.541	.020
Mercury, 32°	13.598	.492	white	.473	.017
60°	13.580	.491	Poplar	.587	.021
Platinum, rolled	22.069	.798			
hammered	20.337	.736	**STONES AND EARTHS.**		
Silver, pure, cast	10.474	.379	Alabaster, white	2.730	.099
hammered	10.511	.381	yellow	2.699	.098
Steel, soft	7.833	.283	Amber	1.078	.039
tempered and hardened	7.818	.283	Asbestos, starry	3.073	.111
Tin, Cornish	7.291	.263	Borax	1.714	.062
Zinc, cast	6.861	.248	Brick	1.900	.069
			Chalk	2.784	.100
WOODS (Dry).			Charcoal	.441	.016
Apple	.793	.029	triturated	1.380	.050
Alder	.800	.029	Clay	1.930	.070
Ash	.845	.031	common soil	1.984	.071
Beech	.852	.031	Coral, red	2.700	.098
Box, Dutch	.912	.033	Coal, bituminous	1.270	.046
French	1.328	.048	Newcastle	1.270	.046
Brazilian	1.031	.037	Scotch	1.300	.047
Campeachy	.913	.033	Maryland	1.355	.049
Cherry	.715	.026	Anthracite {	1.436	.052
Cocoa	1.040	.037		1.640	.059
Cork	.240	.009	Diamond	3.521	.127
Cypress	.644	.023	Earth, loose	1.500	.054
Ebony, American	1.331	.048	Emery	4.000	.144
Elder	.695	.025	Flint, black	2.582	.094
Elm	.671	.024	white	2.594	.094
Fir, yellow	.657	.023	Glass, flint	2.933	.099
white	.569	.021	white	2.892	.098
Hacmetac	.592	.021	bottle	2.732	.099
Lignum vitæ	1.333	.048	green	2.642	.096
Live Oak	1.120	.040	Granite, Scotch	2.625	.095
Logwood	.913	.033	Susquehanna	2.704	.098
Mahogany	1.063	.038	Quincy	2.652	.097
Maple	.750	.027	Patapsco	2.640	.096
Mulberry	.897	.032	Grindstone	2.143	.077
Oak, English	.932	.033	Gypsum, opaque	2.168	.077
heart, 60 years	1.170	.043	Hone, white, razor	2.876	.104
Orange	.705	.025	Ivory	1.822	.066
Pine, yellow	.660	.024	Limestone, green	3.180	.115
white	.554	.020	white	3.156	.114
Poplar	.383	.014	Lime, quick	.804	.029
white	.529	.019	Manganese	7.000	.252
Pear	.661	.024	Marble, African	2.708	.098
Plum	.785	.029	Egyptian	2.668	.097
Quince	.705	.025	Parian	2.838	.103
Sassafras	.482	.017			

* Ordnance Manual, 1841.

N

TABLE—(Continued).

Divide the Specific Gravity by 16, and the quotient is the weight of a Cubic Foot in pounds.	Specific Gravity	Weight of a Cubic In.	Divide the Specific Gravity by 16, and the quotient is the weight of a Cubic Foot in pounds.	Specific Gravity	Weight of a Cubic In.
STONES AND EARTHS.		*Lbs.*	**MISCELLANEOUS.**		*Lbs.*
Marble, common	2.686	.097	Asphaltum	.905 / 1.650	.033 / .058
French	2.649	.096	Beeswax	.965	.035
white Italian	2.708	.098	Butter	.942	.034
Mica	2.800	.100	Camphor	.988	.362
Millstone	2.484	.090	India rubber	.933	.033
Nitre	1.900	.069	Fat of Beef	.923	.033
Porcelain, China	2.385	.086	Hogs	.936	.034
Pearl, Oriental	2.650	.097	Mutton	.923	.033
Phosphorus	1.770	.065	Gamboge	1.222	.044
Pumice Stone	.915	.033	Gunpowder, loose	.900	.032
Paving Stone	2.416	.088	shaken	1.000	.036
Porphyry, red	2.765	.099	solid	1.550 / 1.800	.056 / .065
Rotten Stone	1.981	.071	Gum Arabic	1.452	.051
Salt, common	2.130	.077	Indigo	1.009	.037
Saltpetre	2.090	.076	Lard	.947	.034
Sand	1.800	.065	Mastic	1.074	.038
Shale	2.600	.095	Spermaceti	.943	.034
Slate	2.672	.097	Sugar	1.606	.058
Stone, Bristol	2.510	.091	Tallow	.941	.034
common	2.520	.091	Atmospheric air	.0012	
Sulphur, native	2.033	.075			
Talc, black	2.900	.105			

LIQUIDS.

	Specific Gravity		Specific Gravity
Acid, Acetic	1.062	Oil, Olive	.915
Nitric	1.217	Essential, turpentine	.870
Sulphuric	1.841	Whale	.923
Muriatic	1.200	Proof Spirit	.925
Alcohol, pure	.792	Vinegar	1.060
of commerce	.835	Water, distilled	1.000
Ether, sulphuric	.715	sea	1.026
Honey	1.450	Dead Sea	1.240
Human blood	1.054	Wine	.992
Milk	1.032	Port	.997
Oil, Linseed	.940	Champagne	.997

ELASTIC FLUIDS.

	Specific Gravity		Specific Gravity
1 cubic foot of atmospheric air weighs 527.04 troy grains. Its assumed gravity of 1 is the unit for elastic fluids.	1.000	Hydrogen	.070
		Oxygen	1.104
		Sulphuretted hydrogen	1.777
Ammoniacal gas	.597	*Steam, 212°	.490
Azote	.976	Nitrogen	.972
Carbonic acid	1.524	Vapour of Alcohol	1.613
Carburetted hydrogen	.555	" of Turpentine spirits	5.013
Chlorine	2.470	" of Water	.623
Chloro-carbonic	3.389	Smoke of bituminous Coal	.102
		" of Wood	.90

* Weight of a cubic foot, 253.3 grains.

APPLICATION OF THE ABOVE.

When the Weight of a Body is required.

RULE.—Find the contents of the body in cubic feet or inches, and multiply it by the factor in the table.

EXAMPLE.—What is the weight of a cube of Italian marble, the sides being 3 feet?

$$3^3 \times 2708 = 73116 \text{ oz.} \div 16 = 4569.7 \text{ lbs.}, \textit{Ans.}$$

Or, of a 2 inch sphere of cast iron, $2^3 \times .5236 \times .260$ weight of a cubic inch $=1.089$ lbs., *Ans.*

Comparative Weight of Timber in a Green and Seasoned State.

Timber.	Weight of a Cubic Foot.	
	Green.	Seasoned.
	lbs. oz.	lbs. oz.
English Oak	71.10	43. 8
Cedar	32.	28. 4
Riga Fir	48.12	35. 8
American Fir	44.12	30.11
Elm	66. 8	37. 5
Beech	60.	53. 6
Ash	58. 3	50.

NOTE.—The average weight of the timber materials in a vessel of war (English) is about 50 lbs. to the cubic foot, and for masts and yards about 40 lbs.—*Edye's N. C.*

Given the Diameter of a Balloon to find what Weight it will raise.

RULE.—As 1 cubic foot is to the specific difference between atmospheric air, and the gas used to inflate the balloon, so is the capacity of the balloon to the weight it will raise.

EXAMPLE.—The diameter of a balloon is 26.6 feet, and the gas used to inflate it is hydrogen; what weight will it raise?

Sp. gr. of air. Grains. Sp. gr. of hydr. Grains.
1.000 : 527.04 : : .070 : 36.89 wt. of 1 cubic foot of hydrogen.

Then $1 : 527.04 - 36.89 : : 26.6^3 \times .5236 : 4830293.$ grains, $\div 7000$ (grains in a lb.), $=690.04$ lbs., *Ans.*

Given the Weight to be raised to find the Diameter of a Balloon.

By inversion of the preceding rule. The weight to be raised is 690.04 lbs.; what is the diameter?

$490.15 = (527.04 - 36.89) : 1 : : 690.04 \times 7000 : 9854.725$ cubic feet, $\div .5236$, the cube root of the quotient, is 26.6 feet, *Ans.*

STRENGTH OF MATERIALS.

COHESION.

The power of cohesion is that force by which the fibres or particles of a body resist separation, and it is therefore proportional to the number of fibres in the body, or to the area of its section.

TABLE OF THE COHESIVE FORCE OF METALS, &c.

Weight or Force necessary to tear asunder 1 Square Inch, in Avoirdupois pounds.

METALS.

Copper, cast	22500	Lead, cast		880
wire	61200	milled		3320
Gold, cast	20000	Platinum, wire		53000
wire	30800	Silver, cast		40000
Iron, cast	18000	Steel, soft		120000
	50000	razor		150000
wire	103000	Tin, cast block		5000
best bar	75000	Zinc, cast		2600
medium bar	60000	sheet		16000
inferior bar	30000			

COMPOSITIONS.

Gold 5, Copper 1	50000	Silver 5, Copper 1		48000
Brass	45000	" 4, Tin 1		41000
Copper 10, Tin 1	32000	Tin 10, Antimony 1		11000
" 8, " 1	36000	" 10, Zinc 1		12914
" 4, " 1	35000	" 10, Lead 1		6800

WOODS.

Ash	16000	Mahogany, Spanish		12000
Beech	11500	Maple		10500
Box	20000	Oak, American white		11500
Cedar	11400	English		10000
Chestnut, sweet	10500	seasoned		13600
Cypress	6000	Pine, pitch		12000
Deal, Christiana	12400	Norway		13000
Elm	13400	Poplar		7000
Fir, strongest	12000	Quince		6000
American	8800	Sycamore		13000
Lance wood	23000	Teak, Java		14000
Lignum vitæ	11800	Walnut		7890
Locust	20500	Willow		13000
Mahogany	21000			

MISCELLANEOUS SUBSTANCES.

Brick	290	Mortar, 20 years		52
Glass plate	9400	Slate		12000
Hemp fibres glued together	92000	Stone, fine grain		200
Ivory	16000	Whalebone		7600
Marble	9000			

To find the Strength of Direct Cohesion.

RULE.—Multiply area of transverse section in inches by the weight given in the preceding tables, and the product is the strength in lbs.

EXAMPLE.—In a square bar of ordinary wrought iron, of 2 inches, what is the resistance?

$$2 \times 2 \times 60000 = 240000 \text{ lbs.}, \textit{Ans.}$$

Also, in a rod of cast steel $\frac{1}{2}$ inch diameter, area of $\frac{1}{2} = .1963 \times 120000 = 23556$ lbs., *Ans.*

The *absolute strength* of materials, pulled lengthwise, is in proportion to the squares of their diameters.

The Lateral or Transverse Strength

Of any beam, or bar of wood, &c., is in proportion to its breadth, multiplied by its depth squared, and in like-sided beams as the cube of the side of a section. Or, one end being fixed, and the other projecting, is inversely as the distance of the weight from the section acted upon, and the strain upon any section is directly as the distance of the weight from that section.

The strength of a projecting beam is only one fourth of what it would be if supported at both ends, and the weight applied in the middle.

The strength of a projecting beam is only one sixth of one of the same length, fixed at both ends, and the weight applied in the middle.

The strength of a beam to support a weight in the centre of it, when the ends rest merely upon two supports, compared to one, the ends being fixed, is as 2 to 3.

TABLES OF THE TRANSVERSE STRENGTH OF TIMBER.

AMERICAN.

One Foot in Length, and 1 Inch Square, Weight suspended from one end.

	Materials.	Breaking weight in lbs.	Greatest deflexion in inches.	Weight borne with safety.	Value for general use.
Seasoned.	White Oak . . .	240	9.	196	72
	Sweet Chestnut . .	170	1.8	115	35
	Yellow Pine . . .	150	1.7	100	30
	White Pine . . .	135	1.4	95	32
	Ash	175	2.4	105	25
	Hickory	270	.8.	200	75

One Foot in Length, and 2 Inches Square.

	Breaking weight in lbs.	Greatest deflexion	Weight borne with safety	Value for general use
White Pine	1087	1.5	800	32

CYLINDER. *One Foot in Length.*

	Breaking weight in lbs.	Weight borne with safety.	Value for general use.
White Pine, 2 inches diameter . .	610	460	20
White Pine, 1 inch diameter . . .	75	56	

TABLES OF THE TRANSVERSE STRENGTH OF CAST AND WROUGHT IRON.

AMERICAN.

Weight suspended from one end.

CYLINDER.   *One Foot in Length, and 3 Inches Diameter.*

Average of 18 experiments with Gun Metal.	Breaking weight in lbs.	Weight borne with safety.	Value for general use.
*Cast Iron, cold blast	12000	10000	350

SQUARE BAR.   *One Foot in Length by 2 Inches.*

Gun Metal.	Breaking weight in lbs.	Weight borne with safety.	Value for general use.
Cast Iron, cold blast	5781	5000	500

The values above given are for iron of more than ordinary strength; if an inferior article is to be used, a corresponding deduction should be made.

SQUARE BAR.   *One Foot in Length by 1 Inch.*

Wrought Iron.	Weight borne with perfect safety	Deflexion from a horizontal plane without rupture.	Weight that gave a permanent bend.	Deflexion in inches with last weight.	Value for general use.
†Wrought Iron . .	1520	53°	600	1	300

MISCELLANEOUS.

Cast Iron.—Square bar, side 2 inches, length 12 inches, supported at both ends, broke with 22728 lbs. applied in the middle.

Cylinder 3 inches diameter, length 8½ inches, broke with 17110 lbs. applied at one end.

White Pine.—Cylinder ⅞ ins. diameter, length 12 inches, broke with 68 lbs. applied at the end.

Yellow Pine.—1 inch square, and 15 inches in length, broke with 125 lbs. applied at the end.

Hickory and White Oak.—1 inch square, and 12 inches in length, required 82 lbs. to deflect them ½ an inch, the weight suspended from the end.

The above and preceding experiments were made by the author in December, 1840.

---

* From the West Point Foundry Association at Cold Spring, Putnam county, N. Y. Specific gravity. 7210.
† From the Ulster Iron Company, Saugerties, N. Y. A fine specimen of machinery iron.
This specimen broke with the greatest weight here given, when filed through the top to the depth of a ¼ of an inch, and the fracture showed but very little fibre.

Mean Result of several Experiments by English Authors on Cast Iron.

Square bar, 1 inch by 32, resting upon two supports, broke with 840 lbs. suspended in the middle.

Square bar, of 1 inch, projecting 32 inches from a wall, broke with 278 lbs. applied; and one, 2 inches deep by $\frac{1}{2}$ an inch, required 543 lbs. to break it.

Square bar, 1 inch by 32, the ends fixed in walls, required 1,170 lbs. suspended from the middle to break it.

TO FIND THE TRANSVERSE STRENGTH.

When a Rectangular Bar or Beam is Fixed at one End, and Loaded at the other.

RULE.—Multiply the *Value* in the preceding table by the breadth, and square of the depth, in inches, and divide the product by the length in feet; the quotient is the weight in pounds.

NOTE.—When the beam is loaded uniformly throughout its length, the result must be doubled.

EXAMPLE.—What are the weights a cast and a wrought iron bar, projecting 30 inches in length, by 2 inches square, will bear?

$$2 \times 2^2 \times 500 \div 2.5 = 1600 \text{ lbs., } Ans.$$
$$2 \times 2^2 \times 300 \div 2.5 = 960 \text{ lbs., } Ans.$$

OR, *if the Dimensions of a Beam be required, to support a Given Weight at its End.*

RULE.—$\dfrac{\text{Weight} \times \text{length}}{\text{value in table}}$ = product of breadth, and square of the depth.

EXAMPLE.—What is the depth of a wrought iron beam, 2 inches square, necessary to support 960 lbs. suspended at 30 inches from the fixed end?

$$\frac{960 \times 2.5}{300} = 8, \text{ and } 8 \div 2 = 4, \text{ and } \sqrt{4} = 2, \, Ans.$$

When the Bar or Beam is Fixed at both Ends, and Loaded in the Middle.

RULE.—Multiply the *Value* in the preceding table by six times the breadth, and the square of the depth, in inches, and divide by the length in feet.

NOTE.—When the weight is laid uniformly along its length, the result must be tripled.

EXAMPLE.—What weight will a bar of cast iron, 2 inches square and 5 feet in length, support in the middle, when fixed at the ends?

$$500 \times \overline{6 \times 2} \times 2^2 \div 5 = 4800 \text{ lbs., } Ans.$$

When the Bar or Beam is Supported at both Ends, and Loaded in the Middle.

RULE.—Multiply the *Value* in the preceding table by the square of the depth, and four times the breadth, in inches, and divide the product by the length in feet.

NOTE.—When the weight is laid uniformly along its length, the result must be doubled.

EXAMPLE.—What are the weights a cast and a wrought iron bar, 60 inches between the supports, and 2 inches square, will bear?

$$500 \times 2^2 \times \overline{2 \times 4} \div 5 = 3200 \text{ lbs., } Ans.$$
$$300 \times 2^2 \times \overline{2 \times 4} \div 5 = 1920 \text{ lbs., } Ans.$$

OR, *if the Dimensions be required to Support a Given Weight.*

RULE.—$\dfrac{\text{Weight} \times \text{length}}{\text{value in table}} = $ product of four times the breadth, and square of the depth.

EXAMPLE.—What is the side of a square cast iron beam 2 feet in length, between supports, that will support 8000 lbs. in the centre?

$$\frac{8000 \times 2}{500} \div \overline{4 \times 1} = 8, \text{ and } \sqrt{8} = 2.828, Ans.$$

When the Breadth or Depth is required.

Divide the product obtained by the preceding rules by the square of the depth, and you have the breadth; or by the breadth, and the square root of the quotient is the depth.

EXAMPLE.—If 128 is the product, and the depth 8, $128 \div 8^2 = 2$, the breadth;

And $\sqrt{(128 \div 2)} = 8$, the depth.

When the Weight is not in the Middle between the Supports

$\dfrac{\text{Distance from nearest end} \times \text{weight}}{\text{whole length}} = $ pressure upon support farthest from the weight.

$\dfrac{\text{Distance from farthest end} \times \text{weight}}{\text{whole length}} = $ pressure upon support nearest the weight.

When a Beam, supported at both Ends, bears two Weights at unequal Distances from the Ends.

Let D = distance of greatest weight from nearest end,
d = distance of least weight from nearest end,
W = greatest weight, w = least weight,
L = whole length, l = length from least weight to farthest end,
l' = distance of greatest weight from farthest end.

Then $\dfrac{D \times W}{L} + \dfrac{l \times w}{L} =$ pressure at w end;

and $\dfrac{d \times w}{L} + \dfrac{l' \times W}{L} =$ pressure at W end.

In cylindrical beams or bars, the lateral strength is as the cube of the diameter.

The strength of a hollow cylinder is to that of a solid cylinder, of the same length and quantity of matter, as the greater diameter of the former is to the diameter of the latter; and the strength of hollow cylinders of the same length, weight, and material, is as their greatest diameters.

To find the Diameter of a Solid Cylinder, Fixed at both Ends, to support a Given Weight in the Middle.

Rule.—Multiply the length between the supports in feet by the weight in pounds; divide by the *value*, and the cube root of one sixth of the quotient is the diameter in inches.

Example.—What should be the diameter for a cylinder 2 feet in length between the supports, to bear 20000 lbs.?

$$\sqrt[3]{\dfrac{20000 \times 2 \div 350}{6}} = 2.67+, \; Ans.$$

To find the Diameter of a Solid Cylinder, to support a Given Weight in the Middle, between the Supports.

Rule.—Multiply the weight in pounds by the length in feet; divide by the *Value*, and the cube root of ¼ the quotient is the diameter in inches.

Example.—What is the diameter of a cast iron cylinder, 8 inches long between the supports, that will support 60000 lbs. suspended in the middle?

$$\sqrt[3]{\dfrac{60000 \times .66 \div 350}{4}} = 3.03, \; Ans.$$

To find the Diameter of a Solid Cylinder when Fixed at one End, the Load applied at the other.

Rule.—Multiply the length of the projection in feet by the weight to be supported in pounds; divide by the given *Value*, and the cube root of the quotient is the diameter.

Example.—What should be the diameter of a cast iron cylinder 8 inches long, to support 15000 lbs.?

8 inches is .66 feet, $\sqrt[3]{(15000 \times .66 \div 350)} = 3+$ inches, *Ans.*

Example.—What should be the diameter for 270000 lbs., at 12 inches from the end?

$$\sqrt[3]{(270000 \times 1 \div 350)} = 9.17, \; Ans.$$

To find the Diameter of a Beam or Solid Cylinder when the Load is uniformly distributed over its Length.

Rule.—Proceed as if the load was suspended at the end or in the middle until the *quotient* is obtained ; then,

If for a cylinder with one end fixed, the cube root of half this quotient is the diameter ;

If the ends rest upon two supports, the cube root of half this quotient is the diameter ;

And if the ends are fixed, the cube root of one third of this quotient is the diameter.

The *Constant Divisor* of 350 is for iron of great strength ; where an inferior article is to be used, it may be decreased to 250.

Thus, 350 represents a weight of 9450 lbs. upon the end of a cylinder 3 inches in diameter and 1 foot in length, and 250 under the same circumstances is equal to a weight of 6750 lbs.

500 represents a weight of 4000 lbs. upon the end of a bar 2 inches square and 1 foot in length, and 400 upon the same bar is equal to a weight of 3200 lbs.

The strength of an equilateral triangle, an edge up, compared to a square of the same area, is as 45 to 28.

To ascertain the Relative Value of Materials to resist a Transverse Strain.

Let V represent this value in a beam, bar, or cylinder one foot in length and one inch square, side or in diameter.

1. *Fixed at one end.* Weight suspended from the other.

$$V = \frac{lW}{bd^2}.$$

2. *Fixed at both ends.* Weight suspended from the middle.

$$V = \frac{lW}{6bd^2}.$$

3. *Supported at both ends.* Weight suspended from the middle.

$$V = \frac{lW}{4bd^2}.$$

4. *Supported at both ends.* Weight suspended at any other point than the middle.

$$V = \frac{mnW}{lbd^2}.$$

5. *Fixed at both ends.* Weight suspended at any other point than the middle.

$$V = \frac{2mnW}{3lbd^2} :$$

W representing the weight, l the length, b the breadth, d the depth, m the distance from one end, and n the distance from the other.

From which the value of any of the dimensions may be found, by the following formulæ :

1. $\dfrac{Vbd^2}{l} = W$. $\dfrac{Vbd^2}{W} = l$. $\dfrac{lW}{Vd^2} = b$. $\sqrt{\dfrac{lW}{bV}} = d$.

In square beams, &c., b and $d = \sqrt[3]{\dfrac{lW}{V}}$.

2. $\dfrac{6bd^2V}{l} = W$. $\dfrac{6bd^2V}{W} = l$. $\dfrac{lW}{6d^2V} = b$. $\sqrt{\dfrac{lW}{6bV}} = d$.

In square beams, &c., b and $d = \sqrt[3]{\dfrac{lW}{6V}}$.

3. $\dfrac{4bd^2V}{l} = W$. $\dfrac{4bd^2V}{W} = l$. $\dfrac{lW}{4d^2V} = b$. $\sqrt{\dfrac{lW}{4bV}} = d$.

In square beams, &c., b and $d = \sqrt[3]{\dfrac{lW}{4V}}$

4. $\dfrac{lbd^2V}{mn} = W$. $\dfrac{mnW}{bd^2V} = l$. $\dfrac{mnW}{ld^2V} = b$. $\sqrt{\dfrac{mnW}{lbV}} = d$.

In square beams, &c., b and $d = \sqrt[3]{\dfrac{mnW}{lV}}$.

5. $\dfrac{3lbd^2V}{2mn} = W$. $\dfrac{2mnW}{3bd^2V} = l$. $\dfrac{2mnW}{3ld^2V} = b$. $\sqrt{\dfrac{2mnW}{3lbV}} = d$.

In square beams, &c., b and $d = \sqrt[3]{\dfrac{2mnW}{3lV}}$.

When the weight is uniformly distributed, the same formulæ will apply, W representing only half the required or given weight.

Mean Results of various Experiments by English Authors.

WOODS.

Fixed at one end.	Length in inches.	Breadth in inches.	Depth in inches.	Breaking weight in lbs
Riga Fir (dry) . . .	60	2	2	153
Riga Fir (wet) . . .	60	2	2	162
Yellow Pine (American) .	60	2	2	176
White Pine (Canadian) .	60	2	2	112

SOLID AND HOLLOW CYLINDERS.

Supported at each end.	Length in inches.	Diameter external in ins	Diameter internal in inches.	Deflexion in inches.	Breaking weight in lbs.
Fir . .	48	2	.	2.	740
Ash . .	46	2	.5	3.	664
Ash . .	46	2	1.	3.6	630

CAST IRON *of various Figures, having equal Sectional Areas.*

Description of bar.	Distance between supports in inches.	Breaking weight in lbs.
Area of 1 square inch.		
Square	36	897
" through the diagonal .	32	851
2 inches deep by $\frac{1}{2}$ inch . .	32	2185
3 inches deep by $\frac{1}{3}$ inch . . .	32	3588
4 inches deep by $\frac{1}{4}$ inch . .	32	3979
Equilateral Triangles.		
Angle up	32	1437
Angle down	32	840

OAK, IN SEASONING, loses at least $\frac{1}{3}$ of its original weight, and this process is facilitated by steaming or boiling.

It loses more by the former process than the latter.

By steaming, the specific gravity of a piece of
oak was reduced from . . . . 1050 to 744
By boiling, from . . . . . 1084 to 788
By exposure to the air, from . . . . 1080 to 928

Weight in air of a cubic foot of	Butt. Ounces.	Top. Ounces.
White Pine, before seasoning . . .	658	432
" " when seasoned . . .	549	416
Pitch Pine, before seasoning . . .	628	597
" " when seasoned . . .	540	529
Spruce Spar, before seasoning . . .	587	580
" " when seasoned . . .	541	554

Stiffness of Oak to Cast Iron is as . . . . 1 to 13
Strength of Oak to Cast Iron is as . . . . 1 to 4.5

Mean Specific Gravity of Yellow Pine . 558
" " " of Pitch Pine . . 777

DEFLEXION OF RECTANGULAR BEAMS.

1. The deflexions of the same beam, resting on props at each end, and loaded in the middle with weights, are as those weights.

2. The deflexion is inversely as the cube of the depth; also, the depth being the same, the deflexion is inversely as the breadth.

3. The deflexion is directly as the cube of the length.

Let l represent the length of a beam, b its breadth, d its depth, and W the weight with which it is loaded; then the deflexion will vary as $\dfrac{l^3 W}{bd^3}$; and if the deflexion is represented by e, then,

When the Beam is Fixed at one End, and Loaded at the other,

$$\frac{l^3 W}{bd^3 e} = C, \text{ a constant quantity.}$$

When uniformly loaded . $\dfrac{3 l^3 W}{8 bd^3 e} = C.$

When Supported at both Ends, and Loaded in the Middle,

$$\frac{l^3 W}{32 \, bd^3 e} = C.$$

When uniformly loaded $\quad \frac{5}{8} \times \frac{l^3 W}{32 \, bd^3} = C.$

Hence it follows, that, to preserve the same stiffness in beams, the depth must be increased in the same proportion as the length, the breadth remaining constant.

The deflexion of different beams arising from their own weight, having their several dimensions proportional, will be as the square of either of their like linear dimensions.

Of three equal and similar beams, one inclined upward, one inclined downward at the same angle, and the other horizontal, it has been determined that that which had its angle upward was the weakest, the one which declined was the strongest, and the one horizontal was a mean between the two.

Barlow furnishes the following as some of the results obtained by him upon the deflexion of beams:

	Length.	Depth.	Breadth.	Lbs.	Deflexion in ins.
Fir .	6 feet	2 inches	1½ inches	180	1.
Fir .	3 "	2 "	1½ "	120	.10
Fir .	6 "	1¼ "	2 "	180	2.

WROUGHT IRON.

Supported at each end. The average of a number of experiments gave, for bars 33 inches in length, 1.9 inches broad, and 2 inches deep, a deflexion for every half ton of .024 inches.

CAST IRON.

Supported at both ends. Bars 33 inches in length, 1.3 inches in breadth, and 0.65 inches deep, deflected 0.27 inches with 162 lbs. applied.

Fir battens. Supported at each end, 15 inches in length, and 1 inch square, broke with a weight of 440 lbs. ; 30 inches in length, and 1 inch square, broke with 240 lbs.

Oak battens. Supported at each end, 2 feet long, 1½ inches deep, and ¾ inch in breadth, deflected 1.1 ins., and supported 408 lbs.

Ash battens. Fixed at one end, 2 feet long, 2 inches deep, and 1 inch in breadth, deflected 6 inches with a weight of 434 lbs.

Fir battens. Fixed at one end, same dimensions as last piece, deflected 3.9 ins. with 276 lbs.

Note 1.—When a weight is uniformly distributed over the length of a beam, the deflexion will be three eighths of the deflexion from the same weight applied at the extremity.

2. If the beam be a cylinder, the deflexion is 1.7 times that of a square beam, other things being equal.

3. If the load is uniformly distributed over the length, the deflexion will be five eighths of the deflexion from the same load collected in the middle.

COHESION.

In page 148, the results given in the table are those of ultimate resistance ; in practice, ¼ of the weight there given will be sufficient

STRENGTH OF THE JOURNALS OF SHAFTS.

When the Weight is in the Middle of the Shaft.

Apply the rule under the head of Strength of Materials, and the result is the diameter of the journals in inches.

EXAMPLE.—What should be the diameter of the journals of a shaft 10½ feet long to support a wheel of 10,000 lbs. in the centre?

Ans. 4.21 ins.

TO RESIST TORSION.

Water Wheels, &c.

RULE.—Multiply pressure on the crank pin, or at the pitch line of the pinion, by the length of the crank or radius of wheel in feet; divide their product by 125, and the cube root of the quotient is the diameter of the journal in inches if of wrought iron. If cast iron is to be used, add $\frac{1}{10}$.

EXAMPLE.—What should be the diameter for the journal of a water-wheel shaft, the pressure on the crank pin being 594,000 lbs., and the crank 5 feet in length?

$$\sqrt[3]{\frac{59400 \times 5}{125}} = 13.5 \text{ inches, } Ans.$$

EXAMPLE.—The pressure on a crank pin is 123.680 lbs., and the length of crank 5 feet.

$$\sqrt[3]{\frac{123680 \times 5}{125}} = 17+, \ Ans.$$

When two Shafts are used, as in Steam Vessels with one Engine.

RULE.—$\sqrt[3]{\left(\dfrac{\text{diameter for one shaft}^3 \times 3}{4}\right)} = $ diameter in inches.

EXAMPLE.—The area of the journal of a single shaft is 113 inches; what should be the diameter if two shafts are used?
Diameter for area of 113 = 12 inches.

$$\sqrt[3]{\frac{12^3 \times 3}{4}} = 10.9, \ Ans.$$

The examples above given are instances in successful practice; where the diameter has been less, fracture has almost universally taken place, the strain being increased beyond the ordinary limit.

Results of Experiments on Torsional Strain.

Square bars, with a Journal 1 inch in diameter and ¼ inch in length.

Wrought Iron (Ulster Iron Co.), twisted with 326 lbs., and broke with 570 lbs. applied at the end of a lever 30 inches in length.

Wrought Iron (Swedes), same length of lever, twisted with 367 lbs., and broke with 615 lbs.

Cast Iron (Foundry), journal 1 inch long, same length of lever, broke with 436 lbs.

The diameters for second and third movers are found by multiplying the diameters ascertained by the above rules by .8 and .793 respectively.

Grier, in his Mechanics' Calculator, gives the following rule for cast iron shafts :

$$\sqrt[3]{\left(\frac{240 \times \text{number horses' power}}{\text{number revolutions per minute}}\right)} = \text{diameter in inches.}$$

For wrought iron, multiply result by .963, for oak by 2.238, and for pine by 2.06.

GUDGEONS AND SHAFTS.

To find the Dimensions of a Gudgeon.

$$0.30 \sqrt[3]{(wl)} = d,$$

w representing the stress in 100 lbs., l the length in inches, and d the diameter in inches.

If a Cylindrical Shaft has no other lateral stress to sustain than its own weight, and is Fixed at one End,

$$d = .000024 l^2.$$

Let the stress supposed to be in the middle be n times the weight of the shaft ; then,

When supported at both Ends,
If the weight of the shaft be not taken into account,

$$d = \sqrt[3]{.00012\, nl^2}.$$

If the weight of the shaft is taken into account,

$$d = \sqrt[3]{.00012\,(n+1)l^2}.$$

When a Hollow Shaft is supported at each End,

$$d = \sqrt[3]{\frac{.00048\, wl}{4} + D^3},$$ w representing the stress in lbs., l the length in inches, D the interior diameter, and d the diameter in inches.

When a Hollow Shaft is Fixed at each End, and Loaded in the Middle,

$$d = \sqrt[3]{\frac{.00048\, wl}{6} + D^3}.$$

For hollow Cylindrical Shafts, supported at one End,

$$d = \sqrt[3]{.00048\, wl + D^3}.$$

If the hollow shaft support the weights at distances m and n from each end, and is supported at each end,

$$d = \sqrt[3]{.00048\frac{mn}{l}w + D^3}.$$

The last four formulas do not take into account the weight of the shaft.

The above is for *Cast Iron.*

For Cylindrical Shafts of Cast Iron to resist Torsion,   (Buchanan.)
Let P be the number of horses' power, and R the revolutions of the shaft in a minute ; then

$$\sqrt[3]{\frac{240\, P}{R}} = d.$$

For *Wrought Iron,* multiply this result by .963 ; for *Oak,* by 2.238 ; for *Pine,* by 2.06.

If a shaft has to sustain both lateral stress and torsion, then,
For cast iron,

$$\sqrt[3]{\left(\frac{240\, P}{R} + \frac{wl^2}{2}\right)} = d.$$

TEETH OF WHEELS.

To Construct a Tooth.

DIVIDE the pitch into 10 parts. Let 3.5 of these parts be below the pitch line, and 3.0 of them above.

The thickness should be 4.7 of the pitch

The length should be 6.5 of the pitch.

The Diameter of a wheel is measured from the pitch line.

The wood used for teeth is about ¼ the strength of cast iron, therefore they should be twice the depth to be of equal strength.

To find the Diameter of a Wheel, the Pitch and Number of Teeth being given.

$$\frac{\text{Pitch} \times \text{number of teeth}}{3.1416} = \text{diameter.}$$

NOTE.—The pitch, as found by this rule, is the arc of a circle; the true pitch required is a straight line, and must be measured from the centres of two contiguous teeth.

To find the Pitch, the Diameter and Number of Teeth being given.

$$\frac{\text{Diameter} \times 3.1416}{\text{number of teeth}} = \text{pitch.}$$

To find the Radius.

$$\frac{\text{Pitch} \times \text{number of teeth}}{3.1416} \div 2 = \text{radius.}$$

To find the Number of Teeth.

$$\frac{2 \times \text{radius} \times 3.1416}{\text{pitch}} = \text{number of teeth.}$$

Dimensions of Wheels in operation.

Diameter.		Breadth.	Pitch.	Length of teeth.	Thickness of teeth.	Velocity per second.	Pressure.
Feet.	Ins.	Inches.	Inches.	Inches.	Inches.	Feet.	Lbs.
10		7.	2.8	1.625	1.3	3.	11000
6		12.	4.2	2.25	1.9	6.6	20000
7	10	4.5	1.9	1.125	.875	1.1	3300
14	4	8.	3.	1.75	1.4	1.87	9000

VELOCITY OF WHEELS.

THE relative velocity of wheels is as the number of their teeth.

To find the Velocity or Number of Turns of the last Wheel to one of the first.

RULE.—Divide the product of the teeth of the wheels that act as drivers by the product of the driven, and the quotient is the number.

EXAMPLE.—If a wheel of 32 teeth drive a pinion of 10, on the axis of which there is one of 30 teeth, acting on a pinion of 8, what is the number of turns of the last?

$$\frac{32}{10} \times \frac{30}{8} = \frac{960}{80} = 12, \text{ } Ans.$$

To find the Proportion that the Velocities of the Wheels in a train should bear to one another.

RULE.—Subtract the less velocity from the greater, and divide the remainder by one less than the number of wheels in the train ; the quotient is the number, rising in arithmetical progression from the less to the greater velocity.

EXAMPLE.—What are the velocities of three wheels to produce 18 revolutions per minute, the driver making 3 revolutions per minute?

$$\frac{18-3 = 15}{3-1 = 2} = 7.5 \text{ ; then } 3+7.5 = 10.5,$$

and $10.5+7.5 = 18$; thus, 3, 10.5, and 18 are the velocities of the three wheels.

To find the Number of Teeth required in a Train of Wheels to produce a certain Velocity.

RULE.—As the velocity required is to the number of teeth in the driver, so is the velocity of the driver to the number of teeth in the driven.

EXAMPLE.—If the driver has 90 teeth, makes 2 revolutions, and the velocities required are 2, 10, and 18, what are the number of teeth in each of the other two?

2d wheel, 10 : 90 : : 2 : 18 teeth.
3d wheel, 18 : 90 : : 2 : 10 teeth.

STRENGTH OF WHEELS.

THE strength of the teeth of wheels is *directly* as their breadth and as the square of their thickness, and *inversely* as their length.

The stress is as the pressure.

To find the Thickness of a Tooth, the Strain at the Pitch Line being given.

RULE.—Divide the pressure in pounds at the pitch line by 3000, and the square root of the quotient is the thickness of the tooth in inches.

EXAMPLE.—The pressure is 9000 lbs., what is the thickness of the tooth required?

$$\sqrt{\frac{9000}{3000}} = 1.732 \text{ inches, } Ans.$$

The Breadth should be 2.5 times the pitch.

Therefore, as the thickness should be 0.47 of the pitch, the pitch for the above example will be 3.685 inches, and the breadth 3.685 ×2.5=9.2125 inches.

To find the Horses' Power of a Tooth, the Dimensions and Velocity being given.

Thickness $^2 \times 3000 =$ pressure.

$$\frac{\text{Pressure} \times \text{velocity in feet per minute}}{33000} = \text{horses' power.}$$

Thickness $\times 2.1277+ =$ the pitch.

Thickness $\times 1.5384+ =$ the length.

To find the Dimensions of the Arms of a Wheel.

RULE.—Multiply the power at the pitch line by the cube of the length of the arms, and divide this product by the product of the number of arms and 280; the quotient will be the breadth and cube of the depth.

EXAMPLE.—If the power be 1600, the diameter of the wheel 10 feet, and the number of arms 6, what will be the dimensions of each arm?

$$\frac{1600 \times \overline{10 \div 2}^3}{6 \times 280} = \frac{200000}{1680} = 119; \text{ if the breadth be 5 inches, then}$$

$$\frac{119}{5} = 23.8, \text{ and } \sqrt[3]{} \text{ of } 23.8 = 2.87, \text{ the depth.}$$

GENERAL EXPLANATIONS CONCERNING WHEELS.

Pitch Lines.—THE touching circumferences of two or more wheels, which act upon each other.

Pitch of a Wheel.—The distance of two contiguous teeth, measured upon their pitch line.

Length of a Tooth.—The distance from its base to its extremity.

Breadth of a Tooth.—The length of the face of the wheel.

Spur Wheels.—Wheels that have their teeth perpendicular to their axis.

Bevel Wheels.—Wheels having their teeth at an angle with their axis.

Crown Wheels.—Wheels which have their teeth at a right angle with their axis.

Mitre Wheels.—Wheels having their teeth at an angle of 45° with their axis.

Spur Gear.—Wheels acting upon each other in the same plane.

Bevel Gear.—Wheels acting upon each other at an angle.

When two wheels act upon one another, the greater is called the *spur* or *driver*, and the lesser the *pinion* or *driven*.

When the teeth of a wheel are made of a different material from the wheel, they are called cogs.

TABLE *of the Strength of Teeth and Arms.*

Pressure in lbs.	Horses' power at 3 feet per second.	Teeth.			With 6 Arms	
		Pitch in inches.	Thickness in inches.	Breadth in inches.	Depth for 1 foot radius in inches.	Breadth of rib in inches.
22	.25	.25	.119	.75	0.87	.25
85	.5	.50	.238	1.25	1.24	.42
191	1.	.75	.357	1.75	1.67	.60
337	2.	1.	.475	2.50	1.76	.80
520	3.	1.25	.590	3.	2.	1.
800	4.	1.50	.730	4.	2.20	1.30
1040	5.	1.75	.835	4.25	2.40	1.40
1370	7.	2.	.955	5.	2.50	1.70
1720	9.	2.25	1.070	5.50	2.70	1.80
2100	10.5	2.50	1.190	6.	2.85	2.
2560	13.	2.75	1.310	6.75	3.	2.20
3000	15.	3.	1.430	7.25	3.20	2.40
3600	18.	3.25	1.550	8.	3.30	2.60
4150	21.	3.50	1.670	8.50	3.40	2.80
4800	24.	3.75	1.790	9.25	3.50	2.90
5700	27.5	4.	1.910	10.25	3.60	3.40
6300	31.5	4.25	2.025	10.50	3.70	3.50
6900	34.5	4.50	2.150	11.	3.80	3.70
7700	38.5	4.75	2.270	11.75	3.90	3.90
8500	42.5	5.	2.390	12.25	4.	4.

Tredgold.

HORSE POWER.

As this is the universal term used to express the capability of first movers of magnitude, it is very essential that the estimate of this power should be uniform ; and as it is customary, in Europe, to estimate the power of a horse equivalent to the raising of 33000 *lbs. one foot high in a minute*, there can be no objection to such an estimate here.

The estimate, then, of a horse's power in the calculations in this work, is 33000 pounds avoirdupois, raised through the space of one foot in height in one minute, and in this I am supported by the practice of a majority of the manufacturers of steam-engines in this country.

ANIMAL STRENGTH.

MEN.

The mean effect of the power of a man, unaided by a machine, working to the best possible advantage, and at a moderate estimation, is the raising of 70 lbs. 1 foot high in a second, for 10 hours in a day.

Two men, working at a windlass at right angles to each other, can raise 70 lbs. more easily than one man can 30 lbs.

Mr. Bevan's results with experiments upon human strength are, for a short period,

With a drawing-knife	a force of 100 lbs.
an auger, both hands	" 100 "
a screw-driver, one hand . . .	" 84 "
a bench vice, handle	" 72 "
a chisel, vertical pressure . . .	" 72 "
a windlass	" 60 "
pincers, compression	" 60 "
a hand-plane	" 50 "
a hand-saw	" 36 "
a thumb-vice	" 45 "
a brace-bit, revolving	" 16 "
Twisting by the thumb and fingers only, and with small screw-drivers . .	" 14 "

By Mr. Field's experiments in 1838, the maximum power of a strong man, exerted for 2½ minutes, is = 18000 lbs. raised one foot in a minute.

A man of ordinary strength exerts a force of 30 lbs. for 10 hours in a day, with a velocity of 2½ feet in a second, = 4500 lbs. raised one foot in a minute, = ⅐ of the work of a horse.

A foot-soldier travels in 1 minute, in common time,	90 steps, = 70 yards.
in quick time,	110 " = 86 "
in double quick-time,	140 " = 109 "

He occupies in the ranks, a front of 20 inches, and a depth of 13, without a knapsack ; the interval between the ranks is 13 inches.

Average weight of men, 150 lbs. each.

5 men can stand in a space of 1 square yard.

A *man* travels, without a load, on level ground, during 8½ hours a day, at the rate of 3.7 miles an hour, or 31¼ miles a day. He can carry 111 lbs. 11 miles in a day.

A porter going short distances, and returning unloaded, carries 135 lbs. 7 miles a day. He can carry, in a wheelbarrow, 150 lbs. 10 miles a day.

The muscles of the human jaw exert a force of 534 lbs.

HORSES.

A *horse* travels 400 yards, at a walk, in 4½ minutes; at a trot, in 2 minutes; at a gallop, in 1 minute.

He occupies in the ranks a front of 40 inches, and a depth of 10 feet; in a stall, from 3½ to 4½ feet front; and at picket, 3 feet by 9.

Average weight = 1000 lbs. each.

A *horse*, carrying a soldier and his equipments (say 225 lbs.), travels 25 miles in a day (8 hours).

A *draught horse* can draw 1600 lbs. 23 miles a day, weight of carriage included.

The ordinary work of a horse may be stated at 22.500 lbs., raised 1 foot in a minute, for 8 hours a day.

In a *horse mill*, a horse moves at the rate of 3 feet in a second. The diameter of the track should not be less than 25 feet.

A *horse power* in machinery is estimated at 33.000 lbs., raised 1 foot in a minute; but as a horse can exert that force but 6 hours a day, one machinery horse power is equivalent to that of 4.4 horses.

The expense of conveying goods at 3 miles per hour per horse teams being 1, the expense at 4½ miles will be 1.33, and so on, the expense being doubled when the speed is 5¼ miles per hour.

The strength of a horse is equivalent to that of 5 men.

TABLE *of the Amount of Labour a Horse of average Strength is capable of performing, at different Velocities, on Canals, Railroads, and Turnpikes.*

Force of traction estimated at 83.3 lbs.

Velocity in miles per hour.	Duration of the day's work.	Useful effect for one day in tons, drawn one mile.		
		On a Canal.	On a Railroad.	On a Turnpike.
Miles.	Hours.	Tons.	Tons.	Tons.
2½	11½	520	115	14
3	8	243	92	12
3½	5 $\frac{9}{10}$	153	82	10
4	4½	102	72	9.
5	2 $\frac{9}{10}$	52	57	7.2
6	2	30	48	6.
7	1½	19	41	5.1
8	1⅛	12.8	36	4.5
9	$\frac{9}{10}$	9.0	32	4.0
10	¾	6.6	28.8	3.6

The actual labour performed by horses is greater, but they are injured by it.

HYDROSTATICS.

HYDROSTATICS treat of the pressure, weight, and equilibrium of non-elastic fluids.

The pressure of a fluid at any depth is as the depth of the fluid.

The pressure of a fluid upon the bottom of the containing vessel is as the base and perpendicular height, whatever may be the figure of the containing vessel.

Fluids press equally in all directions.

The *Centre of Pressure* is that point of a surface against which any fluid presses, to which, if a force equal to the whole pressure were applied, it would keep the surface at rest.

The centre of pressure of a *parallelogram* is at ⅔ of the line (measuring downward) that joins the middles of the two horizontal sides.

In a *triangular plane*, when the base is uppermost, the centre of pressure is at the middle of the line, raised perpendicularly from the vertex; and when the vertex is uppermost, the centre of pressure is at ¼ of a line let fall perpendicularly from the vertex.

OF PRESSURE.

The pressure of a fluid *on any surface*, whether *vertical, oblique,* or *horizontal*, is equal to the weight of a column of the fluid, whose base is equal to the surface pressed, and height equal to the distance of the centre of gravity of the surface pressed, below the surface of the fluid.

To find the Pressure of a Fluid upon the Bottom of the Containing Vessel.

RULE.—Multiply area of base in feet by height of fluid in feet, and their sum by the weight of a cubic foot of the fluid.

EXAMPLE.—What is the pressure upon a surface 10 feet square, the water (fresh) being 20 feet deep?

$$10^2 \times 20 \times 62.5 = 125000 \text{ lbs., } Ans.$$

The side of any vessel sustains a pressure equal to the area of the side, multiplied by half the depth.

The pressure upon an inclined, curved, or any surface, is as the area of the surface, and the depth of its centre of gravity below the fluid.

EXAMPLE.—What is the pressure upon the sloping side of a pond 100 feet square, the depth of the pond being 8 feet?

$$100^2 \times \frac{8}{2} \times 62.5 = 625000 \text{ lbs., } Ans.$$

Or, on a hemisphere just covered with water, and 36 inches in diameter,

$$3 \times 3.1416 \times \frac{36}{2} \times \frac{18}{2} \times 62.5 = 662.5, \text{ } Ans.$$

The pressure upon a number of surfaces is found by multiplying the sum of the surfaces into the depth of their common centre of gravity, below the surface of the fluid.

CONSTRUCTION OF BANKS.

A bank, constructed of a given quantity of materials, will just resist the pressure of the water when the square of its thickness at the base is to the square of its perpendicular height, as the weight of a given bulk of water is to the weight of the same bulk of the material the bank is made of, increased by twice the aforesaid weight of the given bulk of water.

Thus, if the bank is made of a stone 2 times heavier than water, the thickness of the base should be to the height, as 3 to 6.

If the height, compared to the thickness of the base, be as 10 to 7, stability is always ensured, whatever the specific gravity of the material may be.

The bottom of a conical, pyramidal, or cylindrical vessel, or of one the section of which is that of an inverted frustrum of a cone or pyramid, sustains a pressure equal to the area of the bottom and the depth of the fluid.

FLOOD GATES.

To find the Strain which a Fluid will exert to make it turn upon its Hinges, or open.

RULE.—Multiply $\frac{1}{4}$ of the square of the height by the square of the breadth, and take a bulk of water equal to the product.

EXAMPLE.—If the gate is 6 feet square,

$$\frac{6^2}{4} \times 6^2 = 324 \text{ cubic feet, or } 20250 \text{ lbs.}$$

To find the Strain the Water exerts upon its Hinges.

RULE.—Multiply $\frac{1}{6}$ of the breadth by the cube of the height, and take a bulk of water equal to the product.

EXAMPLE.—With the same gate,

$$\frac{6}{6} \times 6^3 = 216 \text{ cubic feet, or } 13500 \text{ lbs.}$$

PIPES.

To find the Thickness of a Pipe.

RULE.—Multiply the height of the head of the fluid in feet by the diameter of the pipe in inches, and divide their product by the cohesion of one square inch of the material of which the pipe is composed.

By experiment it has been found that a cast iron pipe, 15 inches in diameter, and $\frac{3}{4}$ of an inch thick, will support a head of water of 600 feet; and that one of oak, of the same diameter, and 2 inches thick, will support a head of 180 feet.

The cohesive power of cast iron, then, would be 12,000 lbs.; of oak, 1350 lbs.

That of lead is 750 lbs.; and wrought iron boiler plates, riveted together, is from 25 to 30,000 lbs.

In conduit pipes, lying horizontal, and made of lead, their thickness, compared to their diameter, should be,

As 2½, 3, 4, 5, 6, 7, 8 lines,
To 1, 1½, 2, 3, 4½, 6, 7 inches.

And when made of iron,

As 1, 2, 3, 4, 5, &c., lines,
To 1, 2, 4, 6, 8, &c., inches.

The tenacity of lead is increased to 3000 by the addition of 1 part of zinc in 8.

HYDROSTATIC PRESS.

To find the Thickness of the Metal to resist a Given Pressure.

Let p = pressure per square inch in pounds, r = radius of cylinder, and c = cohesion of the metal per square inch.

Then $\dfrac{pr}{c-p}$ = thickness of metal.

The cohesive force of a square inch of cast iron is frequently estimated at 18000 lbs.

P

HYDRAULICS AND HYDRODYNAMICS.

HYDRAULICS treats of the motion of non-elastic fluids, and Hydrodynamics of the force with which they act.

Descending water is actuated by the same laws as *falling bodies.*

Water will fall through 1 foot in $\frac{1}{4}$ of a second, 4 feet in $\frac{1}{2}$ of a second, and through 9 feet in $\frac{3}{4}$ of a second, and so on.

The velocity of a fluid, spouting through an opening in the side of a vessel, reservoir, or bulkhead, is the same that a body would acquire by falling through a perpendicular space equal to that *between the top of the water and the middle of the aperture.*

Then, by rule 4 in Gravitation,

$$\sqrt{\text{height} \times 64.33} = \text{velocity}.$$

EXAMPLE.—What is the velocity of a stream issuing from a head of 10 feet?

$$\sqrt{10 \times 64.33} = 25.36 \text{ feet,} \left. \right\} \; Ans.$$
$$\text{Or, } \sqrt{10 \times 8} = 25.30 \text{ feet,}$$

If the velocity be 50.72 feet per second, what is the head?

$$50.72^2 \div 64.33 = 40 \text{ feet,} \left. \right\} \; Ans.$$
$$\text{Or, } \overline{50.72 \div 8^2} = 40.2 \text{ feet,}$$

This would be true were it not for the effect of friction, which in pipes and canals increases as the square of the velocity.

The mean velocity of a number of experiments gives 5.4 feet for a height of one foot. The theoretical velocity is $(\sqrt{64\frac{1}{3}})$ 8.

OF SLUICES.

To find the Quantity of Water which will flow out of an Opening.

RULE.—Multiply the square root of the depth of the water by 5.4; the product is the velocity in feet per second. This, multiplied by the area of the orifice in feet, will give the number of cubic feet per second.

EXAMPLE.—If the centre of a sluice is 10 feet below the surface of a pond, and its area 2 feet, what quantity of water will run out in one second?

$$\sqrt{10} \times 5.4 \times 2 = 34.1496 \text{ feet, } Ans.$$

NOTE.—If the area of the opening is large compared with the head of the water take $\frac{2}{3}$ of this velocity for the actual velocity.

OF VERTICAL APERTURES OR SLITS.

The quantity of water that will flow out of one that reaches as high as the surface is $\frac{2}{3}$ of that which would flow out of the same aperture if it were horizontal at the depth of the base.

$$\text{Or, } \frac{\text{velocity at bottom} \times \text{depth} \times 2}{3} \times \text{breadth of slit} = \text{number}$$

of cubic feet per second.

OF STREAMS OR JETS.

To find the Distance a Jet will be projected from a Vessel through an opening in the Side.

RULE.—B C will always be equal to twice the square root of A O × O B.

If *o* is 4 times as deep below A, as *a* is, *o* will discharge twice the quantity of water that will flow from *a* in the same time, because 2 is the square root of A *o*, and 1 is the square root of A *a*.

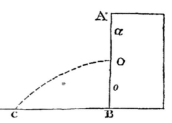

NOTE.—The water will spout the farthest when *o* is equidistant from A and B; and if the vessel is raised above a plane, B must be taken upon the plane.

The quantities of water passing through equal holes in the same time are as the square roots of their depths.

EXAMPLE.—A vessel 20 feet deep is raised 5 feet above a plane; how far will a jet reach that is 5 feet from the bottom?

$$\sqrt{15 \times 10} \times 2 = 24.48 \text{ feet, } Ans.$$

When a prismatic vessel empties itself by a small orifice, in the time of emptying itself, twice the quantity would be discharged if it were kept full by a new supply.

To find the Vertical Height of a Stream projected from a Pipe.

RULE.—Ascertain the velocity of the stream by computing the quantity of water running or forced through the opening; then, by rule 5 in Gravitation, page 140, find the required height.

EXAMPLE.—If a fire-engine discharges 16.8 cubic feet of water through a ¾ inch pipe in one minute, how high will the water be projected, the pipe being directed vertically?

16.8×1728 ÷ area of ¾ ÷ inches in a foot ÷ seconds in a minute = 91.6, or velocity of stream in feet per second; then, by rule, page 140, 91.6÷8 = 11.45, and $11.45^2 = 131.10$ feet, *Ans.*

NOTE.—This rule gives a theoretical result; the result in practice is somewhat less.

VELOCITY OF STREAMS.

In a stream, the velocity is greatest at the surface and in the middle of the current.

To find the Velocity of a River or Brook.

RULE.—Take the number of inches that a floating body passes over in one second in the middle of the current, and extract its square root; double this root, subtract it from the velocity at top, and add 1; the result will be the velocity of the stream at the bottom; and the mean velocity of the stream is equal the velocity at the surface — $\sqrt{}$ velocity at the surface +.5.

EXAMPLE.—If the velocity at the surface and in the middle of a stream be 36 inches per second, what is the mean velocity?

$$\sqrt{36 \times 2 - 36 + 1} = 25, \text{ the velocity at bottom.}$$
$$36 - \sqrt{36} + .5 = 30.5, \text{ Ans.}$$

To find the Velocity of Water running through Pipes.

RULE.—Divide height of head in inches by length of pipe in inches, and the square root of the quotient, multiplied by 23.3, will give the velocity in inches at the orifice.

EXAMPLE.—What is the velocity when the head is 9 feet, the pipe 24 inches long and 2½ inches bore?

$$\sqrt{108 \div 24} \times 23.3 = 49.49 \text{ inches per second, Ans.}$$

Quantities of Water discharged from Orifices of various forms, the Altitude being constant, at 34.642 Inches.

Nature and dimensions of the tubes and orifices.	Cubic inches discharged in a minute.
1. A circular orifice in a thin plate, the diameter being 1.7 inches	10783
2. A cylindrical tube 1.7 inches in diameter, and 5.117 inches long	14261
3. A short conical adjutage, 1.7 inches in diameter	10526
4. The same, with a cylinder 3.41 inches long added to it	10409
5. The same, the length of the cylinder being 13.65 inches long	9830
6. The same, the length of the cylinder being 27.30 inches long	9216

Results prove that the discharge of water through a straight cylindrical pipe of an unlimited length may be increased only by altering the form of the terminations of the pipe, by making the inner end of the pipe of the same form as the *vena contracta*, and the extremity a truncated cone, having its length about 9 times the diameter of the cylinder or pipe attached, and the aperture at the outlet to the diameter of the cylinder as 18 is to 10.

By giving this form, the discharge is over what it would be by the cylinder alone as 24 is to 10.

WAVES.

The undulations of waves are performed in the same time as the oscillations of a pendulum, the length of which is equal to the breadth of a wave, or to the distance between two neighbouring cavities or eminences.

TABLE *showing the Head necessary to overcome the Friction of Water in Horizontal Pipes,*

By Mr. SMEATON.

Velocity of Water in Pipe per Second.

(Each velocity column gives the required head as Feet and Inches per 100 feet of pipe.)

Feet 0, Inches	Feet 1, Inches 0	Feet 1, Inches 6	Feet 2, Inches 0	Feet 2, Inches 6	Feet 3, Inches 0	Feet 3, Inches 6	Feet 4, Inches 0	Feet 4, Inches 6	Feet 5, Inches 0	Bore of the Pipes.
4.5	1 · 4.7	2 · 11.1	4 · 9.7	7 · 1.7	10 · 1.0	13 · 8.0	17 · 10.	22 · 6.7	28 · 0.2	½ inch
3.0	11.1	1 · 11.3	3 · 2.5	4 · 9.2	6 · 8.6	9 · 1.3	11 · 10.6	15 · 0.5	18 · 8.1	¾ "
2.2	8.4	1 · 5.5	2 · 4.9	3 · 6.9	5 · 0.5	6 · 10.	8 · 11.	11 · 3.4	14 ·	1 "
1.8	6.7	1 · 2.	1 · 11.1	2 · 10.3	4 · 0.4	5 · 5.6	7 · 1.6	9 · 0.3	11 · 2.5	1¼ "
1.5	5.6	11.7	1 · 7.2	2 · 4.6	3 · 4.3	4 · 6.7	5 · 11.3	7 · 6.2	9 · 4.1	1½ "
1.3	4.8	10.	1 · 4.5	2 · 0.5	2 · 10.6	3 · 10.9	5 · 1.1	6 · 5.4	8 · 0.1	1¾ "
1.1	4.2	8.7	1 · 2.4	1 · 9.4	2 · 6.9	3 · 5.	4 · 5.5	5 · 7.7	7 ·	2 "
1.0	3.7	7.8	1 · 0.8	1 · 7.	2 · 3.9	3 · 0.4	3 · 11.6	5 · 0.1	6 · 2.7	2¼ "
.9	3.3	7.0	11.5	1 · 5.1	2 · 0.9	2 · 8.8	3 · 6.8	4 · 6.1	5 · 7.2	2½ "
.7	2.8	7.0	9.6	1 · 2.3	1 · 10.	2 · 3.3	3 · 1.6	3 · 9.1	4 · 8.	2¾ "
.6	2.4	5.0	8.2	1 · 0.2	1 · 8.2	2 ·	2 · 6.6	3 · 4.8	4 ·	3 "
.6	2.1	5.0	7.2	10.7	1 ·	1 · 11.4	2 · 2.7	3 · 0.1	3 · 6.	3¼ "
.5	1.9	4.4	6.4	9.5	1 ·	1 · 8.5	1 · 11.7	2 · 9.8	3 · 1.4	3½ "
.4	1.7	3.9	5.8	8.6	1 ·	1 · 6.2	1 · 9.1	2 · 6.1	2 · 9.6	4 "
.4	1.4	3.5	4.8	7.1		1 · 3.3	1 · 7.	2 · 3.1	2 · 4.	4½ "
.3	1.2	2.9	4.1	6.1		1 · 1.7	1 · 4.4			5 "
.3	1.0	2.5	3.6	5.4			1 · 2.7	1 · 10.6		6 "
.25	.9	2.2	3.2	4.8			1 · 0.1	1 · 9.6		7 "
.2	.9	1.9	2.9	4.3						8 "
.2	.8	1.7	2.6	3.9				1 · 6.7	1 · 9.	9 "
.19	.8	1.6	2.4	3.6				1 · 4.8	1 · 6.7	10 "
	.7	1.5						1 · 3.3	1 · 4.8	11 "
								1 · 2.0	1 · 2.0	12 "

Look for the velocity of water in the pipe in the upper line, and in the column beneath it, and opposite to the given diameter, is the height of the column or head requisite to overcome the friction of such pipe for 100 feet in length, and obtain the required velocity.

GENERAL RULES.

Discharge by Horizontal Pipes.

1. THE less the diameter of the pipe, the less is the proportional discharge of the fluid.

2. The greater the length of the discharging pipe, the greater the diminution of the discharge. Hence, the discharges made in equal times by pipes of different lengths, of the same diameter, and under the same altitude of water, are to one another in the inverse ratio of the square roots of their lengths.

3. The friction of a fluid is proportionally greater in small than in large pipes.

4. *The velocity of water flowing out of an aperture is as the square root of the height of the head of the water.*

Theoretically the velocity would be $\sqrt{}$ height $\times 8$. In *practice* it is $\sqrt{}$ height $\times 5.4 =$ velocity in feet per second.

Discharge by Vertical Pipes.

The discharge of fluids by vertical pipes is augmented, on the principle of the gravitation of falling bodies; consequently, the greater the length of the pipe, the greater the discharge of the fluid.

Discharge by Inclined Pipes.

A pipe which is inclined will discharge in a given time a greater quantity of water than a horizontal pipe of the same dimensions.

Deductions from various Experiments.

1. The areas of orifices being equal, that which has the smallest perimeter will discharge the most water under equal heads; hence circular apertures are the most advantageous.

2. That in consequence of the additional contraction of the fluid vein, as the head of the fluid increases the discharge is a little diminished.

3. That the discharge of a fluid through a cylindrical horizontal tube, the diameter and length of which are equal to one another, is the same as through a simple orifice.

4. That the above tube may be increased to four times the diameter of the orifice with advantage.

5. The velocity of motion that would result from the direct, unretarded action of the column of a fluid which produces it, being a constant, or   . 8.
The velocity through an aperture in a thin plate, with the same pressure, is 5.
Through a tube from two to three diameters in length, projecting outward, 6.5
Through a tube of the same length, projecting inward 5.45
Through a conical tube of the form of the contracted vein .   .   . 7.9
Curvilineal and rectangular pipes discharge less of a fluid than rectilineal pipes.

Discharge from Reservoirs receiving no Supply of Water.

For prismatic vessels the general law applies, that twice as much would be discharged from the same orifice if the vessel were kept full during the time which is required for emptying itself.

Discharges from Compound or Divided Reservoirs.

The velocity in each may be considered as generated by the difference of the heights in the two contiguous reservoirs; consequently, the square root of the difference will represent the velocity, which, if there are several orifices, must be inversely as their respective areas.

Discharge by Weirs and Rectangular Notches.

The quantity of water discharged is found by taking $\frac{2}{3}$ of the velocity due to the mean height, using 5.1 for the coefficient of the velocity.

EXAMPLE.—What quantity of water will flow from a pond, over a weir 102 inches in length by 12 inches deep?

$\frac{2}{3}\sqrt{}$1 foot $\times 5.1 \times 8.5$ area of weir $= 28.9$ cubic feet in one second.

TABLE *of the Rise of Water in Rivers, occasioned by the erection of Piers, &c.*

Velocity of current in feet per sec.	Amount of obstruction compared with area of section of the river.								$\frac{9}{10}$
	$\frac{1}{10}$	$\frac{2}{10}$	$\frac{3}{10}$	$\frac{4}{10}$	$\frac{5}{10}$	$\frac{6}{10}$	$\frac{7}{10}$	$\frac{8}{10}$	
	Feet.	Feet.	Feet.	Feet.	Feet.	Feet.	Feet.	Feet.	Feet.
1	.0157	.0377	.0698	.1192	.2012	.3521	.6780	1.609	6.639
2	.0277	.0665	.1231	.2102	.3548	.6208	1.196	2.838	11.71
3	.0477	.1144	.2118	.3618	.6107	1.069	2.058	4.885	20.15
4	.0760	.1822	.3372	.5759	.9719	1.701	3.276	7.775	32.07
5	.1165	.2793	.5168	.8782	1.490	2.607	5.020	11.92	49.15
6	.1558	.3736	.6912	1.181	1.993	3.487	6.715	15.94	65.75
7	.2078	.4983	.9221	1.575	2.658	4.651	8.958	21.26	87.71
8	.2678	.6423	1.188	2.030	3.426	5.995	11.54	27.40	113.0
9	.3359	.8054	1.490	2.557	4.296	7.517	14.48	34.36	141.7
10	.4119	.9877	1.827	3.122	5.268	9.219	17.75	42.14	173.8

Velocity of Water in Pipes or Sewers.

The time occupied in an equal quantity of water through a pipe or sewer of equal lengths, and with equal falls, is proportionally as follows:

In a right line as 90, in a true curve as 100, and in passing a right angle as 140.

The resistance that a body sustains in moving through a fluid is in proportion to the square of the velocity.

The resistance that any plane surface encounters in moving through a fluid with any velocity is equal to the weight of a column whose height is the space a body would have to fall through in free space to acquire that velocity, and whose base is the surface of the plane.

EXAMPLE.—If a plane, 10 inches square, move through water at the rate of 8 feet per second, then $8^2 \div 64 = 1. =$ the space a body would require to fall to acquire a velocity of 8 feet per second; and as 1 foot $= 12$ inches, then $10 \times 12 = 120$ cubic inches, $=$ the column of water whose height and base are required.

      Cub. Inches.   Ounces.

As 1728 : 120 : : 1000 : 69.4, or 4.3 lbs., which is the amount of resistance met with by the plane at the above velocity.

And it is the same, whether the plane moves against the fluid or the fluid against the plane.

The following Table shows the results of experiments with a plane one foot square, at an immersion of 3 feet below the surface, and at different velocities per second.

Velocity.	Resistance.	Velocity.	Resistance.	Velocity.	Resistance.
5 feet	29.5 lbs.	8 feet	71.7 lbs.	11 feet	136.3 lbs.
6 "	40. "	9 "	90.6 "	12 "	162.1 "
7 "	54.6 "	10 "	112. "	13½ "	213. "

WATER WHEELS.

THIS subject belongs properly to Hydrodynamics, but a separate classification is here deemed preferable.

WATER WHEELS are of three kinds, viz., the *Overshot, Undershot,* and *Breast.*

The *Overshot Wheel* is the most advantageous, as it gives the greatest power with the least quantity of water. The next in order, in point of efficiency, is the *Breast Wheel*, which may be considered a mean between the overshot and the *Undershot.* For a small supply of water with a high fall, the first should be employed ; where the quantity of water and height of fall are both moderate, the second form should be used. For a large supply of water with a low fall, the third form must be resorted to.

Before proceeding to erect a water wheel, the area of the stream and the head that can be used must be measured.

Find the velocity acquired by the water in falling through that height by the rule, viz. : Extract the square root of the height of the head of the water (from the surface to the middle of the gate), and multiply it by 8.

NOTE.—Where the opening is small, and the head of water is great, or propor tionally so, use from 5.5 to 8 for the multiplier.

EXAMPLE.—The dimensions of a stream are 2 by 80 inches, from a head of 2 feet to the upper surface of the stream ; what is the velocity of the water per minute, and what is its weight ?

2 feet and $\frac{1}{2}$ of 2 inches $= 25$ inches $= 2.08$ feet, $\sqrt{2.08} \times {}^{*}6.5 \times 60 = 561.60$ feet velocity per minute.

And $80 \times 2 \times \overline{561.6 \text{ feet}} \times 12$ inches, $\div 1728 = 624$ cubic feet, $\times 62\frac{1}{2}$ lbs. $= 39000$ lbs. of water discharged in one minute.

To find the Power of an Overshot Wheel.

RULE.—Multiply the weight of water in lbs. discharged upon the wheel in one minute by the height or distance in feet from the lower edge of the wheel to the centre of the opening in the gate ; divide the product by 50000, and the quotient is the number of horses' power.

EXAMPLE.—In the preceding example, the weight of the water discharged per minute is 39000 lbs. If the height of the fall is 23 feet, the diameter of the wheel being 22, what is the power of the wheel ?

23 feet — 8 inches clearance below $= 22.4 = 22.33.$
$39000 \times 22.33 \div 50000 = 17.41$ horses' power, *Ans.*

To find the Power of a Stream.

RULE.—Multiply the weight of the water in lbs. discharged in one minute by the height of the fall in feet ; divide by 33000, and the quotient is the answer.

---

* Estimate of velocity.

EXAMPLE.—What power is a stream of water equal to of the following dimensions, viz. : 1 foot deep by 22 inches broad, velocity 350 feet per minute, and fall 60 feet ; and what should be the size of the wheel applied to it ?

$12 \times 22 \times \overline{350 \times 12} \div 1728 \times 62\frac{1}{2} \times 60$ feet $\div 33000 = 72.9$, Ans.

Height of fall 60 feet, from which deduct for admission of water, and clearance below, 15 inches, which gives 58.9 feet for the diameter of the wheel.

$$\text{Clearance above } 3 \atop \text{`` below } 12 \Big\} \text{ 15 inches.}$$

The power of a stream, applied to an overshot wheel, produces effect as 10 to 6.6.

Then, as 10 : 6.6 : : 72.9 : 48 horses' power equal that of an overshot wheel of 60 feet applied to this stream.

When the fall exceeds 10 feet, the overshot wheel should be applied.

The higher the wheel is in proportion to the whole descent, the greater will be the effect.

The effect is as the quantity of water and its perpendicular height multiplied together.

The weight of the arch of loaded buckets in pounds, is found by multiplying $\frac{4}{9}$ of their number, $\times$ the number of cubic feet in each, and that product by 40.

To find the Power of an Undershot Wheel when the Stream is confined to the Wheel.

RULE.—Ascertain the weight of the water discharged against the floats of the wheel in one minute by the preceding rules, and divide it by 100000 ; the quotient is the number of horses' power.

NOTE.—The 100000 is obtained thus: The power of a stream, applied to an undershot wheel, produces effect as 10 to 3.3 ; then 3.3 : 10 : : 33000 : 100000.

When the opening is above the centre of the floats, multiply the weight of the water by the height, as in the rule for an overshot wheel.

EXAMPLE.—What is the power of an undershot wheel, applied to a stream 2 by 80 inches, from a head of 25 feet ?

$\sqrt{25} \times 6.5 \times 60 = 1950$ feet velocity of water per minute, and $2 \times 80 = 160$ inches $\times 1950 \times 12 \div 1728 = 2166.6$ cubic feet $\times 62.5 =$ *135412 lbs. of water discharged in one minute ; then $135412 \div 100000 = 1.35$ horses' power.

NOTE.—The maximum work is always obtained when the velocity of the wheel is half that of the stream. Let V represent velocity of float boards, and v velocity of water; then $\dfrac{(v-V)^2}{V^2} \times$ force of the water, will be the force of the effective stroke.

The effect of an undershot wheel to the power expended is, at a medium, one half that of an overshot wheel.

The virtual or effective head being the same, the effect will be very nearly as the quantity of water expended.

When the fall is below 4 feet, an undershot wheel should be applied.

To find the Power of a Breast Wheel.

RULE.—Find the effect of an undershot wheel, the head of water of which is the difference of level between the surface and where it strikes the wheel (breast), and add to it the effect of that of an overshot wheel, the height of the head of which is equal to the differ-

---

* Equal $160 \times 12 \div 1728 \times 62.5 \times 1950 =$ momentum of water and its velocity.

ence between where the water strikes the wheel, and the tail water; the sum is the effective power.

EXAMPLE.—What would be the power of a breast wheel applied to a stream 2×80 inches, 14 feet from the surface, the rest of the fall being 11 feet?

$\sqrt{14}×6.5×60 = 1458.6$ feet velocity of water per minute.

And $2×80×1458×12÷1728 = 1620$ cubic feet $×62.5 = 101250$ lbs. of water discharged in one minute.

Then $101250÷100000 = 1.012$ horses' power as an undershot.

$\sqrt{11}×6.5×60 = 1290$ feet velocity of water per minute.

And $2×80×1290×12÷1728 = 1433$ cubic feet $× 62.5 = 89562$ lbs. of water discharged in one minute.

$×11$ height of fall $÷50000 = 19.703$ horses, which, added to the above, $=20.715$, *Ans.*

When the fall exceeds 10 feet, it may be divided into two, and two breast wheels applied to it.
When the fall is between 4 and 10 feet, a breast wheel should be applied.
The power of a water wheel ought to be taken off opposite to the point where the water is producing its greatest action upon the wheel.

BARKER'S MILL.

The effect of this mill is considerably greater than that which the same quantity of water would produce if applied to an undershot wheel, but less than that which it would produce if properly applied to an overshot wheel.

For a description of it, see Grier's Mechanics' Calculator, page 234.

Make each arm of the horizontal tube, from the centre of motion to the centre of the aperture of any convenient length, not less than $\frac{1}{9}$ of the perpendicular height of the water's surface above these centres.

Multiply the length of the arm in feet by .61365, and the square root of the product will be the proper time for a revolution in seconds; then adapt the geering to this velocity. Or, if the time of a revolution be given, multiply the square of it by 1.6296 for the proportional length of the arm in feet.

Divide the continued product of the breadth, depth, and velocity of the stream in feet by 14.27; multiply the quotient by the square root of the height, and the result is the area of either aperture.

Multiply the area of either aperture by the height of the head of water, and this product by 56; the result is the moving force in lbs. at the centre of the apertures.

EXAMPLE.—If the fall be 18 feet from the head to the centre of the apertures, then the arm must not be less than 2 feet (as $\frac{1}{9}$ of 18 = 2), $\sqrt{2×.61365} = 1.107$, the time of a revolution in seconds; the breadth of the race 17 inches, the depth 9, and the velocity 6 feet per second; what is the moving force?

17 inches = 1.41 feet, 9 inches = .75 feet; then $1.41×.75×6÷14.27×\sqrt{18}×18×56 = 1895$ lbs., *Ans.*

To find the Centre of Gyration of a Water Wheel.

RULE.—Take the radius of the wheel, the weight of its arms, and the weight of its rim, as composed of floats, shrouding, &c.

Let R represent the weight of rim,
" r " the radius of the wheel,
" A " the weight of arms,
" W " the weight of the water in action when the buckets are filled, as in operation.

Then $\sqrt{(R \times r^2 \times 2 + A \times r^2 \times 2 + W \times r^2 \div \overline{R + A + W} \times 2)}$ = centre of gyration.

EXAMPLE.—In a wheel 20 feet diameter, the weight of the rim is 3 tons, the weight of the arms 2 tons, and the weight of the water 1 ton ; what is the distance of the centre of gyration from the centre of the wheel ?

$R = 3$ tons $\times 10^2 \times 2 = 600$
$A = 2$ " $\times 10^2 \times 2 = 400$
$W = 1$ " $\times 10^2$ . . $= 100$

$$3 + 2 + 1 = 6 \times 2 = \frac{\overline{1100}}{12} = 91.6,$$ the square root of which is 9.5, or $9\frac{1}{2}$ feet, *Ans.*

NOTES.—At the mill of Mr. Samuel Newlin, at Fishkill Creek, N. Y., 5 barrels of flour can be ground, and 400 bushels of grain elevated 36 feet per hour with a stream and overshot wheel of the following dimensions, viz.:

Height of head to centre of opening, $24\frac{4}{8}$ inches; opening, $1\frac{3}{4}$ by 80 inches; wheel, 22 feet diameter by 8 feet face ; 52 buckets, each 1 foot in depth.

The wheel making $3\frac{1}{2}$ revolutions, driving 3 run of $5\frac{1}{2}$ feet stones 130 turns in a minute, with all the attendant machinery.

This is a case of maximum effect, in consequence of the gearing being well set up, and kept in good order.

At the furnace of Mr. Peter Townsend, Monroe Works, N. J., 30 to 34 tons of No. 1 Iron are made per week, with the blast from two 5 feet by 5 feet 1 inch blowing cylinders. The wheel (overshot) being 24 feet diameter, by 6 feet in width, having 70 buckets of 14 inches in depth. The stream is $\frac{3}{4}$ by 51 inches, having a head $6\frac{1}{2}$ feet; the wheel and cylinders each making $4\frac{1}{4}$ revolutions per minute.

Rocky Glen Factory, Fishkill, N. Y., containing 6144 self-acting mule spindles, 160 looms, weaving printing cloths 27 inches wide of No. 33 yarn (33 hanks to a pound), and producing 24,000 hanks in a day of 11 hours, is driven by a breast wheel and stream of the following dimensions, viz.:

Stream 18 feet by 2 inches, head 20 feet, height of water upon wheel 16 feet, diameter of wheel 26 feet 4 inches, face of wheel 20 feet 9 inches, depth of buckets $15\frac{3}{4}$ inches, number of buckets 70.

Revolutions, $4\frac{5}{7\pi}$ per minute.

PNEUMATICS.

WEIGHT, ELASTICITY, AND RARITY OF AIR.

THE pressure of the air at the surface of the earth is, at a mean rate, equal to the support of 29.5 inches of mercury, or 33.18 feet of fresh water. It is usually estimated in round numbers at 30 inches of mercury and 34 feet of water, or 15 lbs. pressure upon the square inch.

The *Elasticity* of air is inversely as the space it occupies, and directly as its density.

When the altitude of the air is taken in arithmetic proportion, its *Rarity* will be in geometric proportion.

Thus, at 7 miles above the surface of the earth, the air is 4 times rarer or lighter than at the earth's surface; at 14 miles, 16 times; at 21 miles, 64 times, and so on.

The weight of a cubic foot of air is 527.04 grains, or 1.205 ounces avoirdupois.

At the temperature of 33°, the mean velocity of sound is 1100 feet per second. It is increased or diminished half a foot for each degree of temperature above or below 33°.

To compute Distances by Sound.

RULE.—Multiply the time in seconds by 1100, and the product is the distance in feet.

EXAMPLE.—After observing a flash of lightning, air at 60°, it was 5 seconds before I heard the thunder; what was the distance of the cloud?

$$1100 + \frac{50-33}{2} \times 5 \div 5280 = 1.049 \text{ miles, } Ans.$$

To compute what Degree of Rarefaction may be effected in a Vessel.

Let the quantity of air in the vessel, tube, and pump be represented by 1, and the proportion of the capacity of the pump to the vessel and tube by .33; consequently, it contains $\frac{1}{4}$ of the air in the united apparatus.

Upon the first stroke of the piston this fourth will be expelled, and $\frac{3}{4}$ of the original quantity will remain: $\frac{1}{4}$ of this will be expelled upon the second stroke, which is equal to $\frac{3}{16}$ of the original quantity; and, consequently, there remains in the apparatus $\frac{9}{16}$ of the original quantity. Calculating in this way, the following table is easily made:

No. of Strokes.	Air expelled at each stroke.		Air remaining in the vessel.	
1	$\frac{1}{4}$	$= \frac{1}{4}$	$\frac{3}{4}$	$= \frac{3}{4}$
2	$\frac{3}{16}$	$= \frac{3}{4\times4}$	$\frac{9}{16}$	$= \frac{3\times3}{4\times4}$
3	$\frac{9}{64}$	$= \frac{3\times3}{4\times4\times4}$	$\frac{27}{64}$	$= \frac{3\times3\times3}{4\times4\times4}$
4	$\frac{27}{256}$	$= \frac{3\times3\times3}{4\times4\times4\times4}$	$\frac{81}{256}$	$= \frac{3\times3\times3\times3}{4\times4\times4\times4}$
5	$\frac{81}{1024}$	$= \frac{3\times3\times3\times3}{4\times4\times4\times4\times4}$	$\frac{243}{1024}$	$= \frac{3\times3\times3\times3\times3}{4\times4\times4\times4\times4}$

And so on, continually multiplying the air expelled at the preceding stroke by 3, and dividing it by 4; and the air remaining after each stroke is found by multiplying the air remaining after the preceding stroke by 3, and dividing it by 4.

Measurement of Heights by Means of the Barometer.

Approximate Rule. For a mean temperature of 55°,

x = required difference in height in feet,
h = the height of the mercury at the lower station,
h' = the height of the mercury at the upper station,

$x = 55.000 \times \dfrac{h-h'}{h+h'}$. Add $\frac{1}{440}$ of this result for each degree which the mean temperature of the air at the two stations exceeds 55°, and deduct as much for each degree below 55°.

Velocity and Force of Wind.

Miles in an hour.	Feet in a minute.	Pressure on a square foot in pounds avoirdupois.	Description.
1	.88	.005	Barely observable.
2	176	.020	Just perceptible.
3	264	.045	
4	352	.080	Light breeze.
5	440	.125	Gentle, pleasant wind.
6	528	.180	
8	704	.320	
10	880	.500	Brisk blow.
15	1320	1.125	
20	1760	2.000	Very brisk.
25	2200	3.125	
30	2640	4.500	High wind.
35	3080	6.125	
40	3520	8.000	Very high.
45	3960	10.125	
50	4400	12.500	Storm.
60	5280	18.000	Great storm.
80	7040	32.000	Hurricane.
100	8800	50.000	Tornado, tearing up trees, &c.

To find the Force of Wind acting perpendicularly upon a Surface.

RULE.—Multiply the surface in feet by the square of the velocity in feet, and the product by .002288; the result is the force in avoirdupois pounds.

Q

STATICS.

PRESSURE OF EARTH AGAINST WALLS.

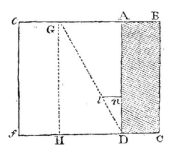

Let A B C D be the vertical section of a wall, behind which is a bank of earth, A D *fe*; let D G be the line of rupture, or *natural slope* which the earth would assume but for the resistance of the wall.

In sandy or loose earth, the angle G D H is generally 30°; in firmer earth it is 36°, and in some instances it is 45°.

The angle formed with the vertical by the earth, A D G, that exerts the greatest horizontal stress against a wall, is half the angle which the natural slope makes with the vertical.

If the upper surface of the earth and the wall which supports it are both in one horizontal plane,

Then the resultant *l n* of the pressure of the bank, behind a vertical wall, is at a distance D *n* of $\frac{1}{3}$ A D.

In vegetable earths, the friction is $\frac{1}{2}$ the pressure; in sands, $\frac{4}{10}$.
The line of rupture A G in a bank of vegetable earth is = .618 of A D.
When the bank is of sand, it is .677 of A D.
If of rubble, it is .414 of A D.

Thickness of Walls, both Faces Vertical.

Brick. Weight of a cubic foot, 109 lbs. avoirdupois, bank of vegetable earth behind it, A B = .16 A D.
Unhewn stones. 135 lbs. per cubic foot, bank as before, A B = .15 A D.
Brick. Bank clay, well rammed, A B = .17 A D.
Hewn freestone. 170 lbs. per cubic foot, bank of vegetable earth, A B = .13 A D; if the bank is of clay, A B = .14 A D.
Bricks. Bank of sand, A B = .33 A D.
Unhewn stone. Bank of sand, A B = .30 A D.
Hewn freestone. Bank of sand, A B = .26 A D.

When the bank is liable to be saturated with water, the thickness of the wall must be doubled.

For farther notes, and for the *Equilibrium of Piers*, see *Gregory's Mathematics*, pages 220 to 234.

DYNAMICS.

DYNAMICS is the investigation of *body, force, velocity, space,* and *time.*

Let them be represented by their initial letters *b f v s t,* gravity by *g,* and *momentum* or quantity of motion by *m;* this is the effect produced by a body in motion.

Force is motive, and accelerative or retardative.

Motive force, or momentum, is the absolute force of a body in motion, and is the product of the weight or mass of matter in the body, multiplied by its velocity.

Accelerative or retardative force is that which respects the velocity of the motion only, accelerating or retarding it, and is found by the force being divided by the mass or weight of the body. Thus, if a body of 4 lbs. be acted upon by a force of 40 lbs., the accelerating force is 10 lbs. ; but if the same force of 40 act upon another body of 8 lbs., the accelerating force then is 5 lbs., only half the former, and will produce only half the velocity.

Uniform Motion.

The space described by a body moving uniformly is represented by the product of the velocity into the time.

With momenta, *m* varies as *b v.*

EXAMPLE.—Two bodies, one of 20, the other of 10 lbs., are impelled by the same momentum, say 60. They move uniformly, the first for 8 seconds, the second for 6 ; what are the spaces described by both ?

$$\frac{b}{v} = v, \text{ or } \frac{60}{20} = 3, \text{ and } \frac{60}{10} = 6.$$

Then $t v = 3 \times 8 = 24 = s,$ and $6 \times 6 = 36 = s.$

Thus the spaces are 24 and 36 respectively.

Motion Uniformly Accelerated.

In this motion, the velocity acquired at the end of any time whatever, is equal to the product of the accelerating force into the time, and the space described is equal to the product of half the accelerating force into the square of the time.

The spaces described in successive seconds of time are as the odd numbers, 1, 3, 5, 7, 9, &c.

Gravity is a constant force, and its effect upon a body falling freely is represented by *g.*

The following theorems are applicable to all cases of motion uniformly accelerated by any constant force :

$$s = \tfrac{1}{2} tv = \tfrac{1}{2} g F t^2 = \frac{v^2}{2 gF}.$$

$$v = \frac{2s}{t} = gFt = \sqrt{2 gfs}.$$

$$t = \frac{ts}{v} = \frac{v}{gF} = \sqrt{\frac{s}{\tfrac{1}{2} gF}}.$$

$$F = \frac{v}{gt} = \frac{2s}{gt^2} = \frac{v^2}{2 gs}.$$

When gravity acts alone, as when a body falls in a vertical line, F is omitted, and we have,

$$s = \tfrac{1}{2} g t^2 = \frac{v^2}{2 g} = \tfrac{1}{2} tv.$$

$$v = gt = \frac{2s}{t} = \sqrt{2 gs}.$$

$$t = \frac{v}{g} \quad = \frac{2s}{v} = \sqrt{\frac{2s}{g}}.$$

$$g = \frac{v}{t} \quad = \frac{2s}{t^2} = \frac{v^2}{2s}.$$

NOTE.—*g is obviously 32.166 from what has been given in rules for Gravitation, and is the force of gravity.*

If, instead of a heavy body falling freely, it be propelled vertically upward or downward with a given velocity, v, then

$$s = tv \mp \tfrac{1}{2} gt^2 ;$$

an expression in which — must be taken when the projection is upward, and + when it is downward.

Motion over a Fixed Pulley.

Let the two weights which are connected by the cord that goes over the pulley be represented by W and w; then

$$\frac{W-w}{W+w} = F \text{ in the formulæ where F is used ; so that}$$

$$s = \frac{W-w}{W+w} \tfrac{1}{2} gt^2.$$

Or, if the resistance of the friction and inertia of the pulley be represented by r, then

$$s = \frac{W-w}{W+w+r} \tfrac{1}{2} gt^2.$$

EXAMPLE.—If by experiment it is ascertained that two weights of 5 and 3 lbs. over a pulley, the heavier weight descended only 50 feet in 4 seconds, what is the measure of r?

If r is not considered, the heavier weight would fall $64\frac{1}{3}$ feet.

$$\text{Then} \frac{W-w}{W+w+r} \tfrac{1}{2} gt^2 = 50 \text{ feet.}$$

And, as $5+3+r : 5+3 :: 64\frac{1}{3} : 50;$
That is   . $r : 5+3 :: 14\frac{1}{3} : 50.$

Whence . . . $r = \frac{8 \times 14\frac{1}{3}}{50} = 2.293$ lbs., *Ans.*

TABLE *of the Effects of a Force of Traction of 100 lbs. at different Velocities, on Canals, Railroads, and Turnpikes.*

Velocity.		On a Canal.		On a Railroad.		On a Turnpike.	
Miles per hr.	Feet per second.	Mass moved.	Useful effect.	Mass moved.	Useful effect.	Mass moved.	Useful effect.
		lbs.	lbs.	lbs.	lbs.	lbs.	lbs.
$2\frac{1}{2}$	3.66	55.500	39.400	14.400	10.800	1.800	1.350
3	4.40	38.542	27.361	14.400	10.800	1.800	1.350
$3\frac{1}{2}$	5.13	28.316	20.100	14.400	10.800	1.800	1.350
4	5.86	21.680	15.390	14.400	10.800	1.800	1.350
5	7.33	13.875	9.850	14.400	10.800	1.800	1.350
6	8.80	9.635	6.840	14.400	10.800	1.800	1.350
7	10.26	7.080	5.026	14.400	10.800	1.800	1.350
8	11.73	5.420	3.848	14.400	10.800	1.800	1.350
9	13.20	4.282	3.040	14.400	10.800	1.800	1.350
10	14.66	3.468	2.462	14.400	10.800	1.800	1.350
13.5	19.9	1.900	1.350	14.400	10.800	1.800	1.350

The load carried, added to the weight of the vessel or carriage which contains it, forms the total mass moved, and the useful effect is the load.

The force of traction on a canal varies as the square of the velocity; on a railroad or turnpike the force of traction is constant, but the mechanical power necessary to move the carriage increases as the velocity.

PENDULUMS.

THE Vibrations of Pendulums are as the square roots of their lengths. The length of one vibrating seconds in New-York at the level of the sea is 39.1013 inches.

To find the Length of a Pendulum for any Given Number of Vibrations in a Minute.

RULE.—As the number of vibrations given is to 60, so is the square root of 39.1013 (the length of the pendulum that vibrates seconds) to the square root of the length of the pendulum required.

EXAMPLE.—What is the length of a pendulum that will make 80 vibrations in a minute?

As $\sqrt{39.1013} \times 60 = 375$, a constant number,

Then $\dfrac{375}{80} = 4.6875$, and $4.6875^2 = 21.97$ inches, *Ans.*

The lengths of pendulums for less or greater times is as the square of the times; thus, for $\frac{1}{2}$ a second it would be the square of $\frac{1}{2}$, or $\dfrac{39.1013}{4} = 9.7753$ inches, the length of a $\frac{1}{2}$ second pendulum at New-York.

To find the Number of Vibrations in a Minute, the Length of the Pendulum being given.

RULE.—As the square root of the length of the pendulum is to the square root of 39.1013, so is 60 to the number of vibrations required.

EXAMPLE.—How many vibrations will a pendulum of 49 inches long make in a minute?

$\sqrt{49} : \sqrt{39.1013} : : 60 :$ number of vibrations.

Or, $\dfrac{375}{\sqrt{49}} = 53.57$ vibrations, *Ans.*

To find the Length of a Pendulum, the Vibrations of which will be the same Number as the Inches in its Length.

RULE.—Square the cube root of *375, and the product is the answer.

EXAMPLE.—$\sqrt[3]{375} = 7.211247$, and $7.211247^2 = 52.002$, *Ans.*

The Length of a Pendulum being given, to find the Space through which a Body will fall in the Time that the Pendulum makes one Vibration.

RULE.—Multiply the length of the pendulum by 4.93482528, and it will give the answer.

---

* 375 is the constant for the latitude of New-York; in any other place, multiply the square root of the length of the pendulum at that place by 60.

EXAMPLE.—The length of the pendulum is 39.1013 inches ; what is the distance a body will fall in one vibration of it ?

$39.1013 \times 4.9348 = 192.9578$ inches, or 16.8298 feet, *Ans.*

All vibrations of the same pendulum, whether great or small, are performed very nearly in the same time.

In a *Simple Pendulum*, which is, as a ball, suspended by a rod or line, supposed to be inflexible, and without weight, the length of the pendulum is the distance from its centre of gravity to its point of suspension. Otherwise, the length of the pendulum is the distance from the point of suspension to the *Centre of Oscillation,** which does not coincide with the centre of gravity of the ball or bob.

CENTRE OF GYRATION.

THE Centre of Gyration is the point in any revolving body, or system of bodies, that, if the whole quantity of matter were collected in it, the angular velocity would be the same; that is, the momentum of the body or system of bodies is centred at this point.

If a straight bar, equally thick, was struck at this point, the stroke would communicate the same angular velocity to the bar as if the whole bar was collected at that point.

To find the Centre of Gyration.

RULE 1.—Multiply the weight of the several particles by the squares of their distances in feet from the centre of motion, and divide the sum of the products by the weight of the entire mass ; the square root of the quotient will be the distance of the centre of gyration from the centre of motion.

EXAMPLE.—If two weights of 3 and 4 lbs. respectively be laid upon a lever (which is here assumed to be without weight) at the respective distances of 1 and 2 feet, what is the distance of the centre of gyration from the centre of motion (the fulcrum)?

$$3 \times 1^2 = 3. \qquad\qquad 4 \times 2^2 = 16.$$

$$\frac{3+16}{3+4} = \frac{19}{7} = 2.71, \text{ and } \sqrt{2.71} = 1.64 \text{ feet, } Ans.$$

That is, a single weight of 7 lbs., placed at 1.64 feet from the fulcrum, and revolving in the same time, would have the same impetus as the two weights in their respective places.

---

* See Centre of Oscillation.

Rule 2.—Multiply the distance of the centre of oscillation, from the centre or point of suspension, by the distance of the centre of gravity from the same point, and the square root of the product will be the answer.

Example.—The centre of oscillation is 9 feet, and that of gravity is 4 feet from the centre of the system, or point of suspension; at what distance from this point is the centre of gyration?

$$9 \times 4 = 36, \text{ and } \sqrt{36} = 6 \text{ feet, } Ans.$$

The following are the distances of the centres of gyration from the centre of motion in various revolving bodies, as given by Mr. Farey:

In a straight, uniform Rod, revolving about one end; length of rod $\times.5773$.

In a circular Plate, revolving on its centre; the radius of the circle $\times.7071$.

In a circular Plate, revolving about one of its diameters as an axis; the radius $\times.5$.

In a Wheel of uniform thickness, or *in a Cylinder* revolving about the axis; the radius $\times.7071$.

In a solid Sphere, revolving about one of its diameters as an axis; the radius $\times.6325$.

In a thin, hollow Sphere, revolving about one of its diameters as an axis; the radius $\times.8164$.

In a Cone, revolving about its axis; the radius of the circular base $\times.5477$.

In a right-angled Cone, revolving about its vertex; the height of the cone $\times.866$.

In a Paraboloid, revolving about its axis; the radius of the circular base $\times.5773$.

In a straight Lever, the arms being R and r, the distance of the centre of gyration from the centre of motion $= \sqrt{\dfrac{R^3 + r^3}{3(R - r)}}$.

Note.—*The weight of the revolving body, multiplied into the height due to the velocity with which the centre of gyration moves in its circle, is the energy of the body, or the mechanical power which must be communicated to it to give it that motion.*

Example.—In a solid sphere revolving about its diameter, the diameter being 2 feet, the distance of the centre of gyration is $12 \times .6325 = 7.59$ inches.

CENTRES OF PERCUSSION AND OSCILLATION.

The Centres of Percussion and Oscillation being in the same point, their properties are the same, and their point is, that in a body revolving around a fixed axis, which, when stopped by any force, the whole motion, and tendency to motion, of the revolving body is stopped at the same time.

It is also that point of a revolving body which would strike any obstacle with the greatest effect, and from this property it has received the name of percussion.

As in bodies at rest, the whole weight may be considered as collected in the centre of gravity; so in bodies in motion, the whole force may be considered as concentrated in the centre of percussion: therefore, the weight of a bar or rod, multiplied by the distance of the centre of gravity from the point of suspension, will be equal to the force of the rod, divided by the distance of the centre of percussion from the same point.

EXAMPLE.—The length of a rod being 20 feet, and the weight of a foot in length equal 100 oz., having a ball attached at the under end weighing 1000 oz., at what point of the rod from the point of suspension will be the centre of percussion ?*

The weight of the rod is $20 \times 100 = 2000$ oz., which, multiplied by half its length, $2000 \times 10 = 20000$, gives the momentum of the rod. The weight of the ball $= 1000$ oz., multiplied by the length of rod, $= 1000 \times 20$, gives the momentum of the ball. Now the weight of the rod multiplied by the square of the length, and divided by 3, $= \dfrac{2000 \times 20^2}{3} = 266666$, the force of the rod, and the weight of the ball multiplied by the square of the length of the rod, $1000 \times 20^2 = 400000$, is the force of the ball: therefore, the centre of percussion $= \dfrac{266666 + 400000}{20000 + 20000} = 16.66$ feet.

EXAMPLE.—Suppose a rod 12 feet long, and 2 lbs. each foot in length, with 2 balls of 3 lbs. each, one fixed 6 feet from the point of suspension, and the other at the end of the rod; what is the distance between the points of suspension and percussion ?

$$12 \times 2 \times 6 = 144, \text{ momentum of rod,}$$
$$3 \times 6 \quad = 18 \quad \text{``} \quad \text{of 1st ball,}$$
$$3 \times 12 \quad = \underline{36} \quad \text{``} \quad \text{of 2d ``}$$
$$198$$

$$\frac{24 \times 144}{3} = 1152, \text{ force of rod,}$$
$$3 \times 36 = 108 \quad \text{`` of 1st ball,}$$
$$3 \times 144 = \underline{432} \quad \text{`` of 2d ball,}$$
$$1692$$

therefore the centre of percussion $= \dfrac{1692}{198} = 8.545$ feet from the point of suspension·

As the centre of percussion is the same with the centre of oscillation in the non-application to practical purposes, the following is the easiest and simplest mode of finding it in any beam, bar, &c.:

Suspend the body very freely by a fixed point, and make it vibrate in small arcs, counting the number of vibrations it makes in any time, as a minute, and let the number of vibrations made in a minute be called n; then shall the distance of the centre of oscillation from the point of suspension be $= \dfrac{140850}{n^2}$ inches. For the length of the pendulum vibrating seconds, or 60 times in a minute, being $39\frac{1}{8}$ inch-

---

* $a = 20$ feet long,
$b = 100$ oz. weight of a foot in length, $\left. \right\} \dfrac{\frac{1}{3} ab \times a^2 + ca^2}{\frac{1}{2} ab \times a + ac} =$ centre of percussion.
$c = 1000$ " fixed at end,

es, and the lengths of the pendulums being reciprocally as the square of the num ber of vibrations made in the same time, therefore $n^2 : 60^2 : : 39\frac{1}{8} : \frac{60^2 \times 39\frac{1}{8}}{n^2} = \frac{140850}{n^2}$, being the length of the pendulum which vibrates n times in a minute, or the distance of the centre of oscillation below the axis of motion.

There are many situations in which bodies are placed that prevent the application of the above rule, and for this reason the following data are given, which will be found useful when the bodies and the forms here given correspond :

1. If the body is a heavy, straight line of uniform density, and is suspended by one extremity, the distance of its centre of percussion is $\frac{2}{3}$ of its length.

2. In a slender rod of a cylindrical or prismatic shape, the breadth of which is very small compared with its length, the distance of its centre of percussion is nearly $\frac{2}{3}$ of its length from the axis of suspension.

If these rods were formed so that all the points of their transverse sections were equidistant from the axis of suspension, the distance of the centre of percussion would be exactly $\frac{2}{3}$ of their length.

3. In an Isosceles triangle, suspended by its apex, and vibrating in a plane perpendicular to itself, the distance of the centre of percussion is $\frac{3}{4}$ of its altitude. A line or rod, whose density varies as the distance from its extremity, or the point of suspension ; also *Fly-wheels, or wheels in general*, have the same relation as the isosceles triangle, the centre of percussion being distant from the centre of suspension $\frac{3}{4}$ of its length.

4. In a very slender cone or pyramid, vibrating about its apex, the distance of its centre of percussion is nearly $\frac{4}{5}$ of its length.

The distance of either of these centres from the axis of motion is found thus :

If the Axis of Motion be in the vertex of the figure, and the motion be flatwise ; then, in a right line, it is $\frac{2}{3}$ of its length.

In an Isosceles Triangle $= \frac{3}{4}$ of its height.

In a Circle $= \frac{3}{4}$ of its radius.

In a Parabola $= \frac{5}{7}$ of its height.

But if the bodies move sidewise, it is,

In a Circle $= \frac{3}{4}$ of its diameter.

In a Rectangle, suspended by one angle, $= \frac{2}{3}$ of the diagonal.

In a Parabola, suspended by its vertex, $= \frac{5}{7}$ axis $+ \frac{1}{3}$ parameter ; but if suspended by the middle of its base, $= \frac{4}{7}$ axis $+ \frac{1}{2}$ parameter.

In the Sector of a Circle $= \dfrac{3 \times \text{arc} \times \text{radius}}{4 \times \text{chord}}$

In a Cone $= \frac{4}{5}$ axis $+ \dfrac{\text{radius of base }^2}{5 \times \text{axis}}$.

In a Sphere $= \dfrac{2 \times \text{radius }^2}{5(t \times \text{radius})} +$ radius $+ t$, t representing the length of the thread by which it is suspended.

EXAMPLE.—What must be the length of a rod without a weight, so that when hung by one end it shall vibrate seconds ?

To vibrate seconds, the centre of oscillation must be 39.1013 inches from that of suspension ; and as this must be $\frac{2}{3}$ of the rod,
Then $2 : 3 : : 39.1013 : 58.6519$, *Ans.*

EXAMPLE.—What is the centre of percussion of a rod 23 inches long ?
$\frac{2}{3}$ of $23 = 15.3$ inches from the point of suspension or motion.

EXAMPLE.—In a sphere of 10 inches diameter, the thread by which it is suspended being 20 inches, where is the centre of percussion or oscillation ?
$\dfrac{2 \times 5^2}{5(20+5)} + 5 + 20 = \dfrac{50}{125} + 25 = 25.4$, *Ans.*

These centres are in the same point only when the body is symmetrical with regard to the plane of motion, or when it is a solid of revolution, which is commonly the case.

CENTRAL FORCES.

ALL bodies moving around a centre or fixed point have a tendency to fly off in a straight line : this is called the *Centrifugal Force;* it is opposed to the *Centripetal Force*, or that power which maintains the body in its curvilineal path.

The *centrifugal force* of a body, moving with different velocities in the same circle, is proportional to the square of the velocity. Thus, the centrifugal force of a body making 10 revolutions in a minute is four times as great as the centrifugal force of the same body making 5 revolutions in a minute.

To find the Centrifugal Force of any Body.

RULE 1.—Divide the velocity in feet per second by 4.01, also the square of the quotient by the diameter of the circle; the quotient is the centrifugal force, assuming the weight of the body as 1. Then this, multiplied by the weight of the body, is the centrifugal force.

EXAMPLE.—What is the centrifugal force of the rim of a fly-wheel 10 feet in diameter, running with a velocity of 30 feet in a second ?

$$30 \div 4.01 \times 7.48 \div 10 = 5.59 \text{ times the weight of the rim, } Ans.$$

NOTE.—When great accuracy is required, find the centre of gyration of the body and take twice the distance of it from the axis for the diameter.

RULE 2.—Multiply the square of the number of revolutions in a minute by the diameter of the circle in feet, and divide the product by the constant number 5870; the quotient is the centrifugal force when the weight of the body is 1. Then, as in the previous rule, this quotient, multiplied by the weight of the body, is the centrifugal force.

EXAMPLE.—What is the centrifugal force of a grindstone, weighing 1200 lbs., 42 inches in diameter, and turning with a velocity of 400 revolutions in a minute ?

$$\frac{400^2 \times 3.5}{5870} \times 1200 = 114480 \text{ lbs., } Ans.$$

The central forces are as the radii of the circles directly, and the squares of the times inversely; also, the squares of the times are as the cubes of the distances.

Hence, let v represent velocity of body in feet per second,
  w "   weight of body,
  r "   radius of circle of revolution,
  c "   centrifugal force.

$$\text{Then } \frac{v^2 \times w}{r \times 32} = c, \quad \text{and } \frac{v^2 \times w}{c \times 32} = r ;$$

$$\text{and } \frac{c \times 32 \times r}{v} = w, \text{ and } \sqrt{\left(\frac{r \times 32 \times c}{w}\right)} = v.$$

Dr. Brewster has furnished the following :

1. The centrifugal forces of two unequal bodies, having the same velocity, and at the same distance from the central body, are to one another as the respective quantities of matter in the two bodies.

2. The centrifugal forces of two equal bodies, which perform their revolutions in the same time, but are different distances from their axis, are to one another as their respective distances from their axis.

3. The centrifugal forces of two bodies, which perform their revolutions in the same time, and whose quantities of matter are inversely as their distances from the centre, are equal to one another.

4. The centrifugal forces of two equal bodies, moving at equal distances from the central body, but with different velocities, are to one another as the squares of their velocities.

5. The centrifugal forces of two equal bodies, moving with equal velocities at different distances from the centre, are inversely as their distances from the centre.

6. The centrifugal forces of two unequal bodies, moving with equal velocities at different distances from the centre, are to one another as their quantities of matter multiplied by their respective distances from the centre.

7. The centrifugal forces of two unequal bodies, having unequal velocities, and at different distances from their axis, are, in the compound ratio of their quantities of matter, the squares of their velocities, and their distances from the centre.

The weight of the rim of a fly-wheel for a 20 horse engine is 6000 lbs., the diameter 16 feet, and the revolutions 45 ; what is its centrifugal force ?

33120 lbs., *Ans.*

SUMMARY.—Let b represent any particle of a body B, and d its distance from the axis of motion, S.

G, O, R, the centres of Gravity, Oscillation, and Gyration.

Then $\dfrac{bd}{B} = S\,G.$

$$\frac{bd^2}{S\,G\,B} = S\,O.$$

$$\sqrt{\frac{bd^2}{B}} = S\,R.$$

FLY-WHEELS.

To find the Weight of Fly-wheels.

RULE.—Multiply the horses' power of the engine by 2240, and divide the product by the square of the velocity of the circumference of the wheel in feet per second; the quotient will be the weight in 100 lbs.

EXAMPLE.—The power of an engine is 35 horses, the diameter of the wheel 14 feet, and the revolutions 40; what should be the weight of the wheel?

$$35 \times 2240 \div \overline{40 \times 14 \times 3.1416 \div 60^2} = \frac{78400}{858.5} \times 100 = 9130 \text{ lbs.}$$

The weight of the wheel in engines that are subjected to irregular motion, as in the cotton-press, rolling-mill, &c., must be greater than in others where so sudden a check is not experienced, and 3000 would be a better multiplier in such cases.

GOVERNORS.

THE Governor acts upon the principle of central forces.

When the balls diverge, the ring or the vertical shaft raises, and that in proportion to the increase of the velocity squared; or, the square roots of the distances of the ring from the top, corresponding to two velocities, will be as these velocities.

EXAMPLE.—If a governor make 6 revolutions in a second when the ring is 16 inches from the top, what will be the distance of the ring when the speed is increased to 10 revolutions in the same time?

As $10'' : 6' :: \sqrt{16}$ inches : 2.4 inches, which, squared, is 5.76 inches, the distance of the ring from the top.

A governor performs in one minute half as many revolutions as a pendulum vibrates, the length of which is the perpendicular distance between the plane in which the balls move and the centre of suspension.

GUNNERY.

It has been ascertained by experiment that the velocity of the ball projected from a gun varies as the square root of the charge directly, and as the square root of the weight of the ball reciprocally.— *Hutton.*

The same author furnishes the following practical rules :

To find the Velocity of any Shot or Shell.

Rule.—As the square root of the weight of the shot is to the square root of the weight of treble the weight of the powder, both taken in pounds, so is 1600 to the velocity in feet per second.

Example.—What is the velocity of a shot of 196 lbs., projected with a charge of 9 lbs. of powder?

$$14 : 5.2 : : 1600 : 594, \textit{Ans.}$$

When the Range for one Charge is given, to find the Range for another Charge, or the Charge for another Range.

Rule.—The ranges have the same proportion as the charges ; that is, as one range is to its charge, so is any other range to its charge, the elevation of the piece being the same in both cases.

Example.—If, with a charge of 9 lbs. of powder, a shot range 4000 feet, how far will a charge of $6\frac{3}{4}$ lbs. project the same shot at the same elevation?

$$9 : 6.75 : : 4000 : 3000, \textit{Ans.}$$

Given the Range for one Elevation, to find the Range at another Elevation.

Rule.—As the sine of double the first elevation is to its range, so is the sine of double another elevation to its range.

Example.—If a shot range 1000 yards when projected at an elevation of 45°, how far will it range when the elevation is 30° 16′, the charge of powder being the same?

$$\text{Sine of } 45° \times 2 \quad = 100000,$$
$$\text{Sine of } 30° \ 16′ \times 2 = \ 87064.$$

Then, as 100000 : 1000 : : 87064 : 870.64, *Ans.*

Example.—The range of a shell at 45° elevation being 3750 feet, at what elevation must a gun be set for a shell to strike an object at the distance of 2810 feet with the same charge of powder?

As 3750 : 100000 : : 2810 : 74934, the sine for double the elevation of 24° 16′, or of 65° 44′, *Ans.*

R

FRICTION.

EXPERIMENTS upon the effect of this branch of mechanical science are as yet not of such a nature as to furnish deductions for very satisfactory rules.

The friction of planed woods and polished metals, without lubrication, upon one another, is about $\frac{1}{4}$ of the pressure.

Friction does not increase with the increase of the rubbing surfaces.

The friction of metals is nearly constant; that of woods seems to increase with action.

The friction of a cylinder rolling upon a plane is as the pressure, and inversely as its diameter.

The friction of wheels is as the diameter of their axes directly, and as the diameter of the wheel inversely.

Friction is at a maximum after a state of rest; the addition is as the fifth root of the time.

The following are the results of some experiments, *without lubrication*, as given by Adcock:

FRICTION AFTER A STATE OF REST.

At a maximum, oak on oak, $\frac{1}{2.28}$ to $\frac{1}{2.39}$ of the weight, according to the magnitude of the surface; for oak on pine, $\frac{1}{1.5}$; for pine on pine, $\frac{1}{1.73}$; for elm on elm, $\frac{1}{2.13}$ of the weight, the fibres moving longitudinally.

When they cross at right angles, the friction of oak is $\frac{1}{3.76}$; for iron on oak, $\frac{1}{5.5}$; for iron on iron, $\frac{1}{3.5}$; for iron on brass, $\frac{1}{6}$, the surfaces well polished; but when larger, and not so smooth, $\frac{1}{3.8}$.

For iron on copper, with tallow, the friction is $\frac{1}{11}$ of the weight; when olive oil is used, the friction is increased to $\frac{1}{6}$.

The Friction on a level Railroad of a Locomotive is about $\frac{1}{5}$; that is, an engine weighing 10 tons has a tractive power of 2 tons by the friction of the surfaces of its wheels upon the rails.

FRICTION OF BODIES IN MOTION,
Without Lubrication.

When the surfaces are large, the friction increases with velocity.

For a pressure of from 100 to 4000 lbs. on a square foot, for oak on oak, the friction is about $\frac{1}{9.5}$, besides a resistance of about $1\frac{2}{3}$ lbs. for each square foot, independent of the pressure. When the surface is very small, the friction is somewhat diminished. For oak on pine, the friction is $\frac{1}{6.3}$; for pine on pine, $\frac{1}{6}$; for iron or copper on wood, $\frac{1}{13}$, which is much increased by an increase of the velocity; for iron on iron, $\frac{1}{3.55}$; for iron on copper, $\frac{1}{4.15}$; after much use, $\frac{1}{6}$ at all velocities.

Where the unctuous matter is interposed between the surfaces, the hardest were found to diminish the friction most where the weight was great. Tallow, applied between oak, reduced the friction to $\frac{1}{28}$ of the pressure. When the surfaces are very small, tallow loses its effect, and the friction is increased to $\frac{1}{14}$; the adhesion was about 7 lbs. per square foot.

With tallow between iron on oak, the friction is $\frac{1}{35}$; with brass on oak, $\frac{1}{47}$; for iron on iron, the friction is $\frac{1}{10}$, adhesion 1 lb. for 15 square inches; on copper, $\frac{1}{11}$, adhesion 1 lb. for 13 square inches; with soft grease or oil, the friction of iron on copper and brass was $\frac{1}{7}$ and $\frac{1}{8}$.

On the whole, in most machines, $\frac{1}{6}$ of the pressure is a fair estimate of the friction.

FRICTION ON AXES.

For axes of iron on copper, $\frac{1}{11}$ where the velocity was small, the friction being always a little less than for plane surfaces. An axis of iron, with a pulley of gua iacum, gave, with tallow, $\frac{1}{20}$.

FRICTION AND RIGIDITY OF CORDAGE.

Wet ropes, if small, are a little more flexible than dry; if large, a little less flexible. Tarred ropes are stiffer by about $\frac{1}{6}$, and in cold weather somewhat more.

FRICTION OF PIVOTS.

When the angle of the summit of the pivot is about 18° or 20°, the friction for garnet is $\frac{1}{1008}$ to $\frac{1}{1050}$; agate, $\frac{1}{880}$; rock crystal, $\frac{1}{784}$; glass, $\frac{1}{570}$; and steel (tempered), $\frac{1}{500}$. At an angle of 45° the friction is much reduced, and the friction of agate and steel are then nearly equal.

NOTES.—*In general, friction is increased in the ratio of the weight.*

Between woods, the friction is less when the grains cross each other than when they are placed in the same direction.

Friction is greater between surfaces of the same kind than between surfaces of different kinds.

The best *Lubricators* are, and in the following order: Tallow, Soft Soap, Lard, Oil, and Black-lead.

HEAT.

HEAT, in the ordinary application of the word, signifies, or, rather, implies the sensation experienced upon touching a body hotter, or of a higher temperature than the part or parts which we bring into contact with it ; in another sense, it is used to express the cause of that sensation.

To avoid any ambiguity that may arise from the use of the same expression, it is usual and proper to employ the word *Caloric* to signify the principle or cause of the sensation of heat.

CALORIC is usually treated of as a material substance, though its claims to this distinction are not decided ; the strongest argument in favour of this position is that of its power of radiation. On touching a hot body, caloric passes from it, and excites the feeling of warmth ; when we touch a body having a lower temperature than our hand, caloric passes from the hand to it, and thus arises the sensation of cold.

COMMUNICATION OF CALORIC.

Caloric passes through different bodies with different degrees of velocity. This has led to the division of bodies into *conductors* and *non-conductors* of caloric ; the former includes such as metals, which allow caloric to pass freely through their substance, and the latter comprises those that do not give an easy passage to it, such as stones, glass, wood, charcoal, &c.

TABLE *of the relative Conducting Power of different Bodies.*

Gold	.	.	.	1000	Platinum	.	.	.	981
Silver	.	.	.	973	Copper	.	.	.	898
Iron	.	.	.	374	Zinc	.	.	.	363
Tin	.	.	.	304	Lead	.	.	.	180
Marble	.	.	.	24	Porcelain	.	.	.	12.2
Fire-brick	.	.	.	11	Fire-clay	.	.	.	11.4

With Water as the Standard.

Water	.	.	.	10	Elm	.	.	.	32
Pine	.	.	.	39	Ash	.	.	.	31
Lime	.	.	.	39	Apple	.	.	.	28
Oak	.	.	.	33	Ebony	.	.	.	22

Relative Conducting Power of different Substances compared with each other.

Hare's fur	.	.	1.315	Cotton	.	.	.	1.046
Eider-down	.	.	1.305	Lint	.	.	.	1.032
Beaver's fur	.	.	1.296	Charcoal	.	.	.	.937
Raw silk	.	.	1.284	Ashes (wood)	.	.	.	.927
Wool	.	.	1.118	Sewing-silk	.	.	.	.917
Lamp-black	.	.	1.117	Air	.	.	.	.576

Relative Conducting Power of Fluids.

Mercury	.	.	.	1.000	Proof Spirit	.	.	.	.312
Water	.	.	.	.357	Alcohol (pure)	.	.	.	.232

RADIATION OF CALORIC.

When heated bodies are exposed to the air, they lose portions of their heat, by projection in right lines into space, from all parts of their surface.

Bodies which radiate heat best absorb it best.

Radiation is affected by the nature of the surface of the body; thus, black and rough surfaces radiate and absorb more heat than light and polished surfaces.

TABLE *of the Radiating Power of different Bodies.*

Water 100	Blackened tin 100
Lamp-black 100	Clean " 12
Writing paper 100	Scraped " 16
Glass 90	Ice 85
India ink 88	Mercury 20
Bright lead 19	Polished iron 15
Silver 12	Copper 12

REFLECTION OF CALORIC is the reverse of *Radiation*, and the one increases as the other diminishes.

SPECIFIC CALORIC.

SPECIFIC CALORIC is that which is absorbed by different bodies of equal weights or volumes when their temperature is equal, based upon the law, acknowledged as universal, *that similar quantities of different bodies require unequal quantities of caloric at any given temperature.* Dr. Black termed this, *capacity* for caloric; but as this term was supposed to be suggested by the idea that the caloric present in any substance is contained in its pores, and, consequently, the capacities of bodies for caloric would be inversely as their densities; and such not being the case, this word is apt to give an incorrect notion, unless it is remembered that it is but an expression of fact, and not of cause; and to avoid error, the word specific was proposed, and is now very generally adopted.

It is important to know the relative specific caloric of bodies. The most convenient method of discovering it is by mixing different substances together at different temperatures, and noting the temperature of the mixture; and by experiments it appears that the same quantity of caloric imparts twice as high a temperature to mercury as to an equal quantity of water; thus, when water at 100° and mercury at 40° are mixed together, the mixture will be at 80°, the 20° lost by the water causing a rise of 40° in the mercury; and when weights are substituted for measures, the fact is strikingly illustrated; for instance, on mixing a pound of mercury at 40° with a pound of water at 160°, a thermometer placed in it will stand at 155°. Thus it appears that the same quantity of caloric imparts twice as high a temperature to mercury as to an equal volume of water, and that the heat which gives 5° to water will raise an equal weight of mercury 115°, being the ratio of 1 to 23. Hence, if equal quantities of caloric be added to equal weights of water and mercury, their temperatures will be expressed in relation to each other by the numbers 1 and 23; or, in order to increase the temperature of equal weights of those substances to the same extent, the water will require 23 times as much caloric as the mercury.

The rule for finding by calculation, combined with experiment, the relative capacities of different bodies, is this :

Multiply the weight of each body by the number of degrees lost or gained by the mixture, and the capacities of the bodies will be inversely as the products.

Or, if the bodies be mingled in unequal quantities, the capacities of the bodies will be reciprocally as the quantities of matter, multiplied into their respective changes of temperature.

The general facts respecting specific caloric are as follows :

1. Every substance has a specific heat peculiar to itself, whence a change of composition will be attended by a change of capacity for caloric.

R 2

2. The specific heat of a body varies with its form. A solid has a less capacity for caloric than the same substance when in the state of a liquid; the specific heat of water, for instance, being 9 in the solid state, and 10 in the liquid.

3. The specific heat of equal weights of the same gas increases as the density decreases; the exact rate of increase is not known, but the ratio is less rapid than the diminution in density.

4. Change of capacity for caloric always occasions a change of temperature. Increase in the former is attended by diminution of the latter, and *vice versa*.

TABLES *of the Specific Heat of various Substances.*

1. Air taken as unity.

	Equal volumes.	Equal weights.
Air	1.000	1.000
Hydrogen	.903	12.340
Carbonic acid	1.258	.828
Oxygen	.976	.884
Olefiant gas	1.553	1.576

The specific heat of the foregoing compared with that of an equal quantity of water.

Water	1.000	Hydrogen	3.293
Air	2.669	Carbonic acid	.221
Oxygen	2.361	Olefiant gas	.420

2. Water taken as unity.

Bismuth	.0288	Tellurium	.0912
Lead	.0293	Copper	.0949
Gold	.0298	Nickel	.1035
Platinum	.0314	Iron	.1100
Tin	.0514	Cobalt	.1498
Silver	.0557	Sulphur	.1880
Zinc	.0927	Mercury	.0330

ILLUSTRATION.—If 1 lb. of coal will heat 1 lb. of water to 100º, $\frac{1.0000}{.0330}\left(\frac{1}{30}\right)$ of a lb. will heat 1 lb. of mercury to 100º.

The term *Capacity* for heat means the relative powers of bodies, in receiving and retaining heat, in being raised to any given temperature; while *Specific* applies to the actual quantity of heat so received and retained.

When a body has its density increased, its capacity for heat is diminished. The rapid reduction of air to $\frac{1}{4}$ of its volume evolves heat sufficient to inflame tinder.

TABLE *showing the relative Capacity for Heat of various Bodies.*

	Equal weights.	Equal vol.		Equal weights.	Equal vol.
Glass	.187	.448	Silver	.082	.833
Iron	.126	.993	Tin	.060	—
Brass	.116	.971	Gold	.050	.966
Copper	.114	1.027	Lead	.043	.487
Zinc	.102	—			

LATENT CALORIC is that which is insensible to the touch, or incapable of being detected by the thermometer. The quantity of heat necessary to enable ice to assume the fluid state is equal to that which would raise the temperature of the same weight of water 140º; and an equal quantity of heat is set free from water when it assumes the solid form.

If 5½ lbs. of water, at the temperature of 32º, be placed in a vessel, communicating with another one (in which water is kept constantly boiling at the temperature of 212°), until the former reaches this temperature of the latter quantity, then let it be weighed, and it will be found to weigh 6½ lbs., showing that 1 lb. of water has been received in the form of steam through the communication, and reconverted into water by the lower temperature in the vessel.

Now this pound of water, received in the form of steam, had, when in that form, a temperature of 212°. It is now converted into the liquid form, and still retains the same temperature of 212°; but it has caused 5½ lbs. of water to rise from the temperature of 32° to 212°, and this without losing any temperature of itself. It follows, then, that in returning to the liquid state, it has parted with 5½ times the number of degrees of temperature between 32° and 212°, which are equal 180°, and 180°×5½ = 990°. Now this heat was combined with the steam; but as it is not sensible to a thermometer, it is called *Latent.*

It is shown, then, that a pound of water, in passing from a liquid at 212° to steam at 212°, receives as much heat as would be sufficient to raise it through 990 thermometric degrees, if that heat, instead of becoming latent, had been *Sensible.*

The sum of the Sensible and Latent heat of Steam is always the same at any one temperature; thus, 990°+212° = 1202°.

If to a pound of newly-fallen snow were added a pound of water at 172°, the snow would be melted, and 32° will be the resulting temperature.

Latent Heat of Steam, and several Vapours.

Steam	.	.	990°	Nitric acid	.	.	532°
Alcohol	.	.	442°	Vinegar	.	.	875°
Ether	.	.	302°	Lead	.	.	610°

SENSIBLE CALORIC is free and uncombined, passing from one substance to another, affecting the senses in its passage, determining the height of the thermometer, and giving rise to all the results which are attributed to this active principle.

To reduce the Degrees of a Fahrenheit Thermometer to those of Reaumur and the Centigrade.

FAHRENHEIT TO REAUMUR.

RULE.—Multiply the number of degrees above or below the freezing point by 4, and divide by 9.

Thus, 212°—32 = 180×4 = 720÷9 = 80, *Ans.*
   —24°—32 =   8×4 =   32÷9 = 3.5, *Ans.*

FAHRENHEIT TO CENTIGRADE.

RULE.—Multiply the number of degrees above or below the freezing point by 5, and divide by 9.

Thus, 212°—32 = 180×5 = 900÷9 = 100, *Ans.*

MEDIUM HEAT of the globe is placed at 50°; at the torrid zone, 75°; at moderate climates, 50°; near the polar regions, 36°.

The extremes of *natural heat* are from —70° to 120°; of *artificial heat,* from —91° to 36000°.

EVAPORATION.

Evaporation produces cold, because heat must be absorbed to form vapour.

Evaporation proceeds only from the surface of the fluids, and therefore *other things equal* must depend upon the extent of surface exposed.

When a liquid is covered by a stratum of dry air, evaporation is rapid, even when the temperature is low.

As a large quantity of caloric passes from a sensible to a latent state during the formation of vapour, it follows that cold is generated by evaporation.

CONGELATION AND LIQUEFACTION.

Freezing water gives out 140° of heat. Water may be cooled to 20°. All solids absorb heat when becoming fluid.

The particular quantity of heat which renders a substance fluid is called its caloric of fluidity, or latent heat.
The heat absorbed in liquefaction is given out again in freezing.

Fluids boil in vacuo with 124° less of heat than when under the pressure of the atmosphere. On Mont Blanc water boils at 187°.

DISTILLATION.

Distillation is the depriving vapour of its latent heat, and, though it may be effected in *vacuo* with very little heat, no advantage in regard to a saving of fuel is gained, as the latent heat of vapour is increased in proportion to the diminution of sensible heat.

TABLE *of Effects upon Bodies by Heat.*

	Wedgewood.	Fahrenheit.
Chinese porcelain, softened .	156°	21357°
Cast iron, thoroughly smelted	150°	20577°
" " begins to melt .	130°	17977°
Smith's forge, greatest heat	125°	17327°
Stone-ware, bakes	102°	14337°
Welding heat of iron (greatest)	95°	13427°
" " (least)	90°	12777°
Plate glass, working heat	57°	8487°
Fine gold, melts .	32°	5237°
Fine silver, melts .	28°	4717°
Copper, melts	27°	4587°
Brass, melts .	21°	3807°
Red heat, visible by day	—	1077°
Iron, red hot in twilight	—	884°
Common fire	—	790°
Iron, bright red in the dark .	—	752°
Zinc, melts .	—	700°
Quicksilver, boils	—	660°
Linseed oil, boils .	—	600°
Lead, melts .	—	594°
Bismuth, melts	—	476°
Tin, melts .	—	442°
Tin and bismuth, equal parts, melt .	—	283°
Tin 3 parts, bismuth 5, and lead 2, melt	—	212°
Alcohol, boils	—	174°
Ether, boils .	—	98°
Human blood (heat of)	—	98°
Strong wines, freeze .	—	20°
Brandy, freezes .	—	7°
Mercury, melts .	—	—39°

Wedgewood's zero is 1077° of Fahrenheit, and each of his degrees is equal to 130° of Fahrenheit.

MISCELLANEOUS.

FRIGORIFIC MIXTURES.

Mixtures.		Thermometer falls, or degrees of cold produced.	Degrees of Fahrenheit.
Nitrate of Ammonia Water . . .	1 part 1 "	46°	From $+ 50^{\circ}$ to $+ 4^{\circ}$
Phosphate of Soda Nitrate of Ammonia Dilute Nitric Acid	9 parts 6 " 4 "	71°	From $+ 50^{\circ}$ to $- 21^{\circ}$
Sulphate of Soda Muriatic Acid	8 parts 5 "	50°	From $+ 50^{\circ}$ to 0°
Snow . . . Muriate of Lime .	2 parts 3 "	53°	From $- 15^{\circ}$ to $- 68^{\circ}$
Snow . . . Dilute Sulphuric Acid	8 parts 10 "	22°	From $- 68^{\circ}$ to $- 90^{\circ}$
Snow . . . Potash . . .	3 parts 4 "	83°	From $+ 32^{\circ}$ to $- 51^{\circ}$

EFFECTS OF HEAT.

Fahrenheit.	Wedgewood.	
-90°	—	Greatest cold ever produced.
-50°	—	Natural cold at Hudson's Bay.
0	—	Snow and salt, equal parts.
$+43^{\circ}$	—	Phosphorus burns.
60° to 77°	—	Vinous fermentation.
78°	—	Acetous fermentation begins.
88°	—	Acetification ends.
638°	—	Lowest heat of ignition of iron in the dark.
800°	—	Charcoal burns.
8490°	57	Working heat of plate glass.
14337°	102	Stone ware, fired.
16807°	124	Greatest heat of plate glass.
25127°	185	Greatest heat observed.

EXPANSION OF SOLIDS.

At 212°, the length of the bar at 32° considered as 1.0000000.

Glass . . .	.0008545	Gold . . .	.0014950
Platina . . .	.0009542	Copper . . .	.0017450
Cast Iron . .	.0011112	Brass . . .	.0019062
Steel . . .	.0011899	Silver . . .	.0020100
" annealed .	.0012200	Tin . . .	.0026785
Forged Iron . .	.0012575	Lead . . .	.0028436
Iron wire . .	.0014410	Zinc . . .	.0029420

To find the expansion in Surface, double the above; in Volume, triple them.

TABLE *of the Expansion of Air by Heat.*

By Mr. Dalton.

Fahrenheit.		Fahrenheit.		Fahrenheit.	
32°	1000	50°	1043	80°	1110
33°	1002	55°	1055	85°	1121
34°	1004	60°	1066	90°	1132
35°	1107	65°	1077	100°	1152
40°	1021	70°	1089	200°	1354
45°	1032	75°	1099	212°	1376

MELTING POINT OF ALLOYS.

Lead 2 parts, Tin 3 parts, Bismuth 5 parts, melts at . . . . 212°
" 1 " " 4 " " 5 " melts at . . . . 246°
" " 1 " " 1 " melts at . . . . 236°
" " 2 " " 1 " melts at . . . . 336°
Lead 2 parts, " 3 " melts at . . . . 334°
" " 8 " " 1 " melts at . . . . 392°
" 2 " " 1 " common solder melts at . . . . 475°.
" 1 " " 2 " soft solder   melts at . . . . 360°

GUNPOWDER.

PROPORTIONS OF INGREDIENTS.

		Saltpetre.	Charcoal.	Sulphur.
IN THE UNITED STATES.				
Military service	{	75.	15.	10.
	{	76.	14.	10.
Sporting	{	78.	12.	10.
	{	77.	13.	10.
IN ENGLAND.				
Military service		75.	15.	10.
Sporting	{	78.	14.	8.
	{	75.	17.	8.
IN FRANCE.				
Military service		75.	12.5	12.5
Sporting	{	78.	12.	10.
	{	76.	14.	10.
Blasting		62.	18.	20.

GRANULATION.

Diameter of sieve holes for Cannon powder	. .	.070 to .100 inches
" " Musket "	. .	.050 " .070 "
" " Rifle "	. .	.025 " .035 "

DENSITY OF POWDER.

Size of Grain.	Specific Gravity.	Number of grains in 10 troy grains.	Weight of 1 cubic foot.		Cubic ins. in 1 lb. loose.
			Loose.	Shaken.	
			oz.	oz.	
*Cannon . . .	1.630	350	922	1.000	30
Musket . . .	1.533	700	900	990	31
Rifle	1.535	16.000	860	960	32
Sporting . . .	1.800	35.000	885	1.035	31

To find how much Powder will fill a Shell.

Multiply the cube of the interior diameter in inches by .01744.

EXAMPLE.—How much powder will fill a shell, the internal diameter being 9 inches?

$$9^3 \times .01744 = 12.71 \text{ lbs., } Ans.$$

DIMENSIONS OF POWDER BARRELS.

Whole length	20.5 inches.
Length, interior in the clear	18. "
Interior diameter at the head	14. "
" " at the bilge	16. "
Thickness of staves and heads	.5 "
Weight of barrels about	25 lbs.

Proof of Powder.—One oz. with a 24 lb. ball. The mean range of new, proved at any one time, must not be less than 250 yards; but none ranging below 225 yards is received.

Powder in magazines that does not range over 180 yards is considered unserviceable.

Good powder averages from 280 to 300 yards; *small grain* from 300 to 320 yards.

The greatest initial velocity is obtained by powder of great specific gravity and of very coarse grain, giving 130 grains to 10 grains troy.

LIGHT.

LIGHT is similar to caloric in many of its qualities, being emitted in the form of rays, and subject to the same laws of reflection.

It is of two kinds, *Natural* and *Artificial;* the one proceeding from the sun and stars, the other from heated bodies.

Solids shine in the dark only when heated from 600° to 700°, and in daylight when the temperature reaches 1000°.

Relative intensity of light from the burning of various bodies is, for wax, 101 parts; tallow, 100; oil in an Argand lamp, 110; in a common lamp, 129; and an ill-snuffed candle, 229.

By experiments on coal gas, it appears that above 20 cubic feet are required to produce light equal in duration and in illuminating powers to a pound of tallow candles, six to a pound, set up and burned out one after the other.

In distilling 56 lbs. coal, the quantity of gas produced in cubic feet when the distillation was effected in 3 hours was 41.3, in 7 hours 37.5, in 20 hours 33.5, and in 25 hours 31.7.

TONNAGE.

By a law of Congress, the tonnage of vessels is found as follows :

FOR A DOUBLE-DECKED.

Take the length from the fore part of the stem to the after side of the sternpost above the upper deck ; the breadth at the broadest part above the main wales ; half of this breadth must be taken as the depth of the vessel ; then deduct from the length $\frac{3}{5}$ of the breadth, multiply the remainder by the breadth, and the product by the depth ; divide this last product by 95, and the quotient is the tonnage.

EXAMPLE.—What is the tonnage of a ship of the line, measuring, as above, 210 feet on deck, and 59 feet in breath?

$$59 \div 2 = 29.5, \text{ depth.}$$
$$210 - \tfrac{3}{5} \text{ of } 59 = 174.6 \times 59 \times 29.5 \div 95 = 3198.8 \text{ tons.}$$

FOR A SINGLE-DECKED.

Take the length and breadth as above directed for a double-decked, and deduct from the length $\frac{3}{5}$ of the breadth ; take the depth from the under side of the deck-plank to the ceiling of the hold ; then proceed as before.

EXAMPLE.—The length of a vessel is (as above) 223 feet, the breadth $39\frac{1}{2}$ feet, and the depth of hold $23\frac{1}{2}$ feet ; what is the tonnage?

$$223 - \tfrac{3}{5} \text{ of } 39.5 = 199.3 \times 39.5 \times 23.5 \div 95 = 1947.3 \text{ tons.}$$

A ton will stow $3\frac{1}{2}$ bales cotton.

NOTE.—*The burden of similar ships are to each other as the cubes of their like dimensions.*

CARPENTERS' MEASUREMENT.

FOR A SINGLE-DECKED.

Multiply the length of keel, the breadth of beam, and the depth of the hold together, and divide by 95.

FOR A DOUBLE-DECKED.

Multiply as above, taking half the breadth of beam for the depth of the hold, and divide by 95.

To find the Tonnage of English Vessels.

RULE.—Divide the length of the upper deck between the afterpart of the stem and the forepart of the sternpost into 6 *equal parts*, and note the foremost, middle, and aftermost points of division. Measure the *depths* at these three points in feet, and tenths of a foot, also the *depths* from the under side of the upper deck to the ceiling at the limber strake; or, in case of a break in the upper deck, from a line stretched in continuation of the deck. For the *breadths*, divide each depth into 5 equal parts, and measure the inside breadths at the following points, viz.: at ¼ and at ⅘ from the upper deck of the foremost and aftermost depths, and at ⅓ and ¼ from the upper deck of the midship depth. Take the *length*, at half the midship depth, from the afterpart of the stem to the forepart of the sternpost.

Then, to twice the midship depth, add the foremost and aftermost depths for the *sum of the depths;* and add together the foremost upper and lower breadths, 3 times the upper breadth with the lower breadth at the midship, and the upper and twice the lower breadth at the after division for the *sum of the breadths.*

Multiply together the sum of the depths, the sum of the breadths, and the length, and divide the product by 3500, which will give the number of tons, or register.

If the vessel have a poop or half-deck, or a break in the upper deck, measure the inside mean length, breadth, and height of such part thereof as may be included within the bulkhead; multiply these three measurements together, and divide the product by 92.4. The quotient will be the number of tons to be added to the result as above found.

For Open Vessels. The depths are to be taken from the upper edge of the upper strake.

For Steam Vessels. The tonnage due to the engine-room is deducted from the total tonnage calculated by the above rule.

To determine this, measure the inside length of the engine-room from the foremost to the aftermost bulkhead; then multiply this length by the midship depth of the vessel, and the product by the inside midship breadth at 0.40 of the depth from the deck, and divide the final product by 92.4.

S

PILING OF BALLS AND SHELLS.

To find the Number of Balls in a Triangular Pile.

RULE.—Multiply continually together the number of balls in one side of the bottom row, and that number increased by 1 ; also, the same number increased by 2 ; $\frac{1}{6}$ of the product will be the answer.

EXAMPLE.—What is the number of balls in a pile, each side of the base containing 30 balls ? ·

$$30 \times 31 \times 32 \div 6 = 4960, \textit{ Ans.}$$

To find the Number of Balls in a Square Pile.

RULE.—Multiply continually together the number in one side of the bottom course, that number increased by 1, and double the same number increased by 1 ; $\frac{1}{6}$ of the product will be the answer.

EXAMPLE.—How many balls are there in a pile of 30 rows ?

$$30 \times 31 \times 61 \div 6 = 9455, \textit{ Ans.}$$

To find the Number of Balls in an Oblong Pile.

RULE.—From 3 times the number in the length of the base row subtract one less than the breadth of the same ; multiply the remainder by the same breadth, and the product by one more than the same, and divide by 6.

EXAMPLE.—Required the number of balls in an oblong pile, the numbers in the base row being 16 and 7 ?

$$16 \times 3 - \overline{7 - 1} \times 7 \times \overline{7 + 1} \div 6 = 392, \textit{ Ans.}$$

To find the Number of Balls in an Incomplete Pile.

RULE.—From the number in the pile, considered as complete, subtract the number conceived to be in the upper pile which is wanting.

WEIGHT AND DIMENSIONS OF BALLS AND SHELLS.

THE weights of these may be found by the rules in Mensuration ; also, in the tables, pages 233, 236, and 255.

To find the Weight of an Iron Ball from its Diameter.

An iron ball of 4 inches diameter weighs 8.736 lbs. Therefore, $\frac{8.736}{64}$ of the cube of the diameter is the weight, for the weight of spheres is as the cubes of the diameters.

EXAMPLE.—What is the weight of a ball 10 inches in diameter ?

$$\frac{8.736}{64} \text{ of } 10^3 = 136.5 \text{ lbs., } Ans.$$

To find the Diameter from the Weight.

EXAMPLE.—What is the diameter of an iron ball, its weight being 99.5 lbs. ?

$$\sqrt[3]{\frac{64}{8.736} \times 99.5} = 9 \text{ inches, } Ans.$$

Or, multiply the cube of the diameter in inches by .1365, and the sum is the weight. And divide the weight in pounds by .1365, and the cube root of the product is the diameter.

To find the Weight of a Leaden Ball.

A leaden ball of 4 inches diameter weighs 13.744 lbs. Therefore, $\frac{13.744}{64}$ of the diameter is the weight.

EXAMPLE.—What is the weight of a leaden ball 10 inches in diameter?

$$\frac{13.744}{64} \text{ of } 10^3 = 214.7 \text{ lbs., } Ans.$$

Inversely, $\sqrt[3]{\frac{64}{13.744} \times \text{weight}} = \text{diameter.}$

Or, multiply the cube of the diameter in inches by .2147, and the sum is the weight. And divide the weight in pounds by .2147, and the cube root of the product is the diameter.

To find the Weight of a Cast Iron Shell.

Multiply the difference of the cubes of the exterior and interior diameter in inches by .1365.

EXAMPLE.—What is the weight of a shell having 10 and 8.50 inches for its diameters?

$$10^3 - 8.5^3 \times .1365 = 52.6 \text{ lbs., } Ans.$$

WINDING ENGINES.

In winding engines, for drawing coals, water, &c., out of a pit; where it is wanted to give a certain number of revolutions, it is necessary to know the diameter of the *drum* and the thickness of the rope.

Where flat ropes are used, and are wound one part over the other,

To find the Diameter of the Drum.

RULE.—Multiply the depth of the pit in inches by the thickness of the rope in inches for a dividend.

Multiply the number of revolutions by 3.1416, and the product by the thickness of the rope in inches for a divisor.

Divide the one by the other, and from the quotient subtract the product of the thickness of the rope and the number of revolutions; the remainder is the diameter in inches.

EXAMPLE.—If an engine make 20 revolutions, the depth of the pit being 600 feet, and the thickness of the rope 1 inch, what is the diameter of the drum?

$$600 \times 12 \times 1 \div \overline{20 \times 3.1416 \times 1} - \overline{1 \times 20} = 94.5 \text{ inches, } Ans.$$

To find the Diameter of the Roll.

RULE.—To the area of the drum add the area or edge surface of the rope, and the diameter of the circle having that area is the diameter of the roll.

EXAMPLE.—What is the diameter of the roll in the preceding example?

Area of 94.5 = 7013.8+ area of $\overline{7200 \times 1}$ = 14213.8, and $\sqrt{}$ of this sum ÷.7854 = 134.5, *Ans.*

Or, the radius of the drum is increased the number of the revolutions, multiplied by the thickness of the rope; as, $\frac{94.5}{2} + \overline{20 \times 1} =$ 67.25.

To find the Number of Revolutions.

RULE.—To the area of the drum add the area of the edge surface of the rope; then find by inspection in the table of areas, or by calculation, if necessary, the diameter that gives the exact area; subtract the diameter of the drum from this, and divide the remainder by twice the thickness of the rope; the quotient is the number of revolutions.

EXAMPLE.—The length of a rope is 2600 inches, its thickness 1 inch, and the diameter of the drum 20 inches. Required the number of revolutions.

Area of 20 + area of rope = 314.15+2600 = 2914.15, the diameter of which is 60.91, and 60.91—20÷$\overline{1 \times 2}$ = 20.45 revolutions.

To find the Place of Meeting of the Ascending and Descending Buckets when two or more are used.

Meetings will always be below half the depth of the pit, and

To find this Depth,

Take the circumference of the drum for the length of the first turn; then, to the diameter of the drum add twice the thickness of the rope, multiplied by the number of revolutions, less 1, for a diameter, and the circumference of this diameter is the length of the last turn; add these two lengths together, multiply their sum by half the number of revolutions, and the product is the depth of the pit.

EXAMPLE.—The diameter of a drum is 9 feet, the thickness of the rope 1 inch, and the revolutions 20; what is the depth of the pit, and at what distance from the top will buckets meet?

$9 \times 3.1416 = 28.27$, length of first turn;

$$9 + \frac{2 \times 1 \times \overline{20-1}}{12} = 12.166 \times 3.1416 = 38.23, \text{ length of last turn};$$

$$28.27 + 38.23 \times \frac{20}{2} = 665 \text{ feet, or depth of pit.}$$

At 10 revolutions the buckets will meet. Therefore, add 9 times twice the thickness of the rope to the diameter of the drum; to the circumference of this diameter add the length of the first turn, multiply their sum by half the number of turns to meetings, and the product is the distance from the bottom of the pit at which the buckets will meet.

$$\frac{9 \times 1 \times 2}{12} = 1.5 + 9 \times 3.1416 + 28.27 \times \frac{10}{2} = 306.25 \text{ feet, } Ans.$$

FRAUDULENT BALANCES.

IN *order to detect them*, after an equilibrium has been established between the weight and the article weighed, transpose them, and the weight will preponderate if the article weighed is lighter than the weight, and contrariwise. Then,

To ascertain the True Weight,

Let the weight which will produce equilibrium after transposition be found, and with the former weight be reduced to the same denomination of weight; and let the two weights thus expressed be multiplied together, and the square root of the product will be the true weight.

EXAMPLE.—If one weight be 7 lbs., and the other $9\frac{1}{7}$, $7 \times 9\frac{1}{7} = 64$, and the square root of 64 is 8; hence 8 lbs. is the true weight.

Or, let $a =$ length of longest arm, | $A =$ greatest weight,
$b =$ length of shortest arm, | $B =$ least weight.

Then $Wa = Ab$, and $Wb = Ba$; multiplying these two equations, we have $W^2 ab = ABab$, or $W^2 = AB$, and $W = \sqrt{AB}$.

MEASURING OF TIMBER.

Sawed or hewn timber is measured by the cubic foot.

The unit of *board measure* is a superficial foot 1 inch thick.

To measure Round Timber.

Multiply the length in inches by the square of ¼ the mean girth in inches, and the product, divided by 1728, will give the contents in cubic feet.

When the length is given in feet, and the girth in inches, divide by 144.
When all the dimensions are in feet, the product is the content without a division.

Or, $\dfrac{L \times C^2}{16} \div 144$, L the length in feet, and C half the sum of the circumferences of the two ends in inches.

Or, ascertain the contents by the rules in Mensuration of Solids, page 82, and multiply by .75734.

Example.—The girths of a piece of timber are 31.416 and 62.832 inches, and its length 50 feet; required its contents.

$\dfrac{31.416 + 62.832}{2} \div 4 = 11.781$, and $11.781^2 \times 50 \div 144 = 48.1916$ cubic feet, *Ans.*

Or, $\dfrac{50 \times 47.124^2}{16} \div 144 = 48.1916$ cubic feet.

Or, $10^3 - 20^3 \div \overline{20 - 10} \times .7854 \times \dfrac{600}{3} = 63.632 \times .75734 = 48.1916$ cubic feet, *Ans.*

To measure Square Timber.

Multiply the length in inches by the breadth in inches, and the product by the depth in feet; divide by 144, and the quotient is the content.

Note.—When all the dimensions are in feet, omit the divisor of 144.

BOARD MEASURE.

Multiply the length by the breadth, and the product is the content.

Note.—This rule only applies when all the dimensions are in feet. When either the length or breadth are given in inches, divide their product by 12; and when all the dimensions are in inches, divide it by 144.

Pine spars, from 10 to 4½ inches in diameter inclusive, and spruce spars, are to be measured by taking the diameter, clear of bark, at ⅓ of their length from the large end.

Spars are usually purchased by the inch diameter; all under 4 inches are considered *poles.*

Spruce spars of 7 inches and less should have 5 feet in length for every inch diameter. Those above 7 inches should have 4 feet in length for every inch diameter.

STEAM.

STEAM, arising from water at the boiling point, is equal to the pressure of the atmosphere, which is in round numbers 15 lbs. on the square inch.

TABLE *of the Expansive Force of Steam, from* 212° *to* 352½°.

(From experiments of Committee of Franklin Institute.)

The unit is the atmospheric pressure, 30 inches of mercury.

Degrees of heat.	Pressure.	Degrees of heat.	Pressure.	Degrees of heat.	Pressure.
212.°	1.	298.5°	4.5	331.°	7.5
235.°	1.5	304.5°	5.	336.°	8.
250.°	2.	310.°	5.5	340.5°	8.5
264.°	2.5	315.5°	6.	345.°	9.
275.°	3.	321.°	6.5	349.°	9.5
284.°	3.5	326.°	7.	352.°	10.
291.5°	4.				

Under the pressure of the atmosphere alone, water cannot be heated above the boiling point.

It has already been stated (see Heat) that the sum of sensible and latent heats is 1202°, and that 140° of sensible heat becomes latent upon the liquefaction of ice; also, that 1 lb. of water converted into steam at 212° will heat 5¼ lbs. of water at 32° to 212°, and that the sum is 6¼ lbs. of water.

TABLE *of the Volume of Air and Force of Vapour.*

Temperature.	Volume of air or vapour.	Force of vapour in inches of mercury.	Temperature.	Volume of air or vapour.	Force of vapour in inches of mercury.
0°	1000	.032	132°	1491	5.070
32°	1071	.172	152°	1689	8.330
52°	1123	.401	172°	1930	13.170
72°	1183	.842	192°	2287	20.160
92°	1255	1.629	212°	2672	30.
112°	1354	2.950			

To ascertain the Number of Cubic Inches of Water, at any Given Temperature, that must be mixed with a Cubic Inch of Steam to reduce the Mixture to any Required Temperature.

RULE.—From the required temperature subtract the temperature of the water; then find how often the remainder is contained in the given temperature, subtracted from 1202°, and the quotient is the answer.

EXAMPLE.—The temperature of the condensing water of an engine is 80°, and the required temperature 100°; what is the proportion of condensing water to that evaporated?

$$\overline{100-80} \div \overline{1202-100} = \frac{1102}{20} = 55.5, \textit{Ans.}$$

Again, the temperature is 60°, and the required temperature 100°.

$$1202—100\div(100—60)=\frac{1102}{40}=27.5,\ \textit{Ans.}$$

Or, let w represent temperature of condensing water, t the required temperature, and h the sum of sensible and latent heats.

$$\text{Then}\ \frac{h—t}{t—w}=\text{water required.}$$

To ascertain the Quantity of Steam required to raise a Given Quantity of Water to any Given Temperature.

Rule.—Multiply the water to be warmed by the difference of temperature between the cold water and that to which it is to be raised, for a dividend; then to the temperature of the steam add 990°, and from that sum take the required temperature of the water for a divisor; the quotient is the quantity of steam in the same terms as the water.

Example.—What quantity of steam at 212° will raise 100 cubic feet of water at 80° to 212°?

$$\frac{100\times\overline{212°—80}}{212°+990°—212°}=13.3\text{ cubic feet of water formed into steam, occupying (13.3}\times$$
1694) 22586.6 cubic feet of space.

Table of the Boiling Points corresponding to the Altitudes of the Barometer between 26 and 31 Inches.

Barometer.	Boiling point.	Barometer.	Boiling point.	Barometer.	Boiling point.
26.	204.91°	28.	208.43°	30.	212.°
26.5	205.79°	28.5	209.31°	30.5	212.88°
27.	206.67°	29.	210.19°	31.	213.76°
27.5	207.55°	29.5	211.07°		

A cubic inch of water, evaporated under the ordinary atmospheric pressure, is converted into 1694 cubic inches of steam, or, in round numbers, 1 cubic foot, and gives a mechanical force equal to the raising of 2200 lbs. 1 foot high.

The Pressure of Steam being given, to find its Temperature.

Rule.—Multiply the 6th* root of the pressure in inches by 177, and subtract 100 from the product.

Example.—If the pressure is 240 inches of mercury, what is the temperature?
$$\sqrt[6]{240}=2.493\times177—100=341.61,\ \textit{Ans.}$$

For sea water, multiply by 177.6; when $\frac{2}{3}$ saturated, by 178.3; and when $\frac{3}{3}$ saturated, by 179.

Table of the Density of Steam under different Pressures.

Atmospheres.	Density.	Volume.	Atmospheres.	Density.	Volume.
1	.00059	1694	10	.00492	203
2	.00110	909	12	.00581	172
3	.00160	625	14	.00670	149
4	.00210	476	16	.00760	131
5	.00258	387	18	.00849	117
6	.00306	326	20	.00937	106
8	.00399	250			

The volumes are not direct, in consequence of the increase of heat. See observations, page 198.

---

* See page 118 for rule to find this root.

TABLE *of the Expansive Force of Steam in Atmospheres.*

Temperature.	Pressure in atmospheres.	Temperature.	Pressure in atmospheres.	Temperature.	Pressure in atmospheres.
212.°	1	331.2°	7	413.8°	19
242.°	1½	341.8°	8	418.5°	20
250.6°	2	350.8°	9	423.°	21
264.°	2½	359.°	10	427.3°	22
277.2°	3	366.8°	11	431.4°	23
285.2°	3½	374.°	12	435.6°	24
293.8°	4	380.6°	13	438.7°	25
301.°	4½	387.°	14	457.2°	30
308.°	5	392.6°	15	472.8°	35
314.4°	5½	398.5°	16	486.6°	40
320.4°	6	403.8°	17	499.1°	45
326.3°	6½	409.°	18	510.6°	50

NOTE.—*This table gives results slightly differing from that furnished by the Franklin Institute, being about 3.5° for every 5 atmospheres.*

TABLE *of the Pressure, Specific Gravity, and Weight of a Cubic Foot of Steam at different Temperatures.*

Pressure in ins. of mercury.	Weight of a cub. foot in grains.	Spec. gravity, air being 1.	Pressure in ins. of mercury.	Weight of a cub. foot in grains.	Spec. gravity, air being 1.
.55	6.10	.0115	75.	593.50	1.123
1.	10.70	.0202	90.	700.	1.33
2.	20.50	.0388	105.	810.	1.53
3.	30.	.0568	120.	910.	1.728
4.	39.	.0744	150.	1110.	2.12
7.5	71.	.134	180.	1317.	2.5
15.	135.	.255	210.	1520.	2.88
22.5	196.	.371	240.	1660.	3.25
30.	254.70	.484	270.	1910.	3.61
35.	292.	.553	300.	2100.	3.97
45.	363.	.687	600.	3940.	7.44
52.5	427.	.810	900.	5670.	10.75
60.	483.	.915	1200.	7350.	13.88

A pressure of 1, 5, 10, 20, 40, and 50 lbs. on a square inch, will raise a mercurial gauge respectively 1.01, 5.08, 10.16, 20.32, 40.65, and 50.80 inches.

The mean is 1.0159 inches.

A column of mercury 2 inches in height will counterbalance a pressure of .98 lbs. on a square inch.

The practical estimate of the velocity of steam, when flowing into a vacuum, is about 1400 feet in a second when at an expansive power equal to the atmosphere; and when at 20 atmospheres, the velocity is increased but to 1600 feet.

And when flowing into the air under a similar power, about 650 feet per second, increasing to 1600 feet for a pressure of 20 atmospheres.

The elasticity of the vapour of spirit of wine, at all temperatures, is equal to 2.125 times that of steam.

STEAM ACTING EXPANSIVELY.

To find the Mean Pressure of the Steam on the Piston.

RULE.—Divide the length of the stroke, added to the clearance in the cylinder at one end, by the length of the stroke at which the steam is cut off, added to the clearance, and the quotient will express the relative expansion it undergoes.

Find in the following table, in the column of expansion, a number corresponding to this ; take out the multiplier opposite to it, and multiply it into the full pressure of the steam per square inch as it enters the cylinder.

TABLE *showing the Mean Pressure of Steam.*

Expansion.	Multiplier.	Expansion.	Multiplier.	Expansion.	Multiplier.
1.0	1.000	3.4	.654	5.8	.479
1.1	.995	3.5	.644	5.9	.474
1.2	.985	3.6	.634	6.	.470
1.3	.971	3.7	.624	6.1	.466
1.4	.955	3.8	.615	6.2	.462
1.5	.937	3.9	.605	6.3	.458
1.6	.919	4.	.597	6.4	.454
1.7	.900	4.1	.588	6.5	.450
1.8	.882	4.2	.580	6.6	.446
1.9	.864	4.3	.572	6.7	.442
2.	.847	4.4	.564	6.8	.438
2.1	.830	4.5	.556	6.9	.434
2.2	.813	4.6	.549	7.	.430
2.3	.797	4.7	.542	7.1	.427
2.4	.781	4.8	.535	7.2	.423
2.5	.766	4.9	.528	7.3	.420
2.6	.752	5.	.522	7.4	.417
2.7	.738	5.1	.516	7.5	.414
2.8	.725	5.2	.510	7.6	.411
2.9	.712	5.3	.504	7.7	.408
3.	.700	5.4	.499	7.8	.405
3.1	.688	5.5	.494	7.9	.402
3.2	.676	5.6	.489	8.	.399
3.3	.665	5.7	.484		

EXAMPLE.—Suppose the steam to enter the cylinder at a pressure of 20 lbs. per square inch, and to be cut off at ¼ the length of the stroke of the piston. The stroke being 8 feet,

8 feet = 96 inches + 1 for clearance = 97,
¼ = 24 inches + 1 " = 25.

Then 97÷25 = 3.88, the relative expansion which falls between 3.8 and 3.9. Referring to the table, the multiplier for 3.8 is .615, and the difference between that and the multiplier for 3.9 is .010. Hence, multiplying .010 by .8, and subtracting the product .008 from .615, the remainder, .607, is the multiplier for 3.88. Therefore, .607 ×20 lbs. = 12.140 lbs. per square inch, the mean effective pressure of the piston required.

Specific gravity of steam at the pressure of the atmosphere .490, air being 1.

FOR WARMING APARTMENTS.

Every cubic foot of water evaporated in a boiler at the pressure of the atmosphere will heat 2000 feet of enclosed air to an average temperature of 75º, and each square foot of surface of steam-pipe will warm 200 cubic feet of space.

The force of steam is the same at the boiling point for every fluid.

LOSS BY RADIATION.

To ascertain the Loss of Heat per Square Foot in a Second.

Let T = temperature of pipe, which is, say $\frac{1}{20}$ less than that of the steam,
t = temperature of the air,
l = length of the pipe in feet,
d = diameter in inches,
v = velocity in feet per second,
R = radiation in degrees of heat.

$$\frac{1.7l\,(T-t)}{dv} = R.$$

Tredgold.

STEAM-ENGINE.

It is not consistent with the plan of this work to enter fully into details of the steam-engine, and this article will be confined exclusively to some practical rules, the utility of which have been tested and their use adopted.

CONDENSING ENGINES.

Cylinder. The thickness of the metal is found by the following formula :

$$\frac{3 \cdot P \cdot d}{10000} \times \frac{d}{d-2.5} \div \tfrac{1}{2} = \text{thickness in inches, P representing pressure of steam in lbs., and } d \text{ diameter of cylinder.}$$

For cylinders over 30 inches diameter, divide by 9000 ; over 40 inches, by 8000 ; over 50 inches, by 6000 ; and over 60 inches, by 5000.

Condenser. The capacity of it should be $\frac{1}{4}$ that of the cylinder.

Air-pump. The capacity of it should be $\frac{1}{8}$ that of the cylinder.

Steam and Exhaust Valves. Their diameter should give an area of 10 square inches for every 10000 cubic inches contained in the cylinder, and should lift $\frac{1}{4}$ their diameter.

Foot and Delivery Valves. Their dimensions should give an area of $\frac{8}{10}$ that of the airpump.

Force Pumps. Their capacity should be $\frac{1}{100}$ to $\frac{1}{150}$ that of the cylinder.

Injection Cocks. Their area should be sufficient to supply 70 times the quantity of water evaporated when the engine is working at its maximum, and in marine engines there should be three of them to each condenser, viz., a Side, Bottom, and Bilge.

The Side injection should have $\frac{1}{12}$ of an inch diameter of pipe for every inch diameter of cylinder, the Bottom injection should have $\frac{1}{10}$* of an inch diameter of pipe for every inch diameter of cylinder ; ; the Bilge injection is usually a branch of the Bottom injection pipe, and may be of less capacity.

Piston Rod. Its diameter should be $\frac{1}{10}$ that of the cylinder.

Beam. Its length from centres should be twice the stroke of the piston, and its depth $\frac{9}{20}$ of its length. The *strap* at its smallest dimensions should have at least $\frac{9}{10}$ the area of the piston rod, and its depth equal half of its breadth.

---

* The proportion here given will admit of a sufficient quantity of water when the engine is in operation in the Gulf Stream, where the water is at times at the temperature of 84°, and the quantity of water (when the steam is at 10 lbs. pressure) required to give it and the water of condensation a temperature of 100°, is 70 times that of the quantity evaporated

Beam Centres. The end centres should have each one, and the main centre two and a half times the area of the piston rod.

The proportion for the strap, is when the depth of the beam is $\frac{1}{8}$ that of the stroke; consequently, when the depth is less, the area must be increased.

Connecting Rods. Their diameter in the neck should be the same as that of the piston rod. The diameter of the centre of the body is found in the following manner:

As .75 the stroke of the piston is to the length of the body of the rod, so is the area of the neck to the area of the centre of the body.

When two rods are used, each diameter should be $\frac{7}{10}$ that of the piston rod.

Key holes. Their width should be $\frac{1}{5}$ that of the strap or head, their length 5 times their width, and their area $\frac{1}{3}$ that of the rod.

Straps of Connecting Rods, &c. Their area at their least section should be $\frac{3}{4}$ that of the piston rod.

Crank Pins. Their area should be $1\frac{1}{2}$ times that of the piston rod.

Cranks. When of *Cast Iron*, the dimensions of their *Hub* should be, in diameter, twice that of the shaft upon which they are to be placed, and in depth $\frac{1}{2}$ their diameter.

The *Small end* should have its diameter twice, and its depth once the diameter of the pin.

When of *Wrought Iron*, the diameter of the hub, compared to the shaft, should be as 8 to 4.5. The same proportion for the small end, compared with the pin.

Water Wheels, or *Fly Shafts.* See Rule, page 158.

BOILERS.

For every cubic foot capacity in the cylinder, when the length of the flues do not exceed 40 feet, they should have from 18 to 20 square feet of fire and flue surface.

There should be at least 10 times the space in the steam room that there is in the cylinder.

Grates. For *Wood,* their area should be $\frac{4}{7}$, and for *Coal* $\frac{2}{3}$ the number of cubic feet in the cylinder.

T

NON-CONDENSING, OR HIGH-PRESSURE ENGINES.

Cylinder. The thickness is found by the same rule that is applied for that of a condensing engine.

Steam Valves. Their area should be the same as given for condensing engines.

Piston Rod. The diameter should be $\frac{1}{5}$ that of the cylinder.

Connecting Rods, Crank Pins, Straps, Cranks, and *End* and *Main Centres,* should bear the same proportion to the piston rod as in condensing engines.

Gibs and Keys. The same as in condensing engines.

Force Pumps. Their capacity, when the pressure of the steam is not to exceed 60 lbs., should be $\frac{1}{75}$ the contents of the cylinder; when not to exceed 130 lbs., $\frac{1}{50}$, and in a similar ratio for higher pressures.

Water Wheel, or *Fly Shafts.* See Rule, page 158.

BOILERS.

With plain cylindrical boilers without flues, there should be 75 square feet of fire and flue surface for every cubic foot capacity in the cylinder, when their length does not exceed 25 feet.

With boilers having flues there should be 125 square feet of fire and flue surface when their length does not exceed 25 feet.

Locomotive Boilers should have 210 square feet of fire and flue surface for every cubic foot capacity in the cylinder.

These proportions are for obtaining a pressure of 60 lbs. to the square inch.

When of greater length, a corresponding increase of fire surface will be required.

Grates. One square foot is sufficient for a horse's power.

GENERAL RULES.

Journals. Their length should exceed the diameter not less than in the proportion of 10 to 9, and in some cases the proportion can be increased in the ratio of 3 to 2 with advantage.

Steam Pipes. Their area should exceed that of the steam valve.

Front Links. $\frac{1}{2}$ the length of the stroke, and $\frac{7}{16}$ the diameter of the piston rod.

Beams. To ascertain the vibration of their end centres at right angles to the plane of the cylinder, let L represent length of beam, and S stroke of piston.

$$\sqrt{(L\div2)^2-(S\div2)^2}-\frac{L}{2}=\text{vibration at each end.}$$

Cast Iron Beams should always have, when of uniform thickness, their thickness $\frac{1}{16}$ of their depth.

Piston Rods of different materials should have their diameters in the following ratios:

Cast iron 8
Wrought iron 5
Tempered steel 4

*Safety Valves,** 10 inches area of valve for every 250 square feet fire surface.

OF SATURATION IN MARINE BOILERS.

100 parts of sea water contains 3 parts of its weight in saline matter, and is saturated when it contains 36 parts; then, if the quantity in the boiler be taken as 100 parts of water, and s parts be used for steam, b parts blowed out; to fix on the degree of saturation to contain x parts of saline matter, the quantity of salt entering and the quantity leaving in the same time, will be equal when $3(s+b)=xb$; hence $b=\dfrac{3s}{x-3}$.

If $x=30$, the water in the boiler will not reach to a higher degree of saturation when $\frac{1}{9}$ of the quantity used for steam is allowed to escape. And as it requires but about $\frac{1}{6}$ of the quantity of fuel to boil water that is required to convert it into steam, the loss of fuel will be $\frac{1}{9}\times\frac{1}{6}=\frac{1}{54}$ part.—*Tredgold.*

---

* Tredgold gives the following rule: Divide the area of the fire surface by the lbs. pressure (per steam gauge) of the steam, and the quotient will be the square of the diameter of the valve in inches.

SMOKE PIPES, OR CHIMNEYS.

Their area at the base should always exceed that of the flue or flues. When wood is used, the area is required to be greater than for coal.

The intensity of the draught is as the square root of the height.

BELTS.

Two 15 inch belts over a driver of six feet in diameter, running with a velocity of 2128 feet in a minute, transmit the power from the water-wheel at Rocky Glen Factory, the dimensions of which are given in page 179.

An 11 inch belt over a driver of 4 feet in diameter, running from 1200 to 2100 feet in a minute, will transmit the power from two 6 inch cylinders having 11 inches stroke, and averaging 125 revolutions per minute, with a pressure of 60 lbs. per square inch.

Two 6 inch belts over a driver of 5.9 feet in diameter, running 2700 feet in a minute, will transmit the power from two 9 inch cylinders having 8 inches stroke, and averaging 150 revolutions per minute, with a pressure of 60 lbs. per square inch.

To find the Power of a Condensing Engine.

Let *v represent vacuum upon cylinder piston in lbs.,

S velocity of cylinder piston in feet per minute,

n velocity of air-pump piston in feet per minute,

*P mean effective pressure upon cylinder piston in lbs.,

m pressure upon cylinder piston necessary to overcome the friction of the air-pump and its gearing,

b the lbs. pressure upon the air-pump piston,

f the lbs. pressure upon the piston necessary to overcome the friction of the engine.

Where an Indicator is not used, estimate the value of v at 9.5 lbs.

The value of m is about 2 lbs. per square inch, that of $b, = v$ in pressure, and f is $\frac{1}{3}$ of the pressure per steam gauge.

$$\text{Then } \frac{\overline{(P+v)-(f+m)} \times S - \overline{nb}}{33000} = \text{horses' power.}$$

EXAMPLE.—The diameter of a cylinder is 60 inches, the stroke of the piston 10 feet, the revolutions 20 per minute, the diameter of the air-pump 46 inches, and the stroke 4 feet; the pressure of the steam 20 lbs. per square inch, cut off at $\frac{1}{4}$ the length of the stroke.

Then $v =$ area of 60×9.5 $= 26860.3,$
$\quad$ S $= 10 \times 2 \times 20$ $= 400,$
$\quad$ $n = 4 \times 2 \times 20$ $= 160,$
$\quad$ P $=$ (per rule, page 214) $12.1 \times 2827.4 = 34211.54,$
$\quad$ $m = 2827.4 \times 2$ $= 5654.8,$
$\quad$ $b =$ area of 46×9.5 $= 15788,$
$\quad$ $f = 20 \times .2 \times 2827.4$ $= 11309.6.$

$$\frac{34211.54 + 26860.3 - 11309.6 + 5654.8 \times 400 - \overline{160} \times 15788}{33000}$$

526.984 horses' power.

To find the Power of a Non-condensing Engine.

$$\frac{S \times \overline{P-f}}{33000} = \text{horses' power;}$$

$f = \frac{1}{8}$ of the pressure per steam gauge.

EXAMPLE 1.—What is the power of an engine, the diameter of the cylinder being 10 inches, the stroke 4 feet, the pressure of the steam, per gauge, 60 lbs., making 45 revolutions?

$$360 \times \overline{60 - 7.5} \times 78.54 \div 33000 = 44.982, \text{ } Ans.$$

2. The same with 30 lbs., cut off at $\frac{1}{3}$ the stroke, and making 25 revolutions?

$$200 \times \overline{21.25 - 3.75} \times 78.54 \div 33000 = 8.02, \text{ } Ans.$$

* These values are best obtained by an *Indicator.*

The usual rule for either engine is, multiply the effective pressure upon the piston in lbs. per square inch by the velocity of the piston in feet per minute, and divide by 33000.

To find the Volume the Steam of a Cubic Foot of Water occupies (separated from the Water), the Elastic Force and Temperature being given.

RULE.—To the temperature in degrees add 459, multiply the sum by 38, and divide the product by the pressure in lbs. per square inch.

EXAMPLE.—The temperature is 291.5°, and the pressure 4 atmospheres, or 120 inches of mercury ; what is the volume?

An atmosphere is $= 14.7$ lbs. per square inch, and $14.7 \times 4 = 58.8$ lbs.

And 2 inches mercury $= .98$ lbs. per square inch; therefore, $58.8 \div .98 = 60 \times 2 = 120$ inches.

Then $\overline{295.1° + 459} \times 38 \div 58.8 = 485.016$ cubic feet, *Ans.*

What quantity of water will an engine of 10 inches cylinder, 4 feet stroke, and making 45 revolutions per minute, require per hour at the pressure above given?

Area of 10 inches $= 78.54 \times 48 \times 2 \times 45 \div 1728 = 196.3$ cubic feet of steam per minute.

Then, as $485.016 : 1 : : 196.3 : .4047$, and $.4047 \times 60$ minutes $= 24.28$ cubic feet of water per hour at a pressure of $58.8 - 14.7 = 44.1$ lbs. steam gauge.

If it were required for 58.8 lbs. per steam gauge, the quantity would be in the proportion of their densities, viz., as .00210 to .00258 (see table, page 212), or 54.18 cubic feet, independent of the quantity lost by waste, and the clearance of the piston in the cylinder.

To find the Power of an Engine necessary to raise Water to any Given Height.

RULE.—Multiply the weight of the column by the velocity in feet per minute, and divide by 33000.

EXAMPLE.—It is required to raise a column of fresh water, 16 inches in diameter by 86 feet high, with a velocity of 128 feet per minute; what power is necessary?

86 feet $\div 2.31$ feet, the height equal to 1 lb. per square inch $= 37.2$ lbs. Area of 16 inches $= 201. \times 37.2$ lbs. $\times 128 = 957081.6 \div 33000 = 29$, horses' power. To which must be added an allowance for friction and waste, say $\frac{1}{8}$.

To find the Velocity necessary to Discharge a Given Quantity of Water in any Given Time.

RULE.—Multiply the number of cubic feet by 144, and divide the product by the area of the pipe or opening.

EXAMPLE.—The diameter of the pipe is 16 inches, and the quantity of water 179 cubic feet; what is the velocity?

$$179 \times 144 \div 201 = 128.2 \text{ feet, } Ans.$$

To find the Area, the Velocity and Quantity being given.

RULE.—Proceed as above, and divide the product by the velocity.

COMBUSTION.

COMBUSTION is one of the many sources of heat, and denotes the combination of a body with any of the substances termed Supporters of Combustion: with reference to the generation of steam, we are restricted to but one of these combinations, and that is Oxygen.

All bodies, when intensely heated, become luminous. When this heat is produced by combination with oxygen, they are said to be ignited; and when the body heated is in a gaseous state, it forms what is called Flame.

No bodies appear visible, even in a faint light, below about 870°.

Carbon exists in nearly a pure state in charcoal and in soot. It combines with no more than $2\frac{2}{3}$ of its weight of oxygen. In its combustion, 1 lb. of it produces sufficient heat to increase the temperature of 13000 lbs. of water 1°.

Hydrogen exists in a gaseous state, and combines with 8 times its weight of oxygen, and 1 lb. of it, in burning, raises the heat of 42000 lbs. of water 1°.

FUEL.

With equal weights, that which contains most hydrogen ought, in its combustion, to produce the greatest quantity of heat where each kind is exposed under the most advantageous circumstances. Thus, pine wood is preferable to hard wood, and bituminous to anthracite coal.

When wood is employed as a fuel, it ought to be as dry as possible. To produce the greatest quantity of heat, it should be dried by the direct application of heat. As usually employed, it has about 25 per cent. of water mechanically combined, the heat necessary for the evaporating of which is lost.

Weight of sundry Fuels to form a Cubic Foot of Water at 52° into Steam at 220°.

	Lbs.						Lbs.
Newcastle coal .	8.	Peat .	.	.	.	.	30.5
Pine wood (dry) .	.	.	20.2	Olive oil	.	.	.	5.9
Oak wood (dry) .	.	.	12.	Coke .	.	.	.	9.

TABLE *showing the Heating Power of different Substances.*

Name.	Composition of combustible portion.		Weight of water in lbs., heated 1° by 1 lb. of the combustible.	Weight of water converted into steam by 1 lb. of combustible, from 52° to 220°.
Olefiant Gas . . .	Hydrogen . $\frac{1}{7}$ Carbon . $\frac{6}{7}$		12300	
Alcohol . . . (Spec. grav. .812) .	Hydrogen . .1224 Carbon . .4785		11000	
Olive Oil . . .	Hydrogen . .133 Carbon . .772		14500	12.
Beeswax, yellow .	Hydrogen . .1137 Carbon . .8069		14000	11.
Tallow . . .			15000	12.
Oak wood, seasoned .	Hydrogen . .057 Carbon . .525		4600	3.90
———, dried on a stove . . .			5960	5.12
———, allowing 20 per cent. loss . .			5660	4.85
Pine, seasoned . .			5466	4.66
Coal, Newcastle .	Hydrogen . .0416 Carbon . .7516		9230	7.90
——, Welsh . .			11840	10.1
——, Anthracite .	Carbon . .88744		9560	8.
——, Cannel .	Hydrogen . .0393 Carbon . .722		9000	7.7
Coke . . .	Carbon . .84		9110	7.7
Peat . . .			3250	2.e

Small coal produces about ¾ the effect of good coal of the same species.

The averages of the above, for practical results, may be set down as follows:

	Heated 1° by 1 lb.			Heated 1° by 1 lb.
Oak	4500 lbs.	Bituminous coal .	.	9200 lbs.
Pine	5000 "	Anthracite .	.	7800 "
Coke	8600 "			

Different fuels require different quantities of oxygen; for the different kinds of coal, it varies from 1.87 to 3 lbs. for each lb. of coal. 60 cubic feet of air is necessary to afford 1 lb. of oxygen; and making a due allowance for loss, nearly 90 cubic feet of air will be required in the furnace of a boiler for each lb. of oxygen.

The quantity of air and smoke for one cubic foot of water converted into steam at 220° is, for coal about 2000, and for hard wood about 4000 cubic feet.

TABLE *showing the Results of Mr. Bull's Experiments upon Wood.*

Woods.	Weight of a cord.	Comparative value per cord.	Woods.	Weight of a cord.	Comparative value per cord.
	Lbs.			Lbs.	
Shell-bark Hickory	4469	100	Hard Maple . . .	2878	60
Pig-nut Hickory .	4241	95	Jersey Pine . . .	2137	54
Red-heart Hickory	3705	81	Yellow Pine . . .	1904	43
White Oak . . .	3821	81	White Pine . . .	1868	42
Red Oak	3254	69			

Pounds of Ice melted by the following Fuels:

Good coal	90	Wood (hard) . . .	92
Coke	94	Peat . . .	19
Charcoal	95	Hydrogen gas . . .	370

When bituminous coal is subjected to destructive distillation, about ⅔ of its weight is left, in the form of coke.

Relative Value of the following Fuels by Weight:

Seasoned oak . . .	125	Charcoal	285
" " artificially .	140	Peat	115
Hickory . . .	137	Welsh coal . .	312
White pine . . .	137	Newcastle " .	309
Yellow pine . . .	145	Belgium " . .	316
Good coke	285	Anthracite, French . .	290
Inferior "	222	" Pennsylvania .	250

ANALYSIS OF FUELS.

	Newcastle Coal, caking kind.	Cannel Coal.	Cumberland Coal, American.
Carbon . . .	75.28	64.72	80.
Hydrogen . .	4.18	21.56	Bitumen, 18.40
Nitrogen . .	15.96	13.72	Ash, 1.60
Oxygen . . .	4.58	0.00	
	100.	100.	100.

	Oak.	Ash.	Maple.	Ches'nut.	Norway Pine.
Volatile matter . .	76.9	81.3	79.3	76.3	80.4
Charcoal . .	22.7	17.9	20.	23.3	19.2
Ashes . . .	.4	.7	.7	.4	.4

An increase in the rapidity of combustion is accompanied by a diminution in the evaporative efficiency of the combustible.

ANTHRACITE COAL.

The results of late and accurate observations upon the burning of anthracite coal, with the aid of a blast, gives an expenditure of 5 lbs. per horse power per hour.

The best anthracites contain about 95 per cent. of inflammable matter, principally carbon.

1.84 tons coal are required for the smelting and heating of the blast to make 1 ton pig iron.

578304 cubic feet of air are required for the blast to make 1 ton of iron.

CHARCOAL.

The best quality is made from oak, maple, beech, and chestnut.

Wood will furnish, when properly burned, about 16 per cent. of coal.

A bushel of coal from hard wood weighs about 30 lbs., and from pine 29 lbs.

COKE.

Sixty* bushels Newcastle coals (lumps) will make 92 bushels good coke, and 60 bushels (fine) will make 85 bushels of a similar quality.

60 bushels Newcastle and Picton coal (one half of each) makes 84 bushels inferior; 60 bushels Picton, or Virginia coal, makes 75 bushels of bad.

A bushel of the best coke weighs 32 lbs.

Coal furnishes 60 to 70 per cent. of coke by weight.

1 lb. in a common locomotive boiler will evaporate $7\frac{1}{8}$ lbs. water at 212° into steam.

MISCELLANEOUS.

One pound of anthracite coal in a cupola furnace will melt 5 lbs. of cast iron; 80 bushels bituminous coal in an air furnace will melt 10 tons cast iron.

When one bushel bituminous coal per hour will produce steam of the expansive force of 15 lbs. per square inch, $1\frac{1}{2}$ bushels will give 50 lbs., and 2 bushels 120 lbs.

One lb. of Newcastle coal converts 7 lbs. of boiling water into steam, and the time, 6 times that necessary to raise it from the freezing to the boiling point. And a bushel will convert 10 cubic feet of water into steam.

---

* *Winchester bushel* $= 2150.42$ *cubic inches.*

WATER.

FRESH WATER. The constitution of it by weight and measure is,

	By weight.	By measure.
Oxygen	88.9	1
Hydrogen	11.1	2

One cubic inch at 62°, the barometer at 30 inches, weighs 252.458 grains, and it is 830.1 times heavier than atmospheric air.

A cubic foot weighs 1000 ounces, or 62½ lbs. avoirdupois; a column 1 inch square and 1 foot high weighs .434028 lbs.

It expands $\frac{1}{9}$ of its bulk in freezing, and averages .0002517, or $\frac{1}{3957}$ for every degree of heat from 40° to 212°. Maximum density, 39.38°.

TABLE *of Expansion at different Temperatures.*

Temperature.	Expansion.	Temperature.	Expansion.
12°	.00236	64°	.00159
22°	.00090	102°	.00791
32°	.00022	212°	.04330
40°	.00000		

Showing an increase in bulk from 40° to 212° of $\frac{04330}{1.00000}$, equal to 1 cubic foot in every 23.09 feet.

The height of a column of water at 60°, equivalent to the pressure of . . . .
$\begin{cases} \text{1 lb. per square inch, is } 2.31 \text{ feet,} \\ \text{1 " " circular " " } 2.94 \text{ "} \\ \text{1 inch of mercury, " } 1.133 \text{ "} \\ \text{the atmosphere . " } 34. \end{cases}$

River or canal water contains $\frac{1}{20}$ $\Big\}$ of its volume of gaseous matter.
Spring or well water " $\frac{1}{14}$

A cubic inch weighs .03611 of a lb., and at 212° has a force of 29.56 inches mercury.

SEA WATER, according to the analysis of Dr. Murray, at the specific gravity of 1.029, contains,

Muriate of soda	220.01 =	$\frac{1}{46}$
Sulphate of soda	33.16 =	$\frac{1}{302}$
Muriate of magnesia . . .	42.08 =	$\frac{1}{238}$
Muriate of lime	7.84 =	$\frac{1}{1276}$
	303.09 =	$\frac{1}{32}$

TABLE *showing the Deposites that take place at different Degrees of Saturation and Temperature.*

When 1000 parts were reduced by evaporation.

Quantity of sea water.	Boiling point.	Salt in 100 parts.	Nature of deposite.
1000	214°	3.	None.
299	217°	10.	Sulphate of lime.
102	228°	29.5	Common salt.

Boiling Point at different Degrees of Saturation.

Proportion of salt in 100 parts by weight.	Boiling point.	Proportion of salt in 100 parts by weight.	Boiling point.
Saturated solution } 36.37	226.°	18.18	219.°
		15.15	217.9°
33.34	224.9°	12.12	216.7°
30.30	223.7°	9.09	215.5°
27.28	222.5°	6.06	214.4°
24.25	221.4°	3.03 }	213.2°
21.22	220.2°	Sea water }	

SALT WATER. A cubic foot of it weighs 64.3 lbs.; a cubic inch, .03721 lbs.

The height of a column of
water at 60°, equivalent to the
pressure of   .   .   .   .
(Specific gravity, 1029).

{ 1 lb. per square inch, is 2.37 feet,
1 " " circular " " 3.02 "
1 inch of mercury, " 1.165 "
the atmosphere . " 34.98 "

MOTION OF BODIES IN FLUIDS.

TABLE *of the Weights required to give different Velocities to several different Figures.*

THE diameter of all the figures but the small hemisphere is 6.375 inches, and the altitude of the cone 6.625 inches.

The small hemisphere is 4.75 inches.

The angle of the side of the cone and its axis is, consequently, 25° 42′ nearly.

Velocity per second.	Cone.		Whole globe.	Cylinder.	Hemisphere.		Small hemisphere.
	Vertex.	Base.			Flat.	Round.	
feet.	oz.	oz.	oz.	oz.	oz.	oz.	oz.
3	.028	.064	.027	.050	.051	.020	.028
4	.048	.109	.047	.090	.096	.039	.048
5	.071	.162	.068	.143	.148	.063	.072
6	.098	.225	.094	.205	.211	.092	.103
7	.129	.298	.125	.278	.284	.123	.141
8	.168	.382	.162	.360	.368	.160	.184
9	.211	.478	.205	.456	.464	.199	.233
10	.260	.587	.255	.565	.573	.242	.287
12	.376	.850	.370	.826	.836	.347	.418
15	.589	1.346	.581	1.327	1.336	.552	.661
16	.675	1.546	.663	1.526	1.538	.634	.754
20	1.069	2.540	1.057	2.528	2.542	1.033	1.196
Propor. number	126	291	124	285	288	119	140

From this table several practical inferences may be drawn.

1. That the resistance is nearly as the surface, the resistance increasing but a very little above that proportion in the greater surfaces.

2. The resistance to the same surface is nearly as the square of the velocity, but gradually increasing more and more above that proportion as the velocity increases.

3. When the hinder parts of bodies are of different forms, the resistances are different, though the fore parts be alike.

4. The resistance on the base of the hemisphere is to that on the convex side nearly as 2.4 to 1, instead of 2 to 1, as the theory assigns the proportion.

5. The resistance on the base* of the cone is to that on the vertex nearly as 2.3 to 1. And in the same ratio is radius to the sine of the angle of the inclination of the side of the cone to its path or axis. So that, in this instance, the resistance is directly as the sine of the

---

* This is a complete refutation of the popular assertion, that a taper spar will tow in water easiest when the base is foremost.

angle of incidence, the transverse section being the same, instead of the square of the sine.

6. Hence we can find the altitude of a column of air, the pressure of which shall be equal to the resistance of a body moving through it with any velocity.

Thus, let a = the area of the section of the body, similar to any of those in the table, perpendicular to the direction of motion,

R = the resistance to the velocity, in the table, and

x = the altitude sought, of a column of air whose base is a and its pressure R.

Then $a x$ = the contents of the columns in feet, and 1.2 $a x$, or $\frac{6}{5} a x$ its weight in ounces.

Therefore, $\frac{6}{5} a x = $ R, and $x = \frac{5}{6} \times \frac{R}{a}$ is the altitude sought in feet, namely, $\frac{5}{6}$ of the quotient of the resistance of any body divided by its transverse section, which is a constant quantity for all similar bodies, however different in magnitude, since the resistance R is as the section a, as by article 1.

When $a = \frac{2}{9}$ of a foot, as in all the figures in the foregoing table except the small hemisphere, then $x = \frac{5}{6} \times \frac{R}{a}$, becomes $x = \frac{1.5}{4} R$, where R is the resistance in the table, to the similar body.

If, for example, we take the convex side of the large hemisphere, whose resistance is .634, or at a velocity of 16 feet per second, then R = .634, and $x = \frac{1.5}{4} R =$ 2.3775 feet, is the altitude of the column of air whose pressure is equal to the resistance on a spherical surface, with a velocity of 16 feet.

And to compare the above altitude with that which is due to the given velocity, it will be $32^2 : 16^2 :: 16 : 4$, the altitude due to the velocity 16, which is near double the altitude that is equal the pressure. And as the altitude is proportional to the square of the velocity; therefore, in small velocities the resistance to any spherical surface is equal to the pressure of a column of air on its great circle, whose altitude is $\frac{1.9}{3.2}$, or .594 of the altitude due to its velocity.

But if the cylinder be taken, where resistance R = 1.526, then $x = \frac{1.5}{4} R = 5.72$, which exceeds the height 4, due to the velocity, in the ratio of 23 to 16 nearly. And the difference would be still greater if the body were larger, and also if the velocity were more.

If any body move through a fluid at rest, or the fluid move against the body at rest, the force or resistance of the fluid against the body will be as the square of the velocity and the density of the fluid; that is, $R = dv^2$.

For the force or resistance is as the quantity of matter or particles struck, and the velocity with which they are struck. But the quantity or number of particles struck in any time are as the velocity and the density of the fluid. Therefore, the resistance or force of the fluid is as the density and square of the velocity.

The resistance to any plane is also more or less, as the plane is greater or less, and therefore the resistance on any plane is as the area of the plane a, the density of the medium, and the square of the velocity; that is, $R = adv^2$.

If the motion be not perpendicular, but oblique to the plane, or to the face of the body, then the resistance in the direction of the motion will be diminished in the triplicate ratio of radius to the sine of the angle of inclination of the plane to the direction of the motion, or as the cube of radius to the cube of the sine of that angle. So that $R = adv^2s^3$, $1 =$ radius, and $s =$ sine of the angle of inclination.

The real resistance to a plane, from a fluid acting in a direction perpendicular to its face, is equal to the weight of a column of the fluid, whose base is the plane, and altitude equal to that which is due to the velocity of the motion, or through which a heavy body must fall to acquire that velocity.

The resistance to a plane running through a fluid is the same as the force of the fluid in motion with the same velocity on the plane at rest. But the force of the fluid in motion is equal to the weight or pressure which generates that motion, and this is equal to the weight or pressure of a column of the fluid, the base of which is the area of the plane, and its altitude that which is due to the velocity.

1. If a be the area of a plane, v its velocity, n the density or specific gravity of the fluid, and $\frac{1}{2}g = 16.0833$ feet; then, the altitude due to the velocity v being $\frac{v^2}{2g}$, therefore $a \times n \times \frac{v^2}{2g} = \frac{anv^2}{2g}$, will be the whole resistance or force R.

2. If the direction of motion be not perpendicular to the face of the plane, but oblique to it, in an angle; then $R = \frac{anv^2s^2}{2g}$.

3. If W represent the weight of the body, a being resisted by the absolute force R; then the retarding force f, or $\frac{R}{w}$, will be $\frac{anv^2s^3}{2gw}$.

The resistance to a sphere moving through a fluid, is but half the resistance to its great circle, or to the end of a cylinder of the same diameter, moving with an equal velocity.

$R = \frac{pnv^2r^2}{4g}$, being the half of that of a cylinder of the same diameter, R representing radius.

ILLUSTRATION.—A 9 lb. iron ball, the diameter being 4 inches, when projected at a velocity of 1600 feet per second, will meet a resistance which is equal to a weight of 132.66 lbs. over the pressure of the atmosphere.

A I R.

100 Cubic Inches of atmospheric air, at the surface of the earth, when the barometer is at 30 inches, and at a temperature of 60°, weighs 30.5 grains, being 830.1 times lighter than water.

Specific gravity compared with water, .001246.

The atmosphere does not extend beyond 50 miles from the earth's surface.

The mean weight of a column of air a foot square, and of an altitude equal to the height of the atmosphere, is equal to 2116.8 lbs. avoirdupois.

It consists of oxygen 20, and nitrogen 80 parts; and in 10.000 parts there are 4.9 parts of carbonic acid gas.

The mean pressure of the atmosphere is usually estimated at 14.7 lbs. per square inch.

13.29 cubic feet of air weigh a lb. avoirdupois, hence 1 ton of air will occupy 29769.6 cubic feet.

The rate of expansion of air, *and all other Elastic Fluids*, for all temperatures, is uniform.

From 32° to 212° they expand from 1000 to 1376, equal to $\frac{1}{470}$* of their bulk for every degree of heat.

See Heat, page 201.

---

* $\frac{1}{470}$ *equal* .002087 *for each degree.*

PRINCIPAL DIMENSIONS AND WEIGHTS OF GUNS, SHOT, AND SHELLS.
U. S. ARMY.

	Diameter of bore. (Inches)	Length: Of bore. (Inches)	Length: From Muzzle to base ring. (Inches)	Length: Total. (Inches)	Diameter Of Trunnions. (Inches)	Of Vent. (Ins.)	Weight Of Gun. (Lbs.)	Diameter Of shot and shells. (Ins.)	Of high gauge. (Ins.)	Of low gauge. (Ins.)	Thickness of shells. (Ins.)	Weight Of shot. (Lbs.)	Weight Of shells. (Lbs.)	Powder in weight of shells. (Lbs.)	Proport. between weights of gun and ball.	Windage. (Ins.)	Diameter of chamber. (Ins.)	Length of chamber. (Ins.)	Pattern.
IRON. — SEA-COAST.																			
10 Inch	10.	96.	112.	124.25	8.	.175	9500	9.85	9.90	9.80	1.60	136.	89.39	5.12	69.8	.15	7.	9.5	1840
8 "	8.	85.5	93.	109.	6.40	.175	5800	7.85	7.90	7.80	1.25	69.5	44.62	2.66	83.4	.15	6.4	7.5	1840
42 Pounder	7.018	109.	117.2	129.4	7.018	.175	8688	6.83	6.86	6.76	1.15	43.3	30.38	1.64	200.	.188	—	—	1831
42 "	7.	110.	117.	129.	7.	.175	8300	6.83	6.86	6.76	1.15	43.3	30.38	1.64	191.7	.17	—	—	1840
32	6.41	107.59	114.	125.2	6.41	.175	7531	6.24	6.27	6.18	1.	33.04	22.41	1.33	227.9	.161	—	—	1840
32	6.4	107.6	114.	125.2	6.4	.175	7100	6.24	6.27	6.18	1.	33.04	22.41	1.33	214.8	.16	—	—	1829
24	5.823	108.17	114.	123.95	5.823	.175	5500	5.68	5.70	5.61	.85	24.92	16.22	1.09	220.7	.143	—	—	1819
Siege. — Sea-coast.																			
8 Inch How'r.	8.	38.5	52.	61.5	5.82	.175	2650	7.85	7.90	7.80	1.25	—	44.62	2.66	59.5	.15	4.62	8.	1840
Siege and Garrison.																			
24 Pounder	5.82	108.	114.	124.	5.82	.175	5600	5.68	5.70	5.61	.85	24.92	16.22	1.09	224.7	.14	—	—	1840
18 Pounder	5.3	109.	114.	123.25	5.3	.175	4750	5.17	5.18	5.10	.80	18.79	12.5	.75	252.6	.13	—	—	1840
12 Pounder	4.62	103.4	108.	116.	4.62	.175	3500	4.52	4.53	4.46	.70	12.5	8.3	.53	280.	.10	—	—	1840
BRONZE. — Field.																			
24 Pound. How'r.	5.82	56.25	65.	71.2	4.2	.175	1320	5.68	5.70	5.61	.85	24.92	16.22	1.09	53.	.14	4.62	4.75	1840
12 "	4.62	46.25	53.	58.6	3.67	.175	785	4.52	4.53	4.46	.70	12.56	8.3	.53	62.8	.10	3.67	4.25	1840
12 " Gun	4.62	74.	78.	85.	4.62	.175	1800	4.52	4.53	4.46	.70	12.56	8.3	.53	144.	.10	—	—	1840
6 "	3.67	57.05	60.	65.6	3.67	.175	880	3.58	3.60	3.54	—	6.24	—	—	141.	.09	—	—	1840
BRONZE. — Mountain.																			
12 Pound. How'r.	4.62	28.16	32.91	37.21	2.7	.175	220	4.52	4.53	4.46	.70	12.56	8.3	.53	17.6	.10	3.34	2.75	1840

WEIGHT AND DIMENSIONS OF LEADEN BALLS.

TABLE *showing the Number of Balls in a Pound, from* $1.\frac{5}{16}$*ths to* $\frac{.237}{1000}$ *of an Inch Bore.*

Diam. in parts of an inch.	Diam. in decimals of an inch.	Number of balls in a pound.	Diam. in parts of an inch.	Diam. in decimals of an inch.	Number of balls in a pound.	Diam. in parts of an inch.	Diam. in decimals of an inch.	Number of balls in a pound.
*$1.\frac{5}{16}$	1.670	1		.570	25		.301	170
	1.326	2		.537	30		.295	180
	1.157	3		.510	35		.290	190
	1.051	4	* $\frac{1}{2}$	.505	36		.285	200
	.977	5		.488	40		.281	210
* $\frac{15}{16}$	.919	6		.469	45		.276	220
* $\frac{7}{8}$	.873	7	* $\frac{7}{16}$	.453	50		.272	230
	.835	8		.426	60		.268	240
* $\frac{13}{16}$	.802	9		.405	70		.265	250
	.775	10		.395	75		.262	260
* $\frac{3}{4}$	.750	11		.383	80		.259	270
	.730	12	* $\frac{3}{8}$	.375	88		.256	280
	.710	13		.372	90		.252	290
* $\frac{11}{16}$	.693	14		.359	100	* $\frac{1}{4}$	.249	300
	.677	15		.348	110		.247	310
	.662	16		.338	120		.244	320
	.650	17		.329	130		.242	330
	.637	18		.321	140		.239	340
* $\frac{5}{8}$	.625	19	* $\frac{5}{16}$	.314	150		.237	350
	.615	20		.307	160			

* The *exact* decimals would be as follows :

$1.\frac{5}{16}$	1.3125	$\frac{13}{16}$	.8125	$\frac{7}{16}$	.4375
$\frac{15}{16}$	.9375	$\frac{11}{16}$	.6875	$\frac{5}{16}$	.3125
$\frac{7}{8}$	.8750	$\frac{1}{2}$	.5000	$\frac{1}{4}$	.2500

EXPANSION OF SHOT *heated to a White Heat.*

Calibres.	42	32	24	18	12	
Expansion .	Inches. 0.11	Inches. 0.10	Inches. 0.08	Inches. 0.06	Inches. 0.04	Experiment at Fort Monroe, 1839.

WEIGHT AND DIMENSIONS OF SHOT.

GRAPE.

CALIBRE OF	8 Inch.	42	32	24	18	12
Diameter of high gauge .	Inches. 3.60	Inches. 3.17	Inches. 2.90	Inches. 2.64	Inches. 2.40	Inches. 2.06
" low gauge .	3.54	3.13	2.86	2.60	2.36	2.02
Mean weight in lbs. . .	6.24	4.25	3.25	2.45	1.83	1.19

CANISTER.

Calibre of	42	32	24 and 8 inch howitzer.	18	12	9 and 24 lb. howitzer.	6	12 lb. howitzer.	
								Field.	Mountain
	Ins.	Ins.	Ins.	Ins.	Ins.	Ins.	Ins.	Ins.	Ins.
Diam. of high gauge,	2.26	2.06	1.87	1.70	1.49	1.35	1.17	1.08	Musket
" low gauge,	2.22	2.02	1.84	1.67	1.46	1.32	1.14	1.05	ball.
Mean weight in lbs.,	1.57	1.19	.90	.67	.45	.33	.235	.17	.056

CARCASSES.

Calibre of	13 inch.	10 inch.	8 inch.	42	32	24	18	12
Mean weight in lbs. . .	194	87.63	43.62	29.45	21.60	15.84	12.15	8

BRONZE FOR CANNON.

Copper 90, Tin 10.

Specific gravity is greater than the mean of copper and tin, viz.'
8.766.

PRINCIPAL DIMENSIONS AND WEIGHTS OF GUNS, SHOT, AND SHELLS.

U. S. NAVY.

Nature of Guns.	Diameter of bore. (Inches.)	Length of bore.* (Inches.)	Diameter: Of shot and shells. (Ins.)	Diameter: Of high gauge. (Ins.)	Diameter: Of low gauge. (Ins.)	Weight: Of shot. (Lbs.)	Weight: Of shells. (Lbs.)	Weight of guns. (Lbs.)	Thickness of shells. (Ins.)	Proportion between weight of ball and weight of gun.	Length: To base ring. (Ft. Ins.)	Length: Total. (Ft. Ins.)	Windage: Maximum. (Ins.)	Windage: Minimum. (Ins.)	Charges: Maximum. (Lbs.)	Charges: Ordinary. (Lbs.)	Charges: Reduced. (Lbs.)	Diameter of vent: At vent field. (Ins.)	Diameter of vent: At the bore. (Ins.)	Pattern.
10 inch, chamber of a 42	10.	106.	9.85	9.90	9.80	127	100.	9800	2.	{ 1 to 77† / 1 to 98‡	9.4	10.4	.200	.100	10.			.25	.20	Navy Commissioners, 1841.
8 inch, chamber of a 32	8.	102.	7.85	7.90	7.80	64	47.	7056	1.4	{ 1 to 110† / 1 to 150‡	8.10	9.9½	.200	.100	8.			.25	.20	Nav.Com.,1841.
42 Pounder, cannon	7.018	102.	6.85	6.90	6.80	42	31.	7952	1.2	1 to 189.3	9.1	10.2	.218	.118	12.			.25	.20	Navy Commiss. 1821, 1824.
32 " " (heavy)	6.41	102.7	6.25	6.30	6.20	32	25.5	6832	1.2	1 to 213.5	9.2	10.2	.210	.110	10.			.25	.20	Nav.Com.,1824.
32 " " (med.)	6.40	105.6	6.25	6.30	6.20	32	25.5	6914	1.2	1 to 217	9.4	10.2	.200	.100	10.			.25	.20	Nav.Com.,1842.
32 " " (short)	6.40	96.	6.25	6.30	6.20	32	25.5	5712	1.2	1 to 180	8.6	9.2	.200	.100	8.			.25	.20	Nav.Com.,1842.
chamber of a 24	6.40	90.5	6.25	6.30	6.20	32	25.5	4704	1.2	1 to 150	8.	8.9	.200	.100	6.			.25	.20	Nav.Com.,1842.
32 Pounder (light)	6.40	67.5	6.25	6.30	6.20	32	25.5	2800	1.2	1 to 87.5	5.10½	6.7½	.200	.100				.25	.20	Ordne'e Bureau, 1843.
24 Pounder	5.82	100.	5.67	5.72	5.62	24	17.	5488	1.	1 to 229	9.	9.11	.200	.100	8.			.25	.20	Nav.Com.,1824.
24 " (med.)	5.82	75.5	5.67	5.72	5.62	24	17.	3384	1.	1 to 150	6.7	7.8½	.200	.100	5.			.25	.20	Nav.Com.,1826.
Carronades. 42 Pounder	7.	54.	6.85	6.90	6.80	42	30.	2912		1 to 69	4.7	5.11	.200	.100	4.8			.25	.20	Nav.Com.,1821.
32 "	6.40	49.	6.25	6.30	6.20	32	22.4	2352		1 to 73.5	4.9	5.5	.200	.100	3.8			.25	.20	Nav.Com.,1821.

* Including chamber. † Solid shot. ‡ Hollow shot.

PENETRATION OF SHOT AND SHELLS.

PENETRATION IN MASONRY.

Experiments at Fort Monroe Arsenal in 1839.

Calibre.	Charge.	Elevation.	Distance.	Mean penetration.		
				Dressed granite.	Potomac freestone.	Hard brick.
Shot.	Lbs.		Yards.	Inches.	Inches.	Inches.
32 Pounder (Gun) .	8	1°	880	3.5	12.	15.25
Shell.						
8 Inch Howitzer } Seacoast } .	6	1° 35'	880	1.	4.5	8.5

The solid shot broke against the granite.

The shells broke into small fragments against each of the three materials.

PENETRATION IN WHITE OAK.

Experiments at New-York Harbour in 1814.

Calibre.	Charge.	Distance.	Penetration.	Remarks.
32 Pounder . { {	Lbs. 11 11	Yards. 100 150	Inches. 60 54	Shot wrapped so as to destroy the windage.

PENETRATION IN COMPACT EARTH

(Half sand, half clay).

Calibre.	Charge.	Distances in yards.			
		27	109	328	1094
Shot.		Inches.	Inches.	Inches.	Inches.
6.885	⅓	109.1	102.4	93.4	69.7
Shells.					
8.782	4.4 lbs.	*48.4	*45.3	38.6	23.2
Musket .	154 grains	9.85	8.6	4.3	—

The penetrations in other kinds of earth are found by multiplying the above by 0.63 for sand mixed with gravel; by 0.87 for earth mixed with sand and gravel, weighing 125 lbs. to a cubic foot; by 1.09 for compact mould and fresh earth mixed with sand, or half clay; by 1.44 for wet potter's clay; by 1.5 for light earth, settled; and by 1.9 for light earth, fresh.

* With this charge, and at these distances, the shells were often broken.

PENETRATION OF SHELLS.

Eleva-tion.	Distance.	In Compact Earth,			In Oak Wood,			In Masonry,		
		8 ins.	10 ins.	12 ins.	8 ins.	10 ins.	12 ins.	S ins.	10 ins.	12 ins.
	Yards.	Inches.	Inches.	Inches.	Inches.	Inches.	Inches.	Inches.	Inches.	Inches.
30° {	656	7.8	17.7	19.6	3.9	7.8	8.6	1.9	3.5	3.9
	1312	9.8	25.6	27.5	4.7	11.8	13.7	2.3	4.7	5.1
45° {	656	11.8	19.6	21.6	5.9	9.8	10.6	3.1	3.9	4.3
	1312	15.7	27.5	29.5	7.8	13.7	15.7	3.9	5.5	5.9
60° {	656	19.6	29.5	31.5	8.6	13.	14.5	4.3	5.9	6.3
	1312	21.6	31.5	33.4	9.8	13.7	15.7	4.7	6.3	6.6
Falling with maximum velocity. {		23.6	33.4	35.4	9.8	13.7	15.7	4.7	6.6	7.

The penetration in other kinds of earth and stone may be obtained by using the coefficients given for the other tables. For woods, use for beech and ash 1, for elm 1.3, for white pine and birch 1.8, and for poplar 2.

144 grains of powder in a musket, at 5 yards' distance, will project a ball 3 inches into seasoned white oak, and 100 grains in a rifle, at the same distance, 2.05 inches.

MISCELLANEOUS.

RECAPITULATION OF WEIGHTS OF VARIOUS SUBSTANCES.

	Cubic foot in pounds.	Cubic inch in pounds.
*Cast Iron	450.55	.2607
†Wrought Iron	486.65	.2816
Steel	489.8	.2834
‡Copper	555.	.32118
Lead	708.75	.41015
Brass	537.75	.3112
Tin	456.	.263
White Pine . . .	29.56	.0171
Salt Water (sea) . . .	64.3	.03721
Fresh Water	62.5	.03611
Air	.07529	—
Steam	.0350	—

Weights of a Cubic Foot of various Substances in ordinary use.

	Lbs.		Lbs.
Loose earth or sand .	95	Clay and stones . .	160
Common soil . . .	124	Cork	15
Strong soil . .	127	Tallow . . .	59
Clay . . .	135	Brick	125

SLATING.

Sizes of Slates.

Doubles	14 by 6 inches,
Ladies'	15 " 8 "
Countess	22 "11 "
Duchess	26 "15 "
Imperial and Patent . . .	32 "26 "
Rags and Queens	39 "27 "

* From the West Point Foundry Association at Cold Spring, N. Y. Other experiments have given .2613 as the weight of a cubic inch.
† Ulster Iron Company, Saugerties, N. Y.
‡ From Phelps, Dodge, & Co.'s Works, in Derby, Conn.

CAPACITY OF CISTERNS IN U. S. GALLONS.

For each 10 *Inches in Depth.*

2 feet diameter	.	19.5	8 feet diameter	.	313.33
$2\frac{1}{2}$ "	. .	30.6	$8\frac{1}{2}$ "	.	353.72
3 "	. .	44.06	9 "	.	396.56
$3\frac{1}{2}$ "	. .	59.97	$9\frac{1}{2}$ "	.	461.40
4 "	. .	78.33	10 "	.	489.20
$4\frac{1}{2}$ "	. .	99.14	11 "	.	592.40
5 "	. .	122.40	12 "	.	705.
$5\frac{1}{2}$ "	. .	148.10	13 "	.	827.4
6 "	. .	176.25	14 "	.	959.6
$6\frac{1}{2}$ "	. .	206.85	15 "	.	1101.6
7 "	. .	239.88	20 "	.	1958.4
$7\frac{1}{2}$ "	. .	275.40	25 "	.	3059.9

TABLE OF COMPOSITIONS—BRASS, ETC.

Copper.	Tin.	Zinc.	
2	0	1	For Yellow Brass.
3	0	1	" Spelter.
4	1	$\frac{1}{4}$	" Lathe brushes.
6	1	0	" Shaft bearings.
5	1	$\frac{1}{2}$	" " " (hard).
8	1	0	" Wheels, boxes, cocks, &c.
9	1	0	" Gun metal.
3	0	1	" Brass.
10	1	0	" Valves.
78	22	.	
80	10	5.6, and lead 4.3 $\}$	" Bells and Gongs.

SIZES OF NUTS, EQUAL IN STRENGTH TO THEIR BOLTS.

Diameter of bolt in inches.	Short diameter of nut in inches.	Diameter of bolt in inches.	Short diameter of nut in inches.	Diameter of bolt in inches.	Short diameter of nut in inches.
$\frac{1}{4}$	$\frac{3}{8}$	$1\frac{3}{8}$	$2\frac{7}{16}$	$2\frac{1}{2}$	$4\frac{7}{16}$
$\frac{3}{8}$	$\frac{5}{8}$	$1\frac{1}{2}$	$2\frac{11}{16}$	$2\frac{5}{8}$	$4\frac{3}{4}$
$\frac{1}{2}$	$\frac{7}{8}$	$1\frac{5}{8}$	$2\frac{7}{8}$	$2\frac{3}{4}$	$4\frac{15}{16}$
$\frac{5}{8}$	$1\frac{1}{16}$	$1\frac{3}{4}$	$3\frac{1}{8}$	$2\frac{7}{8}$	$5\frac{1}{8}$
$\frac{3}{4}$	$1\frac{5}{16}$	$1\frac{7}{8}$	$3\frac{3}{8}$	3	$5\frac{3}{8}$
$\frac{7}{8}$	$1\frac{9}{16}$	2	$3\frac{9}{16}$	$3\frac{1}{4}$	$5\frac{7}{8}$
1	$1\frac{3}{4}$	$2\frac{1}{8}$	$3\frac{3}{4}$	$3\frac{1}{2}$	$6\frac{5}{16}$
$1\frac{1}{8}$	2	$2\frac{1}{4}$	4	$3\frac{3}{4}$	$6\frac{3}{4}$
$1\frac{1}{4}$	$2\frac{1}{4}$	$2\frac{3}{8}$	$4\frac{1}{4}$	4	$7\frac{1}{8}$

NOTE.—The depth of the head should equal the diameter of the bolt; the dep..
of the nut should exceed it in the proportion of 9 or 10 to 8.

SCREWS.

TABLE *showing the Number of Threads to an Inch in V thread Screws.*

Diam. in inches,	$\frac{1}{4}$	$\frac{5}{16}$	$\frac{3}{8}$	$\frac{7}{16}$	$\frac{1}{2}$	$\frac{5}{8}$	$\frac{3}{4}$	$\frac{7}{8}$	1	$1\frac{1}{8}$	$1\frac{1}{4}$	$1\frac{3}{8}$
No. of threads,	20	18	16	14	12	11	10	9	8	7	7	6

Diam. in inches,	$1\frac{1}{2}$	$1\frac{5}{8}$	$1\frac{3}{4}$	$1\frac{7}{8}$	2	$2\frac{1}{4}$	$2\frac{1}{2}$	$2\frac{3}{4}$	3	$3\frac{1}{4}$	$3\frac{1}{2}$
No. of threads,	6	5	5	$4\frac{1}{2}$	$4\frac{1}{2}$	4	4	$3\frac{1}{2}$	$3\frac{1}{2}$	$3\frac{1}{4}$	$3\frac{1}{4}$

Diam. in inches,	$3\frac{3}{4}$	4	$4\frac{1}{4}$	$4\frac{1}{2}$	$4\frac{3}{4}$	5	$5\frac{1}{4}$	$5\frac{1}{2}$	$5\frac{3}{4}$	6
No. of threads,	3	3	$2\frac{7}{8}$	$2\frac{7}{8}$	$2\frac{3}{4}$	$2\frac{3}{4}$	$2\frac{5}{8}$	$2\frac{5}{8}$	$2\frac{1}{2}$	$2\frac{1}{2}$

The depth of the threads should be half their pitch.

The diameter of a screw, to work in the teeth of a wheel, should be such that the angle of the threads does not exceed 10°.

TABLE *of the Strength of Copper at different Temperatures.*

Temperature.	Strength in lbs.	Temperature.	Strength in lbs.	Temperature.	Strength in lbs.
122°	33079	482°	26981	801°	18854
212°	32187	545°	25420	912°	14789
302°	30872	602°	22302	1016°	11054
392°	27154				

Franklin Institute.

DIGGING.

23 cubic feet of sand, or 18 cubic feet of earth, or 17 cubic feet of clay, make a ton.

18 cubic feet of gravel or earth before digging, make 27 cubic feet when dug.

COAL GAS.

A chaldron of bituminous coal yields about 10.000 cubic feet of gas.

Gas pipes $\frac{1}{2}$ inch in diameter supply a light equal to 20 candles.

1.43 cubic feet of gas per hour give a light equal to one good candle.

1.96 cubic feet equal four candles.

3.   "   "   "   ten   "

X

ALCOHOL

Is obtained by distillation from fermented liquors.

Proportion of Alcohol in 100 *parts of the following Liquors:*

Scotch Whiskey	. 54.32	Sherry . . .	19.17
Irish " .	. 53.9	Claret . . .	15.1
Rum . .	. 53.68	Champagne . .	13.8
Brandy . .	. 53.39	Gooseberry . .	11.84
Gin . . .	. 51.6	Elder . . .	8.79
Port . . .	. 22.9	Ale . . .	6.87
Madeira . .	. 22.27	Porter . . .	4.2
Currant . .	. 20.55	Cider . . . 9.8 to 5.2	
Teneriffe . .	. 19.79	*Prof. Brande.*	

WEIGHT OF COMPOSITION SHEATHING NAILS.

Number.	Length in inches.	Number in a pound.	Number.	Length in inches.	Number in a pound.	Number.	Length in inches.	Number in a pound.
1	$\frac{3}{4}$	290	6	1	190	10	$1\frac{5}{8}$	101
2	$\frac{7}{8}$	260	7	$1\frac{1}{8}$	184	11	$1\frac{3}{4}$	74
3	1	212	8	$1\frac{1}{4}$	168	12	2	64
4	$1\frac{1}{8}$	201	9	$1\frac{1}{2}$	110	13	$2\frac{1}{4}$	59
5	$1\frac{1}{4}$	199						

CEMENT.

Ashes, 2 parts }
Clay, 3 " } Mixed with oil, will resist the weather equal to
Sand, 1 " } marble.

HYDRAULIC CEMENT.

A barrel contains 300 lbs., equal to 4 struck bushels.

BROWN MORTAR.

One third Thomaston lime,
Two thirds sand, and a small quantity of hair.

BRICKS, LATHS, ETC.

Dimensions.

Common brick . . . 8 to $7\frac{3}{4} \times 4\frac{1}{4} \times 2\frac{1}{2}$ inches.
Front brick . . . . $8\frac{1}{4}$ $\times 4\frac{1}{2} \times 2\frac{1}{2}$ "

20 common bricks to a cubic foot, when laid ;
15 " " " a foot of 8 inch wall, when laid.

Laths are $1\frac{1}{4}$ to $1\frac{1}{2}$ inches by four feet in length, are usually set $\frac{1}{4}$ of an inch apart, and a bundle contains 100.

Stourbridge fire-brick, $9\frac{1}{4} \times 4\frac{1}{8} \times 2\frac{3}{4}$ inches.

HAY.

10 cubic yards of meadow hay weigh a ton. When the hay is taken out of large or old stacks, 8 and 9 yards will make a ton.

11 to 12 cubic yards of clover, when dry, weigh a ton.

HILLS IN AN ACRE OF GROUND.

40 feet apart	.	27 hills,	8 feet apart	.	680 hills,
35 " "	. .	35 "	6 " "	. .	1210 "
30 " "	. .	48 "	5 " "	. .	1742 "
25 " "	. .	69 "	$3\frac{1}{2}$ " "	. .	3556 "
20 " "	. .	108 "	3 " "	. .	4840 "
15 " "	. .	193 "	$2\frac{1}{2}$ " "	. .	6969 "
12 " "	. .	302 "	2 " "	. .	10890 "
10 " "	. .	435 "	1 " "	. .	43560 "

DISPLACEMENT OF ENGLISH VESSELS OF WAR, WHEN LAUNCHED AND WHEN READY FOR SEA.

Rate of Guns.	120	80	74	Razee. 50	52	46	28	Corv. 18	Brig. 18
	Tons.	Tons.	Tons.	Tons.	Tons.	Tons.	Tons.	Tons.	Tons.
Weight of hull, launched .	2467	1882	1617	1448	1042	795	413	281	213
Weight received on board .	2142	1723	1359	1044	1067	670	370	326	242
Weight complete	4609	3605	2976	2492	2109	1465	783	607	455

Edye's N. C.

WEIGHT OF LEAD PIPE PER YARD,

From ¼ to 4½ Inches Diameter.

			Weight in lbs. and oz					Weight in lbs. and oz.
¼ inch	medium	.	3	—	1½ inch	extra light	9	—
"	strong	.	4	—	"	light .	13	—
½ inch	light	.	3	—	"	medium .	15	8
"	medium	.	4	—	"	strong .	19	—
"	strong	.	5	—	1¾ inch	medium .	16	—
"	extra strong		6	6	"	strong .	20	—
⅝ inch	light	.	5	—	2 inch	light .	16	12
"	medium	.	6	8	"	medium .	20	—
"	strong	.	7	8	"	strong .	23	—
"	extra strong		8	4	2½ inch	light .	25	—
¾ inch	extra light		5	—	"	medium .	30	—
"	light	.	6	4	"	strong .	35	—
"	medium	.	8	—	3 inch	light .	30	—
"	strong	.	9	12	"	medium .	35	—
"	extra strong		10	8	"	strong .	44	—
1 inch	extra light		6	14	3½ inch	medium .	45	—
"	light	.	8	5	"	strong .	54	—
"	medium	.	10	5	"	extra strong	70	—
"	strong	.	12	4	4 inch	waste, light,		—
1¼ inch	extra light		8	5	"	" medium,	21	—
"	light	.	9	12	"	" strong,	26	—
"	medium	.	11	—	4½ inch	" light,	—	—
"	strong	.	12	8	"	" medium,	24	—
"	extra strong		14	10	"	" strong,	29	—

Very light Pipe.

Diameter.			Weight in lbs. and oz.		Diameter.			Weight in lbs. and oz.
¼ inch	.	.	1	—	¾ inch	.	.	3	6
⅜ "	.	.	1½	—	1 "	.	.	5	10
½ "	.	.	2	—	1¼ "	.	.	6	14
⅝ "	.	.	2½	—				

TIN.

Description.	Size of sheet.	Mean thickness.		Mean weight of one sheet.
		No. on wire gauge.	Thickness of sheet.	
	Inches.		Inches.	Lbs.
Single .	10 × 14	31	.0125, (or 80 to 1 inch)	0.5
Double X	10 × 14	27	.0181, (or 55 to 1 inch)	0.75

There are usually 225 sheets in a box.

RELATIVE PRICES OF AMERICAN WROUGHT IRON.

Round.			Square.		
4 inches	. .	27	4 inches	. .	27
3½ to 2¼ inches	.	26 to 21	3½ to 2¼ inches	.	26 to 20
2⅛ " ¾ "	.	19	2⅛ " ¾ "	.	21
11/16 " 3/16 "	.	20 to 29	11/16 " ¼ "	.	19 to 26

Flat.			Hoops.		
⅜ and ¼ inch to ⅛		26 to 28	1½ to ¼ inch	.	24 to 33
⅜ " 1 " " 1×4		19	Band	. .	20
1¼ " ½ " " ½×5/16		19 to 23			

ILLUSTRATION.—If 4 inch round iron is worth $135 per ton, then band iron is worth $100 per ton, for 27 is to 20 as 135 to 100.

POWER REQUIRED TO PUNCH IRON AND COPPER PLATES.

Through an Iron Plate, with a Punch ½ Inch in Diameter.

.08 inches thick	.	.	.	.	.	6025 lbs.
.17 " "	.	.	.	.	.	11950 "
.24 " "	.	.	.	.	.	17100 "

Through a Copper Plate, with a Punch ½ Inch in Diameter.

.08 inches thick	.	.	.	.	.	3983 lbs.
.17 " "	.	.	.	.	.	7833 "

The force necessary to punch holes of different diameters through metals of various thicknesses, is directly as the diameter of the hole and the thickness of the metal.

To ascertain the Force necessary to Punch Iron or Copper Plates.

RULE.—Multiply, if for iron, 150000, and if for copper, 96000, by the diameter of the punch and the thickness of the plate, each in inches; the product is the pressure in pounds.

The use of oil reduces the above 8 per cent.

X 2

IRON.

Cast Iron expands $\frac{1}{102000}$ of its length for one degree of heat; greatest change in the shade in this climate, $\frac{1}{1170}$ of its length; exposed to the sun's rays, $\frac{1}{1000}$; shrinks in cooling from $\frac{1}{85}$ to $\frac{1}{98}$ of its length; is crushed by a force of 93,000 lbs. upon a square inch; will bear, without permanent alteration, 15,300 lbs. upon a square inch, and an extension of $\frac{1}{1200}$ of its length.

Weight of modulus of elasticity for a base of an inch square, 18,400,000 lbs.; height of modulus of elasticity, 5,750,000 feet.

Wrought Iron expands $\frac{1}{143000}$ of its length for one degree of heat; will bear on a square inch, without permanent alteration, 17,800 lbs., and an extension in length of $\frac{1}{1400}$; cohesive force is diminished $\frac{1}{3000}$ by an increase of 1 degree of heat.

Weight of modulus of elasticity for a base of an inch square, 24,920,000 lbs.; height of modulus of elasticity, 7,550,000 feet.

Compared with cast iron, its strength is 1.12 times, its extensibility 0.86 times, and its stiffness 1.3 times.

WEIGHT OF SQUARE ROLLED IRON,

From ¼ Inch to 12 Inches,

AND ONE FOOT IN LENGTH.

Size in inches.	Weight in pounds.	Size in inches.	Weight in pounds.	Size in inches.	Weight in pounds.	Size in inches.	Weight in pounds.
$\frac{1}{16}$	.013	2.	13.520	4.$\frac{3}{8}$	64.700	7.$\frac{1}{2}$	190.136
$\frac{1}{8}$	.053	2.$\frac{1}{8}$	15.263	4.$\frac{1}{2}$	68.448	7.$\frac{3}{4}$	203.024
$\frac{3}{16}$	.118	2.$\frac{1}{4}$	17.112	4.$\frac{5}{8}$	72.305	8.	216.336
$\frac{1}{4}$	.211	2.$\frac{3}{8}$	19.066	4.$\frac{3}{4}$	76.264	8.$\frac{1}{4}$	230.068
$\frac{3}{8}$	.475	2.$\frac{1}{2}$	21.120	4.$\frac{7}{8}$	80.333	8.$\frac{1}{2}$	244.220
$\frac{1}{2}$	.845	2.$\frac{5}{8}$	23.292	5.	84.480	8.$\frac{3}{4}$	258.800
$\frac{5}{8}$	1.320	2.$\frac{3}{4}$	25.560	5.$\frac{1}{8}$	88.784	9.	273.792
$\frac{3}{4}$	1.901	2.$\frac{7}{8}$	27.939	5.$\frac{1}{4}$	93.168	9.$\frac{1}{4}$	289.220
$\frac{7}{8}$	2.588	3.	30.416	5.$\frac{3}{8}$	97.657	9.$\frac{1}{2}$	305.056
1.	3.380	3.$\frac{1}{8}$	33.010	5.$\frac{1}{2}$	102.240	9.$\frac{3}{4}$	321.332
1.$\frac{1}{8}$	4.278	3.$\frac{1}{4}$	35.704	5.$\frac{5}{8}$	106.953	10.	337.920
1.$\frac{1}{4}$	5.280	3.$\frac{3}{8}$	38.503	5.$\frac{3}{4}$	111.756	10.$\frac{1}{4}$	355.136
1.$\frac{3}{8}$	6.390	3.$\frac{1}{2}$	41.408	5.$\frac{7}{8}$	116.671	10.$\frac{1}{2}$	372.672
1.$\frac{1}{2}$	7.604	3.$\frac{5}{8}$	44.418	6.	121.664	10.$\frac{3}{4}$	390.628
1.$\frac{5}{8}$	8.926	3.$\frac{3}{4}$	47.534	6.$\frac{1}{4}$	132.040	11.	408.960
1.$\frac{3}{4}$	10.352	3.$\frac{7}{8}$	50.756	6.$\frac{1}{2}$	142.816	11.$\frac{1}{4}$	427.812
1.$\frac{7}{8}$	11.883	4.	54.084	6.$\frac{3}{4}$	154.012	11.$\frac{1}{2}$	447.024
		4.$\frac{1}{8}$	57.517	7.	165.632	11.$\frac{3}{4}$	466.684
		4.$\frac{1}{4}$	61.055	7.$\frac{1}{4}$	177.672	12.	486.656

EXAMPLE.—What is the weight of a bar of rolled iron 1½ inches square and 12 inches long?

In column 1st find 1½, and opposite to it is 7.604 pounds, which is 7 lbs. and $\frac{604}{1000}$

of a lb. If the lesser denomination of ounces is required, the result is obtained as follows: Multiply the remainder by 16, pointing off the decimals as in multiplication of decimals, and the figures remaining on the left of the point indicate the number of ounces.

$$\text{Thus, } \frac{604}{1000} \text{ of a lb.} = .604$$
$$\underline{\quad 16}$$
$$9.664 \text{ ounces.}$$

The weight, then, is 7 lbs. $9.\frac{664}{1000}$ ounces.

If the weight for less than a foot in length was required, the readiest operation is this:

EXAMPLE.—What is the weight of a bar 6¼ inches square and 9¾ inches long?

In column 5th, opposite to 6¼, is 132.040, which is the weight for a foot in length.

6¼×12 inches			= 132.040
6.	"	is ½	= 66.020
3.	"	is ½ of 6	= 33.010
.½	"	is ⅙ of 3	= 5.5016
.¼	"	is ½ of ½	= 2.7508
9.¾			$= 107.\frac{2824}{1000}$ pounds.

WEIGHT OF ROUND ROLLED IRON,

From ¼ Inch to 12 Inches Diameter,

AND ONE FOOT IN LENGTH.

Diameter in inches.	Weight in pounds.	Diameter in inches.	Weight in pounds.	Diameter in inches.	Weight in pounds.	Diameter in inches.	Weight in pounds.
.1/16	.010	2.⅛	11.988	4.½	53.760	7.¾	159.456
.⅛	.041	2.¼	13.440	4.⅝	56.788	8.	169.856
.3/16	.119	2.⅜	14.975	4.¾	59.900	8.¼	180.696
.¼	.165	2.½	16.688	4.⅞	63.094	8.½	191.808
.⅜	.373	2.⅝	18.293	5.	66.752	8.¾	203.260
.½	.663	2.¾	20.076	5.⅛	69.731	9.	215.040
.⅝	1.043	2.⅞	21.944	5.¼	73.172	9.¼	227.152
.¾	1.493	3.	23.888	5.⅜	76.700	9.½	239.600
.⅞	2.032	3.⅛	25.926	5.½	80.304	9.¾	252.376
1.	2.654	3.¼	28.040	5.⅝	84.001	10.	266.288
1.⅛	3.360	3.⅜	30.240	5.¾	87.776	10.¼	278.924
1.¼	4.172	3.½	32.512	5.⅞	91.634	10.½	292.688
1.⅜	5.019	3.⅝	34.886	6.	95.552	10.¾	306.800
1.½	5.972	3.¾	37.332	6.¼	103.704	11.	321.216
1.⅝	7.010	3.⅞	39.864	6.½	112.160	11.¼	336.004
1.¾	8.128	4.	42.464	6.¾	120.960	11.½	351.104
1.⅞	9.333	4.⅛	45.174	7.	130.048	11.¾	366.536
2.	10.616	4.¼	47.952	7.¼	139.544	12.	382.208
		4.⅜	50.815	7.½	149.328		

The application of this table is precisely similar to that of the preceding one.

WEIGHT OF FLAT ROLLED IRON,

From ⅛ × ½ Inch to 5¾ × 6 Inches,

AND ONE FOOT IN LENGTH.

Breadth in inches.	Thickness in inches.	Weight in pounds.	Breadth in inches.	Thickness in inches.	Weight in pounds.	Breadth in inches.	Thickness in inches.	Weight in pounds.
.1/2	1/8	0.211	1 3/8	1 1/4	5.808	2.	1/8	0.845
	1/4	0.422	1 1/2	1/8	0.633		1/4	1.689
	3/8	0.634		1/4	1.266		3/8	2.534
.5/8	1/8	0.264		3/8	1.900		1/2	3.379
	1/4	0.528		1/2	2.535		5/8	4.224
	3/8	0.792		5/8	3.168		3/4	5.069
	1/2	1.056		3/4	3.802		7/8	5.914
.3/4	1/8	0.316		7/8	4.435		1.	6.758
	1/4	0.633		1.	5.069		1 1/8	7.604
	3/8	0.950		1 1/8	5.703		1 1/4	8.448
	1/2	1.265		1 1/4	6.337		1 3/8	9.294
	5/8	1.584		1 3/8	6.970		1 1/2	10.138
.7/8	1/8	0.369	1 5/8	1/8	0.686		1 5/8	10.983
	1/4	0.738		1/4	1.372		1 3/4	11.828
	3/8	1.108		3/8	2.059		1 7/8	12.673
	1/2	1.477		1/2	2.746	2 1/8	1/8	0.898
	5/8	1.846		5/8	3.432		1/4	1.795
	3/4	2.217		3/4	4.119		3/8	2.693
1.	1/8	0.422		7/8	4.805		1/2	3.591
	1/4	0.845		1.	5.492		5/8	4.488
	3/8	1.267		1 1/8	6.178		3/4	5.386
	1/2	1.690		1 1/4	6.864		7/8	6.283
	5/8	2.112		1 3/8	7.551		1.	7.181
	3/4	2.531		1 1/2	8.237		1 1/8	8.079
	7/8	2.956	1 3/4	1/8	0.739		1 1/4	8.977
1 1/8	1/8	0.475		1/4	1.479		1 3/8	9.874
	1/4	0.950		3/8	2.218		1 1/2	10.772
	3/8	1.425		1/2	2.957		1 5/8	11.670
	1/2	1.901		5/8	3.696		1 3/4	12.567
	5/8	2.375		3/4	4.435		1 7/8	13.465
	3/4	2.850		7/8	5.178		2.	14.362
	7/8	3.326		1.	5.914	2 1/4	1/8	.950
	1.	3.802		1 1/8	6.653		1/4	1.900
1 1/4	1/8	0.528		1 1/4	7.393		3/8	2.851
	1/4	1.056		1 3/8	8.132		1/2	3.802
	3/8	1.584		1 1/2	8.871		5/8	4.752
	1/2	2.112		1 5/8	9.610		3/4	5.703
	5/8	2.640	1 7/8	1/8	0.792		7/8	6.653
	3/4	3.168		1/4	1.584		1.	7.604
	7/8	3.696		3/8	2.376		1 1/8	8.554
	1.	4.224		1/2	3.168		1 1/4	9.505
	1 1/8	4.752		5/8	3.960		1 3/8	10.455
1 3/8	1/8	0.580		3/4	4.752		1 1/2	11.406
	1/4	1.161		7/8	5.544		1 5/8	12.356
	3/8	1.742		1.	6.336		1 3/4	13.307
	1/2	2.325		1 1/8	7.129		1 7/8	14.257
	5/8	2.904		1 1/4	7.921		2.	15.208
	3/4	3.484		1 3/8	8.713		2 1/8	16.158
	7/8	4.065		1 1/2	9.505	2 3/8	1/8	1.003
	1.	4.646		1 5/8	10.297		1/4	2.006
	1 1/8	5.227		1 3/4	11.089		3/8	3.009

Table—(Continued).

Breadth in inches.	Thickness in inches.	Weight in pounds.	Breadth in inches.	Thickness in inches	Weight in pounds.	Breadth in inches.	Thickness in inches.	Weight in pounds.
2.3/8	1/2	4.013	2.3/4	1/4	2.323	3.	1.3/4	17.742
	5/8	5.016		3/8	3.485		1.7/8	19.010
	3/4	6.019		1/2	4.647		2.	20.277
	7/8	7.022		5/8	5.808		2.1/4	22.811
	1.	8.025		3/4	6.970		2.1/2	25.346
	1.1/8	9.028		7/8	8.132		2.3/4	27.881
	1.1/4	10.032		1.	9.294	3.1/4	1/8	1.373
	1.3/8	11.035		1.1/8	10.455		1/4	2.746
	1.1/2	12.038		1.1/4	11.617		3/8	4.119
	1.5/8	13.042		1.3/8	12.779		1/2	5.492
	1.3/4	14.045		1.1/2	13.940		5/8	6.865
	1.7/8	15.048		1.5/8	15.102		3/4	8.237
	2.	16.051		1.3/4	16.264		7/8	9.610
	2.1/8	17.054		1.7/8	17.425		1.	10.983
	2.1/4	18.057		2.	18.587		1.1/8	12.356
2.1/2	1/8	1.056		2.1/8	19.749		1.1/4	13.730
	1/4	2.112		2.1/4	20.910		1.3/8	15.102
	3/8	3.168		2.3/8	22.072		1.1/2	16.475
	1/2	4.224		2.1/2	23.234		1.5/8	17.848
	5/8	5.280		2.5/8	24.395		1.3/4	19.221
	3/4	6.336	2.7/8	1/8	1.215		1.7/8	20.594
	7/8	7.392		1/4	2.429		2.	21.967
	1.	8.448		3/8	3.644		2.1/4	24.712
	1.1/8	9.504		1/2	4.858		2.1/2	27.458
	1.1/4	10.560		5/8	6.072		2.3/4	30.204
	1.3/8	11.616		3/4	7.287		3.	32.950
	1.1/2	12.672		7/8	8.502	3.1/2	1/8	1.479
	1.5/8	13.728		1.	9.716		1/4	2.957
	1.3/4	14.784		1.1/8	10.931		3/8	4.436
	1.7/8	15.840		1.1/4	12.145		1/2	5.914
	2.	16.896		1.3/8	13.360		5/8	7.393
	2.1/8	17.952		1.1/2	14.574		3/4	8.871
	2.1/4	19.008		1.5/8	15.789		7/8	10.350
	2.3/8	20.064		1.3/4	17.003		1.	11.828
2.5/8	1/8	1.109		1.7/8	18.218		1.1/8	13.307
	1/4	2.218		2.	19.432		1.1/4	14.785
	3/8	3.327		2.1/8	20.647		1.3/8	16.264
	1/2	4.436		2.1/4	21.861		1.1/2	17.742
	5/8	5.545		2.3/8	23.076		1.5/8	19.221
	3/4	6.654		2.1/2	24.290		1.3/4	20.699
	7/8	7.763		2.5/8	25.505		1.7/8	22.178
	1.	8.872		2.3/4	26.719		2.	23.656
	1.1/8	9.981	3.	1/8	1.267		2.1/4	26.613
	1.1/4	11.090		1/4	2.535		2.1/2	29.570
	1.3/8	12.199		3/8	3.802		2.3/4	32.527
	1.1/2	13.308		1/2	5.069		3.	35.485
	1.5/8	14.417		5/8	6.337		3.1/4	38.441
	1.3/4	15.526		3/4	7.604	3.3/4	1/8	1.584
	1.7/8	16.635		7/8	8.871		1/4	3.168
	2.	17.744		1.	10.138		3/8	4.752
	2.1/8	18.853		1.1/8	11.406		1/2	6.336
	2.1/4	19.962		1.1/4	12.673		5/8	7.921
	2.3/8	21.071		1.3/8	13.940		3/4	9.505
	2.1/2	22.180		1.1/2	15.208		7/8	11.089
		1.162		1.5/8	16.475		1.	12.673

TABLE—(Continued).

Breadth in inches.	Thickness in inches.	Weight in pounds.	Breadth in inches.	Thickness in inches.	Weight in pounds.	Breadth in inches.	Thickness in inches.	Weight in pounds.
3.¾	1.⅛	14.257	4.½	2.¼	34.217	5.¼	2.½	44.355
	1.¼	15.841		2.½	38.019		2.¾	48.791
	1.⅜	17.425		2.¾	41.820		3.	53.226
	1.½	19.009		3.	45.623		3.¼	57.662
	1.⅝	20.594		3.¼	49.425		3.½	62.097
	1.¾	22.178		3.½	53.226		3.¾	66.533
	1.⅞	23.762		3.¾	57.028		4.	70.968
	2.	25.346		4.	60.830		4.¼	75.404
	2.¼	28.514		4.¼	64.632		4.½	79.839
	2.½	31.682	4.¾	.¼	4.013		4.¾	84.275
	2.¾	34.851		.½	8.026		5.	88.710
	3.	38.019		.¾	12.039	5.½	.¼	4.647
	3.¼	41.187		1.	16.052		.½	9.294
	3.½	44.355		1.¼	20.066		.¾	13.940
4.	.⅛	1.690		1.½	24.079		1.	18.587
	.¼	3.380		1.¾	28.092		1.¼	23.234
	.½	6.759		2.	32.105		1.½	27.881
	.¾	10.138		2.¼	36.118		1.¾	32.527
	1.	13.518		2.½	40.131		2.	37.174
	1.¼	16.897		2.¾	44.144		2.¼	41.821
	1.½	20.277		3.	48.157		2.½	46.468
	1.¾	23.656		3.¼	52.170		2.¾	51.114
	2.	27.036		3.½	56.184		3.	55.761
	2.¼	30.415		3.¾	60.197		3.¼	60.408
	2.½	33.795		4.	64.210		3.½	65.055
	2.¾	37.174		4.¼	68.223		3.¾	69.701
	3.	40.554		4.½	72.235		4.	74.348
	3.¼	43.933	5.	.¼	4.224		4.¼	78.995
	3.½	47.313		.½	8.449		4.½	83.642
	3.¾	50.692		.¾	12.673		4.¾	88.288
4.¼	.⅛	1.795		1.	16.897		5.	92.935
	.¼	3.591		1.¼	21.122		5.¼	97.582
	.½	7.181		1.½	25.346	5.¾	.¼	4.858
	.¾	10.772		1.¾	29.570		.½	9.716
	1.	14.364		2.	33.795		.¾	14.574
	1.¼	17.953		2.¼	38.019		1.	19.432
	1.½	21.544		2.½	42.243		1.¼	24.290
	1.¾	25.135		2.¾	46.468		1.½	29.148
	2.	28.725		3.	50.692		1.¾	34.006
	2.¼	32.316		3.¼	54.916		2.	38.864
	2.½	35.907		3.½	59.140		2.¼	43.722
	2.¾	39.497		3.¾	63.365		2.½	48.580
	3.	43.088		4.	67.589		2.¾	53.437
	3.¼	46.679		4.¼	71.813		3.	58.296
	3.½	50.269		4.½	76.038		3.¼	63.154
	3.¾	53.860		4.¾	80.262		3.½	68.012
	4.	57.450	5.¼	.¼	4.436		3.¾	72.870
4.½	.¼	3.802		.½	8.871		4.	77.728
	.½	7.604		.¾	13.307		4.¼	82.585
	.¾	11.406		1.	17.742		4.½	87.443
	1.	15.208		1.¼	22.178		4.¾	92.301
	1.¼	19.010		1.½	26.613		5.	97.159
	1.½	22.812		1.¾	31.049		5.¼	102.017
	1.¾	26.614		2.	35.484		5.½	106.876
	2.	30.415		2.¼	39.920		6.	116.592

EXAMPLES.—What is the weight of a bar of iron 5¼ inches in breadth by ¾ inches thick?

In column 4, page 250, find 5¼, and below it, in column 5, ¾; and opposite to that is 13.307, which is 13 lbs. and $\frac{307}{1000}$ of a lb.

For parts of a lb. and of a foot, operate precisely similar to the rule laid down for table, page 247.

WEIGHTS OF A SQUARE FOOT OF IRON IN AVOIRDUPOIS POUNDS.

THICKNESS BY WIRE GAUGE.

No. on gauge	1	2	3	4	5	6	7	8	9	10	11
Pounds	12.5	12	11	10	9	8	7.5	7	6	5.68	5

No. on gauge	12	13	14	15	16	17	18	19	20	21	22
Pounds	4.62	4.31	4	3.95	3	2.5	2.18	1.93	1.62	1.5	1.37

Number 1 is $\frac{5}{16}$, number 4 is $\frac{1}{4}$, and number 11 is $\frac{1}{8}$ of an inch.

CAST IRON.

To ascertain the weight of a cast iron Bar or Rod, find the weight of a wrought iron bar or rod of the same dimensions in the preceding tables, and from the weight deduct the $\frac{2}{27}$th part; or say,

As 486.65 : 450.55 : : the weight in the table : to the weight required.   Thus,

What is the weight of a piece of cast iron 4×3¾×12 inches?

In table, page 250, the weight of a piece of wrought iron of these dimensions is 50.692 lbs.

486.65 : 450.55 : : 50.692 : 46.93 lbs.

Or, by an easier mode, though not so minutely correct,

As 281 : 260 : : 50.692 : 46.90 lbs.

To find the Weight of a piece of CAST or WROUGHT IRON of any size or shape.

By the rules given in Mensuration of Solids (see page 81), ascertain the number of cubic inches in the piece, multiply by the weight of a cubic inch, and the product will be the weight in pounds.

EXAMPLES.

What is the weight of a block of wrought iron 10 inches square by 15 inches in length?

$$10 \times 10 \times 15 = 1500 \text{ cubic inches.}$$
$$.2816 \text{ weight of a cubic inch.}$$
$$\overline{422.4000 \text{ pounds.}}$$

What is the weight of a cast iron ball 15 inches in diameter?

By table, page 255 = 176.7149 cubic inches.
$$.2607 \text{ weight of a cubic inch.}$$
$$\overline{460.6957 \text{ pounds.}}$$

WEIGHT OF CAST IRON PIPES OF DIFFERENT THICKNESSES,

From 1 Inch to 36 Inches Bore,

AND ONE FOOT IN LENGTH.

Bore.	Thickness	Weight.	Bore.	Thickness	Weight.	Bore.	Thickness	Weight.
Inches.	Inches.	Pounds.	Inches.	Inches.	Pounds.	Inches.	Inches.	Pounds.
1.	1/4	3.06	6.	3/4	49.60	11.1/2	1/2	58.82
	3/8	5.05		7/8	58.96		5/8	74.23
1.1/4	1/4	3.67	6.1/2		34.32		3/4	90.06
	3/8	6.			43.68		7/8	106.14
1.1/2	3/8	6.89			53.30		1.	122.62
	1/2	9.80			63.18	12.	1/2	61.26
1.3/4	3/8	7.80	7.		36.66		5/8	77.36
	1/2	11.04			46.80		3/4	93.70
2.	3/8	8.74			56.96		7/8	110.48
	1/2	12.23			67.60		1.	127.42
2.1/4	3/8	9.65		1.	78.39	12.1/2	1/2	63.70
	1/2	13.48	7.1/2	1/2	39.22		5/8	80.40
2.1/2	3/8	10.57		5/8	49.92		3/4	97.40
		14.66		3/4	60.48		7/8	114.72
		19.05		7/8	71.76		1.	132.35
2.3/4		11.54		1.	83.28	13.	1/2	66.14
		15.91	8.		41.64		5/8	83.46
		20.59			52.68		3/4	101.08
3.		12.28			64.27		7/8	118.97
		17.15			76.12		1.	137.28
		22.15		1.	88.20	13.1/2	1/2	68.64
		27.56	8.1/2	1/2	44.11		5/8	86.55
3.1/4		18.40			56.16		3/4	104.76
		23.72		3/4	68.		7/8	123.30
		29.64		7/8	80.50		1.	142.16
3.1/2		19.66		1.	93.28	14.	1/2	71.07
		25.27	9.		46.50		5/8	89.61
		31.20			58.92		3/4	108.46
3.3/4		20.90			71.70		7/8	127.60
		26.83			84.70		1.	147.03
		33.07		1.	97.98	14.1/2	1/2	73.72
4.	1/2	22.05	9.1/2		48.98		5/8	92.66
	5/8	28.28			62.02		3/4	112.10
	3/4	34.94			75.32		7/8	131.86
4.1/4		23.35			88.98		1.	151.92
		29.85		1.	102.90	15.	1/2	75.96
		36.73	10.	1/2	51.46		5/8	95.72
4.1/2		24.49		5/8	65.08		3/4	115.78
		31.40		3/4	78.99		7/8	136.15
		38.58			93.24		1.	156.82
4.3/4		25.70		1.	108.84	15.1/2	1/2	78.40
		32.91	10.1/2		53.88		5/8	98.78
		40.43			68.14		3/4	119.48
5.		26.94			82.68		7/8	140.40
		34.34			97.44		1.	161.82
		42.28		1.	112.68	16.	1/2	80.87
5.1/2		29.40	11.		56.34		5/8	101.82
		37.44			71.19		3/4	123.14
		45.94			86.40		7/8	144.76
6.		31.82			101.83		1.	166.60
		40.56		1.	117.60	16.1/2	1/2	83.30

TABLE—(Continued).

Bore.	Thickness	Weight.	Bore.	Thickness	Weight.	Bore.	Thickness	Weight.
Inches.	Inches.	Pounds.	Inches.	Inches.	Pounds.	Inches.	Inches.	Pounds.
$16,\frac{1}{2}$	$\frac{5}{8}$	104.82	22.	$\frac{5}{8}$	138.60	30.	1.	303.86
	$\frac{3}{4}$	126.79		$\frac{3}{4}$	167.24		$1\frac{1}{8}$	343.20
	$\frac{7}{8}$	149.02		$\frac{7}{8}$	196.46	31.	$\frac{3}{4}$	233.40
	1.	171.60		1.	225.38		$\frac{7}{8}$	273.40
17.	$\frac{1}{2}$	85.73	23.	$\frac{5}{8}$	144.77		1.	313.68
	$\frac{5}{8}$	107.96		$\frac{3}{4}$	174.62		$1\frac{1}{8}$	354.24
	$\frac{3}{4}$	130.48		$\frac{7}{8}$	204.78	32.	$\frac{3}{4}$	240.76
	$\frac{7}{8}$	153.30		1.	235.28		$\frac{7}{8}$	281.94
	1.	176.58	24.	$\frac{5}{8}$	150.85		1.	323.49
$17,\frac{1}{2}$	$\frac{1}{2}$	88.23		$\frac{3}{4}$	181.92		$1\frac{1}{8}$	365.29
	$\frac{5}{8}$	111.06		$\frac{7}{8}$	213.28	33.	$\frac{3}{4}$	248.10
	$\frac{3}{4}$	134.16		1.	245.08		$\frac{7}{8}$	290.50
	$\frac{7}{8}$	157.59	25.	$\frac{5}{8}$	156.97		1.	333.24
	1.	181.33		$\frac{3}{4}$	189.28		$1\frac{1}{8}$	376.26
18.	$\frac{5}{8}$	114.10		$\frac{7}{8}$	221.94	34.	$\frac{3}{4}$	255.45
	$\frac{3}{4}$	137.84		1.	254.86		$\frac{7}{8}$	298.88
	$\frac{7}{8}$	161.90	26.	$\frac{3}{4}$	196.62		1.	342.88
	1.	186.24		$\frac{7}{8}$	230.56		$1\frac{1}{8}$	387.13
19.	$\frac{5}{8}$	120.24		1.	264.66		$1\frac{1}{4}$	431.76
	$\frac{3}{4}$	145.20	27.	$\frac{3}{4}$	204.04	35.	$\frac{3}{4}$	262.70
	$\frac{7}{8}$	170.47		$\frac{7}{8}$	239.08		$\frac{7}{8}$	307.62
	1.	195.92		1.	274.56		1.	352.86
20.	$\frac{5}{8}$	126.33	28.	$\frac{3}{4}$	211.32		$1\frac{1}{8}$	398.10
	$\frac{3}{4}$	152.53		$\frac{7}{8}$	247.62		$1\frac{1}{4}$	443.96
	$\frac{7}{8}$	179.02		1.	284.28	36.	$\frac{3}{4}$	270.18
	1.	205.80	29.	$\frac{3}{4}$	218.70		$\frac{7}{8}$	316.36
21.	$\frac{5}{8}$	132.50		$\frac{7}{8}$	256.20		1.	362.86
	$\frac{3}{4}$	159.84		1.	294.02		$1\frac{1}{8}$	409.34
	$\frac{7}{8}$	187.60	30.	$\frac{3}{4}$	226.20		$1\frac{1}{4}$	456.46
	1.	215.52		$\frac{7}{8}$	264.79			

NOTE.—These weights do not include any allowance for spigot and faucet ends.

Y

WEIGHT OF A SQUARE FOOT OF CAST AND WROUGHT IRON, COPPER, AND LEAD,

From $\frac{1}{16}$th to 2 Inches thick.

Thickness.	Cast Iron.	Wrought Iron. Hard rolled.	Copper. Hard rolled.	Lead.
	Pounds.	Pounds.	Pounds.	Pounds.
$\cdot\frac{1}{16}$	2.346	2.517	2.890	3.691
$\cdot\frac{1}{8}$	4.693	5.035	5.781	7.382
$\cdot\frac{3}{16}$	7.039	7.552	8.672	11.074
$\cdot\frac{1}{4}$	9.386	10.070	11.562	14.765
$\cdot\frac{5}{16}$	11.733	12.588	14.453	18.456
$\cdot\frac{3}{8}$	14.079	15.106	17.344	22.148
$\cdot\frac{7}{16}$	16.426	17.623	20.234	25.839
$\cdot\frac{1}{2}$	18.773	20.141	23.125	29.530
$\cdot\frac{9}{16}$	21.119	22.659	26.016	33.222
$\cdot\frac{5}{8}$	23.466	25.176	28.906	36.913
$\cdot\frac{11}{16}$	25.812	27.694	31.797	40.604
$\cdot\frac{3}{4}$	28.159	30.211	34.688	44.296
$\cdot\frac{13}{16}$	30.505	32.729	37.578	47.987
$\frac{7}{8}$	32.852	35.247	40.469	51.678
$\cdot\frac{15}{16}$	35.199	37.764	43.359	55.370
1 inch	37.545	40.282	46.250	59.061
1.$\frac{1}{8}$	42.238	45.317	52.031	66.444
1.$\frac{1}{4}$	46.931	50.352	57.813	73.826
1.$\frac{3}{8}$	51.625	55.387	63.594	81.210
1.$\frac{1}{2}$	56.317	60.422	69.375	88.592
1.$\frac{5}{8}$	61.011	65.458	75.156	95.975
1.$\frac{3}{4}$	65.704	70.493	80.938	103.358
1.$\frac{7}{8}$	70.397	75.528	86.719	110.740
2.	75.090	80.563	92.500	118.128

NOTE.—The SPECIFIC GRAVITY of the Wrought Iron is that of Pennsylvania plates, and of the Copper, that of plates from the works of Messrs. Phelps, Dodge, & Co., in Connecticut. The Lead, a mean from several places.

WEIGHT AND CAPACITY OF CAST IRON AND LEAD BALLS,

From 1 to 20 Inches in Diameter.

Diameter in inches.	Capacity in cubic inches.	CAST IRON. Pounds.	LEAD. Pounds.
1.	.5235	.1365	.2147
1.½	1.7671	.4607	.7248
2.	4.1887	1.0920	1.7180
2.½	8.1812	2.1328	3.3554
3.	14.1371	3.6855	5.7982
3.½	22.4492	5.8525	9.2073
4.	33.5103	8.7361	13.744
4.½	47.7129	12.4387	19.569
5.	65.4498	17.0628	26.843
5.½	87.1137	22.7206	35.729
6.	113.0973	29.4845	46.385
6.½	143.7932	37.4528	58.976
7.	179.5943	46.8203	73.659
7.½	220.8932	57.5870	90.598
8.	268.0825	69.8892	109.952
8.½	321.5550	83.8396	131.883
9.	381.7034	99.5103	156.553
9.½	448.9204	117.0338	184.121
10.	523.5987	136.5025	214.749
11.	696.9098	181.7648	285.832
12.	904.7784	235.8763	371.096
13.	1150.346	299.6230	471.806
14.	1436.754	374.5629	589.273
15.	1767.145	460.6959	724.781
16.	2144.660	559.1142	879.616
17.	2572.440	670.7168	1055.066
18.	3053.627	796.0325	1252.422
19.	3591.363	936.2708	1472.970
20.	4188.790	1092.0200	1717.995

WEIGHT OF COPPER RODS OR BOLTS,

From ¼ to 4 Inches in Diameter,

AND ONE FOOT IN LENGTH.

Diameter.	Pounds.	Diameter.	Pounds.	Diameter.	Pounds.
$\frac{1}{4}$	.1892	1.$\frac{1}{16}$	3.4170	2.$\frac{1}{8}$	13.6677
$\frac{5}{16}$	.2956	1.$\frac{1}{8}$	3.8312	2.$\frac{1}{4}$	15.3251
$\frac{3}{8}$	.4256	1.$\frac{3}{16}$	4.2688	2.$\frac{3}{8}$	17.0750
$\frac{7}{16}$	.5794	1.$\frac{1}{4}$	4.7298	2.$\frac{1}{2}$	18.9161
$\frac{1}{2}$	.7567	1.$\frac{5}{16}$	5.2140	2.$\frac{5}{8}$	20.8562
$\frac{9}{16}$	.9578	1.$\frac{3}{8}$	5.7228	2.$\frac{3}{4}$	22.8913
$\frac{5}{8}$	1.1824	1.$\frac{7}{16}$	6.2547	2.$\frac{7}{8}$	25.0188
$\frac{11}{16}$	1.4307	1.$\frac{1}{2}$	6.8109	3.	27.2435
$\frac{3}{4}$	1.7027	1.$\frac{9}{16}$	7.3898	3.$\frac{1}{8}$	29.5594
$\frac{13}{16}$	1.9982	1.$\frac{5}{8}$	7.9931	3.$\frac{1}{4}$	31.9722
$\frac{7}{8}$	2.3176	1.$\frac{3}{4}$	9.2702	3.$\frac{3}{8}$	34.4815
$\frac{15}{16}$	2.6605	1.$\frac{7}{8}$	10.6420	3.$\frac{1}{2}$	37.0808
1.	3.0270	2.	12.1082	3.$\frac{5}{8}$	39.7774
				3.$\frac{3}{4}$	42.5680
				3.$\frac{7}{8}$	45.4550
				4.	48.4330

WEIGHT OF RIVETED COPPER PIPES,

From 5 to 30 Inches in Diameter, from 3 to $\frac{5}{16}$ths thick,

AND ONE FOOT IN LENGTH.

Diam. in ins.	Thickness in 16ths.	Weight in pounds.	Diam. in ins.	Thickness in 16ths.	Weight in pounds.	Diam. in ins.	Thickness in 16ths.	Weight in pounds.
5.	3	12.497	9.$\frac{1}{2}$	4	30.598	19.	4	60.142
5.	4	16.880	10.	4	32.208	19.	5	75.233
5.$\frac{1}{4}$	3	13.628	11.	4	35.200	20.	5	78.208
5.$\frac{1}{2}$	4	18.395	12.	4	38.456	21.	5	82.984
6.	3	14.765	13.	4	41.456	22.	5	86.771
6.	4	19.908	14.	4	44.640	23.	5	90.571
6.$\frac{1}{4}$	3	15.897	15.	4	47.646	24.	5	94.308
6.$\frac{1}{2}$	4	21.415	15.	5	59.588	25.	5	98.122
7.	3	17.034	16.	4	50.752	26.	5	101.897
7.	4	22.932	16.	5	63.470	27.	5	105.700
7.$\frac{1}{2}$	4	24.447	17.	4	53.856	28.	5	109.446
8.	4	25.961	17.	5	67.344	29.	5	113.221
8.$\frac{1}{4}$	4	27.471	18.	4	57.037	30.	5	116.997
9.	4	28.985	18.	5	71.258			

The above weights include the laps on the sheets for riveting and caulking.

The weights of the rivets are not added; the *number* per lineal foot of pipe depends upon the distance they are placed apart, and their *size* upon the diameter of the pipe.

COPPER.

To ascertain the Weight of Copper.

RULE.—Find by calculation the number of cubic inches in the piece, multiply them by .32118, and the product will be the weight in pounds.

EXAMPLE.—What is the weight of a copper plate $\frac{1}{2}$ an inch thick by 16 inches square ?

$$16^2 = 256$$
$$.5 \text{ for } \tfrac{1}{2} \text{ an inch.}$$
$$\overline{128.0} \times .32118 = 41.111 \text{ pounds.}$$

LEAD.

To ascertain the Weight of Lead.

RULE.—Find by calculation the number of cubic inches in the piece, and multiply the sum by .41015, and the product will be the weight in pounds.

EXAMPLE.—What is the weight of a leaden pipe 12 feet long, $3\frac{3}{4}$ inches in diameter, and 1 inch thick ?

By rule in Mensuration of Surfaces, to ascertain the area of cylindrical rings,

$$\text{Area of } (3\tfrac{3}{4}+1+1) = 25.967$$
$$\text{`` `` } 3\tfrac{3}{4} \qquad = 11.044$$
$$\text{Difference, } \overline{14.923}, \text{ or area of ring.}$$
$$\underline{144} \qquad = 12 \text{ feet.}$$
$$\overline{2148.912} \times .41015 = 881.376 \text{ pounds.}$$

BRASS.

To ascertain the Weight of ordinary Brass Castings.

RULE.—Find the number of cubic inches in the piece, multiply by .3112, and the product will be the weight in pounds.

Y 2

CABLES AND ANCHORS.

Table *showing the Size of Cables and Anchors proportioned to the Tonnage of Vessels.*

Tonnage of vessel.	Cables. Circumference in inches.	Chain Cables. Diameter in inches.	Proof in tons.	Weight of Anchor in pounds.	Weight of a fathom of Chain.	Weight of a fathom of Cable.
5	3.	$\frac{5}{16}$	$\frac{3}{4}$	56	$5.\frac{1}{2}$	2.1
8	4.	$\frac{3}{8}$	$1.\frac{3}{4}$	84	8.	4.
10	$4.\frac{1}{2}$	$\frac{7}{16}$	$2.\frac{1}{2}$	112	11.	4.6
15	$5.\frac{1}{2}$	$\frac{1}{2}$	4.	168	14.	6.5
25	6.	$\frac{9}{16}$	5.	224	17.	8.4
40	$6.\frac{1}{2}$	$\frac{5}{8}$	6.	336	24.	9.8
60	7.	$\frac{11}{16}$	7.	392	27.	11.4
75	$7.\frac{1}{2}$	$\frac{3}{4}$	9.	532	30.	13.
100	8.	$\frac{13}{16}$	10.	616	36.	15.
130	9.	$\frac{7}{8}$	12.	700	42.	18.9
150	$9.\frac{1}{2}$	$\frac{15}{16}$	14.	840	50.	21.
180	$10.\frac{1}{2}$	1.	16.	952	56.	25.7
200	11.	$1.\frac{1}{16}$	18.	1176	60.	28.2
240	12.	$1.\frac{1}{8}$	20.	1400	70.	33.6
270	$12.\frac{1}{2}$	$1.\frac{3}{16}$	21.	1456	78.	36.4
320	$13.\frac{1}{2}$	$1.\frac{1}{4}$	$22.\frac{1}{2}$	1680	86.	42.5
360	14.	$1.\frac{5}{16}$	25.	1904	96.	45.7
400	$14.\frac{1}{2}$	$1.\frac{3}{8}$	27.	2072	104.	49.
440	$15.\frac{1}{2}$	$1.\frac{7}{16}$	30.	2240	115.	56.
480	16.	$1.\frac{1}{2}$	33.	2408	125.	59.5
520	$16.\frac{1}{2}$	$1.\frac{9}{16}$	36.	2800	136.	63.4
570	17.	$1.\frac{5}{8}$	39.	3360	144.	67.2
620	$17.\frac{1}{2}$	$1.\frac{11}{16}$	42.	3920	152.	71.1
680	18.	$1.\frac{3}{4}$	45.	4200	161.	75.6
740	19.	$1.\frac{13}{16}$	49.	4480	172.	84.2
820	20.	$1.\frac{7}{8}$	52.	5600	184.	93.3
900	22.	$1.\frac{15}{16}$	56.	6720	196.	112.9
1000	24.	2.	60.	7168	208.	134.6

The proof in the U. S. Naval Service is about $12\frac{1}{2}$ per cent. less than the above.

The utmost strength of a good hemp rope is 6400 lbs. to the square inch; in practice it should not be subjected to more than half this strain. It stretches from $\frac{1}{5}$ to $\frac{1}{7}$, and its diameter is diminished from $\frac{1}{4}$ to $\frac{1}{7}$ before breaking.

A difference in the quality of hemp may produce a difference of $\frac{1}{4}$ in the strength of ropes of the same size.

The strength of Manilla is about $\frac{1}{2}$ that of hemp.

White ropes are one third more durable.

CABLES.

TABLE *showing what Weight a good Hemp Cable will bear with Safety.*

Circumference.	Pounds.	Circumference.	Pounds.	Circumference.	Pounds.
6.	4320.	10.25	12607.5	14.50	25230.
6.25	4687.5	10.50	13230.	14.75	26107.5
6.50	5070.	10.75	13867.5	15.	27000.
6.75	5467.5	11.	14520.	15.25	27907.5
7.	5880.	11.25	15187.5	15.50	28830.
7.25	6307.5	11.50	15870.	15.75	29767.5
7.50	6750.	11.75	16567.5	16.	30720.
7.75	7207.5	12.	17280.	16.25	31687.5
8.	7680.	12.25	18007.5	16.50	32670.
8.25	8167.5	12.50	18750.	16.75	33667.5
8.50	8670.	12.75	19507.5	17.	34680.
8.75	9187.5	13.	20280.	17.25	35707.5
9.	9720.	13.25	21067.5	17.50	36750.
9.25	10267.5	13.50	21870.	17.75	37807.5
9.50	10830.	13.75	22687.5	18.	38880.
9.75	11407.5	14.	23520.	18.25	39967.5
10.	12000.	14.25	24367.5		

To ascertain the Strength of Cables.

Multiply the square of the circumference in inches by 120, and the product is the weight the cable will bear in pounds, with safety.

To ascertain the Weight of Manilla Ropes and Hawsers.

Multiply the square of the circumference in inches by .03, and the product is the weight in pounds of a foot in length.

This is but an approximation, and yet it is sufficiently correct for many purposes.

TABLE *showing what Weight a Hemp Rope will bear with Safety.*

Circumference.	Pounds.	Circumference.	Pounds.	Circumference.	Pounds.
1.	200.	3.$\frac{1}{2}$	2450.	6.	7200.
1.$\frac{1}{4}$	312.5	3.$\frac{3}{4}$	2812.5	6.$\frac{1}{4}$	7812.5
1.$\frac{1}{2}$	450.	4.	3200.	6.$\frac{1}{2}$	8450.
1.$\frac{3}{4}$	612.5	4.$\frac{1}{4}$	3612.5	6.$\frac{3}{4}$	9112.5
2.	800.	4.$\frac{1}{2}$	4050.	7.	9800.
2.$\frac{1}{4}$	1012.5	4.$\frac{3}{4}$	4512.5	7.$\frac{1}{4}$	10512.5
2.$\frac{1}{2}$	1250.	5.	5000.	7.$\frac{1}{2}$	11250.
2.$\frac{3}{4}$	1512.5	5.$\frac{1}{4}$	5512.5	7.$\frac{3}{4}$	12012.5
3.	1800.	5.$\frac{1}{2}$	6050.	8.	12800.
3.$\frac{1}{4}$	2112.5	5.$\frac{3}{4}$	6612.5		

To ascertain the Strength of Ropes.

Multiply the square of the circumference in inches by 200, and it gives the weight the rope will bear in pounds, with safety.

To ascertain the Weight of Cable-laid Ropes.

Multiply the square of the circumference in inches by .036, and the product is the weight in pounds of a foot in length.

To ascertain the Weight of Tarred Ropes and Cables.

Multiply the square of the circumference by 2.13, and divide by 9; the product is the weight of a fathom in pounds.

Or, multiply the square of the circumference by .04, and the product is the weight of a foot.

For the *ultimate strength*, divide the square of the circumference in inches by 5; the product is the weight in tons.

A square inch of hemp fibres will support a weight of 92000 lbs.

BLOWING ENGINES.

THE object of a blast is to supply oxygen to furnaces.

The quantity of oxygen in the same bulk of air is different at different temperatures. Thus, dry air at 85° contains 10 per cent. less oxygen than when at the temperature of 32°; when saturated with vapour, it contains 12 per cent. less.

Hence, if an average supply of 1500 cubic feet per minute is required in winter, 1650 feet will be required in summer.

The pressure ordinarily required for smelting purposes is equal to a column of mercury from 3 to 7 inches.

The capacity of the Reservoir should exceed that of the cylinder or cylinders, and the area of the pipes leading to it should be $\frac{1}{10}$ of the area of the cylinder.

The quantity of air at atmospheric density delivered into the reservoir, in consequence of escapes through the valves, and the partial vacuum necessary to produce a current, will be about $\frac{1}{3}$ less than the capacity of the cylinder.

To find the Power when the Cylinder is Double Acting.

Let P represent pressure in lbs. per square inch,
    v "   the velocity of the piston in feet per minute,
    a "   the area of the cylinder in inches,
    1.25   "   the friction necessary to work the machinery.
Then Pva 1.25 = the power in lbs. raised 1 foot high per minute.

When Single Acting.

$$\frac{Pva\ 1.25}{2} = \text{the power in lbs. raised 1 foot high per minute.}$$

Air expands nearly 2½ times its bulk while in the fire of an ordinary furnace.

Dimensions of a Furnace, Engines, &c.

Furnace. At Lonakoning (Md.). Diameter at the boshes 14 feet, which fall in, 6.33 inches in every foot rise.

Engine. Diameter of cylinder 18 inches, length of stroke 8 feet.
Averaging 12 revolutions per minute, with a pressure of 50 lbs. per square inch.

Boilers. Five: each 24 feet in length, and 36 inches in diameter.

Blast Cylinders. 5 feet diameter, and 8 feet stroke.
At a pressure of from 2 to 2½ lbs. per square inch, the quantity of blast is 3770 cubic feet per minute, requiring a power of about 50 horses to supply it.

180 tons air is required to make 10 tons pig iron, and burn the coke from 50 tons coal. The ore yielding about 33 per cent. of iron.

Steam Boilers. Two cylinders, 12 inches in diameter and 12 inches stroke, aided by exhausting into a condenser, and with steam of 30 lbs. pressure per square inch, will make 50 revolutions per minute, and drive 4 blowers, each 54 inches in diameter, and 30 inches wide, 300 revolutions in a minute, furnishing the necessary blast for burning anthracite coal on a grate surface of 108 square feet; supplying 4400 cubic feet steam per minute, at a pressure of 30 lbs. per square inch.

35 cubic feet of steam used in the cylinder of a blowing engine will drive blowers 4 feet in diameter by 26 inches face, and furnish the necessary blast to an anthracite fire, for generating 1150 cubic feet steam, the time 1 minute, and pressure per square inch 35 lbs.

MISCELLANEOUS NOTES.

ON MATERIALS, ETC.

Wood is from 7 to 20 times stronger transversely than longitudinally.

In Buffon's experiments, b, d, and l being the breadth, depth, and length of a piece of oak in inches, the weight that broke it in pounds was $bd^2\left(\dfrac{54.25}{l}10\right)$.

The *hardness of metals* is as follows : Iron, Platina, Copper, Silver, Gold, Tin, Lead.

A piece spliced on to strengthen a beam should be on its convex side.

Springs are weakened by use, but recover their strength if laid by.

A pipe of *cast iron* 15 inches in diameter and .75 inches thick will sustain a head of water of 600 feet. One of *oak*, 2 inches thick, and of the same diameter, will sustain a head of 180 feet.
When the cohesion is the same, the thickness varies as the height × the diameter.

When one *beam* is let in, at an inclination to the depth of another, so as to bear in the direction of the fibres of the beam that is cut ; the depth of the cut *at right angles to the fibres* should not be more than $\frac{1}{5}$ of the length of the piece, the fibres of which, by their cohesion, resist the pressure.

Metals have five degrees of lustre—*splendent, shining, glistening, glimmering,* and *dull.*

THE *Vernier* Scale is $\frac{11}{10}$, divided into 10 equal parts ; so that it divides a scale of 10ths into 100ths when the lines meet even in the two scales.

A *luminous point*, to produce a *visual* circle, must have a velocity of 10 feet in a second, the diameter not exceeding 15 inches.

Tides. The difference in time between high water averages about 49 minutes each day.

In *Sandy soil*, the greatest force of a pile-driver will not drive a *pile* over 15 feet.

A *fall* of $\frac{1}{10}$ of an inch in a mile will produce a *current* in rivers.

Melted snow produces about $\frac{1}{8}$ of its bulk of water.

All solid bodies become *luminous* at 800 degrees of heat.

At the depth of 45 feet, the *temperature of the earth* is uniform throughout the year.

A *Spermaceti candle* .85 of an inch in diameter consumes an inch in length in 1 hour.

Silica is the base of the mineral world, and *Carbon* of the organized.

Sound passes in water at a velocity of 4708 feet per second.

SOLDERS.

For *Lead*, melt 1 part of Block tin ; and when in a state of fusion, add 2 parts of Lead. Resin should be used with this solder.

For *Tin*, Pewter 4 parts, Tin 1, and Bismuth 1 ; melt them together. Resin is also used with this solder.

For *Iron*, tough Brass, with a small quantity of Borax.

CEMENTS.

Glue. Powdered chalk added to common glue strengthens it.

A glue which will resist the action of water is made by boiling 1 pound of glue in 2 quarts of skimmed milk.

Soft Cement. For steam-boilers, steam-pipes, &c. Red or white lead in oil, 4 parts ; Iron borings, 2 to 3 parts.

Hard Cement. Iron borings and salt water, and a small quantity of sal ammoniac with fresh water.

PAINTS.

White Paint.

	Inside work.	Outside work.
White-lead, ground in oil	80.	80
Boiled oil	14.5	9
Raw oil	—	9
Spirits turpentine	8.	4

New wood work requires about 1 lb. to the square yard for 3 coats.

Lead Colour.

White-lead, ground in oil, 75	Litharge	.5
Lampblack . . 1	Japan varnish	.5
Boiled linseed oil . 23	Spirits turpentine	2.5

The turpentine and varnish are added as the paint is required for use or transportation.

Gray, or Stone Colour.

White-lead, in oil . 78.	Spirits turpentine	3.
Boiled oil. . . 9.5	Turkey umber .	.5
Raw oil . . 9.5	Lampblack	.25

1 square yard of new brick work requires, for 2 coats, 1.1 lb. ; for 3 coats, 1.5 lbs.

Cream Colour.

	1st coat.	2d coat.
White-lead, in oil	66.6	70.
French yellow	3.3	3.3
Japan varnish	1.3	1.3
Raw oil	28.	24.5
Spirits turpentine	2.25	2.25

1 square yard of new brick work requires, for 1st coat, 0.75 ; for 2d coat, 0.3 lbs.

Black Paint (for Iron).

Lampblack	28	Linseed oil, boiled	73
Litharge	1	Spirits turpentine	1
Japan varnish	1		

The varnish and turpentine are added last.

Liquid Olive Colour.

Olive paste	61.5	Dryings	3.5
Boiled oil	29.5	Japan varnish	2.
Spirits turpentine	5.5		

Paint for Tarpaulins (Olive).

| Liquid olive colour | 100 | Spirits turpentine | 6 |
| Beeswax | 6 | | |

1 square yard requires 2 lbs. for 3 coats.
Dissolve the beeswax in the turpentine, and mix the paint warm.

LACKER for Iron Ordnance.

Black-lead, pulverized	12	Red-lead	12
Litharge	5	Lampblack	5
Linseed oil	66		

Boil it gently for about 20 minutes, stirring it constantly during that time.

Lacker for Small Arms, or for Water Proof Paper.

| Beeswax | 18. | Spirits turpentine | 80 |
| Boiled linseed oil | 3.5 | | |

Heat the ingredients in a copper or earthen vessel over a gentle fire, in a water bath, until they are well mixed.

Lacker for Bright Iron Work.

| Linseed oil, boiled | 80.5 | Litharge | 5.5 |
| White-lead, ground in oil, | 11.25 | Pulverized rosin | 2.75 |

Add the litharge to the oil; let it simmer over a slow fire for 3 hours; strain it, and add the rosin and white-lead; keep it gently warmed, and stir it until the rosin is dissolved

Staining Wood and Ivory.

Yellow. Dilute nitric acid will produce it on wood.

Red. An infusion of Brazil wood in stale urine, in the proportion of a lb. to a gallon for wood, to be laid on when boiling hot, and should be laid over with alum water before it dries.

Or, a solution of dragon's blood, in spirits of wine, may be used.

Black. Strong solution of nitric acid, for wood or ivory.

Mahogany. Brazil, Madder, and Logwood, dissolved in water and put on hot.

Blue. Ivory may be stained thus: Soak it in a solution of verdigris in nitric acid, which will turn it *green;* then dip it into a solution of pearlash boiling hot.

Purple. Soak ivory in a solution of sal ammoniac into four times its weight of nitrous acid.

THE END.

Lightning Source UK Ltd.
Milton Keynes UK
UKOW021940080512

192200UK00005B/39/P